Books by Brendan Gill

Death in April
The Trouble of One House
The Day the Money Stopped
Cole
Tallulah
Happy Times
Ways of Loving
Here at The New Yorker

Here at
The
New Yorker

Brendan Gill

Here at
The
New Yorker

Random House
New York

Library of Congress Cataloging in Publication Data

Gill, Brendan, 1914–   Here at the New Yorker.

Autobiographical.
1. Gill, Brendan, 1914–   — Biography.   2. The New Yorker.   I.   Title.
PS3513.I468Z52   818'.5'209 [B]   74-23927
ISBN 0-394-48989-6

Manufactured in the United States of America

98765432

Designed by Carole Lowenstein

For William Shawn,
and no wonder

Here at
The
New Yorker

1

Happy writers have histories shorter even than happy families. The whole of my professional career can be summed up by saying that I started out at the place where I wanted most to be — *The New Yorker* magazine — and with much pleasure and very little labor have remained here ever since. Sometimes, and with reason, I boast of never having done an honest day's work in my life. An honest day's play — oh, that I have accomplished on a thousand occasions, or ten thousand, but work implies a measure of drudgery and fatigue, and these are states as yet unknown to me. With *The New Yorker* serving as my passport and letter of credit, how easy I have found it for almost forty years to rush pell-mell through the world, playing the clown when the spirit of darkness has moved me and colliding with good times at every turn!

Such a confession will no doubt make unwelcome reading to my colleagues, for the fashion among them is to hold that writing is a prolonged and disenchanting misery. A friend of mine, Patrick Kavanagh, who was the premier poet in Ireland after Yeats, said of the peasantry from which he sprang that they live in the dark cave of the unconscious and they scream when they see the light. They *scream* when they see the light. Now, most *New Yorker* writers share this attribute with Irish peasants. They tend to be lonely, molelike creatures, who work in their own portable if not peasant darkness and who seldom utter a sound above a groan. It happens that I am not like that. On the contrary, I am among those who enjoy the light and even, to a certain extent, the limelight — a predilection that has its hazards. Once I was showing off at a cocktail party, and I mentioned some very arcane fact that we had dug up for "Talk of the Town," like that Saint Ambrose was the first person in history reputed to have been able to read without moving his lips. Somebody asked me how I knew that, and I replied grandly, "I know everything." And a pretty girl was there, an Italian model, and she looked up at me with great melting dark eyes and said softly, "Tell me about the Battle of Mukden." I burst out in dismay, "Mukden, Mukden, the Battle of Mukden —!" For, sure enough, I knew nothing whatever about that very important event.

Nevertheless, I am always so ready to take a favorable view of my powers that even when I am caught out and made a fool of, I manage to twist this circumstance about until it becomes a proof of how exceptional I am. The ingenuities we practice in order to appear admirable to ourselves would suffice to invent the telephone twice over on a rainy summer morning.

Writer-moles avoid another hazard of the limelight: the public occasion that fails. In my youth, having gained a little fame by some short stories in *The New Yorker*, I was invited to give a talk about the magazine at Indiana University, and it turned out to be a nightmare, because the audience was academic. I didn't know then what I know now — that college professors like a talk to last at least an hour, with everything being said at least three times. The third time they hear a thing, they feel that famous shock of recognition, and a pleased smile begins to play over their faces. Well, in my ignorance on that occasion, I simply got up and talked, and having told them everything I knew about my assigned topic, I found I had consumed only ten minutes. I then went nattering on, in greater and greater panic, about metalinguistics, pendentive arches, and the decline of materialism in third-century Greece. Oh, God! That took but ten minutes more. All I could think of to do was sit down, and I did. Silence. No applause. The audience stared at me and I stared back. Little by little, I perceived that they thought I was having a heart attack, or a massive cerebral hemorrhage, or some such tiresome little thing as that; as soon as it was over, they expected me to get to my feet and go on. No doubt many of *them* had had heart attacks or massive cerebral hemorrhages in the course of those sixty-minute talks of theirs and had gone on speaking without the slightest trace of discomfort. Anyhow, I finally got to my feet, bowed, or, rather, lowered my head in a protective fashion, and slunk offstage.

In the offices of *The New Yorker* is a long corridor off which Joseph Mitchell, Philip Hamburger, and a couple of dozen other writers and editors have their bleak little ill-painted cells. The silence in that corridor is so profound and continuous that Hamburger long ago christened it Sleepy Hollow. At this moment, I am breaking the silence of Sleepy Hollow with the thud and clatter of an ancient sea-green Olivetti 82. Fortunately, my neighbors on either side are away on holiday; their daily naps will not be interrupted by my zeal. I foresee that writing about the magazine will be a lighter task than talking about it proved to be in Indiana. My intention is to follow the principle upon which the "Talk of the Town" department of the magazine is based: I will try to cram these paragraphs full of facts and give them a weight and shape no greater than that of a cloud of blue butterflies.

Ross in 1949, making a rare public appearance. He is testifying before the Public Service Commission of the State of New York, at a hearing to determine whether recorded music and commercial announcements should be allowed to be broadcast in Grand Central Terminal. The New Yorker has published a number of editorials attacking such broadcasts; hence, Ross as witness. An attorney for the New York Central Railroad describes Ross as the "editor of a comic book for adults." On the stand, Ross calls this description "rather heavy-handed." He makes an excellent witness; the upshot of the hearing is that the "canned" music and announcements are stopped. Ross is unusually well turned out, for Ross. His springy hair has been slicked down and he is wearing a tie that bears his monogram.

Not that this is how the principle of "Talk" would have been enunciated by Harold Wallace Ross, the founder and first editor of the magazine. Butterflies, and especially metaphorical butterflies, were the kind of thing that made Ross nervous. He was a self-taught man, and his teaching had been spectacularly hit-or-miss. He was rumored to have read only one book all the way through — a stout volume on sociology by Herbert Spencer. The truth was that he had read other books, but not many. He had the uneducated man's suspicion of the fickleness of words; he wanted them to have a limited, immutable meaning, but the sons of bitches kept hopping about from one sentence to the next. Ross was a foul-tongued man and he used curse-words to curse words. Nor were the goddam dictionaries the allies he thought they ought to be; they nearly always betrayed him by granting a word several definitions, some of which were maddeningly at odds with others. That was why Ross fell back with such relish upon Fowler's *Modern English Usage* — the work of a petty tyrant, who imposed idiosyncrasies by fiat. Ross was awed by Fowler; he would have liked to hold the whip hand over words and syntax as Fowler did. If words in themselves were not to be trusted, figures of speech were suspicious in the extreme. Metaphors and similes were Ross's adversaries; my blue butterflies would have been wiped out by a single sweep of his big nicotine-stained hand, a single agitated "Jesus!"

Ross's way of stating the principle of "Talk" was simple and direct. "If you can't be funny," he would growl, "be interesting." Like so many Ross formulations, this is something easier said than done.

By now I am half-convinced that I came to work for *The New Yorker* as a child. I make up stories to the effect that I was too small to reach above the lowest row of typewriter keys and therefore had to write pieces that consisted largely of words containing the letters z, x, c, v, b, n, and m. In truth, I sold my first short story to the magazine in 1936, when the magazine was eleven and I was approaching my twenty-second birthday. I was well able to strike all those shapely, necessary vowels in the upper row of keys, and I did so with eagerness. I had graduated from Yale in June of that year and had got married the next day. My wife and I spent the summer honeymooning in Europe, from time to time accompanied, not altogether to our convenience, by some seventy members of the Yale Glee Club. I felt thoroughly grown-up at twenty-one — more grown-up, indeed, than I have ever succeeded in feeling since. The confidence of ignorant youth seeps slowly, slowly away and to our astonishment no confidence of sapient age comes surging in to take its place.

When I started at *The New Yorker*, I felt an unshakable confidence in my talent and intelligence. I revelled in them openly, like a dolphin diving skyward out of the sea. After almost forty years, my assurance is less than it was; the revellings, such as they are, take place in becoming seclusion. This steady progress downward in the amount of one's confidence is a commonplace at the magazine — one might almost call it a tradition. Again and again, some writer who has made a name for himself in the world will begin to write for us and will discover as if for the first time how difficult writing is. The machinery of benign skepticism that surrounds and besets him in the form of editors, copy editors, and checkers, to say nothing of fellow-writers, digs a yawning pit an inch or so beyond his desk. He hears it repeated as gospel that there are not three people in all America who can set down a simple declarative sentence correctly; what are the odds against his being one of this tiny elect?

In some cases, the pressure of all those doubting eyes upon his copy is more than the writer can bear. When the galleys of a piece are placed in front of him, covered with scores, perhaps hundreds, of pencilled hen-tracks of inquiry, suggestion, and correction, he may sense not the glory of creation but the threat of being stung to death by an army of gnats. Upon which he may think of nothing better to do than lower his head onto his blotter and burst into tears. Thanks to the hen-tracks and their consequences, the piece will be much improved, but the author of it will be pitched into a state of graver self-doubt than ever. Poor devil, he will type out his name on a sheet of paper and stare at it long and long, with dumb uncertainty. It looks — oh, Christ! — his name looks as if it could stand some working on.

As I was writing the above, Gardner Botsford, the editor who, among other duties, handles copy for "Theatre," came into my office with the galleys of my latest play review in his hand. Wearing an expression of solemnity, he said, "I am obliged to inform you that Miss Gould has found a buried dangling modifier in one of your sentences." Miss Gould is our head copy editor and unquestionably knows as much about English grammar as anyone alive. Gerunds, predicate nominatives, and passive periphrastic conjugations are mother's milk to her, as they are not to me. Nevertheless, I boldly challenged her allegation. My prose was surely correct in every way. Botsford placed the galleys before me and indicated the offending sentence, which ran, "I am told that in her ninth decade this beautiful woman's only complaint in respect to her role is that she doesn't have enough work to do."

I glared blankly at the galleys. Humiliating enough to have buried a dangling modifier unawares; still more humiliating not to be able to disinter it. Botsford came to my rescue. "Miss Gould points out that as the sentence is written, the meaning is that the complaint is in its ninth decade and has, moreover, suddenly and unaccountably assumed the female gender." I said that in my opinion the sentence could only be made worse by being corrected — it was plain that "The only complaint of this beautiful woman in her ninth decade . . ." would hang on the page as heavy as a sash-weight. "Quite so," said Botsford. "There are times when to be right is wrong, and this is one of them. The sentence stands."

2

The celebrated nit-pickiness of Harold Ross has been inherited by his successor, William Shawn, and with this additional cause for alarm: that while Ross was an aggressively ignorant man, with a head full of odd scraps of information and misinformation and with little experience of the arduous discipline of taking thought (in reasoning he could get from A to B and even to C, but he could rarely reach D), Shawn has read in many fields of knowledge, appears to remember everything he has read, and has trained his natural gift for orderly analysis to the point where he is able not merely to make his way from A through D but also to march on into the fastnesses, impenetrable by ordinary mortals, of O and P and Q and R and S and T. Most of Ross's queries could be disposed of without much effort — the classic Rossian query was "Is Moby Dick the whale or the man?" — but Shawn's queries are likely to require time and reflection, being nearly always less concerned with facts than with whether a writer has said what he intended to say. The embarrassment of having failed to do this is nothing to the embarrassment one feels when Shawn discovers in the course of his gently probing cross-examination that the writer no longer has the slightest recollection of what it was that he intended to say. "Why, m-m-m, ah —" is an answer I have often given on such occasions, and it is not an effective one. Usually, I have preferred the strategy of snatching up the galleys on the pretense that I have a train to catch and going off to work anew on the tangled paragraph.

Another difference between the two men is luckily of the sort that causes a writer to feel much less cause for alarm with Shawn than he would have felt with Ross. One was constantly tempted to turn a professional difference of opinion with Ross into a quarrel, because as an editor his posture was that of a belligerent. With a few notable exceptions, of which I was not one, Ross suspected

I-1. Insert good but will work only, $^\perp$ think if repeats phrase

from previous clause, i.e. "in charge of" should follow an "in charge

of" describing someone else.

2. Outside of what. Don't get.

3. Too detailed

4. Where Cutler school. Also, doesn't story get out of sequence here?
Must have given his lectre before going Cutler school.

5. Who he?
6. Did they votex sperately in these three categories, Must have, and
its am amazing coincidence that he came in fifth in all three, and
tied for third at that. Transcends credulence.

7. He means he§s moved to Pennsylvania. Fix wording.

8. Trimming can be done here.

9. Mean she left her husband for a few mos. after marraige?

10. This whole page awfully soft. For God sake, at (a) there's no
point to enumerating all these subididiaries. We haven't space for
such, and its dull.

11. What tanks? Explain.
12 Awful lot of words here. Its this kind of thing that gets repetious.
Hellman has a dozen examples of such adrbitness before x gets through,
probably eight or xix nine of them unneduessary.

ñÑm Part II X. Why single out the 100 mil of domestic business just?
First part says radio o does $160 mil. Mean Turck just has to do with'
domestic business, or what. Indirection her anyway.

4. Indirection. There's been no indication Rockefeller was going to

work there.

5. Not certain I understand this exactly, but it seems like the same

old point again.

6. Has his father the Dr. passed on, or what?

7̶.̶x̶ñ̶k̶x̶x̶x̶x̶x̶x̶ñ̶x̶n̶x̶x̶ñ̶x̶a̶k̶n̶

7. Sheriff who? Who's he?

8. Bushwah.

9. twa As dull and unconvincing a joke as I've heard in some time.

*A characteristic specimen of a Ross query sheet. A Profile might prompt as many as a
hundred and fifty such challenges and ruminations. The Profile under scrutiny here concerned
a businessman named Turck and was written by Geoffrey T. Hellman. The typos and
neologisms are classically Rossian. "Credulence" may well be a needed addition to the
language.*

writers of trying to put something over on him. He knew reporters — after all, he had been a reporter himself, and a conspicuously raffish and incompetent one — and he was convinced that
they would always get away with murder if they could. Again and

again in his notes about a piece he would type, "Given facts will fix," and the impression conveyed by these words was, and was intended to be, that a sorely tried man of superior skills was consenting to improve the work of someone who was at best lazy and at worst an imbecile. Shawn's attitude toward writing, and by extension toward writers as a class, has always been that of reverence. There have been circumstances — never involving one-self, of course, but involving some of one's fellow-writers — in which it has been hard to credit this attitude, but the evidence is that it is genuine. Certainly it has survived decades of work on manuscripts of remarkable ineptitude (in the old days more than now, there were contributors to the magazine who delivered what Hamburger used to call great bundles of wet wash), and if Shawn were only pretending to be reverent, his mask would have slipped at least once or twice during all those years.

Shawn's method in dealing with a writer is to convey such a high regard for a given piece of work that once it has been put in type and the moment comes for the editor to challenge certain phrases and seek certain necessary changes, the writer is pretty well convinced that the corrections will cost Shawn as much pain as they do him — indeed, that the corrections are being made, at no matter what expense of spirit, only in order to bring a master-piece from near-perfection to perfection. No author can fail to recognize the attractive logic of this proposition. The hazard in such cases is not, as it was with Ross, that one will pick a quarrel but that one will give way too quickly and easily. Shawn's delicacy is a negative brute force that gets greater results than Ross's posi-tive one. Because most writers would do anything rather than hurt Shawn's feelings, they begin to babble premature agreements; they hear themselves apologizing for the gaucherie of a phrase that had seemed, up to a few minutes before, a stroke of genius.

The following passage is an exaggeration of Shawn's oral edit-ing technique. It is an attempt to indicate with words what Shawn indicates with silences, hesitations, sidelong glances of his very blue eyes, tentative baton-like strokes in air of his dark-green Venus drawing pencil. Questioning a comma, he will shake his head and say in his soft voice that he realizes perfectly well what a lot of time and thought have gone into the comma and that in the ordinary course of events he would be the first to say that the comma was precisely the form of punctuation that he would have been most happy to encounter at that very place in the sentence, but isn't there the possibility — oh, only the remotest one, to be sure, and yet perhaps worth considering for a moment in the light of the care already bestowed on the construction — that the sentence could be made to read infinitesimally more clearly if, say, instead of a comma a semicolon were to be inserted at just that point? And the author, touched by Shawn's sympathy, aghast with admiration for the skill of his circumlocutions, and determined at all costs to prevent Shawn from suffering the humiliation of having his proposed semicolon rejected, throws up his hands and exclaims, "Much clearer your way!"

New Yorker editors have always been notorious for preoccupying themselves with punctuation. It is a virtue — or a failing — that goes back to Ross's never-ending and never very successful attempt to educate himself. There is reason to believe that he was already cracked on the subject when he was editing the Army newspaper *Stars and Stripes* in Paris during the First World War. In the *New Yorker* years, he would ransack Webster and Roget in search of the ideal word for his purpose: surely it must exist somewhere, waiting to have a pinch of salt put on its tail. Similarly, he was ever in pursuit of an ideal form of punctuation. I have a magpie mind, not unlike Ross's in this respect, and I remember telling him once that I had read in some obscure publication that the laws passed by the English Parliament had to be drawn up without any interior punctuation at all, lest a single misplaced comma cause — as on one occasion a misplaced comma had indeed caused — the law to say the opposite of what it was intended to say.

Ross was enchanted by this information. It was the news he had been waiting for all his life. Much as he loved commas, semicolons, colons, and dashes, they were but a means to an end; he loved them in the hope that they would serve to make a statement as exact as possible, and the notion that they could be dispensed with altogether, in the name of some supreme exactitude, electrified him. For days he experimented with sentences that omitted all forms of punctuation except the period. In vain, for what emerged was a series of curt declarations like those to be found in an old-fashioned child's primer ("Dicky Dare met a cow. It was a nice cow. Dicky thought he would speak to the cow."), and Ross had no more relish for concision than he had for small children. He was contradictory in every aspect of his nature — at once brave and timid, cruel and tender-hearted, shy and overbearing — and his mingled emotions in respect to language were no exception to the rule. The fact is that he wanted everything to be both plain and baroque. His passion for qualifying things as he huffed and puffed his way uphill and downdale after clear-cut meanings led to a staggering multiplicity of modifiers. His sentences bulged with restrictive and non-restrictive clauses, themselves grossly bedecked with a dozen or more prepositional phrases, and the result of all this continuous agglutinative heaping up of particularities was a style that seemed (if one can imagine such a thing) the handiwork of a Henry James with a tin ear.

In the days when Berton Roueché and I were writing a good many "Talk" pieces, we became restive under the literary mutilations ritually practiced upon us by Ross in the sacred name of accuracy. ("Given facts will fix.") We took care to write well, and we were proud of what we achieved, and to have this clumsy water buffalo of an editor come stomping into our neatly laid-out gardens and start crushing all of our delicate litotes underfoot was unendurable. When we protested, Ross replied mildly that, goddam it, it was up to us to rewrite his rewrite; that way we might get some halfway decent stories into the magazine.

I recall on one occasion writing a "Talk" piece about a man who had invented a toy that became, as toys will, a seven days' wonder; it was called a Zoomerang and it sprang into existence as a result of its inventor's having noticed that a certain kind of laminated paper used in adding machines and the like had a tendency, when stretched out and then released, to curl back tightly upon itself. Well! The toy itself was so unimportant and at the same time so difficult to give an accurate account of in words that for what must have been the first time in my writing career, and was certainly the last, I fell back upon applying to it that lamest of adjectives, "indescribable." Ross was on the phone the moment he got my copy. "Nothing is indescribable, Gill," he barked. (Ross had no difficulty turning "Gill" into a bark; moreover, he gave it the same ring of contempt that he gave the "god" in "goddam.") "Send that damn toy down to me. I'll show you."

And so there appeared in the magazine a "Talk" piece in which Ross demonstrated to his satisfaction the triumph of the prose of reason, however lumpy, over the prose of intuition, however graceful. The piece began: "The hottest novelty in the toy line this season is an article called the Zoomerang, which consists of a two-and-a-half-inch-wide strip of tough, resilient red, white, and blue paper attached to and wound around one end of a stick somewhat smaller than a pencil. Using the other end of the stick as a handle, you flick the wrist or flail the arm and whip the coil outward in an elongated spiral for a distance of up to eight feet. The paper then springs back into place (if all goes well and it doesn't get tangled up)." The anticlimactic parenthesis is characteristic of Ross. It effectively drains much of the looked-for playfulness out of the piece by its earnest truth-telling. What had happened was that Ross, by then a grumpy man in his late fifties and one not regularly given to playing with toys, had felt obliged to experiment with the Zoomerang and had found that it didn't always work properly. Who cared? Why, Ross cared, of course. He would no sooner have withheld from the readers of *The New Yorker* the fact that the Zoomerang occasionally failed to recoil than he would have given them an inaccurate measurement of the height of the Washington Monument. Ross clung to facts as a shipwrecked man clings to a spar.

In an attempt to get back at Ross for his rough handling of our well-wrought prose, Roueché and I began a contest to see who could write the longest — and therefore, in our eyes, the worst possible — sentence for "Talk." I won the contest with a cumbersome gigantosaurus of a sentence some twenty-six lines long, but the victory was a hollow one. At least two of the lines had been added by Ross himself, who had observed nothing ungainly about my effort. On the contrary, he congratulated me on it, as he was later to do on a "Talk" piece I wrote about the annual flower show that used to be held at the Grand Central Palace, on Lexington Avenue. We covered the event every year, so every year it became more difficult to invent something fresh for the lead; one year I began the piece with what I assumed was a obvious borrowing from Shakespeare: "The daffodils that come before the swallow dares and take the winds of March with beauty took Grand Central Palace last week, etc., etc." To my embarrassment, Ross sent me a note praising my lead in a way that indicated that he had not recognized the source. There was nothing for me to say except

Ross permitted no indirection or physical implausibility in the text of the magazine, and he exercised a similar strictness in respect to drawings. For a long time he resisted running this brilliant drawing by Arno, on the grounds that it was based on an impossible situation. If the faucets in the shower couldn't be turned off, surely the drain in the floor of the shower would let the water out. If the faucets in the shower couldn't be turned off and the drain were stopped up, water would be bound to leak out around the edges of the shower door. Moreover, all shower doors are made with an open space at the top, so there would be at least six inches or so of air available at the top of the shower; ergo, no man in a shower is ever really in danger of drowning.

"Thank you." Similarly, on a still later occasion, I dropped into a "Talk" piece a reference, without attribution, to Tennyson's "nature red in tooth and claw." Not knowing that the phrase was a quotation, Ross felt free to change it to "nature red in claw and tooth." One is bound to wonder why he bothered to tamper with such a trifle. His literal-mindedness being what it was, I suspect that he must have worried it out that an animal seizing its prey would bloody its claws before it got around to bloodying its teeth. Something just as reasonable and just as ridiculous as that.

Otto Soglow has been drawing for the magazine since 1925. This illustrative "spot" drawing for the "Talk of the Town" department has to do with a story about Desmond Guinness and how much easier his task of raising money for the restoration and preservation of eighteenth-century Irish buildings would be if the name of a society he had founded didn't continuously remind the Irish of their hated English masters.

A footnote to Ross on grammar: in my twenties, I was an ardent student of Freud, and one day I undertook to explain, not much to Ross's pleasure, Freud's theory about the profound meanings that can be deduced from slips of the tongue and, by extension, slips of the pen and typewriter as well. "For example," I said to Ross, "you have ulcers and you treat them by drinking milk. This involves the nuisance of keeping a container of milk near your desk at all times. Here in one of your notes on a 'Talk' piece of mine you've intended to write, 'Gill puts too heavy a burden on commas.' Instead, you've written, 'Gill puts too heavy a borden on commas.' Obviously, your unconscious, preoccupied with ulcers and milk, threw up 'Borden' at the very moment that it ought to have thrown up 'burden.'" "Gill," Ross said, "you talk like a goddam fool."

3

Once upon a time, we had a writer on the magazine whose breezy motto was, "Don't get it right, get it written!" He didn't stay with us long. His careless practices but not his high spirits were shared by another writer of a good many years ago, a man whom I think of as the classic loser among the many losers who have worked their way, nearly always by means mysterious to me, into and then away from the not very turbulent whirlpool of *The New Yorker,* vanishing after a while as if they were so much foam. But they were not foam, or not altogether, and it is often the case that ten or twenty years after their departure from the magazine, an obituary of one or another of them will appear in *The New York Times* — an obituary whose importance the *Times* evidently will have judged according to the dead man's connection with the magazine. It may turn out that few of us who read the obituary will be able to remember a word of what the dead man wrote, or even perhaps what he looked like: was he the hawk-faced little man who used to flatten himself like the crushed corpse of a crow against the wall of a corridor when anyone passed him, though the corridor was wide enough for two big men to pass in comfort? Or was he the sour blond boy who spent much of the day in the nearby Cortile bar, writing his pieces in cramped wheels of words along the circumference of innumerable cardboard beer coasters, which he would gather up at nightfall and deposit in the storm-sewer on the corner of Forty-fourth Street and Fifth Avenue?

Scores and hundreds of faces have blurred, and the names affixed to them have been blotted out; if I remember my classic loser vividly, it is because it was a portion of the only genius he possessed to make me feel guilty for disliking him. It was a guilt I had no reason to feel — had I not the right to dislike a dislikable man? — and yet I go on unreasonably feeling it to this day. I perceive that even writing about him now, so long after his death, will not diminish my guilt. He has me locked in an embrace that nothing as simple as his death or the passage of time can release me from. It was his gift to gather a person in against his will and then never let go; I will try to tell the truth about the Loser, but not in the hope that I can slough him off at last.

He was lame. One had to feel sympathy for him because of that inescapable burden, and it didn't occur to any of us on the magazine not to feel it, at least for a time. I have always assumed that Shawn hired the Loser in part because of his disability; I have assumed, too, that the Loser was well aware that this was one of the reasons he had been hired. For it became plain early in his stay with us that, whether consciously or unconsciously, he trafficked in his lameness. His limp was much more pronounced on the days when he was in particular need of encouragement than it was on the days when he was not. Approaching Shawn's door for help, his gait would be almost literally tumble-down; leaving Shawn's door, it would be close to normal. Moreover, with a cunning that one couldn't fail to admire, he managed to make the low quality of his work a function of his lameness. He was a lazy reporter, who sought constantly to borrow other reporter's notes, and he was a writer of little talent, but these professional failings had nothing to do with the condition of his legs; how, then, did he contrive to trick us into feeling that if we didn't admire his work, we were despising him as a cripple?

It was a blackmail that he practiced with mastery in half a dozen forms. One of the most contemptible of these forms was the device of praising a colleague above his worth, at the same time flagrantly abasing himself. One would cringe at the extravagance of his compliments and one would cringe equally at the intimacy of his confession of self-loathing. He would come up to me, I remember — *very* close up to me, for it was among his disagreeable mannerisms to make every encounter an eyeball-to-eyeball affair — and assure me that never in a thousand years would he be able to write a piece as excellent as one of mine. It was a remark that presented difficulties. On the one hand, what he said was true: any piece of work that reached a certain level of competence was far beyond the Loser. On the other hand, for this very reason the compliment, despite its immense thousand-year scale, was a tiny one. To make matters worse, the Loser, though he happened to be speaking the truth, was the last man on earth by whom one wished to be judged. Even less did one want to be warmly congratulated by him. I would feel his valueless praise fastening itself to me like some odious poultice, but any protest on my part would be in vain. He would hail it as demonstrating that my modesty was a match for my great gifts; more slovenly glop of commendation would come flooding in on me. Worst of all was the fact that he really did admire me and really did deplore his ineradicable second-rateness. He saw plainly enough that he was not fit to succeed, but to insist that the rest of us see this, and then that our seeing it be a means of his making good —! That was one of his forms of blackmail, and so was his indirectly conveying to us that if we didn't consent to let him become a peer, we would be forcing him to become a pariah. All or nothing, said the silent, outrageous threat: there was no middle ground. None of us could bear to pronounce anathema upon him; he was, alas, a member of the human race. And so he trapped us one by one into a seeming friendship with him; we became accomplices in his mediocrity. He linked arms with ours and smiled his classic loser's smile and said how great it was that we were all writers together on such a wonderful magazine.

If how people get hired by *The New Yorker* is often mysterious to me, how they get fired is still more so. The word "fired" is nearly always too strong for the actual event, which will ordinarily consist of reaching the last, negligible step in a long series of failed connections and mutual disappointments. The story goes that in the old days Ross would first take away a writer's typewriter, then his pencils and paper, and then his desk and chair, reducing him by stages to a condition of journalistic paralysis. In the case of the Loser, it was an unlucky and characteristic mingling of slovenly habits in and out of the office that led to a parting of the ways. It appeared that his private life, about which I knew very little, was as ramshackle as his professional one. In the brief time that he was working on *The New Yorker* — a time when four or five pieces came out over his name, and I could imagine the prodigies of skillful editing that had made their publication possible — he was between marriages. His domestic arrangements were evidently every bit as disheveled as his syntax, and the moment came when, deciding to cut corners for financial and perhaps other reasons, he simply moved into the office and set up a bizarre form of light housekeeping there. The gall of the man!

His cubicle was too small to contain a couch, and there must have been many a night when, with some of the editors working very late, he couldn't avail himself of the couch in the hall upon which E. B. White, John McNulty, and other writers occasionally took cat-naps. Perhaps he slept at his desk, or perhaps he stretched out on the linoleum-covered floor; nor am I beyond supposing that from time to time some poor loser of a girl took pity on him and let him share her bed, such as it was. I was later to learn from Daise Terry, our office manager at that time, that the Loser's desk was transformed into a sort of chiffonier — odds and ends of ill-pressed clothing filled the drawers, and an overcoat and a pair of galoshes were kept wrapped in a plastic shopping bag in the knee space of the desk. He brought in an electric hot plate, which he kept concealed in a large orange-cardboard letter file. Other files held cans of instant coffee, boxes of biscuits, jars of marmalade and peanut butter. The blotter on his desk grew soggy; it became a Sargasso Sea of cookie crumbs and specks of cheese. For the first time, the office had a mouse. No doubt the Loser had brought it in with his groceries, in a brown paper bag from the nearest deli. The mouse throve on the Loser's leavings, and for all I know, became his pet.

These unattractive domestic arrangements were to be revealed only after the Loser, true to the temperament of all losers, went too far and by choice became the agent of his doom; which is to say that he expanded his territory to include the men's room. We might never have noticed that he brushed his teeth and shaved there and — I assume — treated himself to an occasional early-morning sponge bath there; what attracted the attention of one of the older editors, a man totally unlike most members of the staff in being always very well-dressed and very short-tempered, was an incident that resulted from the Loser's having the nerve to do his laundry there. The incident gave the magazine a sufficient reason for discouraging his presence on the premises if not for discharging him, and that was welcome news. Still, one has to say in his behalf that, of its peculiar loser's kind, the episode was very fine. According to Miss Terry, once a week the Loser would improvise a cat's cradle of strings from the mirror above the sinks to the stanchions supporting the toilet-booth doors and suspend from these strings an assortment of newly washed hose, boxer shorts, shirts, and handkerchiefs. Doing his laundry early on Saturday night, before setting out on his social rounds, he would take care to have the laundry down and out of the way before anyone turned up on Monday morning.

Unfortunately, his schedule did not allow for chance visits to the office — especially not a chance visit by this particular editor, who, on his way home late one Saturday evening from a supper party at "21," had his taxi-driver stop off at our building; it had occurred to him to pick up some galleys that he wished to finish correcting by the first of the week. He located the galleys in his office and then, passing the men's room door on his way out, and being the most efficient of men, thought to take advantage of his opportunity. He pushed open the door, perhaps a trifle vehemently — his temperament was impulsive to the point of brusqueness — and the door struck the outer reaches of the Loser's cat's cradle of strings. Down on the editor's carefully barbered head as he stood in the dark and fumbled for the light-switch fell the great soft web of the Loser's dripping-wet underwear. It cannot have been pleasant, pulling the clammy, unknown things off one's face and shoulders; nor can the wetness seeping through the galleys and into the editor's Weatherill evening jacket have improved matters. Worst of all must have been the discovery, once the light had been turned on, of what those clammy things were. I've heard that the editor spent a sleepless night and a raging Sunday; be that as it may, the Loser was not often to be seen in the corridors from that moment on. Two office boys filled several paper cartons with his household effects and left them for him by the elevators. It was a week before the mouse was caught, and by then it was half-dead of hunger.

Another exceptional parting had as its leading actors, in what amounted to a thirty-second melodrama, Shawn and a reporter whom I will call Rufus Horgan, because that was not his name. The time was the Second World War, and Horgan was among a number of peculiar figures who joined the staff of the magazine during that period. Many of our writers and editors were being drafted into the armed forces, and Ross, hard-pressed, had fallen back upon his early habit of hiring people seemingly at random, on the basis of chance encounters on trains and in restaurants and sometimes on the recommendation of friends. Adversity strengthened his habitual mild paranoia and this had, as usual, a tonic effect; it stimulated Ross to feel that he was the victim of an unjust fate. The posture he favored in his fantasies about himself was one of total beleaguerment. Seeing the war in personal terms, he found it easy to suspect that in the course of seeking to destroy Hitler, the United States was also seeking to destroy *The New Yorker.*

Ross roared in protest — not only were some of his best people being taken away but the very paper on which to print the goddam magazine was being taken away. The bureaucrats in Washington were an outrage; the war was an outrage; and though it was tactless and perhaps unpatriotic to say so, Ross couldn't help feeling that it was proving a lot less agreeable to live through than the First World War had been.

Ross had fought in that war. Well, not *fought*, exactly — an itinerant young newspaperman working for the moment in San Francisco and having little reputation except for horseplay and gambling, he had enlisted in 1917 in the Eighteenth Engineers Regiment, had gone AWOL after a few weeks in France, had made his way to Paris and talked himself into a job on the newly created *Stars and Stripes*, and had soon become its editor. He remained a private, detached from the Engineers. (The criminal offense of his having gone AWOL was quickly adjusted in the name of getting out the paper.) Ross rejoiced to find himself the boss of men who were his superiors both in Army rank and in professional experience, to say nothing of age. He had a wonderful, peaceable time in Paris; by day he was learning how to become an editor and by night he was playing poker, raising simple-minded hell, and even falling in love with a girl named Jane Grant, who was subsequently to become the first of his three wives. No two ways about it, he and his buddies — Alexander Woollcott, John T. Winterich, Stephen Early — enjoyed the hell out of the war; its successor was obviously a much grimmer affair, and not simply in the theatres of combat but on the home front as well.

PVT. H. W. ROSS

COMPANY C
EIGHTEENTH ENGINEERS RAILWAY U. S. ARMY

UNITED STATES EXPEDITIONARY
FORCE IN FRANCE

CARE OF THE ADJUTANT GENERAL
WASHINGTON, D. C.

Ross's buddy in the First World War, John T. Winterich, wrote once that Ross was the only Army private he knew who carried calling cards. Winterich suspected that Ross had had the cards printed as part of some nefarious private scheme for outwitting the authorities. Soon afterward, he went A.W.O.L. from the Eighteenth Engineers and never returned. He might have been executed for this offense; instead, he was made editor of The Stars and Stripes.

Here he was, the founder and editor of a brilliant humorous magazine, and soon there might be nothing humorous left to write about, or draw pictures about; there might not even be any writers or artists. (On *The New Yorker,* the tradition has been to call cartoonists artists, with the pleasing result that many cartoonists have become artists.) Ross was aided in those parlous times by Shawn, Lobrano, Maxwell, Gibbs, and half a dozen other able editors, who, either for reasons of health, age, or size of family, had been put in a deferred classification, but the gaps in the magazine's little garrison of defenders were widening day by day. No wonder Ross felt besieged; no wonder he felt obliged to people the battlements with second-raters.

Thus, Horgan. He was a Southerner who had been a reporter on the St. Louis *Post-Dispatch,* and it may have been Ross's high regard for the newspaper, from which we had already gained the writer Robert Lewis Taylor, that caused Horgan to be hired. He was a pudgy man, with profuse, oily hair and a smooth skin that I remember as looking always slightly damp, as if, even in winter, he were quietly sweating to himself, as other people quietly mumble to themselves. He talked a great deal, evidently to his satisfaction, but how much writing he did I don't know — the only piece that appeared in the magazine over his name was an undistinguished Profile of a commercial artist. In those wartime days, Shawn worked something like eighteen hours a day, seven days a week; he was a phenomenon of apparently imperturbable industry, but the moment came when at last he was seen to be perturbed. It was Horgan who brought off this unexpected feat and he did so by the simplest possible means: a display of his incomparable vulgarity.

Shawn had come to *The New Yorker* building on a Saturday, no doubt to pick up more work. He got into the elevator and asked the operator to take him to the nineteenth floor, where his office was. He was joined in the elevator by a tipsy Horgan, accompanied by a tipsy girl. Horgan was sweaty and effusive, and Shawn cowered. It is the custom at the magazine for people not to speak to each other in elevators, as it is the custom for them not to whistle in the corridors (a temptation easy for most members of the staff to resist), but it appears that Horgan was in need of his boss's approbation, and he burst out genially, "Guess there's nothin' wrong, is there, Shawn, with a little sexual interco'se in the office on a Saturday afternoon?"

Shawn said to the operator, "Please stop. I must get off this elevator at once."

And he did.

And soon Horgan, too, had drifted off into limbo, no doubt believing himself to be still a member of the staff.

4

The vagaries of memory! Shawn recollects that the magazine hired Taylor, Roueché, and Horgan in that order, but according to Roueché, when he told his wife that Horgan had succeeded in getting a job on *The New Yorker,* Kay Roueché said at once, with a characteristic wifely mingling of tactlessness and love, "If that no-good Rufus Horgan can get a job there, so can you!" Roueché thereupon came East and got his job and has been writing for us ever since — dozens of "Talk" pieces, innumerable "Briefly Noted" 's for "Books," and long pieces for "Annals of Medicine," the celebrated department that Ross encouraged him to originate. Shawn makes it a rule to read every word published in the magazine, often not once but several times, in typescript, galleys, and page proofs. If there are any exceptions to this rule, they must have to do with certain of Roueché's medical pieces, or with such a piece as Rachel MacKenzie's terrifying account, a few years ago, of open-heart surgery. Shawn has a strong aversion to clinical details that concern the human body, especially when they also concern blood, and I have sometimes wondered by what ingenious tricks of optics he contrives to read and, where necessary, correct a particularly gory passage without taking in the words.

Shawn's aversion to the clinical, like his aversion to strong language, is a measure of his radical unlikeness to Ross, who enjoyed reading and talking about diseases and who, when the time came, could speak freely of the disease — cancer of the lung — that was threatening his life. "I got the same goddam thing," he told me one day in the corridor, "as the King of England." And then, as if he suspected that I might be silently accusing him of putting on airs, he screwed up his face into a characteristic comical grimace, pursing his lips and thrusting them forward in monkey-like fashion, at the same time shoving his heavy, dark-rimmed glasses back up the long slope of his nose. I was shocked by what he told me, but I didn't assume that it meant that he was dying, nor do I know whether Ross himself assumed it at that moment. His seeming candor was often a means of trying out on others a hypothesis that he had had reason to formulate but was reluctant to accept. He had a gift for keeping certain realities at a distance as great as Shawn's gift for facing them head-on. Ross would sweep inconvenient truths . . . I was about to say "under the carpet," but the fact is that he would sweep them *onto* the carpet and leave them there, not seeing them. This was literally the case with his clothing. Coming into the office on a winter's morning, he would take off his hat and coat and simply let them drop; sometimes they would come to rest on a chair or table, sometimes on the floor.

In later years, one of his secretaries, Harriet Walden, purchased a wooden coatrack and placed it in Ross's office. Ross affected to be astonished that such an article of furniture existed. Daily Mrs. Walden would pick up his clothes and hang them on the rack and by the end of several months she had succeeded in training Ross to perform the feat by himself. He performed it only in order to please Mrs. Walden; it was an unreasonable thing to have to do, a real time-waster, but women were unreasonable creatures and one got along with them by giving way to them in matters of little importance.

Ross liked to be thought an exemplar of common sense, but all the evidence of his life is to the contrary. He was a reckless and improvident gambler who preached prudence. Very early in my career on the magazine, he gave me a lecture about money, prompted no doubt by my being in want of it. The lecture began on the expected didactic note — "Gill, you don't know a goddam thing about money" — and proceeded to tick off the various means by which I might acquire a mastery of it. I was to learn to draw up an annual budget of household expenses; I was to set aside certain sums for taxes; I was also to set aside a sum for medical emergencies; and so on and so on. It was an impressive program as he sketched it out for me, and I supposed that it was firmly grounded on his own experience. Not at all — it was a fantasy of how things ought to be with him, a goal that Ross, twenty-two years my senior, was even farther from reaching than I.

Though I didn't know it at the time, my lecturer was a man whose financial affairs were in a state of advanced and continuous disarray. It was typical of him to keep a fistful of checks loose in his pockets, to fill them out helter-skelter whenever the occa-

Cutting down the specially grown trees to make paper for THE NEW YORKER. At the right, supervising the work, may be seen Our Mr. Eustace Tilley, one of THE NEW YORKER's special superintendents of forestry.

THE MAKING OF A MAGAZINE

A TOUR THROUGH THE VAST ORGANIZATION OF THE NEW YORKER

I. *Securing Paper for* THE NEW YORKER

THE most essential feature of a magazine is paper. You might assemble all the vast organization of THE NEW YORKER, with its hundreds of thousands of workers in all the innumerable branches of the industry; you might gather all the type, ink, and other accessories of printing; you might even operate the huge presses week in and week out, turning out the 8,657,000 copies of THE NEW YORKER. But if you did not have any paper, the result would not be a magazine; and all those issues of THE NEW YORKER you had worked so hard to produce would have to be thrown away.

The first man to realize the importance of paper in the manufacture of a magazine was Horace Greeley. In 1847 he bought two acres up in Haarlem, on the site where C. C. N. Y. now stands; and upon this property he planted twenty-eight poplar seeds. It was his intention, "God willing," (as he put it), that these seeds should grow into trees, and from those trees THE NEW YORKER should obtain the paper on which to print its issues.

In those early days, paper was derived from a number of sources—the backs of old envelopes, chewing gum wrappers, discarded Lily Cups—anything that came to hand. It was the duty of every member of the staff of THE NEW YORKER to keep his eyes open on his way to the office, bringing in what paper he could secure on the way. Here the paper was assorted into sizes, and a trained staff, equipped with red erasers, rubbed it clean.

Meantime, the circulation of THE NEW YORKER had grown from three to four to five and so on to seven figures; and as the inefficiency of this method grew more apparent, the practicality of Mr. Greeley's plan was realized. For some time thereafter, THE NEW YORKER depended for its paper on what wood it could gather around New York; but as the Bronx began to be built up and Central Park was taken over by the city, THE NEW YORKER bought a vast tract of land in Maine, where they set out 5,260 trees. This scheme was dubbed at the time "The Maine Bubble" and was laughed at by everyone; but people since then have learned to laugh up the other sleeve.

In order to realize the number of trees which must be felled each week, for one issue of THE NEW YORKER, the reader should try to visualize a vast forest of 8,657,000 trees, or sufficient trees when divided by 10 to equal 865,700 trees. In other words, if the reader will picture one tree, and then multiply that tree by 10% of 86,570,000 trees, he may perhaps form some idea of how many trees 8,657,000 trees are. It is typical of the great NEW YORKER organization, that it owns and operates to-day the biggest paper forest in the world, covering 29,000,000 or so acres in Canada, Maine, and northern New Jersey, under the close supervision of THE NEW YORKER's field superintendent, Mr. Eustace Tilley.

Although most of the paper for THE NEW YORKER is made nowadays from these trees, nevertheless, there is a certain percentage which is made in the old way, by picking it up here and there. The material best suited to this work has been found to be an oblong sheet of green paper issued by the United States Government, and bearing the words: "Five Dollars." From this single scrap, enough paper can be procured to print 52 copies; and to any reader who will submit such a bill to THE NEW YORKER, the editors will mail a year's subscription free.

sion demanded, and to keep no record of the amounts. So little attention did he pay to money coming in or going out that a secretary, Harold Winney, in the course of a few years was able to embezzle something over seventy thousand dollars from Ross, without Ross's having the faintest suspicion that anything was awry. In his book *The Years with Ross,* Thurber tells poor Winney's story at length. He was a homosexual who spent large sums on boy friends and on playing the horses; forging Ross's signature on checks that Ross would never take the trouble to examine was a temptation that proved irresistible. It was the business department of the magazine and not Ross that first smelled a rat; sensing that exposure was imminent, Winney went home, turned on the gas, and killed himself.

Ross was sorry to have lost the seventy thousand dollars and sorry as well to have lost a good secretary, for, embezzlement aside, Winney had been a model of efficiency and decorum. Ross had something else to be sorry about, and to fear, and that was his own exposure. Once the story broke in the newspapers, the reputation he wished to possess as a hard-headed man of affairs would be difficult to sustain; he would be shown up before the whole world, or so he thought, as a sap, a sucker, a rube, born to be taken. Being already aware of Ross's careless fiscal practices, his friends would have no reason to be surprised, but they would feign surprise in order to make him the more miserable. How they would relish his public humiliation and seek to prolong it! Much of Ross's comradeship was based on the old Army custom of coarse insult and practical joking; he had spent his life taunting and jeering at his buddies for their repeated follies, and now they would repay him in kind. To help diminish his disgrace, Ross took care to diminish the amount of money that Winney was said to have embezzled; he saw to it that the announced sum came to seventeen thousand dollars instead of seventy. In order further to restore his self-esteem, Ross worked it out that his was a special case: Winney had tried to destroy him because, as the investigation of Winney's private life had disclosed, Winney was a homosexual and that was what homosexuals always tried to do to "normal" men. Thus, Ross established himself in his favorite role of the victim unjustly singled out by fate. How was he to have known, he protested, that Winney was a fairy?

Ross was probably telling the truth; he wouldn't have noticed that Winney was a homosexual for a reason I have already mentioned: that what it was inconvenient for Ross to observe did not exist for him. If challenged, he might have argued that he would never risk hiring a homosexual, on any of a dozen preposterous grounds; the fact was that he hired them often and willingly and took ruthless advantage of their subservience to him, which he called loyalty. In matters of sex, Ross was a notably ignorant man, as well as a prude. (One of his wives confessed that she had never seen him naked; he came to her bed in a nightgown.) He had been born in Aspen, Colorado, in 1892, at the flood-tide of Victorian puritanism, to a Protestant schoolteacher from Kansas and a Protestant immigrant from the north of Ireland, and the views of life with which they furnished his young mind were based on the superstitions of a far earlier time. Talking with Ross in the thirties and forties of this century, one had to remember that if the topic was sex, or black people, or Jews, or Catholics, his attitudes and much of his information had been the ugly commonplaces of almost a hundred years before. He was a throwback and not always an appealing one.

If Ross was unreliable in his opinions about heterosexual relations, when it came to homosexual ones he was all bluff and harsh-tongued male arrogance. He thought of homosexuals as being effeminate — nances, pansies, fairies. (He died before "faggot" became a popular term of derogation; he would have used it with pleasure.) He saw them as failed women, and his estimate of women was far from high. He would not have believed that his stereotype of the homosexual as a limp-wristed lah-de-dah is but a small minority of the homosexual population as a whole; he would have scorned the notion that the majority of homosexuals are undetectable by mannerisms of dress, speech, or bodily movement and that many homosexuals are to be found playing the roughest and bloodiest of body-contact sports. But then, so artless was Ross in this respect that he saw nothing strange — and history must take care to see nothing strange — in the fact that upon his divorce from Jane Grant he moved into an apartment with an actor once known as "the Singing Policeman." Ross was used to having male roommates. He lived with men much more comfortably and therefore much more happily than he did with women; to him it was plainly more "normal."

For his purposes on the magazine, Ross needed a certain kind of homosexual, whom he thought of as the only kind. To preserve the skimpy fiction that he was not surrounded by his supposed natural enemies, he ignored everything about them except their work. Quiet and orderly nest-builders, they took pleasure in being roared at and bullied and pushed to their limits. Hard-driving Ross was a figure worthy of their being chastened by, and a single word of his praise was precious beyond measure — forty years later, they would recall the occasion and shake their heads, marvelling. Indisputably, they gave good value. They worked hard and for comparatively low wages, in part because they could afford to, having no wives and children to support; moreover, they were able to keep longer and more irregular hours than men whose wives expected them to be home for dinner at a certain time each day and perhaps also to come home early on occasion to entertain the little ones at birthday parties. In a word, they were bachelors, and as such, a resource readily manipulable by Ross. (Ross once complained to Shawn that he didn't think I was going to prove loyal to the magazine. By then I had been working on *The New Yorker* for well over ten years. What Ross meant was that I had a wife, children, an independent income, an outlet for my short stories in other magazines, and half a dozen outside interests, from architecture to tennis. Loyalty in Ross's definition was a form of consenting serfdom.) As for the nest-building faculty I have spoken of, it was indispensable in the early days of the magazine; it implied a devotion to planning and tidy workmanship much needed by an editor whose bent was for chaos.

It would have made Ross so edgy to speculate in this open fashion upon his professional relationship with homosexuals that I am beginning to feel a bit edgy myself. I will drop the subject for both our sakes, leaving unexplored the question of how Ross felt about the female homosexuals in his employ, provided he was aware that they existed. As a footnote, let me just recount an anecdote that illustrates the rough-and-ready mid-nineteenth-century nature of Ross's fiercely cherished dogmas. One day over lunch at the Algonquin, I was expounding to Ross my theory that the number of homosexuals in a given culture is probably a constant; what varies is the extent to which they can persuade society to let them be seen to exist. We were talking, of course, a couple of decades before the emergence of the Gay Alliance, at a time when people had started to notice the presence of many homosexuals in the arts; silly gossip was being spread to the effect that the number of homosexuals in the country was increasing at an unprecedented rate and that they would soon be dominating the whole of our so-called cultural scene.

Seeking weapons against such nonsense, I put it to Ross, as an older man, that there must surely have been as many homosexuals in Aspen and Salt Lake City and Denver when he was growing up in those places as there were at present. "Not true, Gill!" Ross said, pushing the proposition aside with a gesture that would have sufficed to push aside a large dog. "There were goddam few of them and we didn't call them homos, we called them amorphodites."

His reply is worth a moment's study. It was wonderfully like Ross to have conflated two or more grimly whispered barnyard credulities of his youth; it was still more wonderfully like him that, having it firmly fixed in mind that homosexuals were hermaphrodites, he got the word wrong. A man who believed in amorphodites was not one who would face sexual facts with equanimity, and Ross never did.

A footnote to a footnote: Ross and I are again having lunch at the Algonquin. (This happened perhaps half a dozen times in all; given the differences in our ages and, more importantly, the difference in our temperaments, there was no likelihood that I would be one of Ross's buddies.) We are sitting on the half-moon-shaped banquette on the right as you enter the Rose Room: a banquette I am to share many times afterward with Ross's enemy, Raoul Fleischmann, the publisher of The New Yorker, and still later with Shawn. As Ross rambles on, I study him sidelong. A doctor's son, I have inherited my father's lifelong interest in the different rates at which people age. Ross in his late forties strikes me as being exceptionally youthful: his skin is smooth and without liver spots or pronounced veins; his hair is thick and dark, more Indian-seeming than Irish. He looks like a man who will live with undiminished energy well into his eighties. Suddenly and unexpectedly he bursts out, "Never try to commit adultery in New York, Gill!"

"Why not?"

"It's too big."

Now, what on earth can this mean? The conventional belief

in respect to adultery is that it is far more discreetly committed in a big city than in a small one — indeed, that the bigger the city, the greater the chance of avoiding discovery and the greater the chance, if by bad luck the deed should happen to be discovered, of comparatively little notoriety being attached to it. As one of the biggest cities on earth, New York is commonly thought to be an ideal place in which to commit adultery; people come to it for this purpose from many thousands of miles away and add much to the attractiveness of the city by doing so. A personal mishap must have lain behind Ross's astonishing dictum. Dimly I took it in that something had happened in which Ross, as usual, had found himself the victim of an outrageous stroke of fortune, but what could this have been? At the time, I was too diffident to ask. I thanked him for his advice, which I saw no reason to follow.

The New Yorker has always been famously timid in respect to sex and strong language. In regard to strong language, the curious thing to observe in Ross's day was the disparity between his personal manner of speech and the manner of speech he permitted to be reproduced in the magazine. This disparity, great as it was, was perhaps not quite so great as the outside world supposed; Ross's boisterous oral vulgarities were reserved for men, and in the presence of women he made an effort to speak a tongue sacerdotally immaculate. When Harriet Walden became his secretary, if she entered his office at some appointed hour with medicine for his ulcers and found Ross in blasphemous spate, he would break off in the very middle of a word and beg her pardon. He said it was his intention to publish nothing that would bring a blush to the cheek of a twelve-year-old girl. This was a peculiar standard to set for a magazine universally acknowledged to be among the most sophisticated in existence — a magazine that Ross had founded, moreover, with the stipulation that it was *not* to be edited for the old lady in Dubuque. He permitted characters in stories to say "Jesus" and "Christ," probably in part because they were expletives as common to him as "pshaw" would have been to his mother, and from time to time priests, nuns, and representatives of the Holy Name Society would wait upon Ross to protest the magazine's careless bandying about of the name of God. Ross was a notorious coward, in matters spiritual as well

"We want to report a stolen car."

The early Arno drawing that was published in the magazine in spite of Ross's puritanical determination to exclude even the mildest sexual innuendos. The drawing created a considerable stir. Ross said afterward that he hadn't got the point of the joke — he had just thought it was funny that there was nothing left of the car but a seat, and he hadn't bothered to speculate about why it was a seat and not, say, a wheel or a mudguard.

as physical; he was in terror of being scolded by a nun, and the moment a figure in a black habit stepped off the elevator on the nineteenth floor she would be hurried along to a member of the staff named Kip Orr, who was armed with spite and feared nothing and nobody.

Of the immediately obvious ways in which Ross and Shawn were unlike, one thinks of voice, vocabulary, and manners. Ross's voice was loud, rasping, Western; Shawn's is soft, rounded, and standard American. Ross spoke billingsgate; the harshest expletive I have ever heard Shawn utter is a whispered "Oh, God!" As for manners, Ross might truly be said not to have had any. At parties and on other social occasions, he was an awkward creature, best off seated with drink in hand, talking with colleagues. Once, in the Oak Room at the Plaza, my wife and I were having dinner with some friends; I felt myself being pelted with spitballs fashioned from the paper wrappings of sugar cubes. I glanced about and, sure enough, Ross was at a distant table. Throwing spitballs was a form of being friendly. In Jerome Zerbe's notable collection of photographs of New York night life is one of Ross, his third wife Ariane, and Gertrude Lawrence. They are at a table in what was then known as the Lark Room of the St. Regis. A benefit dance is being held for some good cause — the time appears to be early in the Second World War — and Ross is wearing a high, frilled paper cap. He is in black tie and is, of course, smoking. On his face is the expression that caused Alexander Woollcott to say of him that he looked like a dishonest Lincoln. He sits there manifestly ill-at-ease and yet eager to see what is going on among people he fears may be his betters.

At another dance, given by the Philip Barrys in honor of Kath-

Ross at a party at the St. Regis, during the Second World War. Ross's companions are Gertrude Lawrence and his third wife, Ariane. Cupped in his hand, the inevitable cigarette.

34

arine Hepburn, Ross took to lighting matches and tossing them out onto the floor, among the dancing couples. It was not a very witty thing to do: a lighted match fell on the skirt of one of the dancers and the skirt caught fire. The woman screamed, and someone intending to douse the flames made matters far worse by tossing a glass of brandy onto them. The woman fell to the floor and half a dozen men smothered the fire with napkins; a close call.

Ross is said to have summoned up old-fashioned nineteenth-century good manners on occasion, especially in the presence of older women. I have no first-hand evidence of this. One evening my wife happened to be seated at dinner next to Ross. He evidently saw no use in making conversation with a pretty and companionable young woman. His mind darted from her to me and then to money, and with what struck my wife as unseemly relish he burst out, "No writer of mine can afford to own a car!" He then turned his back and spoke not a single word to her all evening long.

So much for the man without manners; Shawn by contrast might be a revenant from some small eighteenth-century court. He observes every amenity. Little as he enjoys bodily contact, he takes care to shake hands firmly and look one straight in the eye; he offers one a place to sit with a bow and a gesture that imply that if only it were within his power to arrange such matters, the chair would be a throne and oneself a sovereign.

Shawn has never been known to go through a door ahead of a companion, male or female. The lobby of our building extends from West Forty-third Street to West Forty-fourth Street and is entered and left by revolving doors. Shawn's only rival for good manners has been R. Hawley Truax, now the retired chairman of the board of the magazine, who long served as the sole means of communication between Ross and Fleischmann. In the days when Shawn and Truax used to go out to lunch together, what a prolonged combat of courtesies they waged! The very act of leaving the office presented difficulties: which of them would consent to enter an elevator first? Moments went by, and so did elevators. Age has its bitter privileges, precedence among them; Truax, being many years older than Shawn, was obliged to make the first move. Having reached the lobby, who was to pass first through the revolving doors? In winter Truax was given to wearing a dark, velvety fedora and a cloth overcoat that fell well below his knees. The hat was in a style that had gone out of fashion forty years earlier; it made Truax look like a Balkan spy in some faded newspaper photograph — one of those figures in the crowd that lined the streets of Sarajevo as the Archduke Ferdinand went wheeling by. Shawn in winter (to say nothing of Shawn in early fall and Shawn very late in spring) wears a heavy orlon-lined

Shawn at his desk. Characteristic are the sweater, the pencil, and the ever-rising tide of typescripts.

overcoat, a long woolen scarf, and a low-crowned hat, and he usually carries a briefcase and an umbrella. If Truax has always struck the note of Herzegovina, Shawn's note has been Dickensian. It was charming to see them at the revolving doors, bobbing and bowing to each other, until at last poor Truax yielded up the infinitesimal punctilio and they could proceed across the street

to lunch at the Algonquin, where the challenge of two more sets
of doors remained to be met and mastered.

Another difference between Shawn and Ross: games. As far as I
know, Shawn plays no games whatever, indoors or out. I remember that once, twenty-odd years ago, he was asked to participate
in a parlor game at somebody's house. It was one of those pencil-
and-paper stunts, popular at the time, that were supposed to provide startling insights into the nature of the players' psyches. In
misery, Shawn consented; in misery, he attempted to execute his
assignment, which was to draw the outline of South America.
Shawn's gift is words, not imagery; his South America remained
a pitiable shapeless blob. I defy anyone to believe that the blob
was an insight.

Shawn has little personal interest in sports, or even in recreation. It has been an open secret in the office that when he takes
one of his rare, brief vacations, it is not in eager pursuit of sun,
sea, and physical activity; he prefers to spend his vacations at
home, working precisely as hard as if he were still at his desk —
harder, perhaps, since there are fewer interruptions. Robert Lewis

One rarely thinks of New Yorker editors and writers as being good at games. Here is
an exception — Herbert Warren Wind, who writes about golf and who is evidently unin-
timidated by the stretch of water lying before him at the National Golf Links, on Long
Island. The left arm is superbly unbent.

Taylor, who wrote some of the funniest Profiles we ever published and who in recent years has drifted away from the magazine into wealth and a querulous political recidivism, used to pretend to be unaware of Shawn's low opinion of the sporting life. As Taylor told the story, when Shawn came back to the office from one of his so-called vacations, Taylor would congratulate him on how well he looked: "Bill, you must have had a marvellous time!"

"Yes, very nice, thank you."

"Played a lot of golf?"

"Well, no, not golf, exactly."

"Tennis, then? Got in a good deal of tennis?"

"No, I don't play tennis."

"Swimming? You must have had some great swimming?"

And so on from sport to sport, even to such unlikely Shawnian adventures as surfboarding and water-skiing, with Shawn remaining invincible in his politeness, Taylor ruthless in his persistence.

A mysterious photograph, in the possession of Ross's friend Dorothy Silberberg. The place is not Aspen and Ross is not fishing. Evident are some of the reasons why Ross was the despair of tailors.

Ross was more of an outdoors man than Shawn, but not much. He did not actively disapprove of fresh air and trees, as Shawn appears to do; indeed, the only lyrical passage that I can recollect from Ross's conversation had to do with the look of the aspens for which his birthplace was named — how their leaves, turning bottom side up in the wind, seemed to change color and tremble against a background of dark-green firs. His first wife writes of Ross's having swum and played croquet at Lake Bomoseen, in Vermont, and there is the well-known anecdote concerning the time that the columnist Franklin P. Adams got Ross up to Connecticut for some winter sports. Somebody asked

Ross on a fishing holiday in Aspen. It is lunchtime and someone has provided him with a deviled egg.

F.P.A. what Ross had looked like tobogganing, and F.P.A. replied, "Well, you know what Ross looks like *not* tobogganing."

When badminton became popular, Ross developed a passion for it; soon the passion cooled, for almost everyone he played badminton with proved capable of trouncing him. He liked fishing as an occupation and not as a sport; he fished mostly in Aspen, and Joseph Anthony, of *The New Yorker*, has in his possession a classic snapshot of Ross seated on a dock by a lake high in the Rockies. A crushed homburg on his head, his gat-teeth gleaming, Ross smiles into the camera in a daze of countrified good humor.

But it was games that Ross loved and not sports, and indoor games, not outdoor. Poker, cribbage, and backgammon were among the addictions to which, night after night, he gave himself up with zest, drinking and cursing as the play went against him. For he was a passionate, reckless gambler, and at a time when he could ill afford it he lost many thousands of dollars a year to his more skillful adversaries.

Once, in the earliest days of *The New Yorker*, Ross lost upward of twenty thousand dollars in a single night, playing with Herbert Bayard Swope, Raoul Fleischmann, and other men a great deal richer than he was. Fleischmann, who, according to Jane Grant, thought Ross had been taken unfair advantage of, subsequently paid off a large portion of the debt. No good deed goes unpun-

Ross by Rea Irvin, in a parody issue of The New Yorker *that celebrated its first anniversary. Ross-Tilley is examining not a butterfly but a bug, and the bug is Alexander Woollcott.*

ished, and it may be that Ross never forgave Fleischmann for having helped him out of that dire episode.

Ross's manner of play had much to do with hunches and little to do with an accurate knowledge of odds. He was under the impression that he wished desperately to win, but people who played poker with him have said that what he seemed to want most was simply to remain in the game: an expensive intention. Daniel H. Silberberg, a stockbroker who was one of Ross's closest friends and who has been for many years the specialist in *New Yorker* stock, used to play backgammon with Ross. Silberberg says of him, "Ross always doubled and he always lost. Getting up from the board, he would invariably exclaim, 'I'm cursed! Something I did to God!' But the curse was self-imposed."

"Something I did to God" is an arresting phrase — few people

see themselves as having done something personally offensive to God, and it is all the more unexpected coming from a man who had little or no religious feeling and for whom, throughout his life, God remained at most a convenient epithet. It is yet another aspect of Ross the hero-victim, central figure in a mock-tragedy of his own invention. But to see nothing strange in making his antagonist the Supreme Being —! This was no ordinary Rocky Mountain boy.

Ross at about the time he was founding The New Yorker. *It was Ina Claire who said of his then ungovernable pompadour that she would like to walk barefoot through it. Ross blamed the singular elevation of his hair on the fear he had felt as a small child, when he was injured in a stagecoach accident in the Rockies. With age, the hair subsided.*

5

I perceive that I have been doing something odd and perhaps confusing. In fitting together the mosaic of these paragraphs — "Mosaic?" I hear Ross groaning. "Last I heard, the goddam things were butterflies" — I have been writing about Ross and Shawn as if they existed for me and for the other writers and editors on the magazine in the same unbroken span of time, and of course it is not so. Ross's irascible ghost hovers over my shoulder as I write this, but the fact is that it is only a ghost; the man himself has been dead for nearly a quarter of a century, and Shawn has been editor of the magazine for nearly as long a time as Ross was. The dates make clear what the vividness of memory obscures: the magazine was founded in February, 1925, and Ross was its editor until his death on December 5, 1951. Shawn, who for years before Ross's death had taken a leading part in the production of the magazine, officially succeeded Ross on January 21, 1952.

I remember reading the announcement on the dusty imitation-cork bulletin board in the stretch of twentieth-floor corridor called Sleepy Hollow, among an assortment of scrawled messages, some of them several months old, offering ski boots for sale ("never been worn"), apartments for sublet, and kittens for adoption. The announcement was typed on the letterhead of the office of the publisher and was signed in blue ink, in his usual shaky hand, "Raoul H. Fleischmann." It consisted of a single sentence: "William Shawn has accepted the position of editor of *The New Yorker*, effective today." After a day or so, I removed the announcement from the board and had it framed, on the assumption that one or another of Shawn's children would someday be amused to come into possession of it. Shawn himself is not much of a collector of mementos, in part because, never going anywhere, he has nowhere to bring mementos back from and in part because he is scarcely more of a nest-builder than Ross was. His office accumulates Himalayas of typescripts and galley proofs but few

Photographs of Ross's office taken by "Hobie" Weekes the day after Ross's death. On the table are a Who's Who, *a dictionary, a bottle of medicine for his ulcer, and his sloppy briefcase. Some unpublished Thurber drawings hang on the wall.*

On the desk, more dictionaries, including, of course, Fowler's A Dictionary of Modern English Usage. *Ross regarded the coatrack as a womanly frill.*

trophies. Though many writers have dedicated books to Shawn, the books are elsewhere. His office is ample in scale, carpeted, with large windows facing east and south, and it may be said to have acquired a modest lived-in charm over the years, but only in contrast to the two bleak and ugly rooms in which Ross worked could it be called distinguished.

I strongly suspect that Shawn was the author of that fourteen-word announcement; it is an admirable specimen of his skill at making an apparently simple disclosure serve to convey a complex truth. There is always more than meets the eye in a statement by Shawn, and one can sometimes spend years teasing out the last of its meanings. In the present instance, note that Shawn has not been appointed or elected or designated; something has been offered to him and upon due consideration he has consented to accept it. The implication is clear: if any gratitude is to be felt, it must be felt by management and not by the editor whom management has chosen. This was how things had been with Ross and that was how they were going to be with Shawn. The exercise of power would doubtless be less arbitrary and blustering than it had been, and therefore perhaps less entertaining to bystanders, but the likelihood was great that Shawn would always gently, whisperingly get his iron way.

The
NEW YORKER

25 West 43rd Street
NEW YORK

*Office of the
Publisher*

January 21, 1952.

William Shawn has accepted the
position of editor of The New Yorker,
effective today.

R.H. Fleischmann

The magazine as it appears today is far more nearly a reflection of Shawn's mind than the magazine of twenty-five years ago was a reflection of Ross's. Nevertheless, something of Ross remains inexpungeably present in its pages and is a fact to be reckoned with. Those of us who worked on the magazine during the Rossian years are grateful for certain trifling physical reminders of him and of his efforts to dominate — with, as he thought, superb common sense — an unruly and often inimical environment. One such trifling reminder is to be found in the toilet stalls of the men's rooms, each of which is supplied with two sets of toilet-paper holders. This precaution goes back to a time when Ross took a manuscript with him for leisurely perusal and discovered, too late, that the single holder in the stall boasted only a bare cardboard cylinder. He was obliged to write a letter to the author of the manuscript apologizing for its mysterious disappearance while under editorial consideration; he then fired off a memo to the effect that henceforth there were to be two holders in every stall. It was characteristic of Ross to double everything in an emergency — double his bets when he was losing at backgammon, or, having fired an editor, hire two editors to take his place — but his solution to the toilet-paper problem, elegant as it struck him as being, had a crucial defect: a maintenance man capable of letting one holder go empty was capable of equal negligence with two.

Another reminder of Ross has to do with the design of the building in which the magazine has long had its headquarters. The building is L-shaped, with the base of the L running along West Forty-third Street and the narrow upright stroke facing Forty-fourth Street. The corridor on the nineteenth floor that leads from the elevators to where Ross had his two mangy offices takes a ninety-degree left turn at about the halfway point, and it was just there that Ross had a large mirror installed, at a kitty-cornered angle that allowed people approaching the turn from one direction to catch sight of people approaching from the opposite direction. (I am being mindful of the fact that Ross held that nothing was indescribable; the previous sentence is my pastiche of a Ross "will fix" sentence in "Talk.") Some members of the staff maintain that

The office corridor that Hamburger calls Sleepy Hollow. The first door on the right leads to the elevators, where the reception-ist's cubicle is located. It's typical of The New Yorker that the sign reading "Infor-mation" is on the wrong side of the parti-tion, helpful only to people who have already proceeded farther than they were intended to.

The Rossian mirror, designed to prevent pedestrian collisions and leading to innu-merable pedestrian collisions.

Ross thought up the mirror in order to prevent people from colliding with each other at a presumptively dangerous blind corner, but this seems unlikely; in any event, what happens is that people looking into the mirror from different directions have a tendency to take the same little sideways precautionary skip, and in doing so, heighten the chance of a collision instead of preventing it.

James M. Geraghty, for many years art editor of the magazine, states that Ross had the mirror installed because he was afraid of encountering artists in the corridor — there were certain artists, as well as certain writers, whom Ross was unwilling to talk to and may indeed have been in literal fear of. If he saw one of these fierce dragons bearing down on him from the elevators, he could duck into an adjacent office and hide out there until the risk of a confrontation was past. Once again, there was a defect in Ross's reasoning: obviously, if he could see the dragons, the dragons could see him, and if they were authentic dragons, they would not hesitate to pursue him into his hiding place. Be that as it may, the mirror is there — a monument to Rossian ingenuity and perhaps to Rossian cowardice.

A pertinent Ross anecdote, recorded by Jane Grant: Ross and his buddies Woollcott and Winterich (both of whom were later to join him on *The New Yorker*) were sitting around at lunch in Paris during the war. Woollcott proposed that a single adjective was sufficient to describe any person. When asked what adjective would best serve to describe him, he replied at once, "Noble." Next, Winterich asked what adjective would best serve to describe Ross. "Timid," Woollcott said. "You sneaky son of a bitch!" Ross cried. "You've been in touch with my mother."

And a standard Ross gag-line, which he repeated with undiminished pleasure throughout his life. The original occasion for it was an interview between Ross and Ralph McAllister Ingersoll, a well-born product of Hotchkiss and Yale, who, momentarily penniless at what he thought of as the advanced age of twenty-four, came to ask Ross for a job. It was the summer of 1925 and the magazine was four months old. According to Ingersoll's autobiography, *Point of Departure,* he got the job in part because of his middle name and in part because of Ross's clumsiness. Despite his poverty, Ingersoll had bought a resplendent oyster-white Palm Beach suit in hopes of making a favorable impression on Ross. In a characteristically impassioned gesture in the midst of an extended aria, Ross succeeded in sweeping an open bottle of blue-black ink off his desk and onto Ingersoll and his brand-new suit. That gave the young applicant an immediate advantage. As for Ingersoll's middle name, according to Ingersoll's account:

> . . . Ross had rallied to explain that there simply wasn't such a person as the kind of reporter he had in mind. He would have to be a Richard Harding Davis and a Ward McAllister rolled into one.
>
> "Well," I was able to interject, "I've been a reporter and Ward was my mother's uncle."
>
> "Jee-sus," Ross snarled, as if completely disgusted with himself for having given me this opening.
>
> Then a sigh escaped him, and he looked me sadly in the eye. "Okay, you're on," he said. "Hell, I hire *anybody!*"

And so Ingersoll became the first of Ross's innumerable long-looked-for, loudly welcomed, and eventually crucified "Jesuses" — men who would be able, Ross hoped, to bring order out of the chaos of producing a humorous weekly magazine with little money, a small staff, and a figure as energetic but scatterbrained as Ross as its head. So radical was the turnover of employees in those early days that by the end of six months Ingersoll was the senior editorial employee on the magazine and its titular managing editor. He remained on *The New Yorker* for five years, moving in 1930 a few blocks uptown to Henry Luce's *Fortune.* Ingersoll was an exception among *New Yorker* writers and editors in being able to make a successful career elsewhere, not alone during the years with Luce but subsequently as a publisher of a chain of small weekly newspapers. Most of the rest of us are what one of our oldest and ablest editors, Rogers E. M. Whitaker, has always described as "congenital unemployables" — people whose utility to the magazine appears to be a function of their total inutility to more sensible enterprises. Whitaker himself, mad about cats and trains, writing now about football, now about nightclubs, would be miserable in any organization that observed conventional standards of interoffice deportment; kind though he is to friends, he has the sharpest tongue in the world, and one young editor of whom I will be writing died long ago of what seemed to be spontaneous combustion but was, in fact, chagrined at being unable to exchange insults with Whitaker at Whitaker's high level of murderous urbanity.

In 1934, Ingersoll wrote an admiring fifteen-thousand-word

piece about *The New Yorker* for *Fortune*. In the course of it, he said that Ross was paid a salary of forty thousand dollars a year. Ross put up a notice on the bulletin board: "It is not true that I get $40,000 a year." Many years later, a magazine article mentioned that Shawn was being paid seventy thousand dollars a year; unaware of Ross's crafty tactics, Shawn put up a notice saying that he was not paid seventy thousand dollars a year, or anything like seventy thousand dollars, and that he wouldn't be worth such a sum if he *were* being paid it. Secrecy about almost everything, and especially about money, has been a trait of the magazine since its founding. To this day, I have no idea how much Ross made, or how much Shawn makes. But secrecy has its hazards: when one negatively affirms that one isn't being paid seventy thousand dollars a year, plenty of envious cynics will be quick to guess that one is being paid eighty or a hundred thousand. In this case the cynics will be wrong, but who knows? Perhaps in the presence of greater candor they would have been less likely to become cynics.

"Hell, I hire *anybody!*" Nearly twenty years after Ross first laid this unflattering unction upon Ingersoll, F. Scott Fitzgerald's daughter, Scottie Lanahan, her husband being away at the war, came to *The New Yorker* in search of a job. The quintessential outsider, Ross was always impressed by people who had a social background as formidable as Ingersoll's, or a literary background as formidable as Scottie's. Moreover, because men reporters were subject to being drafted, for the first time Ross was looking with a comparatively unjaundiced eye upon women reporters. It happened that Scottie was a pretty blonde, small and joyous and highly intelligent. Ross liked pretty blondes, but he expected them to be, as he said, "dumb," and he was taken aback and disappointed in them when they were not. In Scottie's case, he swallowed his disappointment and offered her a job as a "Talk" reporter; she would be joining a couple of other newly recruited women, Andy Logan and Roseanne Smith. (Miss Logan has been with us ever since; she is currently the author of a department called "About City Hall." Miss Smith married a lay analyst and was lost to history, or at any rate, to this history. Shawn once gave her the pithiest of instructions. He wished her to cover for "Talk"

a certain large public gathering in Bryant Park. Shawn fears crowds and has taken care never to be in one, but he knew precisely what was needed for the piece. "Go out," he said to Miss Smith, "and mill.") Scottie thanked Ross profusely for giving her the job. As she was leaving the office, she overheard him saying to a secretary, "Hell, I hire *anybody!*" Not knowing that this was a remark as habitual with Ross as "Done and done!" or "God bless you!" or "Jesus Christ!," Scottie went home feeling simultaneously elated and dejected. Ross had that effect on a lot of people, especially when they were young, and Scottie was young.

I escaped Ross's initial mockery by dint of not being hired by him. This came about thanks partly to my selling stories to the magazine from a distance, without ever troubling to set foot on the premises. (I learned afterward that there had been speculation as to whether my first name was that of a man or a woman. The lives of Irish saints — even of a saint reputed to have discovered America — have been little read by *New Yorker* editors.) I had written some fact pieces as well as fiction, and St. Clair McKelway, the fact editor, and William Maxwell, a fiction editor under Katharine White, invited me to come down from Connecticut and have lunch with them at Christ Cella's; later, McKelway invited me to join the staff. I had been installed in a windowless, frosted-glass-and-wood-walled cubbyhole on the nineteenth floor for some weeks before I met Ross, by then familiar to me as a dark-suited simian figure slouching onto and off elevators with a sloppy-looking briefcase in hand. Our first encounter was memorably brief and awkward. Ross stuck his head abruptly through the open doorway; I heard change jingling in his trousers pocket. Our conversation, here given in full, shows neither of us at his best.

Ross: "Ross."

Gill, after a silence: "I know."

Ross: "I told McKelway not to play God, but goddam it, here you are."

McKelway's playing God had consisted of offering me a drawing account of forty dollars a week.

Gill, after another silence: "I —"

Ross, waving: "Good luck, anyhow."

6

I have hinted that the beginnings of my professional career cost me little pain, and I may as well spell out my good fortune in some detail, both for the amusement it affords me in looking back on it and for the encouragement it may be to the young who will be succeeding me and who even in these easygoing seventies hear far too much about what a serious matter life is. In fact, not a shred of evidence exists in favor of the argument that life is serious, though it is often hard and even terrible. And saying that, I am prompted to add what follows out of it: that since everything ends badly for us, in the inescapable catastrophe of death, it seems obvious that the first rule of life is to have a good time; and that the second rule of life is to hurt as few people as possible in the course of doing so. There is no third rule. It also seems obvious to me that having a good time is an art like any other, and must be learned. Some have a knack for it and learn easily; others — how many *New Yorker* writers among them! — are without the knack and so never learn the art at all. In childhood, I found that I was among the lucky ones with a knack; sooner than most, I took care to master the art.

In grammar school and country-day school in Hartford, where I was born, and later at college in New Haven, I was the conventionally gifted student-writer who is bound to be elected chairman of the literary magazine and who upon graduation wins the highest award for literary excellence. Since I had a talent for drawing as well as for writing, I gave extra value; from one issue to the next, schoolboy publications rarely have material enough to fill their pages, and a person who can write stories and poems under two or three different names, can draw illustrations for them under still other names, and who also rejoices in the drudgery of taking copy to the printer, correcting galley proofs, and pasting up dummies gains in his teens a sense of importance likely to elude him in later life.

I had the advantage, moreover, of a doting father, who himself had strong literary leanings. My mother had died when I was seven, leaving a distracted husband and five mettlesome and therefore quarrelsome children, of whom I was the fourth. My father was a brilliant surgeon and physician, with an exceptionally large practice, and he had not the slightest idea of what to do with us children, except to supply us with houses, servants, money, trips to Europe, extravagant gifts, admiration, and love. He was forty-two when I was born, which is to say that I always thought of him as an old man; in my earliest recollections of him, he is white-haired and corpulent, and I am aware that I am lucky to be related to a figure so well spoken of in the community ("Your father saved my life." "Your father is the kindest man alive." "Dr. Gill's boy! Then do your best to live up to him!"). He had been something of a prodigy, graduating from high school at fourteen and practicing medicine in Hartford at twenty-one. He had far more energy, as well as far more intelligence, than ordinary men; impossible for me as a child to imagine that he would ever know what it was to grow tired. For recreation he hunted, fished, hiked, chopped wood, planted trees, and painted houses, barns, sheds, and every other surface a brush could reach, whether it was in need of paint or not, but his favorite outdoor activity was golf. The game amounted to a passion with him. Though most of his companions were content to play thirty-six holes a day, he would often play forty-five holes and then give up only because the coming of darkness made it impossible for him to see the ball. Lighted driving ranges came into existence around Hartford in the thirties, to his great satisfaction; on his way home from the golf course, he would stop off at a range and drive a couple of hundred balls out into the floodlit meadow.

There was a tradition of writing — or, rather, of storytelling — in his mother's family, who were Bowens. His mother had an immense store of Irish tales and songs, which she had learned by heart, with precision, from her emigrant parents and grandparents, and his favorite aunt, Emma Jane Bowen, wrote innumerable stories and a few novels, none of which was published. Aunt Emma, who died in 1965, could be said to have spanned four centuries: her father had been born in the eighteenth century and told her many stories about his father, a breeder of horses in Ireland, and she told the same stories to my grandchildren, who

The only cover drawn by E. B. White. It is a watercolor in pleasing shades of sea-green, blue, purple, and maroon. White invented Thurber's first cover by taking a Thurber drawing and, without Thurber's knowledge, coloring it for him. Of his own cover, White says, "I produced the drawing by borrowing my son's paint set. I got the seahorse from a picture in Webster's, I got the underwater setting from an advertisement in the Saturday Evening Post, *I executed the thing while sick abed, and at the very last minute I loused up the whole business by printing the word 'oats' on the nosebag. Nosebags do not have the word 'oats' printed on them in real life, but I was afraid people might not get the point of my masterpiece."*

will live well into the twenty-first century. Her father had wanted to name her after Jenny Lind, whom he had heard singing in Hartford in the eighteen-forties, but the parish priest in Southington, Connecticut, would have no truck with such pagan shenanigans — Jenny was not a saint's name, so the child must be baptized Emma Jane. (One comic tale that has been passed along orally through five generations of the family contains interesting evidence of its eighteenth-century origins; the speaker is a woman who engages in an argument with a pub-keeper over a drinking debt owed by her husband. The tale begins, "Hear, hear, last night, about six months ago, as I was puttin' a heel in the hole of the old man's stockin' " and at the climax of the tale the woman reaches down and plucks the silver-mounted pewter buckles off her shoes and dashes them onto the counter — " 'Are ye paid?' says I. 'I am,' says he, and I left his doors forever.") Aunt Emma was a devoted and acute reader of *The New Yorker*. Her family realized that she was getting ready to die when she said, "Take *The New Yorker* downstairs. I am too tired to read it." She was a hundred and three.

My father had been educated — first at the Lewis Academy, in Southington, and then at Yale — in the eighties and nineties, at the height of the Victorian period, and he favored an ornate style in both composition and penmanship. When, at fourteen, he was chosen to deliver the valedictory address at the Academy, he spoke on Thomas Jefferson. He remembered and could recite much of the speech in old age; a flowery thing it was. When it came my turn to deliver a valedictory address — I was thirteen, but I had not outstripped him: I was graduating at the usual age from grammar school — it seemed a natural thing for him to sit down and compose the address along with me. He called it helping me, but it is a sign of how great a share of the handiwork must have been his that I, who have almost as good a memory as he had, have forgotten most of it after less than fifty years. I recall that it had something to do with Oxford, for no better reason than that we had happened to visit that city for a day in the course of the previous summer, on one of those trips abroad that my father believed all children should be fortunate enough to experience. Bravely abandoning his medical practice and his cherished golf, he would send himself and his five so often disagreeable and homesick offspring careering across Europe. He gave us a day in Rome, a day in Florence, a day in Milan, while we dreamed sullenly of peanut-butter and jelly sandwiches and thick shakes.

"Travel is the best education," my father would say, understandably a little out of breath, "in the world."

I also recall that my speech began with a quotation from a poet named Winifred Mary Letts, whose name is more provocative than her verse. The poem from which I quoted on that hot June day begins, "I saw the spires of Oxford/As I was passing by,/The gray spires of Oxford/Against a pearl-gray sky./My heart was with the Oxford men/Who went abroad to die." This sentimental fiddle-faddle had evidently caught my father's fancy, though it had not caught mine. A plump, panic-stricken adolescent, sweaty in a blue serge suit and a starched white collar, at the appointed moment I stepped to the edge of the stage in the school auditorium and began, in a carefully rehearsed singsong, "I *saw* the *spires* of *Oxford*/As *I* was *passing by* ..." My father sat beaming in the front row as I launched into the body of the address — *his* address, filled with polysyllabled Latinisms and archaic grammatical flourishes, which had been the very devil for me to memorize. What can my teachers and classmates and the rest of the large audience have made of this unexpected Victorian revenant? It was 1928 and they were being treated to a disquisition in the style of 1888. I cared not a straw for their bewilderment. My father was proud of me; measured against that, nothing else mattered.

In prep school, I began to find my own way literarily. All those thousands of lines of Shakespeare, Samuel Johnson, Cowper, Gray, Coleridge, Wordsworth, Byron, Moore, Poe, Longfellow, Tennyson, and Whittier that my father had stored away in his memory were also, thanks to his affectionate prompting, stored away in mine. They were a burden to me as I struggled to see things freshly, in my fashion and not theirs. My struggle was brave but not very bold — belatedly, I reached out to Whitman, and then chiefly to poets who, simply because they were living at the same moment as I, I thought of as my contemporaries: Edgar Lee Masters, Edwin Arlington Robinson, Robinson Jeffers, and Robert Frost. In senior year, I won a prize for writing a long narrative poem in what everyone must have seen was a pastiche of Frost. (I had not yet read Eliot's dictum: "The immature poet imitates, the mature poet plagiarizes." Nevertheless, I was obeying it.) The only prosodic novelty in the poem was that it was written in alexandrines instead of in iambic pentameter, as Frost would have written it. I assume now that I must have achieved this feat by mistake; perhaps having miscounted the stresses in the opening one or two lines, I plodded unwittingly on — de-dum, de-dum, de-dum — to the poem's intolerably distant finish.

I was later to meet Frost, on an occasion far from happy for him. He came to Yale while I was there and gave a reading one evening in Pierson College, before a small group of under-graduates. Among the poems he read was "The Witch of Coös," in which most of the drama consists of the uncanny moving about in an old house of a skeleton, referred to as "the bones." Now, it happened that a couple of us at the reading were members of the celebrated secret society at Yale known as Skull and Bones, or "Bones" for short. In those days, secret societies in general and that secret society in particular were of great importance; indeed, the very name of Bones was held in awe, and not at Yale alone — people out in the world believed that if the sacred name were ever to be mentioned in the presence of a Bones man, he would immediately get up and leave the room. As for Bones men them-selves, they never uttered the word except to other Bones men and then, by preference, only deep within the windowless stone tomb on High Street in which the society has had its headquarters for nearly a hundred and fifty years.

"The Witch of Coös" is a ghost story told in verse, and Frost was accustomed to reading it to great effect, making his auditors' flesh creep; but that evening in Pierson his hushed reiteration of "the bones" sent my Bones clubmate and me into childish fits of giggles, which, try as hard as we could, we failed to suppress. It was a humiliating moment for us, and still more humiliating for Frost, who hurried the poem to its close and the evening to an end. The scandalous ruin of his reading was entirely our fault, and yet we could not so much as offer him an apology; for to explain our unbecoming conduct would have required us to men-tion the unmentionable word, which in the Yale of that day would have caused a second scandal greater than the first.

Many years later, at about the time of his eightieth birthday (and taking care not to refresh his recollection of our previous encounter), I interviewed Frost for a possible "Talk" piece in the magazine. As it happened, though I took ample notes, I never got around to writing it. I experience failures of this kind often and for a variety of unpredictable reasons. Perhaps I thought Frost had been getting too much newspaper publicity to make a *New Yorker* piece seem desirable at that moment; perhaps, less rationally, I bore a grudge against Frost because he had once caused me to do him an injury, and I was punishing him by failing both him and me. In any event, Frost at eighty was a formidable figure, well worth my study whether I wrote about him or not. He had spent a lifetime perfecting himself in the role of a humorous Yankee cracker-barrel philosopher, and of course he was no such thing. Every gesture and glance and modulation of voice gave proof of his skill as an actor; it was like a game to stand in his presence and try to gauge the degree of his being other and elsewhere — try to catch a glimpse of the hard-as-nails maker of the poems inside the lovable old stager who went around reciting them. The poems themselves were so often truculent, unloving, and unforgiving ("the art of life is passing losses on"), while the speaker on the lecture platform and in the college common room was just the sort of genial foxy grandpa who in his younger days would have seen fit to stop by woods on a snowy evening.

Frost was an exceedingly handsome man. The thickening of his body as he grew older suited him; it provided a proper base for the big, chunky, Roman head, crowned with white hair that appeared to have known only his fingers for a comb. Though born in San Francisco, educated in part at Harvard, and long a resident of England, he had acquired and naturalized the laconic drawl of a New Hampshire hayseed and he moved like one, never in haste. At the time of my interview, I was eager to get behind the skilled actor and come to grips with the cutthroat competitor of whom I had heard. There were stories — the truth of which became evident when his letters began to be published after his death — that much of Frost's life had been devoted to sedulously puffing himself and putting down rivals. I wanted to hear from his own lips at that late point in his fame and age an appraisal of his ruthless behavior. I had wrung a considerable measure of truth out of Frank Lloyd Wright under similar circumstances, but Frost was too wily for me. Again and again to any question that threatened the embittered and embittering author with having to emerge and face examination, he would reply with a superlatively homely "Oh, come!" His eyes would twinkle, not benignly but with the satisfaction of having withheld from me something of value. In the end, I obtained two telltale sentences. "At the top of the steeple," he said, making a steeple out of his freckled old hands, "there's room for only one person at a time." Then he looked at me hard. "I always meant that person to be me."

A greater poet than Frost was living in Hartford in my prep-school days. I was indirectly acquainted with him, but not with his work, the spell of which I wasn't to fall under until I was in my twenties. Wallace Stevens was a neighbor of one of my sisters, and his daughter Holly, when in her teens and forbidden to smoke, would come to my sister's house in order to practice that wicked activity undetected. Stevens was a vice-president of the Hartford Accident & Indemnity Company; his specialty was bonds. The world wanted to believe that as a poet he was misera-ble over having to earn his living as a servant of big business, but in fact he had begun his professional career as a lawyer in New York and had not enjoyed it — a friend of mine who was a beginner in the same firm with Stevens said of him that he would have made a rotten Wall Street lawyer.

Stevens's mind was of the sort that takes pleasure in elegant intricacies, for which the purchase and redemption of millions of dollars' worth of bonds may have proved as good a source as any. If he disliked his job, he was certainly in no hurry to retire from it. I remember hearing rumors to the effect that when the moment for his obligatory retirement on grounds of age arrived, it was found that he had arranged matters in his department in a fashion so complex that no successor could hope to comprehend them without months and perhaps years of study, with the result that Stevens had to be invited to remain with the company well beyond his allotted time. It is a story full of attractive ironies — a world-famous poet, wholly unread by his business colleagues, outwits them at their own hard-headed, statistical game, not in order to escape from them at last but in order to continue as their close but ever-so-distant companion. There are times when my instincts as a writer of fiction overrule my training as a reporter, and this is one of them; I have taken care not to check the facts behind the rumors for fear they might render the poet less clever than I wish him to be.

Stevens had little to do with the usual social activities of Hart-ford. He remained by calculation an outsider, and people assumed that he was a coldly fastidious and indifferent man. The contrary was the case: though an anchorite, he was an anchorite of passion, whose mind blazed continuously with sensual images. He marched like a big tame bear through the streets of our city, but there was nothing tamed about him; he had chosen to imprison his fiercer self in a cage of upper-middle-class decorum, as Frost had hidden himself inside a canny bumpkin. And Stevens, like Frost, had good reason to keep the rest of us at bay, for at all hours and in all weathers he was intent upon his poems.

It was the custom in Hartford in those days for people driving to work to offer rides to people walking to work; the offer was made almost as readily to strangers as to friends. My father, for example, often set out on foot for his office, several miles distant from his house, knowing that someone was sure to stop and give him a lift; in his case, being a prominent figure in the community, he was likely to be greeted by name. Stevens, though not a prominent figure in the community, certainly gave the impression of being one; he was a tall, good-looking, well-tailored man, with white hair neatly parted and powerful shoulders. Morning and evening, he walked the mile or so between his house and his office and even in rain or snow would never accept a ride; people learned to leave the forbidding pedestrian alone. His solitary walking had a purpose: he composed as he walked. *Ursa faber* poised on a curb waiting for a light to change was trying out on his inward ear sweet sounds — "the emperor of ice cream," perhaps, or "the auroras of autumn." Rocking slightly from side to side as he lumbered forward, Stevens was as obviously engaged in putting one foot of verse in front of the other as he was in putting one physical foot in front of the other. Once, my sister, glancing out of a window, saw Stevens going by her house. As she watched, he slowed down, came to a stop, rocked in place for a moment or two, took a step backward, hesitated, then strode confidently forward — left, right, left, right — on his way to work. It was obvious to her that Stevens had gone back over a phrase, dropped an unsatisfactory word, inserted a superior one, and proceeded to the next line of the poem he was making.

Stevens and I met years later, at an annual ceremonial of the National Book Awards Committee. It was an occasion on which he was being given an award for his collected poems and I was being given a special citation for my first novel, *The Trouble of One House.* We pretended to take seriously the wonder of two Hartford "boys" making good in the same year, though two men less like boys and less like Hartford would have been hard, so we thought, to imagine. By then Stevens was growing old and had nothing to fear from fame. He had wisely kept himself in seclusion during the years when his talent flourished, and now that it was waning he could afford to step forward and enjoy the fruits that a lifetime of exquisite hard work had earned for him. To the general astonishment, he proved convivial; he liked to stand around, prize in hand, and drink martinis with strangers who admired him. Better than any of his contemporaries, he had made his life march to his own beat; it was amusing and — what mattered more — comforting to be acclaimed as the beat began to falter. Even with his late fame, he took care not to become, like Frost, a public figure. He was not good copy for reporters. "Words of the world," he had written, "are the life of the world." It is a stunning claim to make for letters, and he was the only writer in America in his time superb enough to make it. In his carefully guarded, magisterial pride, he must have known that he had the right to do so. Not for him an unseemly scrambling to attain a place at the top of the steeple; where he stood on the ground, none stood higher than he.

In my memory is an episode the leading figures of which are Frost and Stevens. I was told it by Stevens and I often play it over in my mind, like a short home movie, for the pleasure it gives me. The time is late at night and the place is Florida. Frost and Stevens, who are staying at the same resort hotel, have been out drinking at a bar somewhere along the beach. Tipsily, in perfect contentment, they are making their way back to the hotel on a boardwalk that runs a foot or so above the sand. They are holding fast to each other, and each is sure that it is he who is supporting his companion. Frost staggers, catches his heel on the edge of the boardwalk, and starts to fall. Stevens strengthens his hold on him, but in vain — over Frost goes, with Stevens on top of him. The two bulky old poets fall in a single knot onto the sand and start rolling over and over in the moonlight down the long slope of the beach to the edge of the sea.

7

The man generally regarded as the greatest poet in English in our time — Yeats — visited Hartford while I was still in school there. It was in the early thirties, in the depths of the Depression, and Yeats, himself a poor man, had come to America to give readings for perhaps fifty or a hundred dollars an appearance, in order to raise money for the Abbey Theatre. I remember the posters that advertised his coming; they showed a handsome, hawk-faced, elderly man with a pince-nez, one who surely ought to have struck any apprentice writer of seventeen as worthy of admiration, if not downright worship. But in those days I had a curious notion about myself. It was that there was no reason for me to prostrate myself at the feet of my more celebrated contemporaries (since we breathed the same global air, Yeats, almost fifty years older than I, was by my reckoning a contemporary); I would meet them as equals, or not at all.

Now, this lofty view of myself had nothing to do with any work that I had accomplished. It was a fantasy based on the mark I intended to make in the world, and faced with the challenge of real life, the fantasy soon dwindled from a powerful conviction into the merest whispered velleity. Unluckily for me, for as long as it lasted it cost me the chance to make the acquaintance of a remarkable number of my betters. "Ah, did you once see Shelley plain?" No, I didn't. And why not? Because, adolescent egotist that I was, I was waiting for Shelley to see me.

At about that time in my literary career, I had advanced from writing solely for the school newspaper and magazine to writing occasional fiery letters to the local morning newspaper, the Hartford *Courant*, whose name in those days was pronounced with terse Yankee flatness as the *Current*. It has always boasted not only of being the oldest daily newspaper in the country but also of having been subscribed to by George Washington, and in retrospect I perceive a further hint of my youthful megalomania;

plainly, if the *Courant* had been good enough for the father of his country to read, it was good enough for Brendan Gill to write for. My letters were all in defense of Karl Marx and International Communism, about neither of which topics I had any substantial information. I used to quote with gusto from *Das Kapital*, though I had read of the whole work scarcely more than the passages I quoted. My father's friends in the community, seeing Reds and bloody revolution on every side, were troubled by my impassioned expoundings of Marxian texts. My father ought to have minded more than he did; he would certainly have preferred my coming to the defense of F.D.R. and the Democrats — my father voted for only one Republican candidate in his life, and learned his lesson: the candidate was Harding — but he was so proud of my growing fame that the actual subject matter to be found over my signature seemed of little moment to him.

In any event, I had begun to exist as an authentic published literary figure, and my feeling was that if William Butler Yeats wanted to meet Brendan Gill when he came to Hartford, he could take the trouble to find me, there in our big brown house on Prospect Avenue. It appeared that Yeats didn't wish to take the trouble, and a few years later he was dead. From time to time, I visit his grave in Drumcliff Churchyard, in the west of Ireland, and silently express my regrets at our having failed to meet. From the tomb, Yeats gives no signs of distress. The icy injunction cut in his stone — "Horseman, pass by!" — does little to encourage lingering, especially on the part of a motorist. I bear in mind, moreover, that a meeting with him in age might not have been a rewarding experience. Years ago, I heard the story of how the American poet Robert Fitzgerald wanted nothing so much as to make Yeats's acquaintance. With considerable difficulty, a meeting was arranged between the young poet and the old; Fitzgerald was ushered into the presence and introduced. Silence, then at last, in the high, birdy voice: "Fitzgerald? Fitzgerald? That's a fine Irish name." And that was all.

It was the discovery that death was taking distinguished figures away from me faster than I was able to approach them that caused me to abandon my stand-offish ways. In defining as a contemporary anyone who happened to share a portion of my lifetime, I had cast too wide a net for any practical purpose. Born in 1914, I was bound to suffer grievous losses in my earliest years, and quickly plucked from me, in most cases without my being aware of it, were such godlike contemporaries as Henry James, Puccini,

Renoir, Duse, Saint-Saëns, Conrad, Proust, Sargent, Degas, Debussy, and Buffalo Bill. I would not have had much to say to them in the cradle, or even in my kindergarten and grammar-school days; still, I embraced them as soon as I could, and to this day, to the extent that I have been one with them in time, they nourish me.

Those old ones I could resign myself to having lost, but soon writers and artists and performers much closer to me in age and therefore much more nearly imaginable as my colleagues began to slip away unmet. A year before Yeats's death, Thomas Wolfe died. I was in my early twenties by then and Wolfe was in his thirties. Because my wife's family was living in Asheville, North Carolina — the Altamont of Wolfe's *Look Homeward, Angel* and *Of Time and the River* — I had made many visits there and had come to know Wolfe's mother and sister and a couple of his brothers, to say nothing of many of the originals of the characters in his novels. (Wolfe's idea of a sufficient disguise for real people when he put them into his fiction was to call a Vanderbilt an Astorbilt.) I could easily have met Wolfe, but no: I was waiting for Big Tom to make the first gesture.

Similarly with Scott Fitzgerald. His wife Zelda was confined to a sanitarium in Asheville, and Scott — for so I always thought of him, my dear but not yet encountered friend — was staying in Asheville in order to be near her. My mother-in-law helped run Jean West's, a smart dress shop in Asheville, and Scott, at loose ends and lonely, would often stop by and chat with her; they had many friends in common. He would sit on a little Empire sofa just inside the big plate-glass shop window and flick through *Vogue* and *Harper's Bazaar* while my mother-in-law was busy with customers; then she would join him on the sofa and they would talk about the years of their young promise, not so very far behind them; for my mother-in-law had had happy times at St. Jean de Luz and Biarritz in the twenties, while Scott and Zelda were having their happy and sad times on the Riviera. I collected Scott's first editions in the second-hand bookshops in Asheville, never paying more than ten cents apiece for them, and it was the understood thing between him and me that we were soon to meet, but I was waiting in vain to have written "May Day," or "A Diamond as Big as the Ritz," and in a little while he was in Hollywood and then he was dead.

Several years earlier, as an undergraduate at Yale, I was at the height of my ill-fated let-them-come-to-*me* period, but events conspired to plunge me willy-nilly into the midst of a stream of living authors. In the Depression, poets were even more in want of money than they habitually are today, and the most famous among them were quick to come to Yale and give readings. Anyone who was known to be literary was counted on to make the poets welcome, give them tea at the Elizabethan Club — real tea, real crumpets, real Quartos and First Folios on the shelves, a real fire on the hearth, a real bowling green in the garden — and, if necessary, shepherd them to and from the railway station, especially if it was late at night and the celebrated guest had been drinking more than tea. It was thus that I met in passing not only Robert Frost but also T. S. Eliot, looking unexpectedly big and speaking in an expectedly costive British voice ("A cold coming we had of it, just the worst time of year for a journey, and such a journey . . ."); John Masefield, so frail that it seemed as if a gust of pipe-tobacco smoke might overturn him, yet he lived for another thirty years; and Edna St. Vincent Millay, who appeared before us dressed in a monk's brown robe with a golden cincture, her red-blond hair falling to her shoulders, and in the tenderest voice recited, "Childhood is the kingdom where nobody dies. Nobody that matters, that is . . ." Thus, too, I met at dinner, in a candlelit room in Calhoun College, Desmond MacCarthy, that great talker; and I met Mrs. Patrick Campbell, down on her luck and giving recitations of poems and scraps of Shakespeare in a style so old-fashioned in its vividness that when she launched herself into Tennyson's "The wind it is raging in turret and tree," the entire undergraduate audience burst out laughing in her face.

It was inevitable that I write for *The Yale Literary Magazine*. Founded in 1836 and vainglorious like the Hartford *Courant*, the *Lit* has always billed itself as "the oldest monthly magazine in America," and perhaps it is. I was being something of a archaist in those days; I had gone from imitating Frost, which was bad enough, to imitating one or another of the Elizabethan sonneteers, which was far worse. I poured out my rhymes a,b,a,b,c,d,c,d as easily and mindlessly as I breathed. I would not be surprised to learn some day, in a scholarly paper, that fluent rhyming is a function of sexual abstinence; it certainly was for me. I recall that the setting of one of my undergraduate sonnets was San Gimignano and that the setting of another was a steep hillside near the Villa San Michele, on Capri — obvious souvenirs of the Gill family's latest whining assault upon Europe — but the contents of the sonnets have mercifully vanished from my mind.

By the time I was elected editor of the *Lit,* late in junior year, we were making plans for a grand centennial issue. It happened that a very well-known group of men had been members of the board of the *Lit,* including Sinclair Lewis, Thornton Wilder, Stephen Vincent Benét, Archibald MacLeish, Henry L. Stimson, Wilmarth S. Lewis, Philip Barry, Thomas Beer, F. O. Matthiessen, Dwight Macdonald, Waldo Frank, Arthur Goodhart, Henry R. Luce, Walter Millis, and Robert M. Coates. It was my intention to solicit contributions — of course without payment — from these eminences, for publication in a single two-hundred-and-eighty-page issue of the magazine in February, 1936. Some of the writers I came to know in person, despite my prejudice in this regard; others I pursued by mail, letter after letter, until in the end nearly all of the sought-for luminaries capitulated. At the time, Sinclair Lewis was by far the most important of them. He was then at the top of his fame; his anti-Fascist novel *It Can't Happen Here* had been a recent best-seller, and his earlier novels, *Main Street, Babbitt, Arrowsmith,* and *Dodsworth,* were famous throughout the world. A few years before, he had been the first American author to win a Nobel Prize.

Lewis was also, I soon discovered, the most restless and elusive of men. He was a great roaring and raging and boring drunk, with a vile temper, a generous disposition, immense energy, and a notable — and often tiresome — gift for mimicry. He had another gift, and that was for turning a simple, friendly gesture on his part into an occasion for making lifelong enemies of everyone within reach of his scalding, vituperative tongue. In 1935, he was filled with animosity toward Yale. A few years before I set out in pursuit of him, he had been driving up from New York to his house in Vermont and on the spur of the moment, inspired by drink, had decided to stop off in New Haven and present his Nobel Prize medal to Yale. He walked unannounced into the Sterling Memorial Library, and finding the librarian absent, attempted to hand the medal to the librarian's assistant. The assistant protested politely that he could not undertake the responsibility of accepting such a gift. (If, as he must have thought, it really *was* a Nobel Prize medal; for could this rufous, gawky, ill-dressed, drunken apparition of a man, with glaring bloodshot pop-eyes and a skin that looked as if it had been peeled and parboiled not once but many times be the world-famous Sinclair Lewis?) When his gift was, in his view, spurned, Lewis went off in a blazing temper, and the story was quickly in all the papers. I gathered from his old professor, William Lyon Phelps, who was helping me solicit contributions for the centennial issue, that it was up to me to mollify him.

Lewis and I grew friendly through an exchange of many letters and telegrams. One minor comment of his had an immediate effect on me. I had been baptized with the single name of Brendan, but as a compliment to my father, upon being confirmed I added his name to mine, becoming Brendan Michael. My letterhead read "Brendan M. Gill," and Lewis, knowing by then that I intended to become a writer, circled the "M" on a letter of mine and returned it with a scrawled inquiry in the margin: "Brendan *M.* Gill? Rudyard *J.* Kipling?" Then and there, I dropped the "M" forever. Lewis was shrewd about names. As an undergraduate on the *Lit*, he had been a commonplace-sounding Harry S. Lewis; dropping his first name and spelling out his second gave him what a novelist is much helped by — a bright battle-flag of a name. Indeed, there are writers remembered not for their novels but for their names: Mazo de la Roche, Ouida, Warwick Deeping.

One day, Lewis telephoned me in New Haven to say that I might come down and visit him at his place in Bronxville. He was living in a big Westchester-Tudor country house at the end of a winding and bumpy gravelled lane, among evergreen woods — a setting uncannily countrified in feeling, given that New York was but sixteen miles away. (The house was later to be lived in by Vincent Sheean and then rented for a couple of summers by Shawn, who didn't like it: too many dark trees closing in on the house, too many strange sounds in the trees at night. The Shawns thereupon tried renting a house in Bronxville with a more open setting — one with a pasture at the end of the garden. To Shawn's dismay, the pasture contained a live cow, which mooed.) Lewis was then married to Dorothy Thompson, who, as a newspaper columnist and lecturer, was shortly to become almost as famous as her husband. At twenty, I was ignorant of many things, and not the least of these was the nature of marriage; my father had been a widower for nearly fifteen years, and in a widower's house the signs of marriage are few. Dorothy Thompson was eight years younger than her husband and, not yet having grown fat, as good-looking as he was ugly; they had a little boy, Michael, then perhaps five or six. I visited the Lewises several times in Bronxville, and I saw to my astonishment that husband and wife, for all their continuous patty-cake praise of each other, were deadly rivals — rivals for a conspicuous place in the world, for Michael's affection, for the attention of their servants, for the admiration even of young strangers like myself, whom they might well never see again.

Once, when Lewis was drunk, Michael irritated him by some trifling question and Lewis smacked the boy hard across the mouth. Michael screamed. It had never occurred to me until then that a father — especially a middle-aged father — could strike a beloved child. Lewis gathered Michael up in his arms, in paroxysms of drunken remorse, crooning and gibbering, of course to no avail. On another occasion, in his wife's absence and upon her instruction, Lewis undertook to discharge an incompetent maid. He had to drink a good deal to find courage enough for such an unwelcome task, and it came out during the course of dinner that evening that Lewis had given the maid several hundred dollars in order to soften the blow for her. In those days, the sum represented perhaps six or seven months' wages. Dorothy Thompson was furious with Lewis for, in her eyes, simply throwing the money away; Lewis started cursing her, she returned his curses, and for the first time I heard on the lips of a woman an expletive that I had supposed was reserved for the use of men. Bitterly mocking his reiterated use of the term, she said to him, "Ah, balls, balls!" I sat aghast with wonder, a long way from Hartford; so this was what marriage between superior people came to.

Lewis wrote an essay for the *Lit*, which he rightly described as "rambling." Its burden was that writers were not going to be able to make much money out of books in future, thanks to the powerful competition of movies and radio, and that all beginning writers would do well to choose a second skill to fall back on — one that ideally would have no connection with writing or with teaching literature. He suggested that it would be sensible on the part of a serious writer to learn how to run a gas station; Lewis himself had always daydreamed of running an inn. The essay then proceeded to mount a brisk attack on Hemingway, whose book *The Green Hills of Africa* had just been published. Lewis corrected galleys on a typewriter, unlike any other writer I have known; the corrections were very neatly done, with sharply angled lines drawn to mark the points at which new matter was to be inserted. In the course of correcting the *Lit* galleys, he added a few lines of verse, which I got by heart:

Mister Ernest Hemingway
Halts his slaughter of the kudu
To remind you that you may
Risk his sacerdotal hoodoo
If you go on, day by day,
Talking priggishly as you do.
Speak up, man! Be bravely heard
Bawling the four-letter word!
And wear your mind décolleté
Like Mister Ernest Hemingway.

It may seem odd that Lewis, a master of foul language, was offended by Hemingway's then comparatively mild use of foul language in his books, but Lewis, like Ross, was an old-fashioned man, out of the Middle West and out of the nineteenth century as well. He and Ross believed in a double standard of language — one for the publicly printed word, the other for private speech.

One day in the spring of 1936, Lewis and I were talking about *The New Yorker.* I had begun sending in poems and stories to the magazine, and the magazine had been rejecting them with a promptness that was itself a form of rejection. (Like any thrifty editor, I used one of the rejected stories as my contribution to the centennial issue of the *Lit.* It looked very good to me in print.) Lewis wrote only two pieces for *The New Yorker;* they were published in 1937, and even then they were unreadable. One was an account of his first day in New York and the other was a fictional profile of a lady shoe manufacturer. Lewis maintained that the magazine was parochial, and I can remember arguing with him that this was precisely its point and the source of its strength, which it was at that time; many years later, we encountered each other at an opening at the Museum of Modern Art and Lewis began at once, splutteringly, "I tell you the fucking thing is parochial."

Our conversation that day in 1936 led from the magazine to Lewis's career, and he mentioned that he had just been invited to accept an honorary doctorate from a certain small second-rate college. He had refused, but he admitted that he would like very much to be a doctor — it pleased him, he said, whenever he was in Germany to be addressed as "Herr Doktor." We were both sons of doctors, as so many writers are; no doubt that was why the honorific seemed especially precious to us. Wasn't it strange, Lewis asked, that his own alma mater had never offered him a degree?

I took the subject up with Professor Phelps, who took it up with the authorities, and the next thing I knew I was given the secret mission of sounding Lewis out: if by any chance he were to be offered an honorary doctorate in June, would he be willing to accept it? He would indeed. I went further — accepting it, would he undertake not to . . . put on a big act?

Lewis said, "Not be drunk, you mean?"

"Something like that."

"Sober as a judge. Make you proud of me."

The university thereupon invited him to accept a doctorate at the Commencement in June, and Lewis wrote a letter to Phelps, thanking him for the dark plots that he "and that agent of the Yale O.G.P.U., Brendan Gill" must have engaged in on his behalf. In June, I was present at Commencement as a member of the graduating class and so was able to observe Lewis's mannerly deportment. Phelps, who read the citations that accompanied the degrees, when he came to Lewis mentioned the fact that Lewis had always borne the nickname "Red" — a nickname, Phelps said, that "now threatens to outlive its applicability." The mild jest was characteristic of Phelps, the vainest of vain old men. Though only fifty-one, Lewis was growing bald as well as gray, and the jest served to call attention to the fact that Phelps, exuberantly boyish in his seventies, was still in possession of a full head of hair. Dorothy Thompson sat in the balcony of Woolsey Hall during the ceremonies and told Mrs. Angell, wife of the president of Yale, that the honorary degree meant more to Lewis than anything that had happened to him in his life. It was a sad remark to make about a man of Lewis's talent; sadder than Dorothy Thompson appears to have realized. But by then everything that befell Lewis, even when it was fortunate, had a note of sadness in it. He asked me to become his secretary-companion after graduation, but I was determined to get married and therefore declined the offer. (My friend and classmate John Hersey later assumed the position and did not find it easy.)

When I saw Lewis next, in the fall of the year, he provided me by chance with the occasion for my first contribution to *The*

New Yorker. Our encounter ought to have been a cheerful one, and so, on the surface, it was, but I felt that I was failing him and was helpless not to fail him; at twenty-one, it is unnerving to stand in the presence of a man riddled by the disease of himself, and so past cure.

It may be wondered at that I had so much free time in my senior year to devote to O.G.P.U. (Russian Secret Police) and other clandestine activities at Yale. The reason is that by judicious planning in earlier years I had reduced the number of classes I was obliged to attend in senior year to one: a survey of English lyric poetry. And this class met but once a week, and I was the only student in the class. My professor, F. E. Pierce, had suffered a stroke and was confined to his house in the western section of New Haven, not far from the Yale Bowl. He lived in the upper half of a turn-of-the-century two-family house, in circumstances that struck me, a spoiled rich boy, as unpleasantly straitened — furniture of oak instead of mahogany, threadbare rugs on the floor. An elderly widower, he was tended by an elderly widowed sister. His intelligence was unimpaired, but he had lost adequate control of his arms and legs, and his speech often faltered and became incoherent. Being unable to shave, he had grown a beard; he attempted to feed himself, but he did so clumsily, and when I made my visits in the early afternoon there would be crumbs in the thicket of his beard and fresh stains on his vest and trousers.

Pierce was, or pretended to be, resigned to his afflictions; when his lips shaped a nonsense word instead of the correct one chosen by his mind, his eyes would twinkle as if in merriment behind gold-rimmed glasses. But there was no merriment in him, and one day he managed to get out of the house, shuffle his way to a gunsmith's shop, purchase a revolver, shuffle home, put the revolver against the roof of his mouth, and blow his brains out. Shocked as I was by the violence of his death — a violence all the more unexpected in so gentle and smiling a man — I thought it admirable. Nothing was left for him in life except a distressful worsening of it; and with the worsening would come a heavier burden to fall upon others.

By an irony, I profited in two ways from Pierce's death. One of the ways would certainly have amused him and the other might have made him proud. I had written only a single paper in the course of our work together, and he had given me a grade of something over ninety on it. The English department, not knowing quite what else to do and having a soft spot in its heart for me because of my labors on the *Lit*, decided to let that solitary grade become my grade for the whole year; with the result that I was suddenly and undeservedly catapulted upward into Phi Beta Kappa and, on graduating, was given my B.A. *magna cum laude:* a scandalous, delightful end to a lazy scholarly career. In the months following Pierce's death, I wrote a long sonnet-sequence, based on what I imagined to be Pierce's feelings in respect to his late wife. The sequence won a prize, which consisted of a comparatively large sum of money. One of the stipulations of the prize was that the poem that won it must be published, so I decided to spend all the money on the printing of a distinguished-looking little book — my first — called *Death in April.* It contained, in handset type upon handmade paper, the sonnet-sequence, a dozen or so love poems, and other tender scraps. I have taken pains not to look at it since, but all books have lives of their own and their own consequences, and that book helped teach me a lesson: never accept a compliment until it has been completed.

A few years ago, an English friend of mine saw me among a group of people in Washington. He came up and began telling the group how the Gills, meeting him and his wife on their first visit to America, had kindly offered them the use of the Gills' country house for an autumn holiday. Late one night during the holiday, he was glancing over our shelves in search of something to read and stumbled on my little book. He read some of the love poems aloud to his wife; they were so moved by them that they immediately made love and she conceived a child. I broke in at that point to say how delighted I was to think that any word of mine could have led not only to lovemaking but to a birth as well. "And furthermore," my friend went on, interrupting my interruption, "I think those poems of yours are the very best work you've ever done." So from the heights, the depths: his compliment had dismissed thirty years of my life's work in a single breath.

8

The reason I waited to marry until the day after graduating from Yale was that in the thirties most university authorities held the view that education and marriage were unrelated and probably antagonistic activities; anyone who felt inclined to marry, or had to marry (by dint of pregnancy, shotgun, or other unbecoming necessity), was well advised to drop out of college altogether. It is hard to realize in the seventies the extent to which, even after the revolution in social behavior purportedly won by "flaming youth" in the twenties, the so-called Ivy League colleges went on reflecting the Jansenist bias of their eighteenth-century origins. Yale had been founded largely for the purpose of training young men to serve God — a particularly nasty, wrathful, and unforgiving Protestant God, who would sooner scourge His children than love them — and the administration of the university appeared to have inherited from its predecessors a conviction that sex was a species of crime, to be rooted out and suppressed except for occasional icy bouts of procreation in one's later years. Since marriage was all too plainly a manifestation of sex, it was frowned on in academe. And not alone among undergraduates: like a throwback to the days at Oxford and Cambridge when dons had to be in holy orders, the Yale of my time had a faculty that boasted an astonishingly high proportion of bachelors. True, there was a Depression to contend with and salaries at Yale were shockingly low, so a good many young men may have put off marriage for economic reasons; but many others, as prosperity returned and they moved up in the world, remained invincibly celibate. No doubt most of them chose to be either homosexual or masturbatory.

In our ignorance, those of us who had come to Yale from small, conventionally inhibited communities were under the impression that the vice of masturbation was reserved for wretched youths like ourselves, doomed sooner or later to go bald and mad; it didn't occur to us that it was not only permissible for grown men but worthy of them. Little as we were able to imagine our teachers and betters as onanists, still less could we imagine them as being actively homosexual; if we suspected that homosexuality was their failing, we assumed as a matter of course that it was passive and without consequences.

We saw our bachelor mentors as chaste creatures, suffering gallantly a deprivation imposed on them by nature. We might gossip about them, but we felt sorry for them in their misfortune; and we were wrong. For it is a maxim I have learned to trust with all my heart that everyone without exception enjoys a sexual life far more active and more rewarding than can be guessed at even by his close friends.

I perceive now that my unmarried teachers at Yale were probably less chaste than the rest of us, being more caught up in continuous gusts of passion than we simpletons supposed as we sat watching them cover their academic gowns with chalk-dust at some classroom blackboard on a gloomy New Haven afternoon. (With irony, Wallace Stevens entitled one of the greatest of his poems "An Ordinary Evening in New Haven." But an ordinary evening in New Haven is nothing like as languid as an ordinary afternoon; and no one speaks of the mornings.) Our teachers were also less sober than we supposed. Indeed, there were a number of alcoholics among them, but their alcoholism, like their sexual lives, remained a fairly well-kept secret. Open alcoholics are often more interesting, and sometimes more amusing, than secret ones, but they are also by their nature more fugitive; they rarely stay in one place for long and so one doesn't get to know them well. At prep school we had an alcoholic French teacher named Finnegan, who, dressed only in a soiled knee-length white nightgown, rejoiced to dash out at midnight and shinny up the wooden flagpole in the middle of the campus, on his way to the moon and baying at it as he climbed. He didn't shinny very far up the pole and he didn't last very long at the school.

I was unaware in my youth of how great a commonplace the alcoholic is in our society. It is only when I travel far back in my mind that I discover, shaking my head in wonder, how friendly I was with notable specimens in my undergraduate days; and how unwittingly. One spends a lifetime reconstructing one's past, and it is not merely in order to find an image of oneself that will prove pleasing; rather, it is in order to approach some tentative, usable truth about oneself by ransacking all the data that have hovered dimly somewhere "out there," helping to form one's nature. If the unexamined life is not worth living, the unexamined past is not worth possessing; it bears fruit only by being held continuously up to the light, and it is as changeable and as full of surprises, pleasant and unpleasant, as the future. I remember my young life as crammed with mysterious hints, gestures, and sounds: a hand suddenly reaching out to seize me and as suddenly drawing back, the scuffle of a chair overturning on the far side of a wall, a distant, monkey-like whimpering at night, in a voice never heard by day . . . How many friends, drunk and sober, I must have failed in those days by being in the presence of their anguish and yet deaf and blind to it!

University authorities were not alone in disapproving of early marriages. In the thirties, most upper-middle-class parents took the same stern view, without regard to whether the couple in love was in or out of school. A young man was expected to prove himself financially before he married. He was to find a place for himself out in the harsh world. He must stand on his own two feet and learn that money doesn't grow on trees. Meanwhile, the girl was to wait for him, uncourted by others and yielding the precious ground of her body stubbornly or perhaps not at all. I am glad to say that this grisly puritan scenario never crossed my mind. At twenty-one, I had every reason to believe that money *did* grow on trees. (To this day, the evidence remains strongly in favor of this hypothesis; the species of tree that money grows best on is, of course, the family tree.) Luckily for me, the conventional scenario never crossed my father's mind, either. That generous man was as far ahead of his time in respect to the links between money and happiness as he was ahead of his time in respect to his profession. He thought that his five children should come into their inheritance at the beginning of their adult lives, when they were most in need of it, and not upon his death, when, being by then middle-aged, they would presumably have solved their financial problems.

My father spoke out vehemently on the disgustingness of aging people who waited about for their still more aged parents to die, in order that they might finally become rich and hang on to become in turn a torment to their aging children. He had such strong feelings on the subject that he must often have encountered it in his practice. To him the most repellent thing of all was the toadying to the senile that he observed on the part not only of relatives but of young lawyers and doctors as well. Whenever one of his colleagues inherited a large sum from some ancient, slobbering, and long since dotty widow, my father would be filled with eloquent contempt. I remember his telling me once about one of his patients — an old man who had outlived his wits and whom a young broker played fawning nursemaid to; the broker called the old man "Junior" and would say to him, "Now, Junior! Time to go wee-wee." Wee-weeing Junior died at last, at ninety, leaving the grey-haired broker well fixed.

A self-made man — there was money on my mother's side of the family, but none on his; he had worked his way through Yale by waiting on tables — my father was unlike most self-made men I have known in not taking money seriously. He was clever about it but not preoccupied with it. Though he never charged high fees and treated innumerable nuns, priests, ministers, rabbis, and impoverished people free of charge, he worked so hard that he easily earned more than he needed to spend and he invested the surplus wisely in Hartford insurance stocks — the sacred litany that begins "Travelers, Aetna Life, Connecticut General, Hartford Fire . . ." As the boom of the twenties proceeded (a boom that down in New York was making possible the precariously sustained early life of *The New Yorker*, as yet scarcely heard of in Hartford), my father became a millionaire. Most wealthy people in Hartford have little knack for living grandly, or even very well, and may take relish in living so meanly that, encountering them on a street-corner, with their frayed cuffs and down-at-heel shoes, one would suppose that they were on their way to pick up a welfare check; they are the ones who give a hundred dollars a year to the Community Fund and die leaving twenty million. By the comparatively low standard of display that Hartford set for millionaires, my father had always lived like one, so there was no marked change in our status as he grew richer. We went on occupying the same big, towery, elm-shaded house in which I had been born, with a millionaire in liquor (Heublein) on one side of us and a millionaire in tobacco (Hartman) on the other, and with department-store millionaires (Auerbachs and Foxes) behind us and across the street; we went on driving the same shiny new Cadillacs; and we employed the same endless procession of incompetent help —

Mary Blake, Petey and Della, Olga, Rosie, Mrs. Burt, whose visages glide like malignant clockwork figures along the velvet backdrop of my youth.

The Depression, though it reduced my father's capital, by no means wiped it out. If I had to travel six miles to school every day, it was not on foot, or even by bus; I went to and fro in a Yellow Cab. It has to be remembered that depressions provide many advantages for the rich; it was for this reason above all others that the rich accused F.D.R. of betraying his class and went off in venomous high spirits, as in Peter Arno's celebrated cartoon, to hiss him at the Trans-Lux. All the necessities of life were cheaper in the thirties than they had been fifty years earlier. My father was distressed to pay less for eggs and butter than his parents had had to pay in the eighteen-seventies; on every hand the rich were gathering up bargains they didn't need and the poor were starving.

There were other, less painful advantages to wealth, which I was not above welcoming. Having failed to pass several of my College Entrance Board examinations, I was nevertheless allowed to enter Yale, in part because my father was able to pay the full tuition. (When my elder son was admitted to Yale many years later, the Dean of Admissions, turning from my son to me, asked me when my time at Yale had been. I said that I had entered in the fall of '32. "Oh, my God!" said the Dean. "We were scraping the bottom of the barrel in those days.")

Having got out of school and being in possession of my share of the family fortune, I felt perfectly free to marry. My share was but a fifth of the whole, and there were moments when I regretted the size of the fraction. In childhood, I had enjoyed a recurrent fantasy in which my father and my four brothers and sisters were all instantly killed in a terrible car accident and I, weeping bravely, became the sole heir. I had had to abandon the fantasy — we owned too many cars and had too many diverse interests to make such a substantial catastrophe a likely one. I consoled myself with the thought that I would gain a new and far greater fortune by my writing. In one of my novels, the hero says, "I've always been so ready to be rich," and the hero is speaking from the author's heart. If I am now something like thirty years behind schedule financially, I am no less ready than I was. Certainly I have no one to blame but myself for having failed, given so enviable a head start. For small as my fifth share of the family fortune was, it produced an income in the late thirties of perhaps three thousand dollars a year — enough to ensure the freedom of choice that a beginning writer needs. In pocketbook, if not in spirit, I could afford to be rejected again and again. I could make reckless mistakes. I could devote all my energy to learning my craft.

I had still another advantage over other beginners, again thanks to my father's unorthodox wisdom. In conversation about my forthcoming marriage, I learned that he felt none of the usual Hartford horror over the dread deed known as dipping into capital. There were wealthy misers in the Hartford of that period who succeeded in living off the income of their income, but even people who took a more reasonable view of the pleasures of wealth were brought up to suppose that capital was inviolable; they would assert that they were "locked into" their holdings, and one gained from them the impression that wealth consisted of a maximum-security prison of the greatest possible luxury, crowded to its gilded iron doors with contented inmates. My father urged it upon me that, if I saw fit, I was to spend capital as well as income — "Spend it when you're young and healthy and can have some fun with it! Before something goes wrong!" he said. A statement not to be expected from the august director of two Hartford banks, but he made it many times, and I was always quick to agree with him. I think behind the statement was the fact that he and my mother had had only fifteen years together. Better than anyone, he knew how little time there might be for young people to be happy in — planning for old age was all very well, but that was planning according to statistics, and the importance to actual flesh-and-blood individuals of their having a good time in their first youth lay far outside the calculations of actuaries.

Anne Barnard and I were married in Norfolk, Connecticut, on June 20, 1936. I was then still a practicing Catholic, so the ceremony took place in the local Catholic church. This must have been distasteful to the Barnard family, which had been inveterately Protestant for centuries and was familiar with Catholics only as servants. Fortunately, they were too polite to give me the least hint of how uncomfortable a religious and social novelty I was to them. Anne's mother was an Episcopalian and her father had once been a deacon of the fashionable Brick Presbyterian Church, in New York; there were a couple of perfectly good Protestant churches in Norfolk, in one or the other of which the Barnards had always assumed their daughter would be married. That disappointment was bad enough; to make matters worse, the Catholic church had a name ideally unsuitable for the celebration of weddings: it was called the Church of the Immaculate Conception. My imminent Protestant in-laws had no idea what the Immaculate Conception might be, but to engrave such a phrase upon wedding invitations that were being sent to a host of Protestant friends struck them as somewhat indecent.

The ceremony itself was not without peculiarities. Anne's wedding dress had a very long train, which, because of the small size of the church, had to be spread out behind her along the floor of the vestibule, through the open front door, and out onto the paved floor of the porch of the church. As the organist, who was my old prep-school Latin teacher, launched *con brio* into the wedding march and Anne and her father started down the aisle — here comes the bride! — a little dog ran up the steps of the porch and seated himself on the end of the train. He rode the train contentedly into the church and proceeded a considerable distance along the aisle — here comes the dog! — until one of the ushers succeeded in scooping him up and dispatching him outdoors.

The ushers were also something of a comic turn. Most of them were clubmates of mine in Bones and had spent the previous twenty-four hours in merry dissipation aboard the Chisholms' yacht in New London. (Hugh Chisholm, Jr., a member of the class of '36, was a poet who had the rare good fortune to look like a poet. He was as pretty and pink-cheeked and rich as Shelley, and he died in a car accident near Biarritz a few years ago, having written much less than his college friends had expected him to.) One of my clubmates had unaccountably lost his shoes somewhere between New London and Norfolk. He seated people with his usual aplomb, dressed in a disheveled white linen suit and greenish, scuffed tennis sneakers, lent him by a friend.

The priest who married us was an alcoholic; he had been rusticated to Norfolk many years earlier because he would be likely to cause less scandal in a small community than in a big one. He was aware that most of the people at the wedding would be of two sorts — either Protestants who were friends and relatives of the bride, or Catholics who were friends and relatives of the bridegroom and would be trying to act as much at ease as possible in alien country. He was determined to behave splendidly; he would refuse to touch a drop of champagne at the reception. The setting for the reception was the garden of a rambling eighteenth-century farmhouse that had once been the summer home of Anne's grandparents and in 1936 belonged to one of her uncles (for many years now, it has belonged to us). In the course of the reception, the ushers and Anne and I repaired to an upstairs study in the heart of the old house, and in a ceremony notable for disorderliness Anne was, in effect, taken into the bosom of the Bones — an occasion altogether astonishing to her. Meanwhile, down in the garden, in the midst of the flowering mountain laurel and the rows of white, blood-flecked peonies, trays of champagne were being passed among the guests, and the priest firmly refused and refused and refused to touch a drop, until at last . . . And so it befell that long after we had left the reception, driving to Hartford to catch a train for New York and from there take ship for England, the priest came to enjoy himself in his usual fashion; and if some of the Catholics present were mortified on behalf of the holy faith, no Protestant appears to have thought the worse of him.

As a beginning writer, charged with dreams of glory, I took care to bring along on our honeymoon a portable typewriter and a ream of yellow copy paper. No matter what our program — walking strenuously in London, cycling still more strenuously in the Cotswolds, sunning ourselves in Oxford on the leads of the Radcliffe Camera, or punting on the Avon, where we fed stale macaroons to the swans that paddled in querulous pursuit of us — every day I pegged away at a novel. The manuscript of this novel has since been conveniently lost; it was entitled *Yankee Kingdom Come,* and the scene was the valley of the Connecticut River just north of Hartford, where the great shade-grown tobacco farms are located. On these farms, under seas of cheesecloth that all summer long turn the level fields into sweltering greenhouses, grow the tobacco plants whose broad leaves, cured in barns scattered among the fields, are used as cigar-wrappers: pound for pound and dollar for dollar, the most valuable crop grown in America. Now, except for that single moderately interesting fact, I knew nothing whatever about the farms, or about the people who owned them, or about the people who worked on them. Not in the least daunted by my ignorance, in the cool of the English summer I started writing the story of a Polish immigrant family and the troubles that I imagined them encountering in that sun-struck, overheated valley.

We flew from England to the Continent, to spend a few days with a sister of mine and her husband, who were staying at the Ritz in Paris. My parents had spent a part of their honeymoon at the Ritz, and our eldest child and her husband were later to spend a part of their honeymoon there; certain family traditions are worth preserving. The tub in our bathroom was big enough to bathe in two at a time — on honeymoons, this seems an indispensable advantage — and above the beds was a battery of brightly polished bell-buttons to push; we tested all but the one marked *"Service Privé,"* fearing that it might open the door to some exotic sexual privilege not yet within our competence. (We later learned that it was simply the bell by which guests of the hotel could summon their own servants from rooms in the attic of the hotel.)

After Paris, we drifted on to Munich, where the Yale Glee Club was singing. The members of the Club were staying in *pensions*, which in those days lacked adequate bathing facilities. Since we were putting up at a first-rate establishment, our friends in the Club took to making frequent and unannounced visits to our bathroom. We would be lying in bed of a morning as, one after another, they streamed through our bedroom into the bathroom to shave, take showers, or enjoy a good soak. On one occasion the manager of the hotel telephoned in a rage to protest that we had used up all the hot water in the hotel. Nothing so monstrous had ever happened in his experience. He hinted that he was reluctant to imagine what practices we newlyweds were engaging in (shades of *service privé!*); whatever they might be, they were surely unnatural and perhaps illegal.

One evening at the Rathskeller, that saving remnant of the Glee Club known as the Whiffenpoofs was putting on an impromptu concert; Hitler and his entourage entered and sat listening with grave approbation to "Aura Lee" and "Shall I Wasting in Despair." It is hard today to imagine a point in history at which Hitler and the Whiffenpoofs could have coincided, but such, for that little while, was the case. Hitler called J. Merrill Knapp, the leader of the Whiffenpoofs and now a professor of music at Princeton, over to his table to congratulate him on the concert; it appeared that Hitler had found "To the Tables Down at Mory's" especially endearing. I have always held it against Knapp that at that moment he didn't leap upon Der Führer and strangle him to death with his bare hands, thereby, at the expense of a single human life — his own, to be sure — preventing the outbreak of the Second World War.

Over the Alps into Italy, where I went on steadily typing. Oh, the sufferings I invented for that poor Polish family on their to-bacco farm by the Connecticut River! The climax of the novel was a terrible hailstorm, which tore the family's precious crop to shreds and pitched them headlong into bankruptcy. This meteor-ological and financial disaster I worked up in a bower of mosquito netting, my Flit gun at the ready, in our luxurious quarters in the Royal Danieli, in Venice; the Excelsior, in Rome; and the Quisi-sana, on Capri. Strange days for Anne, who knew little of Europe and was eager to observe its wonders at first hand, while I, using my work as an excuse, would have none of them.

I was then at the height of my youthful snobbery in respect to sightseeing and sightseers. Having been a member of what was surely one of the most conspicuous families of American tourists to fling itself grumbling across Europe, it was natural for me to despise the breed. I would rather not see the Sistine Chapel at all than see it as a tripper; it was as if I were waiting for the Pope to invite us over for a Punt e Mes under God and Adam, and he never did. Anne was obliged to go out alone to visit churches and museums; being young and pretty and blond, she would accumulate an army of vociferous admirers, some of whom would follow her on foot and others of whom would follow her in natty little coughing and snorting open cars, which now and then nudged their way up onto the sidewalk in order to give the drivers of them a closer look at the prey. Sometimes, irritated beyond endurance, Anne would beg me to accompany her, and I would grudgingly do so. I was all the more grudging when it turned out that my presence did little to lessen the torrents of whistles, cat-calls, and invitations addressed to her.

Toward the end of summer, we sailed for home from beggar-ridden Naples aboard the handsome and fashionable *Conte di Sa-voia*, which in a few years would be a casualty of the Second World War. The passengers were sleek, potbellied, sunbaked Americans, who clustered about the open-air pool and drowsed and drank and rubbed oil into one or another of their hairy folds. I spent my days in our cabin, in a puritan ecstasy of tap, tap, tap. At my father's house in Hartford, I finished the novel and set about preparing a neat typescript of it, at the rate of ten or fifteen thousand words a day (what on earth was the hurry?), in the law offices of my older brother. Then I mailed the typescript off to

John Farrar, in New York. Farrar had been helpful to me in the preparation of the centennial issue of the *Lit* and he was, besides, a devoted Bones man. He was a partner in the publishing house of Farrar & Rinehart, now Farrar, Straus & Giroux.

In a few days, Farrar summoned me to New York and took me to lunch at a hotel on Murray Hill. One remembers, or *can* remember, everything, and the least important things are as easily remembered as the most important; of that lunch I remember that we sat by a window, through which the sun blazed onto the pierced-silver and rose-silk shade of the little lamp that stood lighted, giving no light, in the middle of the table. In the kindest way possible, Farrar told me that while my novel seemed to him publishable, he would advise me not to make my debut with that particular work. I accepted his advice with an alacrity and good grace that puzzle me now. All those weeks of furious typing under the mosquito nettings! Why did I not howl with rage and swear to show Farrar how obtuse he was by immediately taking the novel to another publisher, and then to another, until at last I found one who was downright eager to accept it? The fact is that I didn't, and I surmise that the reason was that in my heart I was already of Farrar's opinion. The ignorant young man who had amassed all those thousands of words had, one might assume, talent; that was far from making him a novelist. "Beauty is so difficult, Yeats!" Beardsley had protested when Yeats urged him to do better. To write well was also, I was beginning to see, difficult. I would lay siege to letters in a different direction.

9

My disappointment in respect to *Yankee Kingdom Come,* somewhat mitigated by my suspicion of its worth, was still further mitigated by a number of agreeable social and architectural diversions of that first autumn out in the world. My father's bounty being without stint, he saw no reason that I shouldn't begin my literary career as if I were already at the peak of it. The result was that without having sold a penny's worth of my writings, I found myself living like some grand Pulitzer Prize-winning novelist in his sixties, with a lifetime of solid and much-praised work behind him. Not for Anne and me the meanness of a small, sensible apartment in town, the grubby saving up for furniture, kitchenware, and perhaps a battered second-hand car to run errands in. What we had in mind was a charming old place in the depths of the country, on a scale that Washington Irving might not have thought inappropriate for a gentleman writer a hundred years earlier. No difficulty for my father there — busy as he was with his practice, he soon located the very thing for us: in the town of Berlin, Connecticut, about halfway between Hartford and New Haven, on what had once been the main highway and was now a little-used side road, stood a white eighteenth-century farmhouse, set among acres of fields and orchards, with a pleasing distant prospect of a mountain called (out of Bunyan? the Bible?) Mount Lamentation, and with a brook that bubbled and purled in strict Tennysonian meter.

The place was known as Old Toll Gate Farm, in recollection of a tollgate that had stood near the site a hundred and fifty years earlier. The farm was for sale because the wealthy couple that had recently restored the house from top to bottom had had a falling-out and were getting divorced. It appeared that they knew how to do everything well except be married; they had seen to it that the house had a new roof, three new bathrooms, a new furnace, new wiring, and a green-tiled conservatory with a fountain and a small pool. A rosy-brick terrace, overhung by clematis,

It was in this delightful old house in Connecticut that I began writing for The New Yorker. *Ross, who also had a big house in Connecticut, didn't approve of his writers living as well, or better, than he did. It made him nervous.*

projected from a wing of the house; in the newly planted garden borders, flowers leapt up in profusion. Because of the divorce, the property had to be sold quickly and therefore cheaply; my father, who enjoyed the give-and-take of hard bargaining, arranged for us to buy it for ten thousand dollars and then arranged for a mortgage that would cover almost the entire amount. We moved into the immaculate house bearing the booty of our hundreds of wedding presents — china, silver, crystal, leather — as well as the further, and still more precious, booty of a large portion of Anne's family's china, silver, and crystal. To house the treasure, we turned a large ground-floor pantry into a miniature Tiffany warehouse, with bars on the windows and, on the only door, an ingenious iron lock, wrought for us by the local blacksmith.

My father had long made it a custom to spend his lunch hour (he ate in a cheap cafeteria, impatiently) shopping for antiques on Mulberry Street in Hartford — a short street running downhill off Main Street toward the Hog River, measliest of streams, which now flows underground into the nearby Connecticut. Mulberry Street was the center of the antiques trade in Hartford at that time. My father had filled his own house to the rafters with old things;

now that he had the excuse of ten or twelve rooms of farmhouse in need of furnishing, he ransacked the shops daily, to our advantage.

A few of the dealers were Yankees, but many of them were immigrant Russian Jews, or Jews of the first generation in this country, who had acquired an astonishing mastery of Early American antiquities. In the thirties, there were still a number of "pickers" roaming the countryside in battered trucks, bringing back to town at nightfall, along with much that was merely second-hand, an occasional fine Windsor side chair, a scalloped corner cupboard, perhaps even a cherry lowboy with its original brasses. My father enjoyed haggling over prices with the dealers, sometimes in sign language in order to keep his transactions secret from other shoppers. Often it would take him days of entering and leaving a certain shop before he succeeded in buying a piece that he especially coveted, but every day he was sure to buy some trifle or other: a dinted pewter plate, a pair of Sheffield candlesticks, a glazed jug. He had a weakness for crude eighteenth-century farm implements — after all, his grandfather, of whom he had vivid recollections, had been a farmer and had been born in the eighteenth century — and the barn at Old Toll Gate Farm was soon full of treadmills, scythes, shingle-splitters, apple-corers, steelyards, spinning wheels, and churns. There was even a bizarre fly-catcher, with a wooden clock mechanism that, on being wound up, turned a notched roller, onto which honey was spread. The honey attracted flies and drew them, steadily gourmandizing, down to where a blade scraped them off into a drawer from which escape was impossible; sullenly buzzing, they met their slow end. Smears of decades-old honey lay on the roller and black beads of long-dead flies lay in the drawer when my father brought the disgusting object home to us in triumph.

As for the gentleman writer, nothing was too good for him. When it came to acquiring equipment worthy of his intentions, how the money flew! I bought a handsome walnut desk with a typewriter platform that moved up and down by means of an apparatus so complex and therefore so costly to manufacture that the company selling it soon went out of business. I also bought a leather swivel chair with thickly padded arms and a headrest adjustable to five positions, and the most expensive "silent" typewriter on the market. Moreover, I took care to purchase a large quantity of paper that had a very high rag content, with the not quite openly acknowledged purpose of making things easy for any possible future biographer of mine; what I wrote would be sure to last as a physical entity for centuries, whether it was worth saving or not. (I hadn't yet discovered that my natural instinct was to destroy or lose possessions and not to preserve them.)

From early morning — for we leapt out of bed at the first light, as if in terror of the sin of sloth — I sat in splendor in my upstairs study, staring out over the autumn fields toward Mount Lamentation. I was in a posture to be struck by lightning, but it turned out to be flickering at a considerable distance. I had retreated from the large scale of the novel to the small and presumably more manageable scale of verse. I was still being too Frostily bucolic for my own good — I can recall rhyming "heft" and "bereft," which sounds ominous — and I met with as little success as I deserved.

Almost as soon as I had sent off a poem to *The New Yorker*, it would be back in our mailbox in Berlin. The postal service in those days was, of course, incomparably faster than it is at present; even so, the magazine appeared to have devised some extra-speedy method of returning my contributions. My poems would be accompanied by the same rejection slip that the magazine uses today; it reads, "We regret that we are unable to use the enclosed material. Thank you for giving us the opportunity to consider it," and it is signed "The Editors." Very civil; moreover, in the margin of the stationery upon which the message of rejection is printed appears the Roman numeral "I." Naturally, I assumed that I was receiving the editors' Number One Rejection Slip and I flattered and consoled myself with the supposition that less talented would-be contributors were receiving the Number Two and perhaps even the Number Three Rejection Slip. Later, I discovered that everyone who submitted a piece to the magazine followed a similar process of deduction and self-congratulation in respect to that mysterious "I." In fact, it is on every rejection slip and it is meaningless; nobody in the office remembers now why it happens to be there.

False reasoning based on nonexistent principles is apparently as common among our readers as it is among would-be contributors. Many of them spend their days searching through the magazine for cabalistic signs of one sort or another and — wonderfully — finding them. Once at a cocktail party in New York, an English publisher, learning that I was on the staff of *The New Yorker*, drew me aside and in a conspiratorial whisper said, "I know what those two little black dots under a *New Yorker* drawing mean." Now, at that moment I didn't recollect that there *were* any dots under drawings in *The New Yorker*, but in order not to disappoint the publisher in the pride of his knowledge, I answered, in

"Is this yours or mine?"

•   •

A Steig drawing showing the two dots that certain close students of the magazine are sure possess a grave cabalistic significance.

an equally confidential fashion, "You do?" My tone hinted that I admired him for having found us out and that henceforth neither of us need risk exchanging a word on the subject in public; our shared secret had made us brothers. Unless I have been deliberately kept in ignorance of their true meaning throughout all these years, the dots (which can indeed be found under some of our drawings) are, like so many other things in the magazine, vestiges of notions of design that originated in the twenties and that have survived, often in a diminished and mutilated form, into the seventies.

The heading of the "Talk of the Town" department is a characteristic example of such an archaeological survival. It is a drawing made by Rea Irvin, who served as the first art director of the

magazine, though in fact he never bore that title, or any title. Irvin adapted it in the late twenties from a heading that he had prepared for the very first issue of *The New Yorker*, in February, 1925. The drawing is wholly out of keeping with any impression of the

nature of the magazine that the present editors would wish to convey to readers; nevertheless, when it was drawn, it must have been intended to symbolize what Ross and his board of advisory editors — Marc Connelly, Rea Irvin, George S. Kaufman, Alice

At top, *the original heading for* "The Talk of the Town," *as drawn by Rea Irvin in* 1925. Middle, *the heading as modified a few years later. The changes are worth puzzling over. The literal-minded Ross may have asked Irvin to add writing to the paper that the fop is looking at; otherwise, why should he be looking at it? Perhaps the owl is more amusing when he winks than when he doesn't. The removal of the border strengthens the drawing and the rays of the rising (or setting) sun give it liveliness, but what are those peculiar star-bursts and bubbles doing above and below the strangely ribbed line?* Bottom, *one of the many headings drawn by Irvin and soon — and wisely — abandoned.*

Duer Miller, Dorothy Parker, and Alexander Woollcott — hoped would prove the spirit of their racy and sophisticated new publication. And what symbol did they choose? Why, of all unexpected and inappropriate things, a Beau Brummell-like dandy: the same preposterous figure out of a dead and alien past that Irvin drew as a cover for the first issue (a cover reproduced every February on the anniversary issue, except when we forget to do so). One is baffled to see how an early-nineteenth-century English fop, scrutinizing through a monocle, with a curiosity so mild that it amounts to disdain, a passing butterfly, could hope to represent the jazzy, new-rich, gangster-ridden, speakeasy-filled New York of the twenties, which Ross claimed to be ready to give an accurate rendering of.

The drawing at the head of "Talk" is in some ways more mysterious even than the cover and deserves examination. The dandy is shown at the left-hand side of the drawing; he is in profile, wearing a high stock, with a monocle on a ribbon screwed into his left eye. He is engaged in writing a missive of some length with a grotesquely exaggerated quill pen. On the right-hand side of the drawing, full-face to the viewer, perches a plump black owl, roguishly winking. Between the dandy and the owl rise some peculiar skyscrapers, topped by cupolas unlike any to be seen in New York. Rays of sunlight, or perhaps moonlight (for the owl's unwinking eye is wide-open), stream from behind the skyscrapers. Dandy, owl, and skyscrapers are drawn along a single notched, curving line, under and over which float a number of wheels with sawtoothed rims. What is this incoherent jumble attempting to say? Nobody alive any longer remembers, and it doesn't matter. There the heading is, and has been, for upwards of fifty years, and every week we see it and yet take care not to see it; it is a mere reassuring blur at the top of the page as we settle down to our reading of Notes and Comment. As such, it remains a continuing witness to the almost total confusion of purpose manifested in those early days by Ross and his so-called advisers. They had been placed on the masthead less because they were capable of giving good advice (plainly, they were not) than because, as celebrated figures in New York's literary and artistic circles, they were needed for window-dressing. They lent the shaky enterprise a much-needed air of professional self-confidence; their names were soon, and wisely, dropped.

"What is the specialty here?"

In its first years, the magazine wobbled between Irvin's world of archaic fancy and the real world that it had promised in its prospectus to chronicle — a world of speakeasies, nightclubs, and chorus girls. Arno was obviously closer in touch with this world than either Irvin or Ross was.

After several weeks of vainly storming the magazine with carefully worked-over poems, I dashed off and submitted an unambitious little bastard of a piece — neither fact nor fiction — about an encounter between the genuine Sinclair Lewis and an invented Dr. McGrady. To my astonishment, the magazine accepted the story. Katharine White wrote to say that in the opinion of people who knew him it was Lewis to the life; she enclosed with her thanks a check for a hundred and sixty dollars. The amount of the check impressed me less than its physical beauty. I liked everything about the way it looked, from the blue ink of its *New Yorker*-style print to its cameo drawing of Eustace Tilley. If I had been somewhat richer, I would have kept the check uncashed and carried it about with me forever, neatly framed, as a souvenir of my first success out in the world. I was never in any doubt that the story was purchased on the strength of Lewis's fame and not on that of its quality as a piece of writing. Unbeknownst to me, it was a genre categorized by *New Yorker* editors as a "casual," which commonly meant a piece that was based on something that had happened in real life, or was to some degree news; as a form of journalism it was likely to be judged by standards somewhat less high than those set for works that were wholly of the imagination.

That first casual of mine has the virtue of brevity, and it may be worth reproducing here, as an example of where I then stood as a writer and where *The New Yorker* stood as a literary publication.

Of Sinclair Lewis and Dr. McGrady

The day Dr. McGrady met Sinclair Lewis was assuredly the proudest of all his life. The Nobel Prize winner was the first celebrity with whom he had actually exchanged a few words, and the impression Dr. McGrady received in five minutes he could not and would not forget in all his days.

It all began very innocently. That was what made it as exciting as it was. The Doctor and his wife had gone down to the Palace Theatre in Hartford, where the WPA were staging "It Can't Happen Here." They took seats in the third row some fifteen minutes before the curtain was due to rise, and Mrs. McGrady commented, as she always did, upon the faces and clothes of those who claimed the seats about them. It was just like every other night on which they had gone to watch a stock company acting in the old Palace. Just before the curtain rose there was a murmur behind them, and Dr. McGrady, always sensitive to such sounds, by half-rising in his seat was able to see a tall, middle-aged man with a baldish head settling himself halfway back in the darkened theatre. A young, bespectacled Jew behind the Doctor whispered to his companion, "That's Sinclair Lewis, who wrote the play. I seen his picture in the *Times.*" The Doctor watched Lewis closely as he sat down: he was wearing a gray suit in spite of the fact that this was an evening performance, for which the Doctor himself had put on a blue serge; and beside Lewis sat the Governor of Connecticut, a little old man with curly white hair, into whose ear Lewis seemed to be pouring a torrent of words.

Dr. McGrady sat back in his seat. "That's Sinclair Lewis," he said. "He wrote the play."

Mrs. McGrady sniffed. "He isn't much to look at," she said.

"No. But you can tell. You can just tell somehow that he's got brains."

"He's a clumsy thing."

The Doctor's ire rose. "I like him," he said.

The curtain lifted on the first scene. Doremus Jessup and Lorinda Pike walked on with a picnic lunch, settling themselves on a log in front of faded blue canvas mountains. The foliage that hung down one side of the stage failed to meet the narrow trunk from which it was supposed to grow, but when Doremus began to speak, the Doctor forgot everything in the play save the plot. He had not read the book, and he listened with intense interest to every word, so that no slightest turn of phrase might escape him. Any play was to the Doctor a mystery story strewn with clues, and he was determined to miss none. When the curtain fell on the last scene of the first act, it caught him, as it always did, unexpectedly and with hurt surprise.

"I don't think it's so wonderful," Mrs. McGrady said.

"I like it. Every real American ought to see it," said the Doctor. "You keep your eyes on that Shad Ledue."

"Don't worry," his wife said. "I will. I read the book."

"I guess I'll go out and get a smoke," he said. He found no need to argue with his wife, and there was the further chance of catching a glimpse of Lewis as he passed.

Lewis was not, however, in his seat as the Doctor mounted the easy slope of the aisle. He hurried out into the bright lobby, with its painted yellow marble and gaudy linoleum floor, and there, standing in front of him, was Sinclair Lewis, alone, and not ·

five feet away. The Doctor longed to take this chance of speaking to him before it was too late, but in spite of himself there was nothing on his tongue for him to say.

And then, suddenly, and without the slightest warning, Lewis walked across the lobby to the Doctor and stood on his toes in front of him, staring down into his eyes as if from a great height.

"Where is the nearest bar?" Lewis asked.

His voice was high and sharp and quick, and the Doctor jumped.

"The Heublein," Dr. McGrady said.

"Show me the way. Do you mind?"

"Oh, no. No, not at all."

Lewis took the Doctor's hand in his. "You are my friend," he said. The Doctor swallowed.

Together they walked out of the theatre into the dark street; together they made their way down the hill to the door of the Heublein Grill.

"Here we are," Dr. McGrady said. They sat down together by the open fire.

"What will you have?" Lewis said.

"Oh. Nothing. Nothing for me."

"A double Scotch-and-soda," Lewis told the waiter. The Doctor blinked and drew in his breath and said, "Make it two." Lewis stared back at him for a moment, perplexed, and then he smiled. They were silent. At last Dr. McGrady managed to say, "I think the play is — well, really fine." He would have said it was marvellous, but he was afraid that Lewis would think he was merely flattering him.

"It was awful," Lewis said. "Rotten. Rotten! O Lord our God, it was impossible!"

The Doctor was silent, numb with silence. He could say neither yes nor no, yet both words trembled on the edge of his tongue.

They were surrounded by strangers now; friends of Lewis, whom the Doctor had never seen before, all laughing and making jokes — if they were jokes — which he could not understand, and he laughed too, feeling his lips freezing into his cheeks.

"I guess I'll go," he said. His drink was still untouched.

Lewis was talking to the person on his right. He could not hear the Doctor's voice. The Doctor did not hold that against Lewis; it was the other person's fault.

"I guess I'll go," he said.

"So long," somebody replied.

The Doctor made his way along the wall to the cashier's desk. He set down five one-dollar bills, "To pay for Mr. Lewis's drinks," he explained. Then he walked quickly up the slope of the street, remembering and ordering in his mind each word that he and Lewis had spoken together, marshalling them for his wife's ears.

At the beginning of the third act he slipped into the seat beside her, flushed and speechless and without anger at having missed the gigantic clue of the whole second act.

"Where have you been?" his wife asked. "Were you called out?"

The Doctor smiled at her through the dark. "I was just down having a drink with Lewis."

He could hear her moving in the seat beside him. "Lewis who?" she asked.

He waited a moment, shocked, but drinking in the silence. Soon, he felt, soon he must burst.

"Sinclair Lewis," he said. "I'll tell you afterwards."

On the stage, Shad Ledue was now in uniform, but by this time the Doctor was much too excited to pick up the threads of the plot again. He knotted his fingers in his lap. When would the play end, when would the play end?

The story had a simple genesis. Anne and I had driven up to Hartford from Berlin one evening to see a performance of *It Can't Happen Here,* not knowing that Lewis would also be attending that performance. I spotted him in the audience before the house lights went down — in his height and ugliness he was always the most striking figure in any group — and I looked him up in the lobby during the first intermission; mildly drunk, he was eager to get much drunker in the shortest possible space of time, so off we went to the nearby Heublein bar. We had a pleasant private chat there before being joined by a number of his older friends and hangers-on. Our conversation ranged from a vehement denunciation of the W.P.A. production of his play to a no less vehement denunciation of my wearing, in sorry imitation of my hero, F.D.R., a Phi Beta Kappa key in the lapel of my jacket. Lewis heaped scorn on me for showing off in such a juvenile fashion, and I was all the more willing to agree with him because, as I was quick to explain, I had won the key by dint of a teacher's suicide and not through any efforts of my own. (Even so, I was less to be criticized than F.D.R., whose election to Phi Beta Kappa was an honorary one. What a vainglorious boy-man he was!) I never wore the key after that evening with Lewis; it became one of many trinkets on a bracelet of Anne's, and soon enough the bracelet was lost.

I must already have taken it in, though I don't know how, that Ross cared little for stories about writers; least of all did he care for stories about writers writing about other writers, and so I had had the cunning to invent Dr. McGrady. One sees that he wasn't a very vivid invention, but he sufficed to launch me on *The New Yorker* and I have always been grateful to him.

My next story, written a few weeks later, was a genuine work of fiction, if not one of high merit; it had to do with a nun in a convent who vexed her Mother Superior by incessantly playing practical jokes. I followed this story with several others in the same general Catholic and conventual vein. It became evident that the editors of *The New Yorker* knew little about Catholics and especially about Catholics in religious orders, and that they were eager to read about them, as occupying a hitherto largely unexplored field of human conduct; this was lucky for me, because although I knew almost as little about nuns and priests as they did, I was feverishly eager to oblige them and was therefore ready to make up anything that I didn't know or was unable to discover. I had yet to go to New York and meet Mrs. White and her assistant, William Maxwell, with whom I was corresponding in respect to queries and corrections in the galley proofs of the stories, and I learned afterward that although they were uncertain whether I was a man or a woman, they assumed that I was a devout Catholic, armed with an intimate knowledge of the rules and customs of my religion.

The facts were otherwise. It was true that with the exception of a never-to-be-accounted-for English great-grandmother (Mary Kirby, a Protestant from Rutlandshire), my family had been bleakly, unerringly Catholic for hundreds of years, first among the green fields and low hills of Leitrim, in Ireland, and then among the green fields and low hills of Connecticut. Nevertheless, by my generation the grim ties were beginning to loosen. A certain amount of money in the family and a certain amount of prestige in the world were having the usual effect, observed and deplored every Sunday morning by the bullying priests in their stone pulpits: our rising kind had lost the humble faith of the good old starving days in Connaught, with its blind submission not only to the errors and superstitions of Rome but also to whatever social and political opinions might be held by the parish priest one heard Mass under and was confessed by and at last anointed and buried by.

If I was still what is called a practicing Catholic, I was but grudgingly so; in a little while, I would be a collapsed one. I had obtained that dread thing a secular education, with the result that most of my friends were Protestants; so were most of my standards. My two sisters having attended convent schools, I elicited such inside information as I could from them, but it was hard enough to devise plots for my stories without having to devise, out of mere scraps of facts, a plausible *mise en scène* as well. Years later, when I wrote *The Trouble of One House,* Richard Rovere, in a review in *The New Yorker,* described the novel as a study of "middle-class Irish-Americans in a middle-sized city — denizens, in short, of the American middle depths." This grisly territory was by no means as well known to me as I had to pretend for the purposes of the book, and I was puzzled and relieved when none of my readers challenged my seeming familiarity with nuns, priests, and rectories. At the time, I had never been inside a rectory, but evidently I sounded as if I had; either that, or — more likely — the kind of people who buy the kind of novel I write are not the kind of people who frequent rectories any more often than I do. I could cheat with impunity and I did.

Within a year or so, I found that I had pretty well exhausted my poor little vein of Catholic lore. Still without having met anyone on the magazine, I arranged to write a couple of "Reporter at Large" pieces for the magazine on topics that happened to be of personal interest. One of them was about the auction of an estate on the Connecticut River that had belonged to the celebrated actor and author William Gillette. A fantastically handsome and gifted man, Gillette had long been a patient of my father. He had been born in the eighteen-fifties, so by the time I came to encounter him in my father's office — an exquisite porcelain old man, tall, slender, and erect, with white hair worn in bangs and a superb, hushed voice — he was in his early eighties. He had written twenty plays, in most of which he had acted; his great hits were *Secret Service,* a Civil War melodrama, and *Sherlock Holmes,* which he drew from the stories of A. Conan Doyle. Gillette in his checked tweeds, cape, pipe, and deerstalker cap was, in the world's eyes, the only imaginable Holmes. In old age, he wrote a mystery novel, which he had the inspiration to call *The Astounding Crime on the Torrington Road.* Who could resist picking up a book with such a title? He made a number of farewell tours in *Sherlock Holmes,* the last of them in 1936; he was as agile onstage as a man thirty years his junior. He died in 1937 and the auction of his property took place the following year. In his memory, I cannot resist quoting the opening paragraphs of my piece about the auction; the excerpt from Gillette's will gives an amusing glimpse of his lively mind and of his exceptional prose style (think of the legal mucilage in which most wills are written!). He had been a friend of Mark Twain, and the older man had evidently taught him a thing or two. I called my piece, with commendable brevity, "Castle for Sale"; it began:

> By April 28, 1937, William Gillette was seriously ill, but he insisted on making plans for a stone bridge on his estate near Hartford to delight his guests in the summer that was to come. "I want the arch of it twisted," he told Hall Cowan, his brother-in-law, who was in charge of the work, "so gently it won't even know it's being bent." A little later he lay back in his narrow bed and died.
>
> In his will he had written, "I would consider it more than unfortunate for me, should I find myself doomed, after death, to a continued consciousness of the behavior of mankind on this planet, to discover that the stone walls and towers and fireplaces of my home — founded at every point on the solid rock of Connecticut; that my railway line with its bridges, trestles, tunnels through solid rock, and stone culverts and underpasses, all built in every particular for permanence (so far as there is such a thing); that my locomotives and cars, constructed on the safest and most efficient mechanical principles; that these, and many other things of a like nature, should reveal themselves to me as in the possession of some blithering saphead who had no conception of where he was or with what surrounded."
>
> After several months of advertising the estate for sale, the executors began to feel that they would have to take the chance of letting the property slip into whatever hands were holding out the money. Their chief duty was to sell the place. On October 15, 1938, a little desperately, they held a public auction, and I drove up to Hadlyme to see what the fate of the castle would be.

My piece went on to describe the auction, which proved a total failure. Few bids were offered, whether by blithering sapheads or by anyone else, and the executors of the estate decided not to accept the highest of them, which amounted to only thirty-five thousand dollars. After a few years, the property became a state park. It is now one of the most popular tourist attractions in Connecticut. Gillette on earth had a low opinion of crowds and Gillette in heaven must be greatly displeased.

10

Having demonstrated that I was capable of writing factual pieces as well as fiction, I was invited to New York, where I met Maxwell (so Brendan was a man's name!), had lunch with him and McKelway, and was offered a position in the "Talk of the Town" department on a drawing account of forty dollars a week. To Ross's credit, when he said indignantly of this offer, "Don't play God, McKelway!" he was thinking not alone of the risk involved for the magazine in having to lay out so much money every week on a still largely untested writer but also of the responsibility of plucking a young man, his wife, and — by then — an infant daughter from the pleasant Connecticut countryside and setting them down in a New York, for which they might prove totally unfitted and which would serve to make them miserable instead of happy. After all, Anne and I were living at Old Toll Gate Farm in a fashion that most people spent many decades of their lives striving to attain. If we were already at the very top of the tree in terms of creature comfort and contentment, why should we descend into the snakepit of the great, swarming, and not necessarily very nice city? For even in the thirties New York was thought to be a snakepit — was universally reproached for being noisy, dirty, expensive, unfriendly, and often dangerous.

A number of my friends shared Ross's doubts as to the wisdom of my giving up the easy rural life. The reason I chose to do so was, of course, that it was too easy; spoiled as I was at every turn, and grateful to be spoiled, still, my New England conscience was dismayed by and at odds with my unearned good fortune. So, for that matter, was my sense of the appropriate. For we passed there, in the ancient white house in Berlin, among our fields and streams and orchards, a life as tranquil and remote from contemporary stress as that of some first-century Roman elder, rusticated at the emperor's command to a villa in the Alban Hills. It was certainly unnatural for us, at twenty-two, to be so detached from the hurly-burly of New York without the excuse of having been banished from it. The days passed in a dream of the convenient; there were not even many domestic tasks to perform. Our valley was peopled by hard-pressed Polish and Ukrainian farmers, all with children eager to increase their families' meager incomes; we became their youthful benefactors.

For a few dollars a week, a sturdy adolescent, John Zehro, acted as a sort of caretaker for Old Toll Gate. John was born when his father was in his late seventies. At the time we first met him, the boy was still subject to fierce pummelings at the hands of his ninety-year-old father, who, in the course of his regular Saturday-night drunks, would beat up as many of his sons as he could catch. John, being the youngest and most tender-hearted, would always take care to let the old man win the unequal race between them; more than once, he came to the farm with a bruised cheek or even a black eye. (Old man Zehro was nearly a hundred when one of his less tender-hearted sons, himself a grandfather, pushed him down a flight of stairs and so brought his undiminished cruelties to an end.)

John, who tended the garden and cut the grass and helped me saw firewood into usable lengths, grew up to be a formidably strong and ambitious man. In his twenties, he acquired an enormous trailer-truck, in which, more often drunk than sober, he hauled goods at terrifying speeds from coast to coast. John was brave as well as kind. Once, stopped at a traffic light, he glanced down from the cab of his truck and saw in a car in the adjoining lane a man to whom he had once lent some money. The man not only had failed to repay the money but had also nefariously come to claim that he had never borrowed it. John hopped out of the cab and began to berate the man, who unexpectedly pulled out a gun and shot John twice in the stomach. Hearing the shots, a policeman ran up and, before booking the suspect, wanted to have John taken to a hospital. Nothing of the kind for John — bleeding profusely, he insisted that whether or not he was going to die, he would proceed at once to the police station and swear out a warrant against his assailant. That done, he consented to be driven to a hospital, where the bullets were successfully removed.

For help inside the house, we hired a girl named Frannie Louchy, a Ukrainian with shining dark eyes, very white teeth, and a pretty body. In hot weather, she served us at table with notable informality. As soon as the temperature rose into the nineties, she appeared barefoot and barelegged, wearing shorts and a bandanna that just covered but did not deny the nipples of her adorable breasts. Frannie had a boy friend, George, who drove a pickup van for a dry-cleaning establishment in New Britain. George was a dude; he wore a heavily belted polo coat with large imitation mother-of-pearl buttons and combed into his hair an unguent that made it shine like black foil. Whenever we went off to Hartford or New Haven for the evening, Frannie and George were granted the use of the living room. On our return, we would take care to circle the turnaround in front of the house a couple of times, in order for the headlights of the car to give Frannie and George ample warning of our arrival. By the time we had made our way into the living room, Frannie would be seated primly on the couch at one side of the room and George would be bolt-upright in a wing chair on the opposite side of the room, tightly wrapped in his polo coat. They would be looking less disheveled than one might have supposed, given the fact that the air in the room still shook with the heat of their so recently interrupted lovemaking.

It turned out that George could not understand why, as the months went by, Anne showed no signs of being pregnant. If she were not pregnant, why on earth had we married? "Didn't you get caught?" he asked me, in honest bewilderment. It was a tradition in the valley to put off marriage until the girl had established her capacity to bear children, and even then there was no particular hurry about performing the wedding ceremony: getting caught was by no means a dire event, as lovemaking was by no means the sinful activity that the local Irish priest kept assuring the young folk it was. The valley was largely Catholic, but not Irish Catholic; pagans and Old Believers were under every hedge and in every hayloft.

One day Frannie came to us at breakfast and in her deep voice (a voice startlingly unsuited to her slender body) announced, "I feel sick." I telephoned a doctor in Meriden, made an appointment for Frannie, and drove her to the doctor's office. Soon he emerged from the examining room to shake my hand and congratulate me on my imminent fatherhood. I thanked him warmly — at that moment, it struck me as too complicated to explain that although it was true that I was soon to become a father, it was not Frannie who would be the mother of my child, and that the father of Frannie's child would not be me. Anne, who had been a month or so later than Frannie in becoming pregnant, assumed that Frannie would wish to regularize her situation as quickly as possible, but Frannie had a different idea: there was a wedding dress to be made, a trousseau to be assembled, parties to be held. When the wedding day finally arrived, Frannie went down the aisle in an exquisite lace-covered dress, her baby cantilevered out a good foot in front of her and providing a sort of shelf upon which Frannie proudly rested her gloved hands, holding in them a bouquet of lilies of the valley and a white Bible. She made a beautiful bride.

In moving to New York, plainly we would be bound to miss Old Toll Gate Farm and John and Frannie and George and the walks through the autumn woods on Mount Lamentation and the swimming in summer in a nearby millpond. We would miss our neighbor, old Mr. Hutton, a teetotaler who stayed half-drunk all day from his imbibing of Atwater's Bitters ("Never knew 'em to gripe anybody") and who brought us every morning fresh milk from his Jersey cow, warm in the pail and with an occasional piece of straw or dead leaf floating on the surface of the milk; for Mr. Hutton had no patience with pasteurization, covered containers, and similar modern fol-de-rol. We would miss our other neighbors, the Tobeys, the interior of whose house remained in a perpetual twilight, thanks to the jungle of plants that hung in clotted disarray at every window. It was a decaying house, whose foundation timbers groaned and slid askew and on occasion gave way, devoured by termites. One hesitated to sit down on any chair or even on any flat surface (if in the green dusk it was possible to discern a flat surface), since they would nearly always prove to be bristling with life. Dogs, cats, guinea pigs, white mice, lovebirds, pupating moths — Mrs. Tobey loved everything that was capable of being born and dying and she strongly disliked housekeeping. Her house smelled of dust and urine and the dried sweat of innumerable generations of ancestral Tobeys, and nothing mattered more to her than coaxing a single African violet into bloom in some shadowy embrasure. She kept her husband alive until he was well over a hundred, and even then he took care not to die in bed; in his daily constitutionals, he had grown used to walking down the middle of the road instead of along the shoulder, and one day a car struck him and sent him spinning head over heels into a cornfield. He was dead when he landed, a bundle of broken bones held together by clothes.

Most of all, we would miss my father's presence. The farm had given him at least as much pleasure as it had given us. He had enjoyed driving out into the country after a hard day at the office, with perhaps as many as forty patients attended to and given some of his extraordinary strength. The back of his car would be piled high with groceries. He always bought canned goods in twenty-four-can cartons, many cartons at a time, as if to make sure that we would be able to survive for months on end some unprecedentedly prolonged natural catastrophe (a series of blizzards? floods? earthquakes?) at Old Toll Gate Farm. On top of the soups and beans and hash and butter and milk and oranges and eggs and beef and bacon and potatoes and bread would be riding a small, choice antiquity of some kind: a brightly colored Currier & Ives, a child's ladderback chair, a Sheraton side table. In selling the farm, we were taking from my father in his late years a source of amusement and consolation, and I am puzzled, looking back, at how little troubled I was by this aspect of our departure. Luckily, he had bought the nearby millpond and was engaged in making over into a cozy cabin for himself a little icehouse on the property. The icehouse occupied a perch of some peril on the apron of a stone dam that had been built in the eighteenth century to provide power for the mill and later for a factory that manufactured German silver spoons. (When the United States Geodetic Survey maps of Connecticut were redrawn in the nineteen-forties, the pond was given our family name, and that pleased him. One can find "Gill's Pond" on the maps to this very day.) My father gave no indication that he felt we were abandoning him; whatever any of his children did became in his eyes what it was best for them to do. And he had, besides, four other children, two of them still living at home and the others within easy reach.

There was the further fact that he was extremely proud of my having been invited to accept a position in New York. He had been born in the little industrial town of Southington, Connecticut — the millpond aside, our family's only geographical recognition consists of a crossroads in Southington called Gill's Corners — and he had become an important citizen of Hartford, but in his eyes the distance between Southington and Hartford was nothing compared to the distance between Hartford and New York.

To him, content as he was to live on a small scale, New York seemed formidably big, remote, and inhuman, and he assumed that it could be conquered only at a great risk. He was impressed by what he thought of as my courage in venturing so far afield; at once, characteristically, he set about assisting me in my assault upon Everest. When my pieces began to appear in *The New Yorker*, he went up and down the streets of Hartford, stopping at any newsstand that sold the magazine and buying out its entire supply. He gathered up no telling how many scores of copies of the magazine in this fashion, in the not very realistic hope that the advertising department of the magazine would observe the fact that issues of the magazine containing a piece by me sold better than issues that did not. Moreover, he wrote letters to the editor of *The New Yorker*, praising my pieces, and he would have these letters signed by his assistant, Dr. McCullough, and by his nurse-secretary, Mrs. Chapman; he would instruct them to post the letters from their home addresses, outside Hartford, in order to conceal the conspiracy of admiration he had mounted in my behalf. Dr. McCullough and Mrs. Chapman would receive a note from "Kip" Orr, the member of the staff whose duty it was to reply to all correspondence, favorable and unfavorable. Kip would assure them that their kind words would be forwarded to Mr. Gill, and so they were; it was thus that I learned what my doting father was up to.

In New York, we found without difficulty a seven-room apartment at 21 East Ninetieth Street. The building was in a charming block. A few steps away was the Carnegie house, in which members of the family were still living. One had only to cross Fifth Avenue to reach Central Park, where our new baby would find playmates among an army of her peers. The apartment building had thick, soundproof walls and high ceilings, and was staffed by half a dozen burly doormen and elevator operators. Our apartment, which had three baths and a wood-burning fireplace in the living room, was on a sufficiently high floor for the sun to stream in all day through its many windows. The year was 1938 and the rent we paid was a hundred and twenty-five dollars a month.

11

When I came to work for *The New Yorker*, I was assigned to a
nasty, interior cell, just big enough to contain a desk, a chair, a
wooden hatrack, and me. For some reason, the hatrack was in
excellent condition, but the desk and chair were barbarously
scarred and battered and, in the case of the chair, unsafe; one of
its legs had worked loose in its socket and had been wired, not
by an expert craftsman, to the other three legs, in an intricate but
insecure arrangement of picture wire and twisted coat hangers.
When one sat in the chair, it listed sharply to the left and gave
off a loud singing sound. Plainly, the furniture had been bought
at second hand, for, hard as reporters notoriously are on the tools
of their trade, the furnishings of my cell would scarcely have
reached such a state of decrepitude in the twelve or thirteen years
since the magazine had been founded. If it was wonderful that
these articles could already have been so ruinous, what is even
more wonderful is that many of them are still in use today. They
are disgusting and immortal, and, observing them as I write these
words, I cannot fail to have mixed feelings at the thought of their
so easily outlasting me.

The typewriter I was given bore a notable accumulation of
coffee, grease, and other stains. I had the uneasy feeling that some
invisible germ of life was in culture deep inside the machine, as
if in a dish of agar-agar in some secret laboratory of the permanently soiled. Here and there, the lacquer of the typewriter had
been eaten through to the bare metal by cigarettes left burning
upon it, and one of my predecessors had laboriously etched out,
perhaps with a paper clip, the initial letter of the typewriter's
name; it was no longer "ROYAL" but "OYAL," and I could feel
the loss. Another and more ominous oddity was that when one
typed an "s," it invariably came out a "w." Thiw led to wingular
effectw on my prowe. And these effects were all the more painful
to me because I was by nature the neatest of typists. Moreover,

as a beginner on the staff I was especially eager to create a favorable impression by handing in faultlessly typed copy. It turned out that if my typewriter had allowed me to do so, it would have been a waste of time; indeed, it might have been considered a black mark against me, because nearly everyone on the magazine took pride in following Ross's bent and typing as badly as possible, editing in the typewriter by hunt and peck as I was later to hear of young moviemakers editing in the camera. Ross's fiercely X'd out passages were the manifestations of canny second thoughts, contradictions introduced and then cancelled, gropings in the name of his sacred rubic "Nothing is indescribable."

The only attractive equipment supplied to me was the copy paper. It was cheap and soft to the touch and it came in a cheerful shade of lemony yellow. We used only that yellow paper in the office until, just over ten years ago, the day came when copy was transmitted to the printer not by messengers but by closed-circuit TV; our new gadgetry required us to adopt a white paper of greater weight than the old, smoother and somehow less willing to accept the benefaction of the word.

My cell was a far cry from the conventional good taste of the study at Old Toll Gate Farm, with its Alken prints and shining brass on the hearth and the bookshelves full of first editions of Henry James, all signalling, so I then proudly assumed, "Brilliant young author at work here." My cell at the magazine struck me as signalling something like "Derelict old author at a total loss here," for I sensed that, young and old, many a writer had sat in the cubicle before me and had vanished forever into that Sheol where all Ross's failed "Jesuses" might be imagined as dwelling — Perth Amboy, perhaps, or the grim fringes of Bridgeport. ("Jesus" was the office corruption of "genius," the epithet that Ross applied to every promising reporter he discovered in the early days of the magazine and upon whom he would immediately thrust the fugitive honor of the managing editorship.)

To make matters worse, the walls of my cubicle, which was one of four identical cubicles forming a small square in the dark heart of the building, were of a particularly unpleasant kind of frosted glass and of skimpily painted wood; everyone else appeared to be favored with offices that had soundproof walls of solid cinder block and plaster and that had at least a single window apiece. Recently, I asked Hawley Truax, the man responsible for much of the physical layout of the editorial department, how such miserable cubicles had happened to come into existence. "I found them," he said simply. In short, they, too, had been picked up at second hand, like their wretched contents. For all I know, Hawley encountered them in a heap of refuse on the street and dragged them single-handedly up to the nineteenth floor.

My dismay was heightened at the start by my being unaware that this was the note that had always been struck at the magazine: squalor had come to be something that members of the staff took considerable pride in. It was as if the magazine, having decided that it could not afford to be beautiful, had decided to be as ugly as possible; in this perverse intention it may be said to have scored an unbroken series of triumphs. The contrast between the elegance of the actual magazine as it appears from week to week and the circumstances in which the editors produce the magazine has always startled the outside world. It used to startle me as well,

A door without a knob. There are many such. Nobody knows where the doors lead to, and nobody cares.

but by now I am nearly as inured as my colleagues to the shabby discomfort in which we pass our days. Paint peels from the walls; chunks of plaster fall from the ceilings. On a high wooden cupboard near my office someone affixed a sign reading "This door does not open." That was years ago; the sign darkens with age, the door remains closed upon no one remembers what. Along the corridors are scattered remains that put one in mind of the sidewalk outside a tenement house on the day of its demolition. One passes chairs whose stuffings leap up in a tangle of uncoiled springs and frayed webbing, bookcases ripped from a wall and bristling with bent spikes, a stepladder with two of its steps missing, innumerable empty ten-gallon jars of Great Bear spring water, said to be filled not from any spring but from the faucet of the janitor's slop-sink on the twentieth floor, dusty framed clippings from newspapers and magazines of the nineteen-forties . . .

It is a palimpsest of an office, a Dead Sea Scroll, and only a scholar learned in urban débris could do it justice. Most of us on the magazine are not scholars; besides, the singular trophies that surround us have grown invisible. A sort of therapeutic blindness spares us what is understandably an occasion for aston-

An alleyway off Sleepy Hollow. Here writers are able to consult Webster's dictionary, and here what is supposed to be spring water is reputed to be drawn from a faucet in the janitor's slop-sink. Once, when an editor protested to Ross in a long memo about the squalor of the office arrangements, Ross wrote back, "If I don't get action on such things, I will damned well fly the coop. The story of how we landed in this hell-hole is a long and fantastic one, hard for a sane man to believe."

The brazier in the lobby on the nineteenth floor. It was given to the magazine almost fifty years ago, in a vain attempt to brighten up the place. The brazier, chairs, table, and lamp constitute the magazine's waiting room. It is often the case that the chairs cannot be sat in.

ishment in strangers. Take the first object that is likely to call itself to your attention when you get off the elevator on the nineteenth floor. It is the same object that called itself to my attention when I got off the elevator on the nineteenth floor, almost forty years ago — a large, shallow brazier of Indian design, set upon carved and painted tabouret legs. The brass of which it is made glints but dully, through lack of polish; sometimes cigarettes are stubbed out in it, sometimes it is filled with rejected rejection slips, crumpled up and left behind by indignant would-be contributors. What is that brazier doing in what passes for our reception room? Well, it was an article of furniture that Ruth Fleischmann, wife of the publisher of the magazine, decided to get rid of in the twenties, when she was fixing over the Fleischmann house on East Seventy-fourth Street. The brazier represents the first and certainly the last attempt ever made to "decorate" the premises. No doubt it was

The fire escape that for many years was the only means of getting from one editorial floor to another. Once, two or three of us were chatting on the fire escape; Shawn stood listening on the fire-door threshold. Emphasizing a point, I happened to kick at the protective iron grillwork behind me, which promptly gave way. Shawn blanched. Soon thereafter, though perhaps not for that reason, interior stairways were constructed.

brought down to the office by Mr. Fleischmann's chauffeur, who was probably thinking, "Good riddance to bad rubbish!" And if the magazine should last another fifty years, one can be sure that the brazier will still be found in its usual place, secure in the immortality of neglect.

One day in my office, I was showing Maxwell a Roman coin that I had purchased at Gimbels. With thousands of similiar coins, it had been buried in the sands of Egypt by Ptolemy's army paymaster, in order to keep it from falling into the hands of the rapidly approaching Caesar. Maxwell jiggled the coin in his palm. "The odds," he said, "are on objects." This is especially true of objects at *The New Yorker*. Though writers wear out, their typewriters never do; on wooden racks in one of the office storerooms are spare typewriters that include the one that Ross used to pound away on and the one that E. B. White used before he gave up residence in New York in favor of a seaside town in Maine. The typewriters are not being saved as precious souvenirs; they are just being saved. The reasoning, I feel pretty sure, is that there may someday be an unprecedented national shortage of typewriters and *The New Yorker* will then be discovered to be sitting pretty. In the same fashion, though most of the offices are air-conditioned, we keep a number of old electric fans on hand, in case. For all I know to the contrary, there may be palmetto fans in storage somewhere on the premises, dating back to before my time. On a hook in one of the offices hung for many years a coonskin cap. No one remembered who its owner was; it remained there untouched except by dust until it decomposed.

Shawn's office. There is room at the far end of the sofa for a single narrow writer to perch in comfort.

If Ross's typewriter has not been considered sacred, there was certainly a feeling on Shawn's part at the time of Ross's death that his office quarters were sacred. The two cluttered and yet naked rooms that Ross occupied were not simply dismantled — the very walls were knocked down and the space they had enclosed divided into different shapes. History, if it were not instructed otherwise, might deduce that these alterations were an attempt to obliterate all memory of Ross; on the contrary, I have always supposed that it was Shawn's way of saying, "I cannot take Ross's place. Nobody can take Ross's place. Therefore the place had better cease to exist, physically as well as symbolically."

When the new walls went up, a warren of tiny cells filled most of what had been Ross's precincts, and Shawn had a pleasing new office — bigger than either of Ross's, as it turned out, and far more agreeable to the eye, with a carpet underfoot instead of linoleum, a couple of long tables instead of desks, and a couch on which, in spite of a continuous spillage of briefcases and manuscripts, it has nearly always been possible for at least one visitor to find room to sit. No air-conditioning, of course; temperatures in the nineties cause Shawn to flourish, as temperatures in the sixties cause him to rummage about in search of his overcoat and scarf. On the counter that runs parallel to the window sills in Shawn's office and helps to conceal its several radiators rests, among other household gods and souvenirs, a framed photograph of Ross. He is gazing off into space, seemingly in the direction of his old office. To my mind, he looks more at ease in that photograph than he ever looked in life. (Ross characteristically ill-at-ease may be seen in the Fabian Bachrach photograph of him that hangs in the nineteenth-floor corridor; miserably aware that he is having a formal portrait taken, he stares into the camera with the air of a small-town crook arrested for having tried to hold up a bank with a water pistol.)

A tradition of continuous reconstruction of the premises of the magazine goes back to its founding, and I cannot resist noting here that Shawn has recently provided a striking example of total architectural incoherence in the course of remodeling some of the space outside his office for the use of his assistant, Mary Painter, and their secretaries. In spite of Ross's dictum that nothing is indescribable, I think a diagram will serve better than words to reveal our office planning at its most characteristic. This is the maze that has been brought into existence at our editor's door, or, rather, doors (two doors of not quite equal size standing mysteriously side by side) — a maze that might be more readily employed as a setting for a production of *Hotel Paradiso* than for the effective publication of a weekly magazine:

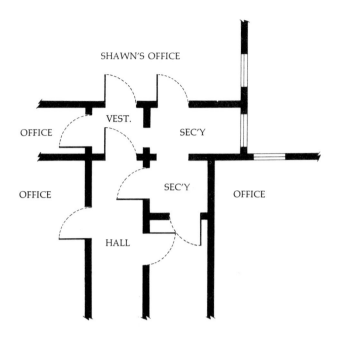

SHAWN'S OFFICE

OFFICE

VEST.

SEC'Y

OFFICE

SEC'Y

OFFICE

HALL

When *The New Yorker* was started, in 1925, it occupied quarters in a building at 25 West Forty-fifth Street. It got space there at a bargain because the building had been put up by a well-known builder of the nineteen-twenties, James T. Lee, one of whose "silent" partners was Russell Fleischmann; Russell was the elder brother of Raoul Fleischmann, our publisher and chief financial backer. (In my day, Russell was a bandy-legged little old man in summer whites, contentedly tottering about the clubhouse and paddock at Belmont and other local tracks. His only connection with the editorial side of the magazine was his friendship with George T. Ryall, who, under the nom de plume of "Audax Minor," has been writing the "Race Track" department for the past forty-eight years.)

If one got off the elevator in the Forty-fifth Street building and turned right, one reached the headquarters of *Time*; if one turned left, *The New Yorker*. The two magazines were not long to be so nearly equal in scale. *Time* became one of the biggest corporations in the country and *The New Yorker* remained one of the smallest. Thanks to the generosity and foresight of Henry R. Luce and the rest of *Time* management, many of the early workers on *Time, Fortune,* and *Life* became millionaires. In sharp contrast, only Fleischmann gained millions from *The New Yorker*, and he took care to offer no inducement to any of the actual creators of the magazine — writers, artists, editors — to acquire a single share. Ross and his wife, Jane Grant, invested twenty thousand dollars of their savings in the founding of the magazine; after they were divorced, Miss Grant held on to her shares and was still in possession of them at the time of her death, in 1972. Ross soon disposed of his holdings, selling by far the greater part of them to Luce. Not that Luce and Ross were friends; they were ideally unsuited to each other in every respect. Ross's sale of his stock to Luce has never been satisfactorily explained. Ross himself subsequently invented as his reason for this astonishing act the theory that no editor should have a financial interest in his own magazine. Ross's real reason appears to have been a combination of an unexpected need for cash and an eagerness to injure Fleischmann, long since his enemy. Luce held his *New Yorker* stock for some years, perhaps with the intention of one day buying out Fleischmann, and then quietly disposed of it.

After a couple of years in the building on West Forty-fifth Street, the magazine needed to expand and so moved into new quarters at 25 West Forty-third Street. Here, over the decades, we have gradually become the tenant renting the greatest amount of space — the eighteenth, nineteenth, and twentieth floors for the editorial department, and the sixteenth and seventeenth floors, as well as portions of several other floors, for the advertising department. The building has been so closely related to the life of the magazine that it is worth paying some attention to. Not by coincidence, the Mr. Lee who built the building on West Forty-fifth Street was also the builder of 25 West Forty-third Street, and Russell Fleischmann was again one of his partners. For reasons of prestige that have escaped being set down, the building was officially known in the twenties as the National Association Building; one can read the name carved in the lintels above the doors.

Lee evidently took a good deal of pride in the buildings he put up; he had a feeling for architectural detail. For example, the building on Forty-fifth Street boasts an extraordinary frieze of giant lion's heads just under the sixteenth-floor cornice, unfortunately at such a height above the street that few pedestrians have ever observed them. On West Forty-third Street, Lee saw to it that the lobby had a floor of travertine, wainscotting of marble, and an intersecting vaulted ceiling, from the crossings of which hung cathedral-like bronze lanterns. The lanterns have gone, and so has a painting of Lee, which, until the building was sold a few years ago to the real-estate firm of Helmsley-Spear, filled the lunette above the Forty-third Street entrance. The painting showed Lee looking over the plans for the building, as drawn for him by the architects Starrett and Van Vleck. He was wearing a pleased expression, and it was not lost upon the viewer that Renaissance princes had often been painted seated in such a posture and wearing such an expression.

The building, which is of red brick with white concrete trim, is, in its upper reaches, faintly Georgian; the terraces that mark the setbacks have classical balustrades, and at their outer corners used to rise handsome obelisks, perhaps three or four feet high. These obelisks were removed for reasons of safety many years ago. I can remember a day when, having graduated from my windowless cubicle to an outside office giving onto the nineteenth-floor terrace, I clambered up onto the balustrade and in an act of youthful bravado walked from the obelisk at one end of the balustrade to the obelisk at the other. It was a two-hundred-foot drop to the street, and I wouldn't be apt to show off in that fashion today.

The building is shaped like an L, with a frontage of approximately one hundred and fifty feet on West Forty-third Street. The upright of the L runs two hundred feet back to a frontage of fifty feet on West Forty-fourth Street (Number 28). Because of its shape, the building is exceptionally well furnished with windows on all four sides, and one of the arguments against our ever moving has been that in the big slab office buildings of the present day few people are in a position to enjoy natural light. A number of our artists — among them Addams, Opie, Weber, Stevenson, Koren, and Lorenz, who recently succeeded Geraghty as art editor — have what amount to studios at *The New Yorker* and are grateful for big windows facing north. For my part, I rejoice at the splendid view my present office gives me of the RCA Building and its adjacent skyscrapers, several blocks uptown. In winter, the sun's rays bounce off the broad side of the RCA Building and through my window with such force as to cast distinct shadows; in the winter dusk, on a day of snow, all those hundreds of lighted windows in Rockefeller Center promise me life — the shortest day of the year will surely be got past safely once again!

A long while ago, a member of the Rockefeller family was in love with a girl I knew, who worked in an office building on Madison Avenue. As I would sit typing by my window, sometimes my eye would be caught by the sight of a bright-orange feather duster suddenly emerging from a window high in the RCA Building. The duster would be shaken violently up and down for a few minutes, then be withdrawn; it was a lover's greeting and was well received by the beloved.

In recent years, part of the twenty-second floor, which is the top floor of the building, has been given over to a facsimile transmitting system, by means of which copy hurtles back and forth all but instantaneously between our office and the Donnelly Press, in Chicago, where the magazine is printed. I would like to describe in precise detail the extraordinary process that makes it possible for me to make any number of fiddling little changes in my galleys as late as two o'clock on a Monday afternoon and have the finished magazine in my hands late the following morning, but I am totally incapable of doing so. No doubt among our writers of a scientific bent, like Daniel Lang, Jeremy Bernstein, and Henry Fenimore Spotswood Cooper, there are those who would have no

Part of the science-fiction quarters on the twenty-second floor of 25 West Forty-third Street, where copy is transmitted in facsimile, over telephone wires, between the magazine and the Donnelly Press, in Chicago. I can go on altering my theatre copy until two o'clock on a Monday afternoon and hold the finished magazine in my hands the following morning. There is no possible way for this to happen.

difficulty saying what it is that is happening up there on the roof. Myself, I am closer in age, ignorance, and temperament to E. B. White, who in the early days of television decided to write a short story upon that subject. He thought it would be wise to have observed an actual TV set in operation before embarking on the story, and he thought further that perhaps he and Katharine would then be tempted to purchase one. This was in the forties, and the radically adventurous Gills were the only people known by the Whites to have taken a chance on the new invention. Andy and Katharine came to the house and stared at our seven-inch screen with little show of admiration. After a while, I led Andy to my bar for a drink, and there his gaze fell upon a Dazey ice-crusher. It had a capped metal container into which ice cubes could be dropped, it had teeth for chopping the ice into varying degrees of fineness, it had a crank that had only to be turned in order to turn the teeth, and it had a little pointed green plastic cup into which the crushed ice would eventually fall. Andy's eyes lighted up: this was something like! Forgetting the TV set, he went home and bought himself a Dazey ice-crusher, and the odds are that he has been cranking away with pleasure ever since.

Incidentally, such are the mysteries of the writer's unconscious that when Andy came to write his story about TV, the villainess of the piece was named Gill. Some compliments are more satisfactory than others.

12

To me in my early weeks and months on the staff of *The New Yorker*, the most startling fact was the total absence of any camaraderie in the office. Among my family and friends, I was accustomed to a continuous manifestation of high spirits in the form of badinage, laughter, and intermittent bursts of song and whistling. At *The New Yorker*, I perceived that a show of high spirits was out of the question; it was not merely unwelcome but impermissible. The custom was to speak as little as possible, and then as dourly as possible. One never touched another person except by accident. Song was as strictly forbidden as whistling, which among reporters has always been thought to invite bad luck. I was willing to get along without whistling, but it was hard to get along without song; and to get along without conversation was surely impossible.

At the magazine, it was plain that *any* ordinary show of friendliness was thought to invite bad luck. No one invited me to pass the time of day with him. The editors and other writers on the staff appeared not to see me; against my will, I had become invisible to everyone except the elevator men. In those days, all four of our elevators were manually operated (now only one of them is, for Shawn's sake: he dislikes running any machine more dangerous than a typewriter), and the operators were, poor devils, the very dregs of the employment market, but oh, how grateful I was to them! They said "Hello," and "Have a good day," and "You too," and "Sure is," and so helped me to remain, though tenuously, a member of the human race.

Everyone I passed in the corridors of *The New Yorker* seemed to be feeling sick. Later, I learned that many of them *were* sick, with hangovers of varying degrees of acuteness. I was not a drinker in those days and so failed to recognize the many telltale signs of distress that have since become commonplaces to me — for example, the conviction that one can feel one's hair growing and that it hurts. In my innocence, I was misled into supposing that the entire staff must have contracted some obscure tribal contagion, for which there was no known medical cure. They glowered, they sulked, they passed one another in silence, or with an inarticulate snarl, and my only consolation in the presence of so much indurated misery was the discovery, made little by little, that none of it was directed at me personally; it was a universal expression of misanthropy and played no favorites. It turned out that another newcomer, E. J. Kahn, Jr., had been undergoing a somewhat similar initiation, but because he had begun on a lower level of buoyant good health than I, he was better adjusted to the grim sourness of the office air. For him that air was natural and even refreshing, and I found out why. Drinking and smoking, he played jazz all night with some friends in a flat off the Bowery, and one day he happened to describe his usual procedure on rising. "I get out of bed," he said, "and throw up and take a shower and shave and have breakfast . . ." "You throw up *every* morning?" I asked, in the bewilderment of a non-smoking, non-drinking, early-to-bed young man from Hartford. "Of course," Kahn said. "Doesn't everyone?"

As a newcomer of a slightly later period, John Bainbridge was as astonished as I by the coldness he encountered at the magazine. A Middle Westerner, brought up in the genial civilities of that part of the world, Bainbridge had always longed to write for *The New Yorker* and rub elbows with Ross, E. B. White, Wolcott Gibbs, and the other great men about whom he had read and heard. At last he found himself on the staff and with an office on the same floor as Gibbs. He knew Gibbs by sight, but had never spoken to him. Bainbridge was in the habit of getting to the office early, and so was Gibbs, on the days when he got there at all. On the morning of a day that happened to follow New Year's Day, Bainbridge stopped at the water-cooler for a drink. Gibbs came up and drew a couple of quick ones. Seizing this opportunity to make conversation, Bainbridge said, "Did you have a nice New Year's, Mr. Gibbs?"

"Fuck you," Gibbs said, tossed his paper cup into the basket, and walked back to his office.

Gibbs's rudeness was a function of his being extremely shy. Contrary to what many shy people like to think, shyness is not necessarily an attractive attribute. It is certainly not one that justifies bad manners; all the less so since there are cases of shyness as extreme as Gibbs's — I am thinking, of course, of Shawn — that lead to the most solicitous good manners. Gibbs's rudeness was his way of keeping the world at a distance, out of fear, and this fear, especially in his youth, wore the mask of a continuous aloof scorn. Like any number of gifted and intelligent but ignorant young men, he affected to despise everything, thus guarding himself against unexpected entrapments by people more knowledgeable than he. Ingersoll recalls in his memoirs that no matter how interesting and perhaps even useful an observation someone in the office might offer, Gibbs would sneer, "Don't be banal!" He abandoned this childish device as he grew older and more confident of his powers and of the body of knowledge at his command, but he never outgrew the shyness and rudeness; they were intrinsic and therefore unalterable.

Gibbs was born in 1902 and joined the staff of the magazine in 1928. He was christened Oliver Wolcott Gibbs and was a descendant of the Oliver Wolcott who signed the Declaration of Independence as a delegate from Connecticut; the "Oliver" was soon dropped. His father, Lucius Tuckerman Gibbs, had a business connection with the Pennsylvania Rail Road, then at the height of its prosperity; his mother came of an old New York family, the Duers. Alice Duer Miller, who was among those listed as one of the founding board of editors of the magazine, was his cousin. (Ross appears to have maintained that she was Gibbs's aunt; there were times when Ross would cling to a demonstrable error as tenaciously as he clung to a demonstrable truth.) Gibbs attended the Hill School, where he was a class behind a boy named Hobart G. Weekes. Weekes joined *The New Yorker* a few months after Gibbs. One of the "old" members of the staff, which then numbered perhaps twenty people in all, was Whitaker, like Weekes a Princeton man (though he never graduated) and unlike Weekes — and unlike most Princeton men — in his practiced acerbity of manner. Whitaker expressed alarm and disgust at the discovery that there were what he called "two Hill snots" on the magazine; surely, he protested, one snot was enough.

It was characteristic of Gibbs at that time that he rather sneakily warned Whitaker against Weekes on the grounds that Weekes was a Christer. It was also characteristic of Gibbs at a somewhat later time that he took care to warn Weekes that Katharine White had developed a theory that all the editors of *The New Yorker* should be writers. As Gibbs knew, Weekes had no intention whatever of being a writer. To protect him against the White theory in case it found favor with Ross, Gibbs generously offered to give Weekes a sure-fire idea for a "casual" — an idea that Gibbs himself had been intending to make profitable use of. Weekes declined the offer with thanks. As it turned out, Mrs. White's theory was soon abandoned. It was certainly a poor one and would have been impossible to put into practice; even Ross, as Thurber once noted, never learned how to become a *New Yorker* writer.

Weekes remembers Gibbs at Hill as a notably well-turned-out little Third Former, wearing handsome English tweed jackets and narrow knickerbockers, with woolen hose drawn up over the bottoned cuffs: not the usual vulgar American plus-fours. Gibbs had a sizable collection of the works of the Canadian humorist Stephen Leacock, whom he greatly admired and copies of whose books he would lend to Weekes. Gibbs was expelled from Hill for some obscure incident having to do with the theft of a wreath from a cemetery; he subsequently attended a cram school but failed to go on to college. Thanks perhaps to his father's business connections, he got a job on the Long Island Rail Road, becoming what Ingersoll in his *Fortune* article on *The New Yorker* called "a gentleman brakeman." The job lasted long enough for Gibbs to marry beneath him — the bride was a railroadman's daughter, and the marriage was of very short duration — and to undergo experiences that, years later, emerged as short stories. He next became a reporter on a suburban Long Island newspaper and from there proceeded to the magazine.

Gibbs always had a chip on his shoulder in respect to not having attended college; in a way that many contemporary young people would find it difficult to understand, this gap in his formal education troubled and embarrassed him. It amounted to a social gaffe, but it was more than that: like his friend John O'Hara, who also had not gone to college, he felt that something important had eluded him. When people who had graduated from college sought to reassure him by saying that this was not the case, he was convinced that his surmise was correct and that they, as possessors of the mystery, considered it too precious to share with the likes of him. People used to make fun of the fact that O'Hara wanted so desperately to have gone to Yale, but it was never a joke to O'Hara, nor was it to Gibbs. O'Hara would have liked to be tapped for Skull and Bones; Gibbs would have liked to be tapped for Bones and then turn it down.

Years before I knew him, Gibbs had fallen in love with and married a girl who worked in the advertising department of the magazine. (This, despite Ross's pronouncement that there was to be no sex on *The New Yorker*, least of all with anybody in the enemy camp of advertising, to whom members of the editorial department were not encouraged to speak.) In the eyes of Gibbs's family and of his snobbish Duer connections, this second bride was as much beneath him as the first, and the bride is said to have taken their low opinion of her to heart. In fact, she was the best-liked girl in the advertising department, full of energy and ideas. Having heard that *Playbill*, the publication distributed free in theatres, was for sale, she proposed that a group of them buy it and turn it into a first-rate magazine. Gibbs would be the editor in chief, Weekes would be the copy editor, Whitaker would do editing and make-up, and she would go out and secure the necessary ads. In the midst of making these plans, she jumped out of the window of their apartment in Tudor City and killed herself. One story goes that she and Gibbs had been quarrelling and that when she threatened to kill herself, Gibbs answered in temper, "Go ahead!" Another story holds that she jumped while O'Hara was in the apartment having breakfast with them and that he was a party to the quarrel. Be all that as it may, Gibbs took her death very hard. He spent some time under psychiatric care and returned to his job on the magazine with a darker view of life than ever and with still less confidence in himself. Not in his powers; in himself. Once, when Weekes and he were speculating on who might become the editor of the magazine if anything should happen to Ross, Weekes said, "Why, you, of course!" Gibbs shuddered with apprehension at the compliment.

And this was strange, because there was simply nothing on the magazine that he couldn't do well. He was a superb editor and he wrote superb stories, verse, Profiles, pieces for "Talk of the Town," book reviews, movie reviews, and play reviews. Probably his greatest skill was as a parodist. It was a skill he developed through the long years of his anonymous editing, when he undetectably imitated other people's styles in the course of perfecting their handiwork. Why he was drawn to parody is worth examining. As a literary form, parody is a method of criticism that amuses as it derogates. The great exception of Joyce aside, it is a form favored by writers of the second and third rank, who take revenge on their betters by putting just the wrong words to just the right tunes. Parodies of writers worse than oneself are scarcely worth troubling with, except as an exercise; Beerbohm mocks Henry James by seeming to become a double of the great man, but the double is a puppet, lifelike only if the original lives. Parody is homage gone sour; it is an accommodation to one's own failings in the very act of pointing out the failings of others. For a writer, it amounts to a kind of gallows humor, in which the executioner is seen to be envious of his victim. The big shark-writers swim on, committing their reckless, unworthy excesses; the little parodist pilot-fish feed off their leavings. In part because Gibbs feared taking big chances, he poked fun at writers who took big chances and miscarried with them, but oh, how he would have liked to be braver than he was! He struggled to produce at least one work on a substantial scale, worth judging his talent by; it was a play called *Season in the Sun,* and, as we shall see, it was a trifle.

Gibbs's first principle in editing was to omit. It was a common practice with him to lop off the first two or three paragraphs of nearly any manuscript; he liked to say, "This will cut like butter," and it almost always did. When I first knew him, he was writing Notes and Comment for the first page of "Talk of the Town." He had succeeded White in this task, the Whites, at Andy's urging and with Katharine's reluctant consent, having retired to their farm in Maine; there White was playing countryman and writing monthly pieces for *Harper's.* (Mrs. White believed herself to be giving up the best job held by any woman in America when she followed her husband to Maine, and no doubt she was right. The retirement proved temporary, but Mrs. White was unable to regain her lofty place in the editorial hierarchy of the magazine.) As was to be expected, Gibbs felt that he would never be able to write Comment as good as White's, and as was also to be expected, it turned out that he did Comment brilliantly, if in a different fashion from his predecessor.

By then Gibbs had married for a third time; fortunately, Elinor Gibbs had been gently born and reared and so measured up to the strict Duer standards. Gibbs and his wife and two small children were living in a house near Beekman Place. Even before I met Gibbs, I formed a strong impression of him, thanks to an exchange of half a dozen words between St. Clair McKelway and his secretary, Betty Thurlow. I was in McKelway's office late one morning, waiting to be given a "Talk" assignment. McKelway had put in a call to Gibbs, evidently because his copy was overdue, and Betty Thurlow put her head through the doorway to say, "Mr. Gibbs is out walking." McKelway smiled, and there was something about his smile that led me to believe that this was a euphemism for Gibbs's nursing a terrific hangover. Maybe he really *was* out walking, I thought, but maybe he was always said to be out walking when he felt bad. I got the impression that McKelway and Gibbs had been drinking together the night before and that McKelway was silently congratulating himself on having survived the occasion in better shape than Gibbs had.

The first time I ever spoke to Gibbs was when we both had offices on the nineteenth floor. I had graduated from my wretched little wood-and-glass box to a normal plaster-walled cell, grubby and ill-shaped, with a single window facing north. On the terrace outside the window was a striped canvas deck chair, placed there by a staff writer named Eugene Kinkead, who had apparently once contemplated taking sun baths in it. The rickety chair crouched on the terrace winter and summer for years, slowly disintegrating. I don't recall seeing anyone seated in it, much less sunbathing in it. (Kinkead, who still writes occasional pieces for the magazine, is both a dreamer and a pragmatist; having read somewhere that fruit flies and other small insects never flew higher than the sixth floor of buildings in New York, he opened a bottle of sweet wine at his desk on the nineteenth floor and was content to see that within a few minutes a number of fruit flies were busily encircling it.)

Small as my office was, for a time I shared it with the newly arrived Philip Hamburger, also a "Talk" reporter. Kip Orr — gentle, venomous, red-eyed Kip — said of us in our cramped quarters that he could not tell the black Irishman from the black Jew. A couple of doors away from us was Gibbs. One morning he burst out of his office bearing an object that some enterprising manufacturer had just sent him by mail: a birthday cake that, on being wound up, revolved on its pedestal, played a tinnily tuneful "Happy Birthday to You," and blazed with tiny electric lights instead of candles. Gibbs was trembling at the enormity of the invention. It was no more calculated to please him than TV was calculated to please Andy White, and it lacked the engaging practicality of a Dazey ice-crusher. We marvelled together over the revolving cake and Gibbs retired in a cloud of unprintable expletives, to compose a charming paragraph about it for the following week's page of Comment.

Gibbs was a small, handsome man, with delicately modelled features. Like all small men, he wished to be taller than he was, and like many small men, he was a natty dresser. Indeed, he was something of a dude, though in his cups the dudishness gave way to a sort of suave dishevelment. He once composed a Profile of Lucius Beebe, a celebrated man about town in the thirties, who

The newspaper columnist Lucius Beebe, a notable man about town in the nineteen-thirties. Well-born, wealthy, homosexual, and good-hearted, he worked up a prose so rococo that one could have built grottoes out of it. Gibbs wrote an admiring Profile of him, telling how many suits he took with him for a weekend in Hollywood: nine.

wrote a column for the New York *Herald Tribune* called "This New York." (The column contained so many references to Beebe's intimate friend Jerome Zerbe, another fashionable man about town, that Walter Winchell, writing in the *Mirror*, suggested that the column should be called not "This New York" but "Jerome Never Looked Lovelier.")

Gibbs and Beebe drank and played the match game together at a bar called Bleeck's, hard by the *Herald Tribune* building. Gibbs was filled with admiration for the variety and richness of Beebe's wardrobe and for the variety and richness of his language, which bore little relationship to ordinary English. "Ingrained in his character," Gibbs wrote, in his Profile of Beebe, "there is a profound nostalgia for dead elegance, and his prose is consequently heavy with Gothic ornament. Almost anything on wheels becomes a 'herdic'; a serving dish is a 'firkin'; 'zounds' and 'egad' break up the rolling periods. It is impossible for him to write 'hat' or 'street' or 'policeman.' They are transmuted into *'chapeau,' 'faubourg,'* and *'gendarme,'* and at one time the Gallic inspiration was so strong upon him that 'success foolish' and 'but incredible' threatened to unseat whatever was left of his readers' minds."

Gibbs would have liked to dress like Beebe, but he lacked both the means and the nerve. Beebe was a wealthy homosexual and spent money liberally upon himself; Gibbs had a family to support. Gibbs spoke with awe of the fact that Beebe, paying a weekend visit to Hollywood, would take along nine suits and seventy-two shirts. Beebe was often to be seen in top hat and tails, but Gibbs was content to make do with a tuxedo. I remember encountering him at a theatre opening and being surprised to observe that he was wearing a brown fedora along with his dinner jacket — a sartorial solecism (as Beebe would have called it) that Beebe himself would never have given way to.

Gibbs had light-brown hair, a brown mustache, and fair skin, and he liked lying idle in the sun. He was at his happiest at his house in Ocean Beach, the largest and most garish of the settlements, each so unlike the others, that lie scattered along the narrow barrier reef of Fire Island. He eventually wrote a number of short stories about the island, and out of the stories came his play *Season in the Sun.* Gibbs smoked too much and drank too much and was never in robust health; on one occasion he had to have part of a lung removed. His stay in the hospital was not shortened when Tallulah Bankhead stopped by to visit him. Tallulah was one of his favorite actresses; he was a man often close to panic, and he admired Tallulah for the courage with which she sailed, head high, through terrible plays. She wrote in her autobiography of her attempt to repay him for his many tributes to her: "Eager to divert him, I put on a one-woman show designed to kill or cure.

The nurses swore it was the most exciting vaudeville ever seen on the floor." Given the number of vaudevilles likely to have been presented at Lenox Hill Hospital over the years, this was a modest compliment on the part of the nurses. The truth of the matter is that Tallulah was probably drunk and noisy and that Gibbs must have been mortified; there was nothing he enjoyed less than being made to feel conspicuous.

As close to ordinary bodily well-being as Gibbs ever came was when he was alone with his family on Fire Island. He liked to make up a silver shakerful of ice-cold and very dry martinis, take the shaker onto the beach, bury it up to its neck in sand, and lie there drinking and sunning himself by the hour. His skin would grow very tanned and his hair would bleach to blond, and the transformation prompted one of Russell Maloney's few successful wisecracks about his colleagues. "Gibbs in summer," he said, "looks like a photographic negative."

13

Poor Maloney! I must offer up a blue-butterfly paragraph or two for the repose of his troubled soul. When I arrived at the magazine, Thurber, having begun to enjoy some success as a writer of books, was no longer regularly in the office and Russell Maloney had taken over, largely from Thurber, the job of "Talk" rewrite. In those days, the "Talk" department consisted of an opening page of Notes and Comment, followed by five pages of "Talk" stories and anecdotes. The stories were four in number, ordinarily divided between what were known as "Talk" "personalities" and "Talk" "visits." A good many reporters did the notes for these pieces, which were then handed along to the rewrite man. Some reporters (I among them) made an effort to bring a story into as finished a state as possible; others prided themselves on providing a grab-bag of disorderly but voluminous facts. The anecdotes, also four in number, served to divide the stories and, being of varied lengths, were a handy device in respect to make-up. The anecdotes came mainly from our readers, and I remember with dismay the mind-destroying difficulty of turning their damnable dross into seeming gold. Word for word, it was the highest-paying job I ever had on the magazine, and the nearest thing to being a chore.

Maloney was a sensationally skillful rewrite man. When it came my time to succeed him, Shawn, by then managing editor of the fact side of the magazine, would often send me a sheaf of "Talk" notes with the scribbled suggestion that I "run it through the typewriter." It was never quite that easy for me, but it was evidently that easy for Maloney. Disorderly as the reporter's notes might be, Maloney would take but a few minutes to quarry out of them some four pages of faultless, triple-spaced typescript, ready to be forwarded to Ross for mangling in the name of greater clarity. Though otherwise totally unlike in temperament — I always assumed, however wrongly, that I was a favored party;

Maloney always assumed that he was being discriminated against — Maloney and I were alike in being fastidious about the look of our copy. Unconsciously, I must have modelled my "Talk" writing on his, as I modelled my typing.

At the time we became friends, he was still in his twenties. Born in the suburbs of Boston, with, as they used to say, the map of Ireland on his face, he had graduated from Harvard in 1932 and had at once begun to sell ideas for drawings to the magazine. He had come to work on the staff a couple of years later. He was very plump and not very tall, and his face was perfectly moon-shaped: a baby face, with big blue eyes, smooth skin, and thin hair rising in an unfashionable crew-cut pompadour, through which one caught glimpses of a gleaming pink scalp. It must have been a fact that his skin was actually thinner than other people's, as his nature was less well protected against hard knocks; as soon as he got exercised over anything, a deep blush would cover his face, the color darkening from rose to almost purple, and he seemed to threaten to explode. He was to die of a cerebral hemorrhage at thirty-eight, three years after leaving the magazine, and no doubt even when I first knew him he must have been suffering from high blood pressure. When he laughed, his whole body — chest, big belly, thighs — would roll about and bob up and down with delight.

In order to diminish his baby-look, Maloney eventually grew a small mustache. As it happened, this did not make him look less baby-faced; instead, and rather endearingly, it made him look like a baby with a mustache. Still, it put him on a par, at least in respect to facial hair, with his much-envied rivals in the office, Gibbs, White, and Thurber, all of whom were moderately mustached. Maloney liked to sit on a table in the corridor outside his office dangling his short legs and passing the time of day with us slightly younger reporters. Whitaker, who had an office nearby and who had the cruelest wit of any member of the staff (one of his colleagues speaks of him with awe as "the assassin"), used to engage Maloney in taunting badinage of a particularly venomous kind, and in these exchanges Maloney was always the loser. Valiantly, he would try to match Whitaker's savage thrusts, but in vain; he would think too late — in the elevator, or down on Forty-third Street — of the perfect riposte. Maloney was so prolific a writer of casuals that he had to adopt a couple of pseudonyms in order to keep from seeming to occupy too great a share of the magazine. He also wrote many able Profiles, and of his short stories one has long been celebrated and may prove immortal. The story has to do with a man who heard it said at a cocktail party that if six monkeys were to be put to work typing away at random on six typewriters, it was a mathematical certainty that sooner or later they would succeed in typing out every book in the British Museum, correct down to the last comma and period. What befalls the man when he undertakes an experiment to test this theory makes a brilliant story, brilliantly executed.

Maloney had a lively awareness of his gifts and a foreboding that they would never be sufficiently rewarded. Like so many Irish Catholics who grew up in and around Boston in those days, he felt himself an outsider at Harvard, and at *The New Yorker* he continued to feel himself an outsider. He saw Gibbs, White, and Thurber as insiders, gaining all the glory while he worked hard behind the scenes. There are people — Shawn is one of them — who, far from objecting to anonymity, eagerly cultivate it. Maloney was a different sort. He longed for fame, though he had no particular knack for acquiring it. He married a girl who was making a career in the theatre, and I remember talk of a musical that Maloney would write the book for: surely a Broadway success was the quickest way for a young writer to become famous? But what a pity that the young writer's name should have to be Maloney! He envied Gibbs, White, and Thurber not only their glory but their indisputable Yankee patronymics as well. He hated his own name because it was Irish and because it had for him a comic lower-class ring. When he and his wife had a daughter, after much debate over possible names to bestow on her they settled for "Amelia." "What can you name a child," he asked me, "that can possibly go well with Maloney? One might as well give up and make a bumpy joke of it."

Hating his name, Maloney had to use it to do himself injury. When he brought out a book of some of his *New Yorker* pieces, in a characteristic act of self-abasement he called it "It's Still Maloney" — a title that echoed the popular Rube Goldberg saw, "No matter how thin you slice it, it's still baloney."

With increasing truculence, Maloney took to boasting of how many hundreds of thousands of words — indeed, how many millions of words — he had written for *The New Yorker*. It was a measure of his misery that he should have been reduced to calling attention to quantity instead of quality; moreover, his boast amounted (though no doubt he was unaware of it) to an echo of the feat that provided the plot for his celebrated short story. A man seated at a typewriter and causing hundreds of different articles to stream through the tips of his fingers, each written seemingly without effort and each without an error, was doing something scarcely less wonderful than what Maloney's six monkeys had done; and it had been their fate to be wantonly killed for having performed not badly but so well.

Maloney met a similar if somewhat less violent fate. He quit the magazine, saying in public that the pace had grown too hard for him to maintain at the advanced age of thirty-five; in private, as I remember hearing at the time, he expressed a good deal of bitterness over his departure. It was true, at any rate, that he subsequently made every effort to dissociate himself from the magazine. He had collected bound volumes of *The New Yorker* for many years; when he told me one day that he was going to throw them out, I asked if I could purchase them. No, he would not sell them; I could have them as a gift, or he would toss them into garbage cans, where they belonged. I stopped off at his house with a station wagon and loaded it up with scores of thick black volumes, some of which had had the corners of their bindings chewed off by one or another of Maloney's dogs. He apologized for the condition of the bindings and expressed relief at seeing the last traces of *The New Yorker* removed from the premises. In three years he was dead. He was then holding a literary post of no great importance at the Columbia Broadcasting System. None of his hopes had been realized and he died broke; indeed, the story went that there wasn't money enough in the house to pay for the ambulance that removed his body. *The New Yorker* is said to have taken care of the funeral expenses, as it has done on so many occasions.

This is as good a place as any to interject that in life our rewards from the magazine are comparatively modest. We are not fussed over or made much of, especially if we are in good health. For example, on the twenty-fifth anniversary of my arrival on the scene, I suggested that a substantial check might serve as an amiable souvenir of the occasion; the suggestion fell upon deaf ears. I then proposed that a gold watch could not possibly give offense. Again, no response. Finally, I put it to Shawn that he might at least take me to lunch at what was then reputed to be the most expensive restaurant in town: Lutèce. Very well; we went to Lutèce, whose owner, enchanted to have the elusive Shawn on the premises, hung aggressively above the table, chatted at intolerable length of his own affairs, and at last insisted upon our having the *plat du jour,* which turned out to be Irish stew. Twenty-five years on the magazine, and my reward a plate of Irish stew! In death we can all hope to do better. Presumably because we will be past knowing about it and therefore, in the magazine's reasoning, past seeking to take advantage of it and becoming spoiled by it, Frank Campbell's best will be seen to be none too good for us.

If Maloney was in truth destitute at the time of his death, then it amounts to a rueful jest of the sort that his big belly was quick to shake at. For he had often printed in pencil on his office walls the grim graffito "Death settles all debts." And he had taken pains to be always literally penniless — he despised those trifling coppers and would make sure to keep the change in his pocket free of them. Again and again I have watched as he tossed unwanted pennies up into the glass globes of the lighting fixtures that hung above his head in the *New Yorker* corridors. Given the nature of our housekeeping, many of them are probably there to this day.

Gibbs, too, sought fame on Broadway, more successfully than Maloney. As he had taken over Notes and Comment from White, so he took over play-reviewing from Benchley, who in the late thirties and forties was spending more and more of his time as a sought-after actor in Hollywood. Gibbs had feared that he would never write Comment as well as White did; similarly, he feared that he would never be able to cover Broadway as ably as Benchley. Again he was being a victim of his notion that a college degree — White had gone to Cornell, Benchley to Harvard — bestowed some mystical intellectual superiority upon the possessor of it. Nothing that Benchley had learned at Harvard had fitted him to become a theatre critic; indeed, he was never to be a proper critic at all. From first to last, he remained an admirable amateur reviewer of plays, and his criterion in judging a particular work was simply the measure of his enjoyment of it; he rarely had ideas about why a play succeeded or failed. He had an infectious laugh and, unlike the current breed of calculatedly inscrutable members of the Critics Circle, who sit hunched in the dark of the theatre giving little sign that they are capable of being entertained, he was not afraid to let his laughter be heard; backstage, producers and playwrights bent their ears, listening for him.

Benchley loved going to the theatre, and he was sorry when

Robert Benchley with Louise Macy at the old El Morocco. Benchley enjoyed serving as the theatre critic for The New Yorker, *but more and more of his time was spent in Hollywood, making movies and having a good time, and the moment was reached when Ross deputed McKelway — in these matters, there was always a deputy — to break the news to Benchley that Gibbs was being appointed critic in his place. McKelway and Benchley had drinks together, and McKelway found that he hadn't the heart to tell Benchley the bad news. Finally, Benchley himself brought up the subject, said he understood perfectly, and ordered another round of drinks. It was his knack to take other people's side, especially when they were in trouble. He made everyone around him happy. Like so many* New Yorker *writers and artists, he died in his fifties, far sooner than anybody wished him to.*

he had to say of a play that he disliked it. Gibbs didn't "love" going to the theatre; in the conventional loose meaning of the word, he probably wouldn't have admitted loving anything except Fire Island. As for falling in love, I assume Gibbs had as many affairs as the next man; he was certainly discreet about them. The only affair of his that I was personally cognizant of was with a fiery, very good-looking young actress, for whom Gibbs sought employment on the magazine, in vain. (Ross used to warn his newly hired editors, "Don't fuck the contributors." A natural Rossian corollary to this edict was, "Moreover, we won't hire the people you *do* fuck." Certain exceptions to the edict spring to mind.) With difficulty I can imagine Gibbs infatuated, but I cannot imagine his actually uttering the words "I love you." Even in the act of making love, he, the born editor, would have found that statement overemphatic and not strictly necessary; therefore, to be cut. Nor can I imagine Gibbs's admitting that he enjoyed writing and editing; he often said that he would stop working the moment he was no longer financially in need of doing so. But the evidence is otherwise; he doted on hard work, and nobody on the magazine except Ross and Shawn worked harder. There were issues of the magazine to which Gibbs contributed Comment, a story, verse, and a review, and if he had not contributed any of the drawings, he had most likely passed judgment on them.

Gibbs began his career as a play-reviewer in a gingerly fashion; alarmed lest there be more to Shakespeare than he was ever going to get to know, he patronized him, saying of *Hamlet*, for example, that it was a good thing to take the children to on a rainy afternoon. As he gained confidence, he made fewer and fewer skittish jokes, and his copy came to be less liberally besprinkled with self-protective "I fear" 's and "I'm afraid" 's. Sitting evening after evening through innumerable second- and third-rate comedies, Gibbs must have reached the conclusion that he could not fail to do better, and so, drawing on a number of his Fire Island stories, he set about writing the play *Season in the Sun*.

The text is worth examining in detail because it is the most openly autobiographical writing that Gibbs ever risked; furthermore, it provides some illuminating glimpses of Ross, apotheosized in the play as Horace William Dodd. Ross's baptismal "Harold Wallace" readily transformed itself into "Horace William"; I suspect it is no accident that Dodd rhymes with God and is also an imaginable scrambling of Ross's favorite epithet: "goddam" into "Dodd am." Gibbs would have had little admiration for God, but his admiration for Ross was as unbridled as he ever permitted himself to become. He and Thurber and White tended to believe that Ross had invented them, when what he had done — no small thing, I grant — was to give them the opportunity to invent themselves.

The hero of the play, George Crane, has just resigned from the staff of a weekly humorous magazine, presided over by an importunate, hot-tempered editor named Dodd. In the course of a long stay in the hospital, Crane has been taking the measure of his life; at thirty-five, he feels that he can no longer afford to devote his gifts to the writing of funny paragraphs. He and his wife and two children have rented a bungalow on Fire Island for the summer; there he will undertake the writing of a book worthy of him, the purpose of which will be to demonstrate that people who come to New York with high hopes in youth end up as hard-drinking, rootless no-goods. On doctor's orders, George has himself gone on the wagon and no longer enjoys watching other people drink. Emily, George's wife, protests that his work as a paragrapher is much admired and deserves to be; to prove her point, she picks up a copy of the magazine and quotes the following passage:

> "For more than three years we have been watching a very bothersome and heroic struggle in the publishing world — *Life* magazine trying to figure out a way to print a picture of a living, breathing woman with absolutely no clothes on. The special problem of *Life*, of course, is that everything in it has to have the air of a respectable, high-minded commentary on America. *Life*, that is, can't publish a picture of a woman undressed over the caption 'Woman Undressed.' It has to *say* something. We are glad to be able to tell you that last week, after years of frustration and seventeen million angle shots that almost got there but not quite, the editors have finally found the answer. Like all truly great things, it was simple. They just photographed a life class at the Yale Art School. This had Yale, it had Art, it had Class, it had America; it had everything, including no clothes on. It was *Life*'s dream come true — a girl who had shucked (and no fooling) but had done it for her country. It was a tremendous relief to us. And a very interesting picture, too."

George asks his wife if she seriously thinks that writing such stuff is a good way for him to spend the rest of his life, and the wife goes so far as to hint that she doesn't see why not. Crane then fishes out a telegram newly received from Dodd:

> "YOUR RESIGNATION DECLINED STOP I GOTTA GET OUT FIFTY-TWO ISSUES A YEAR AND NEED ASSISTANCE YOUR ACTIVE IF VACANT LITTLE MIND STOP UNDERSTAND YOU NOW CONTEMPLATE NOVEL RE SEX OR SOME SUCH STOP NO FUTURE THIS TOPIC AS LADY WRITERS GOT IT SEWED UP STOP STRONGLY URGE YOU RETURN WRITING FOR THIS MAGAZINE WHERE UNNECESSARY WORRY WHO SLEEPS WHO STOP PLEASE PHONE AT ONCE ON RECEIPT THIS STOP REGARDS YOUR UNFORTUNATE WIFE SIGNED D STOP."

These excerpts amount to inside jokes, which Gibbs in principle deplored. The paragraph about the picture magazine *Life* happens to be lifted word for word from one of Gibbs's Notes and Comment pieces (characteristically, Yale is equated with superiority of class); and in the telegram the phrase "re sex or some such" is purest Ross. Ross regarded "some such" as very debonair English and often scattered it through his "Talk" rewrites. "Re" was a useful shorthand to him. Ross was haunted by the necessity of turning out fifty-two issues a year; he feared that sooner or later the magazine was doomed to run out of material. He affected not to worry about running out of writers, who were valued by him, as he often snarlingly informed Thurber, at a dime a dozen. It is Shawn who has always openly considered writers rare creatures, to be bound to the magazine by such hoops of steel — and money — as he can find the means of providing.

The plot of *Season in the Sun* concerns the wavering and eventual total collapse of Crane's firm resolve to turn over a new leaf. New leaves imply new friends, and in his case the new friends turn out to be intolerably tiresome. Temptations abound. The madam of a well-known house in New York — a character called Molly Burden in the play and bearing a lively resemblance to an actual madam of the time, Benchley's good friend Polly Adler — causes some welcome excitement, as does a drunken journalist (perhaps based on a boxing writer on the *Herald Tribune* named Don Skene, whose invariable modest boast in his cups was that he was a descendant of the man who discovered Skene's glands, which lubricate the female genitalia). There is also a pretty young blonde, with a figure that would make the famous bishops of Chichester in their breeches stir, and an assortment of raffish island folk. Finally, Dodd arrives to demand Crane's immediate return to the magazine. Gibbs notes in his stage directions that if Harold Ross of *The New Yorker* cannot be persuaded to take the role, then it should be given to an actor capable of playing either Caliban or Mr. Hyde almost without the assistance of make-up. (When one remembers that Ross was sure to read this description of himself, it strikes one as sufficiently harsh; but Ross was used to dishing it out, and he could take it.) Gibbs writes of Ross/Dodd: "He is a dark, untidy man almost continuously engaged in maniacal gestures — sweeping his hand wildly through his upstanding hair, rattling what must be a gargantuan bunch of keys in his pants pocket, throwing his arms about to indicate his perpetual state of derision, amazement, and disgust with a world that seems to him wholly populated by astounding incompetents. This effect can really only be achieved by imitating the real Ross; if it can be described at all, you might say that every gesture, every expression is ten times as large as the stimulus behind it. He is dressed in a blue suit that probably cost a good deal of money but, somehow, perhaps because he is always in such violent motion inside it, nowhere fits him accurately."

Another true-to-life Ross touch: when Crane and Dodd shake hands, Dodd "offers his hand, limply, absently, while he studies his surrounding." One expected Ross to shake hands with vigor; the limpness always came as a surprise. Dodd tells Crane — again, an authentic Ross quote — "I've been living the life of a hunted animal." Translated from the Rossian, this would read, "I've been working quite hard." Dodd pleads for a drink. "Water. Goddam it, you know I can't drink. I got ulcers. I worry too much." He then glances over the first few pages of Crane's projected book. "Christ, it sounds like a parody," he says. "Who was that female

Gibbs taking the sun on Fire Island. In his play about the island, Season in the Sun, *Gibbs has the drunken hero sing, "Nobody loves me, I wonder why?" This was a question that Gibbs seemed often on the verge of asking, but it appears that he never did.*

pinhead who used to write for the *Saturday Evening Post* all the time? Three names, Willa Walla Waters or some such. Hell, they've *all* got three names. Well, it doesn't matter. That's who it sounds like."

It is a defect of the play that Gibbs brings the noisy and rampageous Ross/Dodd onto the stage and then gives him very little to do; he catches a fish, lectures Crane on his unbecoming virtuousness, meets Molly Burden and rejects the possibility of publishing a piece about her career ("You'd never get the damn thing through the mails"), is relieved to learn that Crane will return to the magazine, and then sits down to await an approaching hurricane. It is a phenomenon of which he has had no first-hand experience, and he will welcome it as he welcomes all novelties, with the eager curiosity of a child. Characteristically, he looks up the word "hurricane" in an encyclopedia and, as the real thing begins to blow, is busy memorizing facts about its likely size and speed — "Sometimes as high as a hundred and forty miles an hour."

If Ross as a character goes to waste in the play, so, most of the time, does Gibbs's talent. For it is not, after all, much of a play, especially for a writer with Gibbs's high standards of excellence. Still, he had proved that, unlike Crane, he was more than just a funny paragrapher; he had composed a work on a certain scale, had seen it produced on Broadway, and had received, from professional colleagues who were no doubt more than ordinarily kind-hearted because they were also personal friends, a bouquet of favorable notices. John Mason Brown called it "a highly diverting evening in the theatre," Brooks Atkinson said of it that it was "an original and funny play that is also intelligent," and George Jean Nathan described it as having "a wealth of flush humor," whatever "flush" humor may be. The play was published and so were a couple of collections of Gibbs's *New Yorker* pieces. They amounted to visible, liftable evidence of his having had a career. He was a man of letters and not without a following. When, in 1958, on his beloved Fire Island and with the usual cigarette in his hand, Gibbs suddenly died, he was looking over a newly arrived advance copy of his latest collection; not the worst death in the world for a writer.

14

In my first year or so on the staff, White, Thurber, and Gibbs were figures far too godlike to permit me to feel the sort of envy of them that Maloney did. I dealt mainly with McKelway and Whitaker in respect to fact pieces and with Katharine White and Maxwell in respect to fiction; and from time to time, in respect to either fact or fiction, Ross's heavy hand would give me a necessary whack. The fierce Whitaker was doing what he could to turn me into a writer of workmanlike prose and Ross was doing what he could to turn me into a responsible reporter. I cultivated at that period (shades of my Victorian father!) a style too fancy for its own good and certainly too fancy for "Talk" and other pieces. I remember on one occasion happening to catch a glimpse of a characteristic comment by Whitaker; circling a long and elaborately balanced sentence of mine, he had scribbled in the margin of the galley, "If you tapped this sentence at one end, it would never stop rocking." After that, I took care to be as little Gibbonesque as possible.

Because I admired Whitaker and was willing to stand up against him, he soon stopped practicing on me the cruel sport that he practiced on Maloney; I was determined not to be among the victims awaiting punishment in Whitaker's exceedingly long pecking order, and whenever he drew any blood of mine I made sure that he didn't see it. The result was that we early became fast friends and have remained friends ever since.

Over the years, Whitaker has edited a great number of my "Talk" pieces, Profiles, and book reviews, and our debates over certain sentences and even over certain words in certain sentences have sometimes lasted for days, but it is fair to say that he has never failed to improve my handiwork. Decade after decade, he has sat hunched like Bartleby the Scrivener in a revolting hovel of an office on the nineteenth floor, working away on galleys while all round him rises a flood of yellowing newspapers, magazines,

Whitaker and I in Uncle Arthur's garden, in Norfolk, Connecticut. The time is the Second World War, as one can deduce from the fact that the garden, celebrated for its double dahlias, has been given over to tomatoes.

Whitaker in his warren, 1974. The castellated magazines on the right have mostly to do with railroads. The football books in the foreground bespeak the fact that Whitaker, over the initials J.W.L., has written the football column for the magazine since 1934. Whitaker has proved more durable than the balustrade outside his window, which is twenty years younger than he.

and Penn Central timetables and other railroad memorabilia. The latter are the outward and visible signs of what has been Whitaker's lifelong passion; he is the formost railroad buff in the country and perhaps in the world, and every moment that he has not devoted to *The New Yorker* over the past forty-odd years has been devoted to railroading.

Long ago, I did a couple of pieces about him in "Talk"; because of our wise prejudice against writing about each other in the magazine, it was necessary to disguise him under the name of Mr. Frimbo and to supply him with lexicography as an appropriate profession. His two habitual nicknames on the magazine are Frimbo and Popsie. Frimbo is borrowed from the name of a bloodthirsty African witch doctor, who was a character in a play given in Harlem by the W.P.A. theatre group, back in the thirties; Popsie was bestowed on Whitaker in his comparative youth, when, after a severe illness, his hair turned prematurely white. No one in or out of the office has ever been known to address Whitaker by his proper first name, which is Rogers.

A book by Whitaker and Anthony Hiss, entitled *All Aboard with E. M. Frimbo,* was published in 1974. Much of the book appeared originally in *The New Yorker,* having been written for "Talk" by Hiss. On the credits page, the authors give thanks to "Dr." Brendan Gill for having contributed a portion of the first chapter of the book. A doctor at last! I am very proud.

One of the earliest "Talk" pieces that Ross, Whitaker, and I collided over and at last thrashed into publishable form came out in the waning days of 1938 and served to herald that marvellous event, the New York World's Fair of 1939. Reading the piece now, one sees little in it that might have gone wrong, but Whitaker and I both remember it as having caused us considerable care and pain. I can see clearly enough what pleased Ross about the piece; for one thing, it contained a superlative — it had to do with the biggest wooden statue in the world (even, as noted, including totem poles: that would have been Ross's wary insertion) — and Ross dearly loved a superlative. For another thing, the maker of the statue almost certainly had a screw loose, and it was a screw that if it were ever to be tightened, would only make the possessor of it less interesting. Ross had a weakness for eccentrics, especially eccentrics who prided themselves on having a practical turn of mind, for that was precisely the sort of eccentric Ross himself was.

It happened that the sculptor of the biggest wooden statue in the world had devised a terrible problem for himself; having carved a statue that weighed twenty-five tons, he wasn't sure how to move it to its proposed site at the World's Fair. Ross liked problems of that nature: they were physical and therefore resolvable, while most of the problems he confronted on the magazine were psychological and therefore, so he thought, unresolvable. A proposal mentioned in the piece — that the statue be floated down the Connecticut River and across the Sound to the fairgrounds — may well have come from Ross. Anyhow, here is the story:

There's a great to-do in South Windsor, Connecticut. Lawrence Tenney Stevens is carving there what he thinks is the largest wooden statue in the world, totem poles included. Stevens began with a cross-cut saw and axe and only lately has got down to hatchets and gouges. All his life he has wanted to carve a statue out of a whole elm tree. Little life-sized figures stir his imagination not at all. Back in 1922, he contrived to get a ten-foot block of stone and hammer it into "The Spirit of America" and won the Prix de Rome, but when he returned from Italy his patrons insisted on his modelling busts and statuettes. He got back on the right track year before last, when he was put in charge of statuary at the Dallas Centennial Exposition, and lately he's been carving eucalyptus wood. He likes that because it's practically impossible to work. "When I sweep up my studio, the shavings sound like gravel," he says. When he submitted a model to the Board of Design of the World's Fair, he was given an opportunity to let himself go. It took the Board only fifteen minutes to decide that a statue six stories high would be exactly right near the Contemporary Arts Building. Stevens thinks it will be the most staggering thing at the Fair, and he may be correct. It took a long time to find a suitable elm because Stevens needed not only an enormous trunk but two branches for arms and another for a head. He finally found one and went off to California. The hurricane fractured the tree and he had to come hurrying back. He found another at South Windsor and got permission to take it, but a good many people raised Cain. They didn't know the tree had been condemned by the State Highway Department and had to go anyhow. The elm will make one of a group of three figures. It will be a man-god. The group has been described by Stevens on a mimeographed sheet:

The tree, six feet in diameter and sixty feet in height, depicts a majestic, ethereal spirit, its graceful lines sweeping upwards in rhythms of peace, equanimity, and faith. The sculptured form of the elm is a marriage to the tree's form, not hindering its natural beauty, but rather increasing its significant message of patience and courage to humanity, as depicted in the restless figures of the male and female below on each side of it.

These figures, ten feet high and carved in eucalyptus, lean slightly towards the mighty elm. The wood of the smaller figures is hard, heavy, and red in color — all of which expresses the earthly. The restless attitude of these figures is in direct contrast with the serenity of the elm. They are striving, even though quite blindly, in half-consciousness that what they seek is to be found in the great spirit of the tree.

Privately, Stevens calls the male and female figures "peanuts." The elm has won his heart. The figure is to have a beard, a hat — for the sake of dignity — and a nimbus, which will, unfortunately, be vertical because of the shape of the tree. He will leave his work uncompleted until spring, then finish it off with a chisel and a three-pound sledge. Getting the giant from South Windsor to Flushing will be a problem, as it will weigh twenty-five tons and will have to be handled delicately. Stevens thinks he'll drop it into the nearby Connecticut River and float it into the Sound, and thence to Flushing Meadows. Landing it will be up to Whalen. What to do with the statue after the Fair is an equal problem. "I'd like to have it brought right back here to South Windsor," Stevens says. "They kicked about losing the tree so damned much." He likes to think of the man-god standing in front of the Congregational church.

It is a conventional defect of journalism that one so often fails to learn the end of a story. Did Stevens actually float the statue down the river to the fairgrounds? Did he erect it there? And did he later bring it back to Connecticut, and, if so, by what means? I am sorry to say that I am unable to answer any of those questions. As I have related, poor Maloney in despair of gaining his just share of fame fell back upon boasting of how many millions of words he had written for the magazine, and even the sophisticated Gibbs once made a similar boast, adding the claim that he had written more words for the magazine than anyone else ever had. Records exist to be broken; largely by the grim chance of my having outlived them for so long, I have easily outstripped both Maloney and Gibbs. In sheer quantity of output — most trivial of measurements! — I am by now no doubt something of a nonpareil, though even as I write the words I have a lively sense that some young person down on the eighteenth floor will be boasting some day in the twenty-first century that *he* is the undoubted nonpareil. Be that as it may, a consequence of all those millions of words having entered my head in the line of duty is that a few thousand of them have remained lodged there, distilled into the form of questions, unanswered and in most cases unanswerable. Sometimes at night I wake with a start and wonder: Where is the inventor of the Twirler-Beanie, once saluted with admiration in our pages? Is he well and happy? The inventor of Silly Putty, what of him? Does he prosper? Or the inventor of the Hula hoop? Not fallen, I hope, upon evil days? Graver questions haunt me. Are there people, perhaps not any longer in their first youth, who do not know what a Twirler-Beanie is? What Silly Putty is? Who have never seen a Hula hoop in operation? It is in the nature of *The New Yorker* to be as topical as possible, on a level that is often small in scale and playful in intention. If the magazine does its work well, then a large portion of the references made in its text and in the captions to its drawings becomes, with the passing of only a handful of years, arcane. The guns of the big events rumble through our pages, but the tiny firecrackers are constantly hissing and popping there as well; it appears that much of my life as a journalist has been devoted to sedulously setting off firecrackers.

The New York World's Fair of 1939–40 was Ross's idea of a big event, and how thoroughly we covered it, with covers, drawings, Profiles, "Talk" pieces, and maps, in a continuous outpouring of celebratory particularities! The New York World's Fair of 1964–65 was such a bungle that it has tended to cast a shadow backward over its brilliant predecessor, but for those of us who all but lived on the fairgrounds during the long summer days and nights of 1939, it was indeed an incomparably happy time. We young reporters, with our passes and, therefore, with easy access to such sell-out exhibits as the General Motors Futurama, were much sought after. I scarcely dare glance at the thousand trifling episodes that jostle one another in my memory, pleading for mention: the newspaper cartoonist Denys Wortman arriving at the fair dressed and bewigged as George Washington and bearing an awesome resemblance to Lillian Hellman; Peter Arno having drinks at the French Pavilion with Brenda Frazier, most conspic-

Peter Arno and Brenda Frazier at the French Pavilion during the World's Fair of 1939–40. According to E. J. Kahn, Jr., who wrote a Profile of Miss Frazier, she was the most celebrated debutante of all time, and when, on the eve of her coming-out ball at the Ritz, she was found to be suffering from a cold, the tabloids reported her condition "with all the gravity that might attend the last earthly hours of a dying king or queen."

uous of debutantes; the Cornelius Rathbornes hanging helpless in space, their parachute at the Parachute Jump having become entangled in its own shrouds; woebegone Admiral Byrd seated among a few equally woebegone Antarctic penguins at a concession he had opened in the so-called Amusement Area; nearby, and far more popular than the penguins (though less popular than a display of premature babies in shiny oxygen tanks), a hapless nudie show, sneaked into the fair under the sacred name of education. The girls were allowed to go bare-breasted because they were teaching us the customs of the ancient Amazon warriors and so, by extension, giving us a glimpse of that lost classic world so precious to our elders and betters. From time to time, one or another of the girls would lift a silvery papier-mâché spear and toss it listlessly at some enemy offstage; we would watch her rosy nipples rise and fall, and sigh with gratitude at having our minds so much improved.

It was nonsense, and much of it was charming nonsense; still, contemporary young people might well wonder how we young people of that day could have been so willing to be charmed on the very brink of the greatest and bloodiest war in history; did

The shroud-lines of their parachute having become entangled, the Cornelius Rathbornes spent several hours aloft at the Parachute Jump at the World's Fair. The society photographer Jerome Zerbe, a close friend of the Rathbornes, took this picture from an adjacent parachute. He borrowed the camera from a newspaper photographer in the crowd gathered below the Rathbornes; the photographer was professionally eager to get the picture but was afraid to make the ascent. For ballast, Zerbe pressed into service a fat policeman, who, just as Zerbe was leaning out into space to take the picture, fainted and slumped against him. Nevertheless, the picture proved satisfactory, and the newspaper photographer, to whom Zerbe gave it, sold it for five hundred dollars.

we not perceive the doom that was then plainly hanging over the world? The answer is that although we perceived it and tried to pay proper attention to it, it was often rendered unreal by a spontaneous sense of personal and national well-being. The world that stood on the brink of war was emerging from a prolonged depression and seemed also to stand on the brink of that mingling of peace and prosperity that the fair had been calculated, however meretriciously, to embody. Surely there *was* some exhilarating promise in the air, even as the leaves of the trees turned belly-up and the sky darkened. We were like a man dying of cancer, who, on a sunny morning, rejoicing to find himself still so intensely alive, begins to doubt the reality of his own pain. It was evident that something terrible might be about to happen in Europe, and most of the Americans I knew, though by no means most of the Americans throughout the country, assumed that if England were to be drawn into a war, the United States would be sure to follow. In the summer of 1939, we were intermittently aware that we faced difficulties, but the degree of the desperation we might eventually be confronted with was only beginning to be imagined; we were far from taking an accurate measure of our future, though there were plenty of signs of imminent disaster even at the fair. In a few months, for example, the lovely Polish Pavilion would stand as a silent witness to the fact that the country of Poland no longer existed, having been overrun by its two adjacent tyrannies.

15

Happy as I was at the fair, I was less happy at the magazine. Not that this was a matter of great moment; I had always wanted to write for *The New Yorker*, and I was doing so agreeably enough, but I had expected the experience to be more than merely agreeable. I hadn't been rebuffed by Gibbs or insulted by Whitaker; still, the atmosphere of the office struck me as unsympathetic. There seemed to be no fabric, family-like or tribal, which one could work one's way into and gain support from. McKelway was a symbol of what I missed and looked for. A handsome man in his thirties, with broad shoulders, a graceful walk, and well-cut clothes, he had sandy hair that was beginning to go thin on top (thirty-five years later, it is still going thin on top) and a small, bristling mustache. He was as able an editor as he was a writer, and he had exceptional charm. It was obvious that he made an effort to put his younger colleagues at their ease, but the effort was not always a success. Some inborn diffidence of manner caused him to mumble his words; they rarely emerged with distinctness from his mustache, and some of us used to speak wistfully of the possibility of combing the words one by one from that obstruction and arranging them in a comprehensible form somewhere outside it. Even at Christmastime, when he came round and shook hands with me and said, "Merry Christmas," he spoke so indistinctly that I assumed with my usual optimism that he was congratulating me on a "Talk" piece I had just done. I blurted out, "No, no! It's nothing!"

In July, 1939, my father telephoned from Hartford to say that he and my younger brother Charles, then twenty, were planning a holiday trip to Ireland and would be delighted to have Anne and me join them. I accepted the invitation at once. For one thing, it never occurred to me to refuse any of the manifold bounties of my father; for another, it seemed a graceful way to part company with the magazine. I would slip away without an expression of strong feelings on either side. And I would slip away while I was still financially ahead of the game, and so be spared the fate of many *New Yorker* writers of whom I had heard by then, vanishing into a quicksand of debt and unfinishable pieces.

On being hired, I had made a tactical error of which I was at first entirely unaware. I had instructed the accounting department not to pay me the forty dollars a week I was entitled to on my drawing account; I would get along on my own means and would let such money as I was entitled to be credited to my account. Well! I was to learn later that this sufficiently unimportant proposal created a sensation in the office. It was at once assumed that I was a person of very great means indeed; not a young man with a few thousand a year but one with many tens of thousands. It was thought that, working for *The New Yorker*, I regarded myself as slumming. I was a mere gentleman writer, as Gibbs had once been a gentleman brakeman. Moreover, my request amounted to a declaration of independence of the kind that made Ross edgy. He didn't mind people threatening to quit if he knew that they were fettered to him and the magazine forever by advances impossible for them to repay. He could not hope to receive from me what he termed "loyalty" if I were not, like most of his writers and artists, in a state of permanent fiscal jeopardy.

My error in respect to not seeming to need money was never to be made again, not alone because I had learned how unfavorable an impression it created in the office but also because from that moment on I took care to be always genuinely overextended. Like the total abstainer who discovers, on taking his first drink, that he has always been in fact a raving, staving alcoholic, I had developed in the course of our first year or so in New York an insatiable craving to live better than we could afford. The trip to Ireland with my father and my brother was perhaps the last indulgence I ever treated myself to in a state of conventional solvency; henceforth, all my pleasures were to be made possible by dint of what the government calls deficit financing. For decades, I have bobbed like a cork, cheekily unsinkable, in a maelstrom of loans, mortgages, liens, and I.O.U.'s, engaged in a way of life indistinguishable from that of a millionaire. Once, discussing with me the disparity between my income and my possession of several delightful houses, Shawn was moved to comment on another *New Yorker* writer, A. J. Liebling. Like me, Liebling was always seeking more money from the magazine than the magazine was willing to pay. "Liebling," said Shawn, "wants to live like a stockbroker, but he doesn't want to *be* one."

Something I didn't know was that McKelway was planning to step down from his job as managing editor of fact at the very moment that I was planning to leave the magazine altogether. McKelway, who had enjoyed even less formal education than Gibbs but did not waste any time brooding about it, had been a newspaperman in his teens. In his early twenties, he was appointed editor of the Bangkok, Siam, *Daily Mail,* and in 1933, he returned to this country and joined *The New Yorker.* His interest lay in writing, not editing, but in 1936, as a favor to Ross, he agreed to replace Stanley Walker, one of the editor "Jesuses" that Ross hired so readily in those days and then not so readily fired. (Ross liked to leave the firing to others; being physically timid, he was afraid that even quite small Jesuses might beat him up upon getting the bad news.) Walker, an able newspaperman, had never caught on to the difference between editing a newspaper and editing a magazine. Ross was convinced that only McKelway could do right what Walker was plainly doing wrong.

McKelway had an understandable fear of becoming the latest in Ross's already formidably long line of Jesuses, but he said he would take the job on three conditions: one, that it be set up in a new fashion, establishing for the first time a division between fact and fiction and thereby insuring that Mrs. White would no longer be concerned with editing factual material; two, that McKelway be paid the same salary that Walker had been getting, which, astonishingly for *The New Yorker* of that day, was the high sum of fifteen thousand dollars a year, or about twice what McKelway was able to make as a writer on the magazine; and, three, that he be obliged to keep the job for only three years.

Ross willingly agreed to these conditions, though it turned out that the third of them puzzled him. Over lunch one day, he asked McKelway, "How come you said three years?" McKelway has the kind of mind that likes to play with such problems, and he at once undertook to explain matters to Ross. For one thing, he said, when in his early newspaper days he had been learning to be a bookkeeper on the side, he had found that he preferred totting up sums not, like most people, in units of two, four, six, eight, and ten but in units of three, six, nine, twelve, and so on. For another thing, he said, his life had always seemed to divide itself into periods of three — three years as a newspaper man in Washington, three years in Bangkok, three years as a writer on *The New*

McKelway has dressed himself up in gear suitable for his role as the author of a book called The Edinburgh Caper. *The book described, in the sunniest terms, one of McKelway's recurrent bouts of extreme fantasizing, in the course of which he detects malevolent conspiracies taking place all round him as readily as other people detect grass and trees. During the Second World War, McKelway accused Admiral Nimitz, the supreme commander in the South Pacific, of high treason and claimed that he had the documents to prove it. Painful as this episode may have proved in real life, it eventually became, like* The Edinburgh Caper, *a funny piece in the magazine.*

Yorker. For that matter, it was characteristic of him, he said, to have laid down three conditions on which he would take the job, and it was equally characteristic of him that he should be giving a three-part explanation of the third of those conditions. Ross had a strong dislike for abstract speculations, especially if they threatened to take a mystical or, still worse, a whimsical turn. He held up his hand to interrupt McKelway. "I don't want to hear about it," he said.

In the course of his three years as managing editor of fact, McKelway trained a couple of gifted assistants — Sanderson Vanderbilt and William Shawn. It was always a nuisance to the former to have to explain to new acquaintances that his very grand-sounding name didn't mean that he was one of the *rich* Vanderbilts; he was simply a Vanderbilt and had to live by his wits like anyone else. A small, puckish-looking man with round, heavy-lidded eyes, always with dark circles under them, and with fingers and teeth stained a deep yellow by nicotine, he had an engaging yuk-yuk of a laugh, and as he told stories he would swing back and forth in his swivel chair, rather like a child riding a hobby-horse. City-bred and childless, he and his wife, Tinka, eventually decided to take a chance on country living; they bought a place in the woods in Palisades, New Jersey, where Sandy learned to cut grass and rake leaves — activities that filled him with awe. He had not supposed that he would ever be able to master such unlikely skills. The beauty of trees and fields and summer skies came as a shock to him; he had apparently assumed that nothing in nature could be more ravishing to the eye than West Forty-third Street. He had come to *The New Yorker* from the *Herald Tribune,* bent upon writing; he was content to be deflected into editing, at which he proved to be very good indeed. Like so many of the *New Yorker* group, he smoked and drank more than was good for him and grew prematurely infirm; he died in 1967, at the age of fifty-seven. A lifetime of hard and able work lay concealed in many hundreds of pieces signed by others. It was like Sandy to prefer practicing his skills in inky anonymity; it was also like him that he wished no services of any kind to mark his death. It was as if he had simply gone away, on some errand too trifling to call our attention to.

McKelway's other assistant, Shawn, had joined the staff of the magazine in 1932. He and his wife, Cecille, then in their middle twenties, had come East from Chicago a few years before. Shawn was earning an uncertain living as a composer of music for small ballet companies and other theatrical groups. Admiring *The New Yorker* and hoping to increase his income, he applied for a job and was invited to become something called a free-lance "Talk" reporter. In journalism, "free-lance" is almost always a synonym for "free to starve," and the *New Yorker*'s "Talk" arrangements, arrived at hit-or-miss like so many of its arrangements in those days, proved unfortunate for Shawn. With characteristic conscientiousness, he would often spend two or three weeks reporting a single piece. If his notes were successfully rewritten, Shawn would be paid at the rate of two dollars an inch for the finished story; with luck, he might receive a check for as much as thirty dollars. Sometimes, however, the piece would be killed before publication, for reasons that had nothing to do with Shawn, and then he would be paid nothing. Still worse, there were occasions when Shawn was *too* conscientious; the rewrite man would be so intimidated by the thick sheaf of notes that Shawn handed in that he would never get around to doing the piece at all.

In the course of his perilous free-lancing, Shawn carried out a good deal of research for Alva Johnston, who was the most widely admired reporter on *The New Yorker* in the thirties and forties. Johnston praised Shawn's work to McKelway and Ross. It was plain to both of them that he was a marvel of orderly thoroughness and an excellent source of ideas for "Talk." It was less plain at the beginning that he would prove a marvel in several other respects as well. Shawn was elusive and reticent to a degree that made Gibbs seem by comparison something of a glad-hander, and McKelway feared that he would not be able to deal readily with people; it turned out over the years that this was what Shawn was able to do better than anyone else on the magazine.

At the time that McKelway was stepping down and I was stepping out, Shawn was stepping up, into the position originated by McKelway. For the first time he was testing his abilities on a level worthy of them. Before, he had been known to most members of the staff as a rather shadowy figure, occupying an office at Ross's end of the nineteenth floor. He had been identified to me as the magazine's "idea" man, who pored over newspapers and magazines and found in them possibilities for "Talk" stories, Profiles, and other long pieces. He was said to be brilliant at this task, which was certainly well suited to his temperament. Seated at a desk heaped with newspapers and armed with scissors for cutting out likely items and a typewriter for working the items up into "Talk" suggestion form, he was as safe from the real and imaginary perils of the outside world as a monk in a cell.

For Shawn this protective immurement was important. He was fascinated by the daily rough-and-tumble of street life in New York, but he had no capacity to become a part of it. He would watch and listen and read and keep at the greatest possible distance from the bruising, hearty, mindless collision of people on sidewalks and in buses, trolleys, and subways. When he said to Roseanne Smith, "Go out and mill," he was well aware that he would never experience milling for himself. Many staff members and contributors, both writers and artists, were victims of ineradicable, unreasonable fears, but only Alan Dunn, one of the ablest of our artists, could be said to equal Shawn in the number and variety of phobias — acrophobia, agoraphobia, claustrophobia, and pyrophobia — through which, by dint of courage and discipline, they gallantly found their way.

Given such handicaps, it is extraordinary that Shawn should have chosen journalism for a career. The record shows that he chose it early and that, except for his brief career as a composer, given up not only for financial reasons but also for the stern reason that the kind of music he wrote no longer seemed pleasing to him, he has had no other. One has only to glance at his teasingly brief entry in *Who's Who*, unchanged for twenty years:

SHAWN, WILLIAM, editor; b. Chicago, Ill., Aug. 31, 1907; s. Benjamin W. and Anna Bransky Chon; student U. Mich., 1925–27; m. Cecille Lyon, Sept. 1, 1928; children — Wallace, Allen, Mary. Reporter Las Vegas (N.M.) Optic, 1928; midwest editor Internat. Illustrated News, Chicago, 1929; reporter, The New Yorker, 1933–35, associate editor, 1935–39, mng. editor, 1939–52, editor since 1952. N.Y. office: 25 W. 43rd St. New York City, N.Y.

What could be less likely than Shawn as a reporter on a paper called the *Daily Optic*? Las Vegas isn't, you will note, the wretched scrub town in Nevada that was later to become the grand weirdo nightclub-and-gambling hell but the little health resort of the same name, high in the Sangre de Cristo Mountains of New Mexico, east of Santa Fe. Since he has always looked much younger than his age, Shawn at twenty, with his bright-blue eyes, fair skin, and small, slender body, could surely have passed for fifteen. I recall his telling me long ago that his family in Chicago had dispatched him at eighteen to Wyoming because he was thought to be in need of building up and perhaps toughening up as well. He chose Las Vegas on his own, as a twenty-year-old college undergraduate trying to choose between writing and music as a career. I haven't the slightest idea how he dressed in that period, or what his duties on the *Optic* may have been, and I don't wish to know; I choose to picture him in chaps and sombrero, on horseback, with a gun on each hip and a lariat looped on the pommel. In my imagination, I set him galloping hell-for-leather through some steep mountain pass in pursuit of an exclusive interview with who knows what trigger-happy, blood-drenched desperado. Says Shawn gently, "It was not like that."

There are several other substantial clues to Shawn to be found in that empty-seeming inch of *Who's Who* — the bold change in the spelling of the family name ("I made the mistake of thinking I might become a writer, and I wanted to be taken for an American and not a Chinese"), the different but perhaps equally bold assertion of self-determination implied by his getting married the day after his twenty-first birthday — but what he mostly reveals is how little he wishes to reveal. People who admire Shawn say of him that he has a passion for privacy; less admiring people might call it a passion for secrecy. Certainly if Sandy Vanderbilt welcomed anonymity, Shawn pursued and embraced it, and with an ardor that has had unlooked-for consequences; he has become famous by eschewing fame and is today one of the best-known unknown men in the country. Still, his privacy remains important to him, and if it were possible to write a book about my experiences on *The New Yorker* and omit any reference to the most important person connected with it, I would certainly be tempted for his sake to do so. But even Shawn, with his superlative editorial skills, would be incapable of such a feat of elision, and so I have settled for the next-best thing: to base my sketch of him not on the abundant assortment of hard facts that he would require of me if I were preparing a Profile for *The New Yorker*, but on the random recollections of a long and close friendship. For that reason, it goes almost without saying that *New Yorker* writers who have known

Shawn as long, or longer, than I have — among them Eugene Kinkead, E. J. Kahn, and Bruce Bliven, Jr. — would be apt to offer likenesses of him at considerable variance from mine.

A second warning to readers: in Shawn's case, more even than in Ross's, the oral tradition of the magazine is something that members of the staff tend to fall back upon as if it were gospel, and it isn't; or not necessarily. For example, it is gospel that when Shawn first came to the magazine he was sent out as a "Talk" reporter to cover the workings of a cooperage somewhere across the river in New Jersey. The assignment was a nightmare to him, because it meant taking the Hudson Tubes over and back, and Shawn cannot bear to find himself trapped underground, much less underground *under a river*, with millions of gallons of water sloshing turbulently about above his head. Gospel says that he wrote the story with his usual skill and turned it in, but that he never went out on an assignment again. Now, all this is perfectly plausible: Ross would have liked nothing better in "Talk" than an account of how barrels are made, and nobody would have done the story better than Shawn. Except that no such story was ever printed. Is gospel then in error? Not in this case. Shawn spent three weeks going from borough to borough and over to New Jersey to learn every last thing about barrel-making, and his crisscross travels were indeed a nightmare to him. All in vain. He supposes now that this was one of the times he wrote too much and frightened the rewrite man — Thurber? Maloney? — into silence.

Similarly, oral tradition holds that in one of the most celebrated murder cases of the century — the Loeb–Leopold case, in Chicago, in which two rich young men chose to murder in cold blood a boy named Bobby Frank — the murderers had drawn up a list of alternative victims, one of whom was blue-eyed little Billy Chon. Alas for tradition, not so, or according to Shawn not so; he was already too old for Loeb's and Leopold's purposes.

As for the tradition that he and Cecille went abroad on their honeymoon and that Shawn got a job as a pianist playing jazz in a nightclub in Paris ... well, something like that. And what of the story that he grew a mustache at that time, in order to look twenty-one and not fifteen? Well, yes, something like that, too; for it is mercifully the case that not all the stories that we wish to be true are false.

In his over forty years on the staff, Shawn has published only one signed piece in *The New Yorker*. It is characteristic of him that this piece was signed only with his initials — initials that he shares with the greatest writer in English who has ever lived, and that make a very striking appearance on the page. The story came out in 1936, when its author was still in his twenties. Even by the standards of extreme brevity followed in those days, it was fairly short, being less than a page in length; the rest of the page was occupied by a Thurber drawing exceptional for being not very funny. The story is called "The Catastrophe," and it concerns the total obliteration of the city of New York by a gigantic meteor. It is an exceptionally well-written piece, with, here and there, a wit worthy of Benchley or Parker ("Franchot Tone, who had come to be accepted as the typical extinct New Yorker") and a suavity of tone wonderfully at odds with its subject matter.

"The Catastrophe" would be well worth reprinting in full today, but the odd fact of the matter is that Shawn dislikes it intensely. "Though I was proud to have something in the magazine, I was uneasy about the piece from the moment I wrote it," he says. "It wasn't me. At least, it wasn't the me I thought I was, and think I am. Everyone on the magazine encouraged me to go on writing other, similar pieces, and I never did."

Shawn was writing of a natural catastrophe, and in less than a decade man-made catastrophes of an equal horror if not on an equal scale were to befall Dresden, Hiroshima, and Nagasaki. It is plain that Shawn has always possessed what Henry James calls the imagination of disaster, and among the fruits of this imagination have been the superb reporting, in hundreds of pieces by correspondents on a dozen fronts, of the Second World War; the decision to let John Hersey's account of obliterated Hiroshima be published in its entirety in a single issue of the magazine; the reporting of the war in Vietnam, which many of our readers were eager to have us forget; and the relentless scrutiny, especially in Notes and Comment, of the immorality not only of the war in Vietnam but also of Watergate and its innumerable sequels. At times, one heard grumblings, in the corridors of the magazine and out in the world, that Shawn was a masochist, who took pleasure in wailing and beating his breast in exaggerated trepidation over the debased conduct of our national and international affairs, but as the facts slowly emerged, both in Southeast Asia and in Washington, Shawn's persistence was seen to be justified. Better than any other editor of our time, he has been able to measure the distance of our national fall from grace; better than any other, he measures today the difficulty of regaining that grace.

Long ago, Shawn's close friend S. N. Behrman wrote a play entitled *No Time for Comedy*. For more than twenty years, it has been Shawn's fate to edit a humorous magazine that, holding up a mirror to life, everywhere reflects the darkest shadows and yet manages to make us laugh. And this without supposing, with Scaramouche, that the world is mad. For Shawn supposes something much riskier and more difficult to credit: that the world is sane and well worth working in and fighting for.

16

Having succeeded McKelway as managing editor, Shawn's first official act in that summer of 1939 was to accept my resignation. Long afterward, he told me that the occasion had astonished him. I simply came into his office and blurted out that I was quitting. Because he was new to the job, he assumed that such abrupt and inexplicable departures were a commonplace; with a show of calm and with his usual good manners, he assured me that though I was sure to be missed, I must do whatever I thought best. The scene was a brief one. I see him now, smiling and ducking his head, his dark, slightly curly hair combed sidelong over an increasing bald spot. He had large, notably well-kept hands, which he rested in his lap in a gesture common among pianists. I thought how different Shawn's hands were from Ross's, the fingers of which were smudged yellow and black from nicotine, pencil-lead, and typewriter ink. Ross's nails were often grossly rimmed with dirt, and their condition was not improved by his habit of running them continuously through the thick mat of his hair. From time to time, when his horn-colored nails grew uncomfortably long, Ross would borrow a nail-clipper from one of his male secretaries and set to work *snip-snip*; he never troubled to keep a nail-clipper of his own.

I said, "We're taking a holiday in Ireland."

Shawn must have thought us foolish as well as callous: already the liners returning from Europe were filled with people eager to escape the threatened war. We were obviously crossing the Atlantic the wrong way. "Have a pleasant trip," he said, his blue eyes wide with alarm.

Despite the political situation in Europe, the trip to Ireland did indeed prove a pleasant one. Landing at Cobh, we hired a big Buick and with it a driver named Bill Sharkey, a saturnine distillation of half a century of drink. Though we never saw him with a glass in hand, he reeked all day of Guinness stout — more at night, of course, than in the morning, but even in the morning the first gust of him at curbside would strike us like a blow in the face. My father, a lifelong teetotaler, occupied the seat beside Bill and, especially when the weather was rainy and the windows of the car had to be kept closed, would breathe in enough of Bill's alcoholic fumes during the course of a day's run to be somewhat tipsy by nightfall. We made a leisurely tour of the stony, empty West Country, found sprawled in a ditch in Leitrim a single Gill with whom we could claim cousinage, and survived a midnight fire in a farmhouse inn in Sligo (Bill, well liquored, leapt in his nightshirt out of an attic window onto a blazing thatched roof, slid on his backside through the flames, and landed safely in the barnyard, knee-deep in a pile of manure, with his nightshirt up to his armpits and his hands chastely covering his privates).

In Dublin, I was granted the supposed great privilege of an interview with De Valera, who at the time was not only Prime Minister of the Irish Republic but President of the League of Nations as well. The League had been working feverishly to prevent an outbreak of war, and it was widely assumed that the best-informed man in Europe on the war question was De Valera. During the course of our interview, De Valera assured me that there would be no war.

We sailed for home in the last days of August, on an American liner, the *Washington*, crowded with tourists who evidently took a darker view of the future than De Valera did. The celebrated actor Edward G. Robinson was aboard. He had been visiting in France, and as a Jew, had become alarmed at the prospect of Hitler's launching a blitzkrieg against France, in the course of which all Jews might be rounded up and executed. Finding at Le Havre that the ship was fully booked, Robinson purchased the purser's own cabin, at no telling what egregious price, for himself and his family. Mrs. Sara Delano Roosevelt was also on board, serenely confident that her boy Franklin would be able to solve all problems; she was much pleased when my father addressed her as "Your Majesty."

On landing in New York, I was interviewed by a reporter from the Hartford *Courant* — after all, I was fresh from abroad and might be counted on to have the latest news. At my father's house in Hartford, on the morning of September third, I read the banner headlines running across the top of the first page of the paper, in which it was announced that Hitler had invaded Poland and that England would come to the aid of France: the Second World War was under way. At the foot of the last page of that same issue of the *Courant* was a small item. Understandably, it caught my eye, for the heading of it read "WILL BE NO WAR SAYS BRENDAN GILL."

For the next year or so, I devoted myself to writing short stories. *The New Yorker* published the best of them — "The Knife," "Truth and Consequences," and the like — for though I was no longer a member of the staff, I remained on friendly terms with Mrs. White and Maxwell. I was also enjoying a certain success among the more commercial, mass-circulation magazines, such as the *Saturday Evening Post, Collier's, Liberty,* and *Good Housekeeping.* (Hard for young writers nowadays to realize how many magazines were vying for short stories in the thirties and forties; hard, too, to believe how much they paid!) The *Saturday Evening Post* was then still in its glory, and to have one's stories published in the magazine that had published Fitzgerald and Lardner and was currently publishing Faulkner, Marquand, and Thomas Beer was considered no small thing. I began to sell my stories to the *Post,* and for a while its editors hoped that perhaps I would prove a second Fitzgerald. That hope lasted but a little while, because the *Post* liked longish stories, with elaborate plots, and it turned out that I wasn't especially interested in making up plots.

My agent, Carl Brandt, who represented half a dozen successful *Post* writers, was full of ingenious dodges by which to make stories salable. He had been practicing literary carpentry of this sort for a lifetime, and he may not have noticed how shocked my aesthetic sensibilities were by the drumfire of gross, helpful suggestions he would lay down in respect to a story that didn't, as he would say, work. Smiling and intent, punctuating his sentences with a series of grunted "m-m-m?" 's, he would say, "Why don't you bring in a little dog just here, m-m-m?, who then gets run over by a car?" Or, "Why not have the boy start hitchhiking out West, m-m-m?, and then turn back, m-m-m?, because he hears his father's sick?" To cobble up the stories in that cold-blooded fashion wasn't an impossible task; it was simply tiresome, because it had so little to do with what I thought of as the sacred act of writing.

Still, I wanted to please Carl and I liked being paid so much more for my *Post* stories than I was for my *New Yorker* ones; for a time, I consented to be bored. Following a schedule that a writer twice as old as I and ten times as famous as I would have found reason to envy, I wrote for a week, loafed for a week, wrote for a week, loafed for a week. It was a period of never-to-be-repeated laziness, and looking back, I don't see how I was able to stand it. My nature is such that idleness has always made me nervous; today, it all but unhinges me. Lying on a beach in the sun, I begin to tremble with unease at my good fortune; if nothing else will serve, I get up and start scooping out and heaping up the biggest sand-castle on earth — an intricately moated and be-towered Mont St. Michel, to be drowned in an hour's time by the incoming tide. Or I leap to my feet and start running at top speed along the beach, singing as I run — a middle-aged man who has plainly outlived his wits, and the sooner somebody locks him up the better.

Having given up our apartment in New York, we had rented a shabby old house in Norfolk, Connecticut, where my wife's family, the Barnards, had long had their summer place. Norfolk is a small village in the Berkshires, high and remote and very cold in winter, and its population in the thirties was less than it had been in the eighteenth century, when its abundant water power had made it a thriving industrial community. The Barnards had suffered severe financial losses in the Depression and had moved to Asheville, North Carolina, to live; their little shingled cottage, known to everyone in town simply as the Bungalow, had remained vacant for several years, and they were delighted to turn it over to us.

The Bungalow had been built as a sort of honeymoon cottage for Anne's parents by her paternal grandmother, who owned a considerable amount of property on the edge of town; because the Bungalow was small and cheaply made and therefore out of keeping with its grand neighbors, the senior Mrs. Barnard had arranged for it to be put up in an open field well back from the road and at the farthest possible distance from the main house on the property. The architect had sketched the floor plan on the back of a scorecard while playing golf one Sunday morning with Anne's father; it is fair to say that the Bungalow looked as if something like that had been the occasion of its design. It had open plumbing openly arrived at, and its best feature was a great stone chimney rising through the center of the structure. Our intention in 1939 was to turn it into an all-the-year-round house (the ugly word "winterize" had yet to be invented); meanwhile, the shabby house in the village would prove a convenient base for us. We were expecting a second child in April, and it struck us that it would be good magic to bring a new baby home to what would amount to a new house.

We went South to spend the Christmas holidays with the Barnards, and there I did something inexcusable and, after all these years, largely inexplicable. I sent Ross a wooden skunk for Christmas. This curious deed came about as if it were the most natural thing in the world. We were visiting a roadside shop that specialized in the remarkable carvings made by local mountaineers — sheep, cows, pigs, cocks, and the like, whittled out of cherry, maple, holly, and apple wood. These carved creatures provided the only cash income that many of the mountaineers were able to earn, and we made it a point to buy all our Christmas presents at that shop. The moment I saw among the animals a smooth little shapely skunk, I decided to send it off to Ross. I don't recall any feeling of bitterness toward him — it was just a prank that I felt compelled to perform.

In a few days, Ross wrote me to ask, with no trace of indignation, what on earth the skunk was meant to signify. It was then that I tried for the first time to examine the sources of that unfriendly gift. I said in reply that I blamed Ross for the fact that during my stay on *The New Yorker* nobody had appeared to appreciate me enough: I had missed the love and admiration that, rightly or wrongly, I had been accustomed to from childhood. Now, "love" and "admiration" were words that Ross was exceptionally unready to use; nevertheless, he sat down at his typewriter and hammered out a three-page letter, saying that as far as he was able to judge the matter, he and his colleagues *had* manifested love and admiration for me, and he was sorry if I hadn't noticed.

This was a brave letter for a man like Ross to write and it disarmed me. I felt ashamed of having behaved so childishly; the difficulty was that I had not changed in my childish needs and that Ross had neither the time nor the interest to satisfy them. Though I didn't know it at the time, he had enough to do playing father-uncle-brother-guardian-nursemaid-confessor to Thurber, White, Benson, Gibbs, Benchley, Arno, Woollcott, Perelman, Parker, and the rest of the older generation of *New Yorker* writers. Many years later, I heard him say, "What I'm running here is a goddam bughouse. Not a man in the place without a screw loose. Look at ——, who thinks his balls are swelling, and ——, who thinks his ass-hole is closing. Jesus Christ, aren't there enough real troubles in the world without brooding about crap like that?"

"Brooding" was one of Ross's favorite words. He used it to describe, and simultaneously dismiss, any topic that he didn't care to deal with. Whenever, down the years, I would protest against the miserable wages my fellow-writers and I were being paid, Ross would jingle the coins in his pocket and say, "Stop brooding, Gill!" Once, to his satisfaction, he made a play on the word that left me speechless. In the course of one of my usual vain financial harangues, I pointed out that my family required six quarts of milk a day, seven days a week, four weeks a month, twelve months a year, and that the total amount came to something over two thousand quarts a year, which at a cost of (in those days) some eighteen cents a quart, meant an expenditure of three hundred and sixty dollars. "Stop breeding, Gill!" Ross said, with a pleased grin, and slouched off down the hall. Harsh enough, but not as harsh as I momentarily feared; for at first I thought he had said, "Stop breathing."

By 1942, I was back on the staff of the magazine. I had learned by experience what I had known at first by intuition: that it was the only place I wanted to be. I felt, moreover, a welcome sense of being needed. The war was raging adversely in Europe and in the Pacific, and many of the unmarried and married-but-childless members of the staff had been drafted. Ross was convinced that the government was single-mindedly bent upon putting him and his magazine out of business. Obviously, there was plenty of reporting to be done for *The New Yorker* on the so-called home front. When it came my turn to be drafted, the understanding was that the Air Force would put in a bid for me and, after basic training, I would be assigned to the Office of Flying Safety in Winston-Salem, where I would be set to work writing flight manuals with John Cheever, Max Shulman, and other friends of mine. (The most distinguished member of the group was James Gould Cozzens, who was later to put the knowledge he acquired in the Air

Force to good use in what is probably the best of his novels, *Guard of Honor*.)

Waiting to be called up, I was content to do innumerable "Talk" pieces about wartime New York and many long, serious pieces about, among other topics, a machine-tool factory, a ration board, the O.P.A., the Navy submarine base at Groton, a home for convalescent seamen at Oyster Bay, a Marine fighter pilot, an Air Force bomber pilot, a captain whose freighter had been sunk under him in the North Atlantic, and a colony of British children living as evacuees in the patrician backwater of Tuxedo Park. There were many stories that I took notes on and, for one sorry reason or another, never got around to writing: a story about a school for newly blinded soldiers; another about a cross-country flight that I made with a squadron of young Javanese fliers, reckless and cheerful, many of whom were soon to die; a third about an Air Force major, a doctor in civilian life, who experimented with free falls from a very great height in order to discover whether one necessarily lost consciousness in the course of them, and who one day plummeted, his parachute unopened, into a potato field in Illinois.

For a time, I served as an editor as well as a writer, but the experiment proved uncongenial to my vanity. Especially during the war years, we had writers so inept that one had to rewrite them almost word for word, and when, at a cocktail or dinner party, I would hear a writer praised for a Profile that was, in fact, almost entirely my handiwork, I would grind my teeth with ill-concealed rage. In the many years that I did "Talk" rewrite, it never troubled me that my words were equally anonymous; the magazine was getting the credit, and that was as it should be. Still, to be an editor is to be an invisible, unheralded Pygmalion; it is not in my style to fashion Galateas who are assumed to have fashioned themselves.

Luckily for those of us who wish to be known as writers, there are people — Shawn and Maxwell among them — who are content to perform feats of editorial sleight-of-hand behind the scenes and who, should it occur to a writer to thank them, would pretend that their ingenious "save's" were but the usual tidying up of grammatical loose ends. If I am a writer today, it is because my betters tugged and teased and bullied and seduced me into learning a craft, when all I had to begin with, like so many hundreds of others, was a talent. So I did learn; I go on learning. To the

William Maxwell. Once, in the midst of a lecture at Smith College on "The Writer as Illusionist," Maxwell said in his gentle voice — indeed, in what amounted to a whisper — "It would help if you would give what I am now about to read to you only half your attention." It was surely the first time that anyone had proposed such a thing to the hundreds of girls who made up his audience; they leaned forward in their seats, listening intently to every word. Afterward, they would never forget what he had said. Maxwell's stories are like that, and so are the means by which he makes other writers' stories more nearly their own than they know how to make them.

extent that it is possible to measure such things, perhaps half the quality of the better of my early stories, like "The Knife," is thanks to what Maxwell managed to find in them and make of them. The proportion of credit owed to Maxwell may have diminished with the years, but it is never not there, and to an extent that the world at large might find it hard to believe. Sometimes his secret labors have unexpected consequences. A couple of years ago, I was working on a short story that Maxwell liked but regarded as imperfect. He kept urging me to tell more about the characters in order to make clearer the theme of the story, and so I wrote on and on, adding episode upon episode, until the story ended up as a novella of something over twenty thousand words. To my astonishment, at that moment Maxwell, with a sad shake of his head, said, "Oh, dear, I think I liked it better the way it was at first," and coolly rejected it for the magazine. Though I rarely disagree with Maxwell, on that occasion I did; all the more so because what I liked best in it was precisely what Maxwell had spurred me into putting there. The novella is called "The Malcontents," and it was published last year in a book of my collected fiction called *Ways of Loving.* It is at once, in my eyes, a success, and, in Maxwell's eyes, a failure. We do not talk about it.

Beginning writers are usually under the impression that once one has arrived at a certain eminence, failure is rare, if not unknown. It is hard for them to believe that the big bow-wow writers whose names have been commonly associated with *The New Yorker* over the years have had to suffer continuously throughout their careers the same humiliation of rejection as the stranger mailing in his manuscripts from Ultima Thule. Oh, it is possible to have as many as four or five stories accepted without a rebuff, but if one keeps on writing long enough, that lovely string of successes is sure to be broken! Robert M. Coates sold over a hundred short stories to the magazine, but you can be sure that there were many stories returned to him along the way. Besides the thirty-odd stories of mine that the magazine has published, there stand in silent contrast the equal number that have been deemed unworthy of publication. And the painfulness of being rejected never grows less. In our hearts, we are all six years old, and when Maxwell or Shawn is obliged to hand back to me a manuscript on which my hopes have centered for weeks or perhaps months, they know I will smile and try to get past the dreadful moment with some unconvincing pleasantry; they also know that if they don't turn and hurry away from my office, they may catch sight of that inextinguishable six-year-old staring woebegonely out at them from the face of a middle-aged man.

In my experience, the risk of failure in writing fiction is far greater than the risk of failure in writing all the different sorts of pieces that we lump together under the word "fact." Every short story is a fresh assault upon unmapped and probably dangerous country; except for an awareness of the audacity of the undertaking, little that one has learned from previous marches into other sections of that country is likely to prove of value. One is always a novice, proceeding by intuition and rightly fearing the worst. The goal that seemed attainable on setting out unaccountably recedes, changes position, is veiled by storms, threatens to vanish altogether; one is tempted to settle for a goal closer to hand — a green meadow to lie down in, rather than an icy rock-face to scale.

If one is able at last to finish a story, it is never the story that one began. The reader may be well satisfied; best that he never learn how different a story it is from the one it was intended to be. Have you James's *The Middle Years* to read for the first time? How lucky you are! But it may be that the author of it was striving to give you *The Death of Ivan Ilyich.* I can scarcely bear to look at the two or three stories of mine that have gained a tiny immortality by being repeatedly anthologized; a glimpse of their opening lines brings back the hours devoted to the writing of the stories, and I recall the disparity between the high hopes with which I began them and the gloom with which I brought them to a close. The difficulty of finding a sympathetic general theme (the ignominy of childhood, the humiliations of old age), then of finding a subject that will embody the theme, and then of finding characters who will embody the subject; finally, the difficulty of inventing actions appropriate to the characters and capable of making the theme, the subject, and the characters all fuse into one and be simultaneously fulfilled in a climax that has a certain interest of its own — given the size of the feat to be performed, is it any wonder that, more often than not, one gets lost along the way? And that one's only consolation lies in Eliot's admonitory words, set down after he had spent a lifetime seeking to outwit what he called "the general mess of imprecision of feeling." Sadly, bravely, Eliot wrote, "For us, there is only the trying. The rest is not our business."

Now, in the writing of fact the seasoned writer nearly always knows at the outset what his chances are. The terrain lies open before him; he can see precisely where he is and where he means to go. No general theme need be sought; a subject suffices, and it is possible to measure with accuracy the degree of interest that a given subject will arouse in a reader by dint of its importance and timeliness. Whatever this subject may be, the characters are already there, embodying it; they exist, they are there to be used, and they cannot fail one, because they are certain to act according to their natures. One has only to remain steadfast to one's purpose and to tamper as little as possible with the weight of the facts as one rummages about in the higgledy-piggledy overabundance of real life; work, work, and the thing is done. Should the story threaten at some point to prove intractable, the wise writer is quick to give it up; the world will assume, and in most cases correctly, that it is the subject that has failed and not the person reporting on it, and the writer can proceed to the next task with no loss of self-respect and with scarcely diminished self-confidence.

The so-called triumph of fact over fiction, much commented on in the past couple of decades and given added attention by Truman Capote's amusing, absurd claim to have invented something called the "non-fiction" novel ("Teach my grandmother," Robert Frost would have told Capote, "how to suck eggs"), is a result of the difference in risks posed for the writer of fiction and the writer of fact. Most people assume that fact has become supreme in our culture because real life today is full of wonders that fiction cannot hope to equal, much less surpass, but what a vulgar misrepresentation of the nature of writing this is! For one thing, the number of objects and events that are considered to be wonders hardly varies from one century to the next: aerial observers took part in battles fought in the eighteenth century, in the nineteenth century Tolstoi and Chekhov chatted briskly over the long-distance telephone, and surely rocketing men to the moon is no more wonderful than the hundred-year-old stunt of sending the words "I love you" a thousand miles through thin air. (In 1974, astronauts spent eighty-four days in space, and few people noticed; wonders capable of being repeated dwindle into commonplaces.)

For another thing, none of the subjects that we now deal with in factual terms were less important to readers in our grandfathers' day; they only seemed to them to be less important than the subjects then being dealt with in stories, poems, novels, and plays. It is obvious that something other than the marvellousness of the real has caused the real to become popular, and I think it may be a matter of the uses to which we are tempted to put our emotions nowadays, both as writers and readers. The writing and reading of fiction require strong convictions as well as strong emotions, and this is a time when we find it easier to respond to the social, political, and economic problems besetting man than to lofty speculations about his nature. The great abstractions — God, ourselves as an act of special creation, the hereafter — upon which, however indirectly, the fiction of the past was based, have become irrelevant for most of us and, for some of us, simply do not exist. In the lonely work of writing fiction, we have nothing to fall back on but self-awareness; understandably, we turn from that dark cave, peopled by who knows what attendant horrors, to enter the busily humming, brightly lighted world of concrete and specific facts, where at every turn we are sure to encounter some situation capable of being measured and described ("Nothing is indescribable, Gill!") and therefore suited to our needs and accommodatable to our craft. "The odds are on objects," Maxwell said; he might have added, "And on facts."

17

Ross's success as an editor had certain elements of the fortuitous about it; for example, it was a lucky accident that his unappeasable appetite for facts coincided with a similar appetite on the part of the public. During the Second World War, the volume of information dispensed by what were beginning to be called the media — newspapers, magazines, books, movies, and, a few years later, TV — multiplied to an extent that nobody has been able so far to make an accurate reckoning of. It was a change so great that even the remotest illiterate hermit could not fail to be altered by it; for the first time, with astonishment and sometimes with dismay, one sensed that a Niagara of news was flooding unstoppably in upon us, not by the week and day but by the hour and minute. People sat by their radios and listened with satisfaction to news bulletins, infinitesimally rewritten as they were repeated, about victories and defeats throughout the world, and then went out and bought newspapers and magazines and gorged themselves on the same information for a tenth or twentieth time.

The Second World War was the most thoroughly reported event in history; it implicated hundreds of millions of people in both hemispheres, and the services of literally millions of reporters, editors, broadcasters, cameramen, printers, and distributors were required to keep abreast of it. The news magazines flourished as never before, and so did *The New Yorker*. Far from destroying the magazine, as Ross had noisily predicted, the war helped bring about its transformation into something far more complex and interesting than it had ever been. The transformation was bound to have taken place — impossible to imagine Shawn, intellectually so much more ambitious than Ross, remaining content with the magazine as he had first known it — but the war hastened the event. From a publication deliberately parochial in range and tone, consisting of a few funny drawings, some funny short pieces, an occasional serious short story, and the Profiles, limited enough in both length and intentions to deserve to be called profiles, it became a publication in which it was natural to look for the highest quality of reporting in almost any field of activity, from almost anywhere on earth.

Ross protested continually that he didn't want to see his magazine turned into a goddam *Saturday Evening Post;* as if to spite him (and Ross was a man who had no difficulty discovering in success signs of a conspiracy bent upon destroying him), the magazine expanded into a national institution and then an international one. Even its suspicious founder was impressed to learn during the war that it was being read, and thought highly of, at Number 10 Downing Street; he could scarcely object to having Churchill among his readers, and, for that matter, the King as well. Washington came to see that the magazine, far from being a luxury for wealthy civilians, was an indispensable part of the war effort; a small-size, twenty-four-page "pony" edition, printed by photo-offset and containing no advertising, was made available to the armed forces, as *Time* and *Newsweek* were. By the end of the war, the pony edition had a larger circulation than its parent. By then, too, our readers were accustomed to datelines more exotic than the two old foreign standbys, London and Paris. From the beginning, the magazine's notion of its geographical boundaries had implicitly embraced these cities, as places that New Yorkers frequented and felt happy in. With the passing of years, reluctantly, room was found inside our boundaries for Washington, a city that kept gaining in importance without ever acquiring a style. Until recently, no New Yorker would think of simply visiting Washington; one went there because one had some substantial professional reason for doing so and not otherwise.

The war broadened our physical horizons; it also taught us as writers how to be harder on ourselves, and so broadened our literary horizons. The extent of our newly acquired excellence can be sampled in *The New Yorker Book of War Pieces,* which came out in 1949 and which many critics and historians have called the finest collection of war-reporting ever published in a single volume. Among the contributors were A. J. Liebling, Mollie Panter-Downes, E. J. Kahn, Jr., Rebecca West, St. Clair McKelway, Janet Flanner, Mark Murphy, Walter Bernstein, John Hersey, Daniel Lang, S. N. Behrman, Philip Hamburger, and Joel Sayre.

Ross's sneering reference to the *Saturday Evening Post*, often repeated, deserves a gloss. In Ross's day, the *Post* was considered the best general magazine in the country, and that alone was reason enough for Ross to dislike it; as an editor, he had revolutionary aspirations and the *Post* was the leading champion of the journalistic conventions that he despised, or affected to despise. As was usually the case with Ross, certain childish personal emotions were also involved. In his youth, he had tried to write for the *Post* and had failed. The failure was all the more humiliating to him because the *Post* was his mother's favorite magazine. Ida Martin Ross, having taught school in Kansas before her marriage to the Irish immigrant George Ross, had found her cultural pretensions hard to satisfy during the years in Aspen and, later, in Salt Lake City. She was chagrined that her only child should have been a total failure in school. She deplored his running away to become a footloose, roughneck newspaperman.

Even in middle age, Ross continued to feel uneasy at not having fulfilled his mother's high hopes for him. He had inherited from her side of the family his ugly gat-teeth and ramshackle body; plainly, what he had not inherited, or acquired, were his mother's notions of what it was to be refined and successful. When in his early thirties her seemingly uneducated son somehow managed to found a magazine in New York, Mrs. Ross was astonished and proud, but she considered the magazine itself a puny thing, full of jokes in doubtful taste — Peter Arno's bibulous Whoops Sisters were certainly a discredit to their sex — and slick, big-city flummery. *The New Yorker* never came to grips with the important, down-to-earth matters, the way the *Post* did. To her dying day, Mrs. Ross looked forward to the possibility that if Harold did well enough with his little novelty of a magazine in New York, he would be invited down to Philadelphia to join the staff of the august *Post*.

If Ross disliked the *Post* in part because his mother admired it, he may have disliked Philadelphia in part because it was the home of the *Post*. Indeed, in the old days the Curtis Publishing Company, which published the *Post* and the *Ladies' Home Journal*, seemed to outsiders very nearly synonymous with Philadelphia;

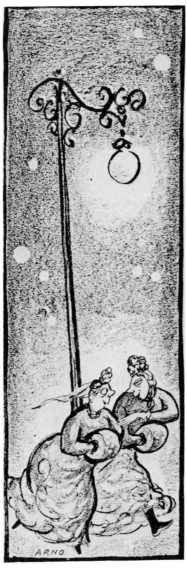

"Tripe? Oh, I'm mad about tripe!"
"Me too. I always say I'd do almost
anything fer a bit o' tripe."

A very early Arno, unlike him even to the
signature. Note the caption, which is not
only unfunny but also requires a dialogue
to be funny in. There were even a few
three- and four-line captions in those
early, floundering days.

the *Post's* editor, George Horace
Lorimer, now wholly forgotten,
was considered a peer of Penn
and Franklin. Whatever the reason, or reasons, for Ross's dislike
of Philadelphia, it was an understood thing that its name was
never to be mentioned in the
magazine except when it was
impossible to avoid it; ideally, it
was then to be treated with derision. I bumped headlong into
this peculiar dictum on an occasion when I wanted to do a
"Talk" story about a banker in
Philadelphia. To make matters
worse, the banker was black, and
that proved to be a violation of
still another of Ross's eccentric
convictions; for if there was anything that Ross disliked more
than Philadelphia, it was blacks.

I have mentioned that Ross
was a consummately nine-
teenth-century figure in the
number and variety of bigotries
that he espoused and didn't hesitate to preach, nearly always at
the top of his voice. With an
equanimity perfectly matched by
ignorance, he uttered nonsense
about blacks and Jews and Catholics and Orientals and Mexi-
cans and every other minority
group except his own, which was
Scotch-Irish-Presbyterian-turned-
freethinker: a small group and
one not subject to much perse-
cution. During the Second World
War — that is to say, during the
days of Hitler's Final Solution,
with millions of Jews dead or

dying in Europe — I remember hearing Ross say to Geoffrey Hellman, over lunch at the Algonquin, in a voice that carried to every corner of the Rose Room, "The trouble with you Jews, Hellman, is . . ." and off he went on some preposterous tirade, the burden of which appeared to be that if only Jews would listen more often to Ross, they would have fewer enemies to contend with.

It was at about this time that Ross became, for perhaps the one time in his life, a controversial public figure. He made a blunder classic in its completeness, revealing far more about himself than he intended. The blunder consisted of an attack upon the inhabitants of the Bronx, which was largely Jewish, and Harlem, which was largely black. According to an account in the *Times*, "Mr. Ross's aspersions on the Bronx and Harlem began six months ago in a letter to Governor Robert A. Hurley of Connecticut. In his letter, repeated last month, he submitted a warm complaint against a proposal for making a public park out of state property adjoining his eleven-acre estate near the junction of the Merritt Parkway and High Ridge Road, Stamford. Such a plan, he wrote, would invite Harlem and the Bronx 'up to Stamford to spend the day.'

" 'Stamford,' complained Mr. Ross, 'is on the verge of becoming the playground of the Borough of the Bronx and the dark, mysterious malodorous stretches of Harlem . . . I do not mean to be undemocratic, but you couldn't choose a more alarming bunch of people in the world.' " Ross went on to say that previous experience with Harlem and Bronx excursionists in his neighborhood had driven him into "panic, alarm, and sheer terror." They had turned his driveway into a lovers' lane and, when swimming in a nearby stream, had been given to "running around naked half the time."

Ross's letter to Governor Hurley drew an indignant response from the Borough President of the Bronx, James J. Lyons, who pointed out that a "more alarming" bunch of people could easily be chosen from among the enemy forces then fighting us on the Continent and that Ross, though taking on the airs of a grandee, was only the "so-called" editor of a "facetious" magazine. Lyons might also have pointed out that Ross, being a coward, was all too quickly given to panic, alarm, and sheer terror (however his beloved Fowler may have distinguished among these states), and that he was also a puritan, made uneasy by lovers' lanes and especially by naked bodies, whether observed running, swimming, or making love. Ross subsequently admitted that he had gone too far in wishing to keep the inhabitants of Harlem and the Bronx at a distance. With his filthy fingernails, coarse speech, and ineptitude at sports, Ross was scarcely the model of a country gentleman, but then, he was never one to linger long over the contradictions in his person and nature. Wasn't he, after all, the man who boasted that none of his writers could afford to drive a car, while he himself took care to drive a Cadillac?

Ross's primitive bigotries were a source of constant embarrassment to Shawn and some of us younger members of the staff; his older associates thought of them as merely ugly and past improving, like his posture, hair, and teeth. For a long time, it was a fact that no black was hired by the magazine, even to serve as a messenger or office boy. This was in accord with a principle that Ross enunciated in a concise and breath-takingly repellent form. "Coons," he would say, "are either funny or dangerous." What had been the source of that maxim? There had been few blacks in Salt Lake City, fewer still in Aspen. Some people held that it sprang from Ross's adventures as an itinerant young newspaperman in Panama. The story that Ross liked to spread about himself was to the effect that he had once bossed a gang of black laborers who were part of the immense work force engaged in digging the Panama Canal. It would certainly have been the case that such laborers would include the dregs of the employment market of the entire Western Hemisphere, whether black or white, and that many of these overworked and underpaid men would be likely, in their cups, to prove dangerous (though not likely, drunk or sober, to prove funny), but the chances are slight that Ross was ever in charge of such a gang. He may have watched the canal being dug, but he didn't assist in digging it. At the time, he was passing through a romantic Jack London–Richard Harding Davis period; as a war correspondent in the Spanish-American War and as an observer of revolutions in one or another of the banana republics of Central America, Davis was a hero to Ross. Probably Ross bummed his way down to Panama in hopeful emulation of Davis, looking for something to write about. "Funny or dangerous"? My guess is that this unsavory prejudice, like so many of Ross's prejudices, preceded his travels and, to a remarkable extent, preceded even his earliest recorded experiences.

Thurber, that malicious man, was a superlative mimic and a confirmed player of practical jokes. (In this respect, Thurber was almost as thoroughly a product of the nineteenth century and its reprehensible preoccupation with horseplay as Ross was. As far as I know, since Thurber's time no practical jokes have been played by anyone on the magazine. Were they to be played today, they would not be found amusing.) Thurber liked to torture Ross with pranks that took advantage of one or another of his failings. Once, knowing how Ross felt about having blacks around the office, Thurber put through a call to Ross in his ordinary voice — quick, high-pitched, nervous — and then, as soon as Ross had picked up the phone, began to address him in the wheedling tones of a ten-year-old Uncle Tom from the remotest backwater of Mississippi: "Mistah Ross, Ah jus' so *eager* to go to work for you! Ah ready to do any kinda writin' you ask this li'l old black boy to put his mind to." Ross attempted to interrupt, in vain: on and on went Thurber–Uncle Tom, explaining that he wanted to work on the magazine not only because he admired the quality of its editing but also because there was so much financial and other trouble in the family — his mother was sick with flu, his grandmother had shingles, and his great-grandmother had just fallen off her front porch and broken her thigh bone in two places. At last light dawned and, trembling with rage, Ross roared, "Now, god*dam* you, Thurber!" and banged down the phone.

So it befell that my desire to write about a black banker in Philadelphia presented certain difficulties for Shawn. Not for the world would he have suggested that I abandon the project; we were both eager to have a piece about a successful black man in the magazine and neither of us took seriously Ross's attempt to destroy Philadelphia by prohibiting the use of its name in *The New Yorker*. I went ahead and reported the story, Shawn O.K.'d it and put it in type, the checking department saw to it that all the facts in it were correct, and the galleys were put on the so-called "bank." Shawn waited until Ross went off on a fishing trip to

Aspen and then ran the piece in "Talk"; here it is, entitled "Banker":

We took advantage of a stopover in Philadelphia last Friday to look up a man we'd long had it in mind to meet — Major Richard Robert Wright, aged ninety-four, founder and president of the Citizens & Southern Bank & Trust Co., of that sedate community, and a former slave. We discovered him sitting in his office, spry, bright-eyed, exceedingly spare, wearing a brown tropical-worsted suit and a figured red tie as jauntily as a seventy-year-old. He told us that he intends to fly to Liberia this month to help celebrate the centennial of that country and to meet the most distant of his depositors, a resident of Monrovia. He also intends to spend three days in London and three in Paris, taking in the sights. His eight children, eleven grandchildren, and four great-grandchildren are all opposed to the trip, but he told us he is going anyhow. "It was the same story back in the nineties," he said, "when Mr. William McKinley wanted to appoint me Minister Plenipotentiary to Liberia. Everybody said I would get jungle fever. I had a growing family then, so I didn't go, but I won't be put off any longer. I don't drink, I don't smoke, I don't carouse, and I don't curse unless I'm pressed real hard. I'm not worrying about jungle fever or anything."

Major Wright was born on a cotton plantation near Dalton, Georgia, in 1853 and passed his early childhood there. He said that his grandmother, who had been brought to this country in a slave ship, used to tell him stories of tribal wars the slave traders stirred up in order to facilitate the capture of natives. He was engaged in keeping flies off the dining-room table in his master's house, swinging a big punkah back and forth above the food, when he heard about the freeing of the slaves. That was in 1865. "The Master, he called my mother in," the Major said, "and he told her, 'Harriet, old Abe Lincoln wants us to run you out of our house and let you starve, but you don't have to go unless you want to.' My mother, she said, 'If you mean I'm free to go out and work for myself and my children, instead of for you and your children, then I'll go tomorrow morning.' And she did. Years afterward, when I'd amounted to a little something, I got a letter from the Master saying he reckoned I owed my success to him — him, who once caught me reading out of a speller and thrashed me and threw the speller in the stove!"

Major Wright's mother walked him and his brother and sister to Atlanta and entered them in a new Negro school there hopefully named Atlanta University, of which the Major is now the oldest living alumnus. After graduation, he taught school in Dalton, and organized (in Augusta) Georgia's first public high school for Negroes and (in Savannah) the Georgia State Industrial College for Negroes, of which he was president until 1921. Back in those days, he was a prominent member of the Republican Party, and he has been active enough politically and socially to have known all the Presidents from Hayes to Truman, inclusive. During the Spanish-American War, McKinley made him a special paymaster, with the rank of major. Woodrow Wilson sent him abroad during the first World War as an official historian of the colored troops. The Major thinks Franklin Roosevelt was the most patient man he ever met. "We talked about Haiti the last time I saw him," he said. "Mr. Roosevelt felt his French hadn't gone over too well down there."

When Major Wright was sixty-seven, he resigned from the college, determined to prove that a Negro could succeed in banking. "All the young Negroes wanted to be lawyers and doctors and ministers," he told us. "They claimed they couldn't get capital to go into business. I said I'd show them." After scouting around the country, the Major hit on Philadelphia as the right environment for a man his age and rented the corner premises that, extensively remodelled, his bank still occupies. The first year, deposits reached fifteen thousand dollars. They now total over three million. Approximately twenty-five percent of the depositors are white. The Major is the founder of the National Negro Bankers Association, the members of which are the heads of the twelve Negro banks in the country. The Citizens & Southern is the only one north of the Mason and Dixon line. We asked the Major how he'd selected the name for his bank, and he swung around in his chair and slapped his desk hard. "There's a bank down in Georgia with this name," he said. "I was a depositor in it. One day, my daughter was insulted there. I spoke to the president of the bank, and I said, 'I'm all for the South, and I'm proud and glad to have been your friend, but if you aren't prepared to run a bank that will be courteous to everybody, black or white, rich or poor, then I'm going to take the name of your bank and put it on a bank of my own, up North.' And that's just what I did."

All very well — I was delighted to have made the acquaintance of an ex-slave, especially such an able and charming one, and I was proud to have been able to tell his story in the magazine. (Soon I will be among the handful of people left alive who has ever met an American born a slave.) As we looked over the rough copy of the magazine a day or two before publication, Shawn and I congratulated each other on having outwitted Ross, but it turned out at once that we had been less clever then we supposed. Unbeknownst to us, poor Major Wright had fallen ill and was dying even as we went to press: by the time the magazine reached the newsstands, he was dead. Ik Shuman, a Ross "Jesus" transmogrified over the years into some sort of general editorial handyman, went up and down the corridors of the magazine, making a terrible face and moaning, in his curious, high-pitched Southern accent, "We got a dead man in the book! We got a dead man in the book!" It was the first time in the magazine's history that this unlucky circumstance had arisen. Of course it confirmed all Ross's surmises in respect to the black race and Philadelphia, as he hastened to point out on his return from Aspen. So, far from having struck a blow in defense of blacks and Philadelphia, we had inadvertently struck a blow against them. Ross hoped we would learn a lesson from this disgraceful episode.

18

To have a dead man in the text of the magazine is awkward enough, but to have dead men on the staff of the magazine is more awkward still. This alarming state of affairs has been experienced not only by me but by most of the other members of the staff as well. It is a consequence of the old tradition that nobody who comes to work for *The New Yorker* is ever properly introduced to anyone else. When I was new on the magazine, I got it into my head that Freddie Packard, head of the checking department, was, in fact, John Mosher, then the movie critic of *The New Yorker*. One day I read in the *Times* that Mosher had died; a few days later, I saw him walking about the corridors of the magazine, and it gave me a terrible turn. Soon I discovered that the man I had supposed to be Mosher was Packard; the man I had supposed to be Packard was a fellow named Anderson, while Anderson . . . I forget now who I thought Anderson was.

In his first weeks at the magazine, Shawn assumed that the tall, fierce-looking Whitaker was Ross; for a long time, Edith Oliver was under the impression that Milton Greenstein, the resident lawyer who checked our copy for libel and performed other legal services for the magazine and who later became its vice-president, was Gus Lobrano, the head fiction editor. She had drawn this conclusion from the fact that only Greenstein ever looked as worried as Shawn, and since Shawn and Lobrano were jointly managing editors, the worried Greenstein *must* be Lobrano — who, to complicate matters, rarely looked worried at all. (Greenstein reads copy for libel as Miss Gould reads it for dangling modifiers. In the course of a Profile of Tallulah Bankhead, I described her sister Eugenia as being eccentric. Galleys in hand, Greenstein gave a doubtful shake of the head. "That *could* be libelous," he said. "Will you give me an example of her eccentricity?" I said, "Well, for one thing, she has been married seven times, and three of those seven times it was to the same man." Greenstein looked relieved. "Eccentric, sure enough," he said.)

In his book on Ross, Thurber quotes from a letter written to him by Edmund Wilson:

"It was only after Russell Maloney's death that I realized that the person I had been thinking was Maloney must actually be somebody else. Since I was seeing him still in the corridors, I knew that it could not be Maloney. I thought Geraghty was Lobrano for years. [Again the wrong man *in loco* Lobrano! Curiously, nobody ever appears to have mistaken Lobrano for someone else.] That girl Lillian Ross with the built-in tape-recorder who did those articles on Hemingway and the Stephen Crane movie — about whom I had a certain curiosity — I have never been able to identify or get anyone to introduce me to.

"I must have been working in the office for years before Ruth Flint identified me correctly, and I should undoubtedly never have known her if she had not been a friend of my wife's. At about the time I started in, a new messenger to the printer's appeared. He was old-fashioned-looking and shabby-genteel, carried a briefcase, wore a black derby and an old dark overcoat; his face was pallid and faded and he walked with averted eyes; his features were rather refined. He looked, Ruth said, like someone who might have absconded from an English bank and come to the United States. She thought that this man was me. When she told me this, I became rather curious about him and found, on inquiry, that she was so far right that he was actually a disbarred Virginia lawyer. At one time I played with the idea of hiring him to impersonate me and deliver the lectures and after-dinner speeches for which I am sometimes asked."

The difficulty we habitually face in attaching the correct names to the people we encounter in the corridors of the magazine is heightened by the fact that some of the most distinguished of our artists and writers rarely set foot in those corridors; they are strangers, who exist for us as benign ghosts, haunting us not by their presence, as proper ghosts would, but by their absence. Myself, I have never met the artist George Price, who has been drawing for us since 1931, and I expect that I never will. Many members of the staff have never met Lewis Mumford, who began his career on *The New Yorker* writing primarily under the heading of "The Sky Line," in the very year that Price began. (After forty years, these veteran colleagues have yet to meet.) If I happen to know Mumford, it is thanks to circumstances that have little to do with

Lewis Mumford

the magazine; throughout most of his long relationship with us, that virtuous and indeed — for one must risk saying it — authentically noble man has been living in the small town of Amenia, New York, and has been sending in his copy by mail. Similarly, Price has been living in Tenafly, New Jersey, and has been sending

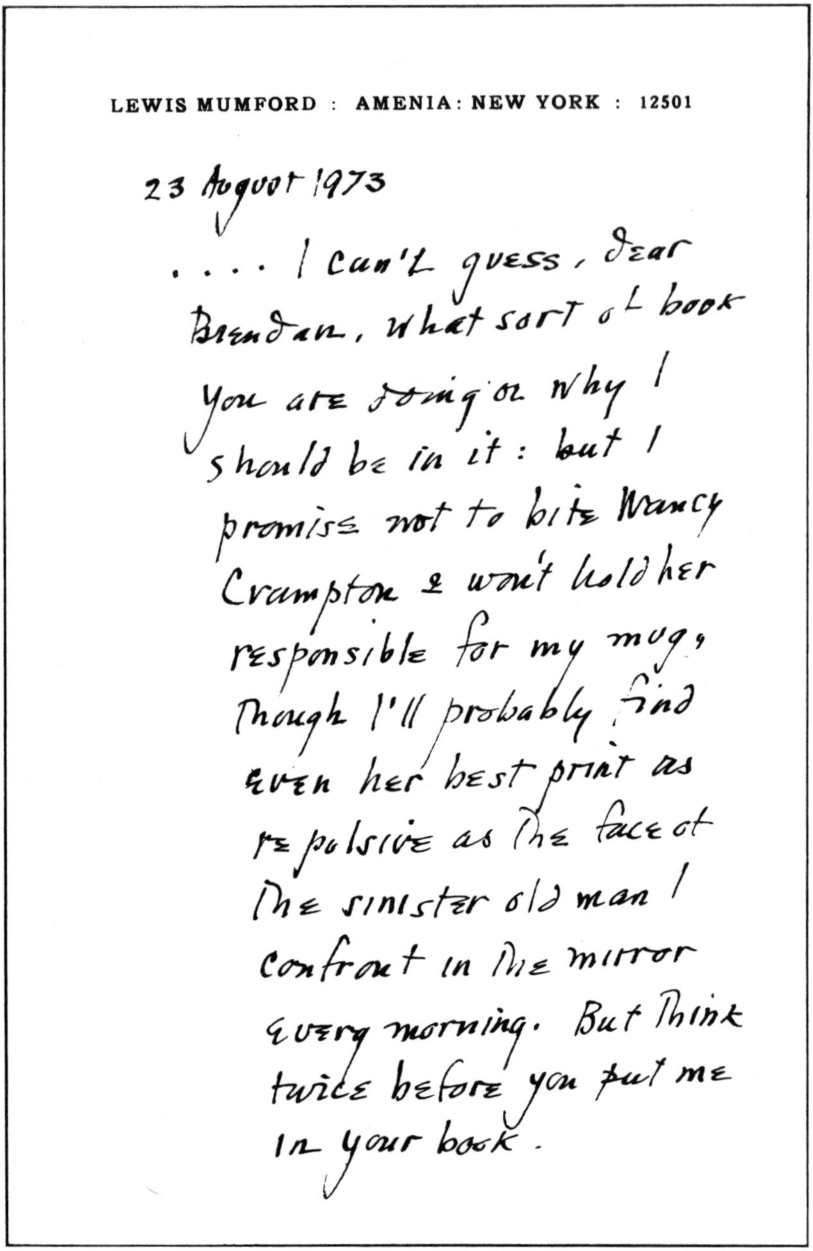

23 August 1973

. . . . I can't guess, dear
Brendan, what sort of book
you are doing or why I
should be in it: but I
promise not to bite Nancy
Crampton & won't hold her
responsible for my mug,
Though I'll probably find
even her best print as
repulsive as the face of
the sinister old man I
confront in the mirror
every morning. But think
twice before you put me
in your book.

in his drawings by mail. Price's avocation is buying antiques, which is easier to accomplish in Tenafly than it is on West Forty-third Street. It is fitting that this superlative depicter of domestic squalor should take care, in his own life, to surround himself with exquisite things.

Our traditional confusion in respect to people's identities has extended to and embraced the jobs people hold. Most of us tend not only to put the wrong names to people but to put them in the wrong jobs as well. There are writers that I assume are editors, editors that I assume are artists, artists that I assume are space salesmen on the business side of the magazine. (The latter mistake is a result of the unexpected way some artists dress, in the pinstripe plumage of Madison Avenue.) Our errors are the result of an ignorance that may have come into existence by chance, in the hysteria of Ross's reckless hiring, firing, and switching about of jobs in the early days of the magazine, but there are those on the staff — our conspiracy seekers? — who suspect its continuance of being cultivated for a reason. To the extent that anything with a structure as meager as *The New Yorker's* may be said to have "management," maybe it is useful for the management to leave writers and editors as much in the dark about each other as possible. What was once a mere awkward not-knowing has been transformed over the years into a secrecy imposed from above, and one can imagine that this secrecy has its Byzantine advantages. Ross could never keep a secret for long, but Shawn relishes keeping them and will go to his grave in happy possession of many thousands of confidences, most of them (for Shawn will surely outlive us all) no longer of the slightest importance. I suspect Truax, the master secret-keeper, of having taught Shawn the art, but how apt a pupil Shawn has proved to be! It was a case of one genius pointing out the way to another. Truax is a man so exceedingly secretive that he would gladly make up a story in order not to be able to tell it to anyone; Shawn does not go that far, but he goes pretty far. Once he said to me, "I hope I am not betraying a confidence, but I have been talking with Joe Liebling and he tells me that he has just finished drinking a full quart of orange juice."

One of the ultimate mysteries at *The New Yorker* is what anyone gets paid. Our compensation, in whatever form (salary, drawing account, payments for individual pieces), is a fact familiar only to Shawn, our accounting department, and the Internal Revenue Service. Since we know so little about each other's duties and since we know nothing whatever about the amount of money at Shawn's disposal, to say nothing whatever about the amount of money that perhaps *ought* to be at Shawn's disposal, we are incapable of arguing our case in regard to more pay and a larger share in the magazine's profits. On the contrary, we find ourselves in the archaic and outrageous position of being totally at Shawn's mercy; if we felt the slightest distrust of his sense of social justice or the slightest doubt of his determination to champion our cause over that of the corporation, we would be unable to go on working for the magazine. Absurd that one man should have the economic destiny of so many of us locked in his bosom and that we should live in constant jeopardy of the loss of his high opinion of our work, but this has been the arrangement since the magazine was founded; we have moved sideways from the benign despotism of Ross to the benign despotism of Shawn, but we cannot be said to have moved forward.

Many years ago, I tried to start a small, informal union among the writers and editors, hoping to establish a means of negotiating with management on a sensible basis, as employees in other publishing enterprises do. What an act of folly on my part! As if the kind of people who want to write for *The New Yorker* were the kind of people who want to act sensibly! Nobody would join me. Nobody would so much as sign a piece of paper that anyone else had signed. Almost to a man, my colleagues, most of them political liberals who wrote and spoke in ardent favor of unions for other people, proved to be Uncle Toms. They preferred lodging their hopes in Ol' Massa to fighting for their freedom. They were being dealt with as if they were untaught and unteachable children, and they appeared to enjoy it. As far as I can tell, they still enjoy it, though younger members of the staff may have more revolution in their hearts than I am able to detect, encountering them in the corridors. As usual, I am too busy wondering who they are to wonder what they are thinking.

For as long as Ross was alive, one wasn't much tempted to consort with his enemy Raoul Fleischmann. Even if the two founders of the magazine hadn't been angrily at odds, we all respected the tradition of an almost complete separation between editorial and business departments. Occupying different floors, the departments mingled only in the elevators and restricted this mingling to nods, constrained smiles, and an occasionally mumbled "Hi." The mild friendliness that now exists between the departments is in marked contrast to the practices of those earlier days; if we do not fraternize, it is less because of the old tabu than because we are temperamentally unsuited to each other. The two ill-matched adversaries are dead, and of their once feverish animosity little remains in history except the anecdote about Fleischmann's getting off the elevator on the nineteenth floor in order to make some necessary call upon Ross and saying to an acquaintance in editorial, "It's all right — I have permission to be here!" It is an anecdote that, if untrue, is well found; and Fleischmann, who told stories well, would not have been above telling it on himself. How he hated Ross for the humiliations Ross had practiced upon him, and how pleased he was to have outlived Ross and to be able to observe that the magazine got along perfectly well without him!

In the period when I knew Fleischmann, he was in his sixties and seventies. (He died in 1969, at eighty-three, leaving as his widow his third wife, an Australian nurse, who had been hired to tend him in his late years.) He was a small, dapper, white-haired man, with blue eyes and smooth pink cheeks; he dressed well, walked with an engagingly jaunty air (especially in summer, with a straw boater upon his head), and lived an easy life that constantly gave him more trouble than he expected it to. He looked down on people in the very act of seeming to look up at them. Truax, for example, was his indispensable go-between in all matters that concerned Ross, but Fleischmann found in Truax many comic traits. Much as he respected the quality of his mind, he often made fun of him to others.

As for Shawn, to Fleischmann he was a figure from another planet — he couldn't begin to take him in. He was relieved to discover that Shawn was the opposite of Ross in person and nature, but as a gambler Fleischmann was uneasy in the presence of a mystery; he didn't know what Shawn wanted and so couldn't make book on him. Nevertheless, he was grateful to him. After his death it was found that he had left Shawn a hundred thousand dollars in his will. If this was less a spontaneous gift than a righting of certain economic injustices that Shawn had suffered at the hands of the magazine on earlier occasions, it had at least the look of generosity. (The present publisher of the magazine is Raoul's only son, Peter. He is a handsome, gentle, ironic man, with blue eyes, prematurely gray hair, and old-fashioned good manners.

Relations between him and Shawn appear to be excellent, which is to say that he allows Shawn to take long chances on writers. It is well known that many of our writers have spent four or five years on the magazine's payroll before finding their voices and coming triumphantly into themselves.)

Like many rich Jews of his time and station in life, Raoul Fleischmann was an anti-Semite; he would speak of Jews he disliked as "kikes," which in its way is even more deplorable than Ross's referring to blacks as "coons," and on one occasion I remember his describing one of the editors of the magazine as having "rabbinical feet." What did that mean? Apparently, that the editor, unlike Fleischmann, wore high black shoes that lacked chic.

Fleischmann had had bad luck with women, and the consequence was that he found them, as a sex, threatening. He was candid in saying that he had never been much of a lover, and the woman whom he admired most — his first wife, Ruth Gardner Botsford Fleischmann Vischer — he admired for qualities that he would have liked to discover in himself as a man. She was exceptional in her beauty and in the quickness of her mind. She was also a superb gambler, playing for high stakes without fear. Fleischmann liked gambling, but when the stakes were high he trembled in terror of the outcome. He took a chance on *The New Yorker* in part because the stakes were so low at the start. It was a foolhardy thing to do, but it was an amusing one as well — more amusing than running a branch of the family's bread-baking business, especially when he had means enough not to be bothered with running anything.

Raoul was the youngest child of one of five Fleischmann brothers, who came to this country from Vienna as a result of a visit that two of the brothers made to the Centennial Exposition in Philadelphia, in 1876, where the Fleischmann family's yeast was on display and much admired. It was decided that the entire family should throw in its lot with the New World. Raoul's father, Louis, was brought over and put in charge of something called the Vienna Model Bakery, next door to Grace Church, on Broadway and Tenth Street. It was a sort of coffeehouse as well as bakery, where Viennese newspapers were kept on racks for customers to read, and it was through Louis that a new word entered our language. In order to call attention to the freshness of Fleischmann's bread and also, it appears, because of an innate generosity, Louis made a practice of giving away at eleven every evening whatever amount of bread had not been sold during the day. The poor lined up to receive it at the bakery door; hence our word "breadline."

Prospering, the five brothers built five big summer houses for themselves in a village in the Catskills, which came to be named after them. The village of Fleischmanns still exists, but without a Fleischmann in it; the family grew apart with the passing of the years, perhaps because its wealth increased at different rates in succeeding generations. Having been in the bread business, Raoul always spoke of himself as one of the "poor" millionaire Fleischmanns; the "rich" millionaire Fleischmanns were the ones that made the yeast and the mayonnaise and the gin. Ross met Fleischmann shortly after Fleischmann had been elected a member of the Thanatopsis Literary and Inside Straight Club, an informal group, consisting mostly of writers and editors, that gathered weekly to drink, smoke, and play poker. The first members of the club had met while working on the *Stars and Stripes* in Paris, during the war; the club had been named by Woollcott, who combined a foul mouth with a sentimentality so extreme that he was sometimes referred to even by friends as "Louisa May Woollcott."

Fleischmann was one of the few members of the club who had no connection with journalism or the arts and he felt honored to belong. When Ross asked Fleischmann to help back a new humorous weekly magazine, Fleischmann consented to put up twenty-five thousand dollars; it was a sum he could easily afford and it would give him an association with the kind of people he admired. (The twenty thousand dollars that Ross and his wife were putting up was all the money they had.) The first issue of the magazine came out on Thursday, February 19, 1925, datelined the following Saturday. From the beginning, it lost money. Week after week, Fleischmann found himself dipping into his pocket to make up a discrepancy of several thousand dollars between income and outgo. He told me once that this act of subtraction was less painful than it might have been because he was speculating in the stock market, and his gains in Wall Street were often sufficient to offset his losses from the magazine. Be that as it may, by the time the magazine began to catch on, Fleischmann had been cajoled and bullied into expending some four hundred thousand dollars upon it — a considerable sum for a "poor" millionaire. Though it was becoming plain by 1926 that the magazine would succeed, it was still in need of financing; Fleischmann proceeded to lend it approximately three hundred thousand dollars, secured by notes. The story goes that within a year he was offered three million dollars for his shares. He did well to turn down the offer. By 1929, the magazine was debt-free and earning a profit of half a million dollars a year.

In short, Fleischmann made a big and reckless gamble and the gamble happened to pay off. It is the gambler's temptation to assume that winning is normal, losing the exception. Egged on by a fast-talking little magazine consultant named John Hanrahan, Fleischmann attempted to repeat his *New Yorker* success with several other new magazines, the most prominent of which was called *Stage.* Fleischmann's divorced wife, by then Mrs. Peter Vischer, and several other substantial stockholders were indignant at the way in which Fleischmann was pouring *New Yorker* profits into these misadventures. He was acting as if the magazine were his private plaything, when it was, in fact, a public corporation, whose shares were being traded over the counter. At the suggestion of Ross's friend Dan Silberberg, himself a stockbroker, another stockholder and close friend of Ross, Hawley Truax, was asked to preside over what threatened to become a dangerous internecine battle, capable of breaking up the magazine. Truax brought in his brother-in-law, Lloyd Paul Stryker, a fee-fi-fo-fum courtroom lawyer of the day. After a brief rummaging about in the books of the corporation, Stryker was able to assert that however innocent Fleischmann's intentions may have been, his casual handling of company funds, in amounts that totalled something over a million dollars, put him in a position where accusations of misfeasance might easily be levelled against him. At first, Fleischmann had been determined to fight his assortment of challengers, but the possibility of being haled into court and the scandalous publicity that this would be sure to arouse was too much for him; he consented to put his shares in escrow for a number of years and to have elected to the board of directors, in place of nameless yes-men, Silberberg, Truax, and Stryker.

It must have been from this moment that Fleischmann, his hands tied and all hope of repeating his *New Yorker* success with other publications permanently dashed, became, in money matters, the disappointed, backward-looking person that I encountered in the thirties and forties. His recollection of the jeopardy in which he had found himself was still very vivid to him, and instead of rejoicing in his good fortune and divising some means of sharing it with those who had made it possible, he fussed and fidgeted over preserving it intact for himself and his heirs. Sitting back, he became richer and richer, to the point where, if *The New Yorker* had been sold in the early nineteen-sixties, when its stock achieved its highest price, Fleischmann and his family would have received some ten or fifteen million dollars for their holdings. Where he might have been expected to be generous, to my astonishment he was selfish, and I did my best to correct this unappealing aspect of his character. Young as I was and old as he was, I lectured him and hectored him and sought to pick a quarrel with him, but he remained invincibly urbane. Since he wished to have

A banquette in the Rose Room at the Algonquin Hotel. Ross used to eat lunch at this table. After his death, Fleischmann took to eating there, and since Fleischmann's death the table is often reserved for Shawn. Few changes are made at the Algonquin from year to year, or even from decade to decade, and no doubt in the year 2000 somebody from The New Yorker *will be seated in that place, pouring coffee from that very pot and sniffing a descendant of that solitary rose.*

friends among the writers and since he had no respect for our judgment about anything except literary matters, which in his opinion were but trifles, it cost him nothing to let me rant on against his miserable business practices.

Early in our acquaintance, he would take me to lunch in the panelled basement grillroom of the Ritz, which then stood on Madison Avenue between Forty-sixth Street and Forty-seventh Street; later, we often ate in the Rose Room of the Algonquin, seated on the half-moon banquette where Ross had formerly held noisy court. Fleischmann liked to drink a couple of very cold and very dry martinis before lunch; because of a congenital tremor in his hands, he would have some difficulty bringing the brimful glass to his lips, but the effort was obviously well worth making. Born in Vienna and gently reared, he had excellent manners; he would always inquire first for my wife and children, in whom, as an older man, he can scarcely have had the slightest interest, and we would then settle down to gossip. Sooner or later, I would get onto the subject of money, which he found distasteful.

About money I took care to speak in general terms, not personal ones. The question of what I was to be paid by the magazine was always something between Shawn and me, though I was aware that Fleischmann would have tucked away in his memory down to the last penny the amount of my income from the magazine — he was notably adept at figures and his quickness at mental arithmetic had turned him, in his youth, into a sort of one-man parlor game. Moreover, I was aware that he held certain notions about payments to writers and artists that were so outrageous as not to be discussible. He sincerely believed that whatever a writer or artist was paid by *The New Yorker* was by definition too much, since the magazine was, as he repeatedly pointed out, a "showcase" for us, especially when we were at the beginning of our careers. It followed that we were lucky to be paid anything at all; if justice were truly to be served, then we should be paying the magazine for the privilege of appearing in it.

In my conversation with Fleischmann, I struck what I hoped was a loftier and, at the same time, a more practical note. My point was simply that the people who had created the magazine ought to have a substantial and continuing share in the fruits of their creation. Fleischmann, already a rich man, had made a single foolish gamble and it had paid off; if the rest of us had striven successfully to bring something new into the world, it was he and a handful of other big stockholders who reaped the profits of our success. Not only reaped them but in Fleischmann's case quite literally threw them away, for as far as I could tell he preferred to pay out hundreds of thousands of dollars in income tax on his *New Yorker* dividends to reducing those dividends and putting the amount saved into an increased budget, with higher wages for writers, artists, editors, and general office personnel (to say nothing of members of the business department); into an adequate pension and retirement plan; and into a stock-acquisition plan that not only would permit members of the staff to purchase shares in *The New Yorker* at less than market value but would also provide them with the means of building up a nest-egg of shares in other corporations. These principles had already been put into practice at *Time* and other magazines; why not at *The New Yorker*? It seemed to be nearly always the case that by ill chance I would be bringing up this battery of questions at the very moment that the waiter would be arriving with the bill for our lunch. Fleischmann would put on his glasses, instantly check the correctness of the figures on the bill, scrawl a shaky signature at the bottom of it, and then, with a little backward wave of the hand, say to me, "Won't work, old boy! Won't work!"

Not another word was ever to be got out of him on that subject. I never learned why something that had proved so beneficial to thousands of other magazine employees would not prove beneficial to the hundreds of employees of *The New Yorker*. Only the wave of that immaculately manicured hand, the blue eyes the dismissive smile: he knew that my colleagues and I were precisely where we wanted to be, no matter how unfortunate the financial circumstances that he imposed on us. We had squeezed ourselves eagerly into the showcase and if we had our way we would leave it only in death. Fleischmann could afford to say behind my back, "Dear Brendan! So young for his age!"

Fleischmann's opinion of me as an aging Peck's Bad Boy may have been shared in part by Ross, who said once to Shawn, "The trouble with Gill is that he hasn't suffered enough." It happened that Shawn and I had often discussed the question of suffering, and we had agreed that anyone who survives to the age of three or four has surely suffered enough to last him a lifetime. But being a puritan, Ross thought people had to be broken to life by pain, as oxen are broken to traces by whip and goad. In his crude, nineteenth-century fashion, he believed in the efficacy of misfortune. What was more remarkable, he appeared to think that the quantity of suffering one ought to undergo was capable of being measured. ". . . hasn't suffered enough." But what on earth is enough? What is too little? Or too much? In his heart, Ross must have had some notion of suffering not unlike the story of the Three Bears and their porridge and chairs and beds. He must have thought there were sufferings that were just right. And he must have thought it would do me good to have them imposed on me.

If Fleischmann engaged in financial hanky-panky in the course of seeking to launch other magazines on the strength of *The New Yorker*'s success, on at least one occasion Ross engaged in editorial hanky-panky with roughly similar intentions. He was given to boasting that he had half a dozen ideas for magazines at least as good as his idea for *The New Yorker.* One of these ideas would have been sure to fail — it was for a daily newspaper devoted to ships' news, and while a tiny newspaper limited to that subject might have enjoyed a mild success in the nineteen-twenties, when scores of passenger ships were constantly entering and leaving the port of New York, it would have sunk without a trace early in the period that saw nearly all transatlantic travel shift from sea to air.

Another of Ross's ideas had to do with a detective-story magazine. Ross liked reading about crimes, even in the trashiest fiction form, but he preferred fact to fiction, and he and Silberberg talked about starting a magazine that would consist entirely of true detective stories. At the time, the idea was a novel one, and it so caught Ross's imagination that he wanted to get it under way at once. In principle, he was obligated to devote all his time to *The New Yorker,* but he figured out a means of getting around this difficulty: he would bring in his old Army buddy, John T. Winterich, as the nominal editor. Behind the scenes, Ross would personally rewrite the factual material as it came in and get it into publishable shape. He believed in the new magazine not only because it seemed to him to be commercially a sure-fire proposition but also because it would give him something to fall back upon in case one of his continual battles with Fleischmann should lead to his having to resign or to his being fired. Silberberg and Ross spent a good deal of time over backgammon thinking up a name for the magazine. Silberberg proposed "Guilty." Ross was not quite satisfied; he hemmed and hawed and took thought and at last hit upon the small, perfect improvement — the addition of a question mark. They would call the magazine "Guilty?"

Daniel H. Silberberg, an adviser to both the editorial and the business sides of the magazine. Between marriages, Ross used to hide out at Silberberg's, fearing, though with little reason, that gossip columnists were bent upon publishing an exposé of his not very startling private life. It was almost always the case that fewer people were out to "get" Ross than Ross thought, but the false prospect kept him on his toes.

Ross urged Silberberg to make an immediate study of the financial prospects. With his usual optimism, Ross was convinced that the magazine could be successfully launched for a maximum of fifty thousand dollars. Since he himself had no money to spare, the burden of the funding of the new enterprise would rest upon Silberberg. It didn't take Silberberg long to discover that the true cost of launching the magazine would come to something like a quarter of a million dollars. (At the time, the country was still in the midst of the Great Depression, so the amount was the equivalent of, say, a couple of million dollars today.) Silberberg had ample means but was a shrewd gambler, not a reckless one. He broke the bad news to Ross that "Guilty?" was economically not feasible. Ross railed in vain. In his heart, he must have known that he was far too busy editing one magazine to take on — and in secret, unknown to Fleischmann — the editing of a second, but the long-shot was always irresistible to him. He cursed and protested and impugned Silberberg's figures, intentions, and friendship. At last he subsided into the outrageous grumble with which he greeted every defeat at cards and backgammon: "Something I did to God!"

According to Joel Sayre, who was an early contributor to the magazine and a close friend of both Ross and Thurber, Ross was not above being tempted by business enterprises that had nothing to do with journalism. "In the thirties," Sayre has written, "when *The New Yorker* was about ten years old, Ross invested in a paint-spraying machine and other ventures; and not only invested in them but insisted on discussing them at depressing length. Certain members of the editorial staff decided that Ross had lost interest in the magazine. After a great deal of debate and soul-searching, they went to Raoul Fleischmann . . . When they had explained their doubts in detail, they asked Fleischmann to find a replacement for Ross.

"The first Thurber knew about this was when Fleischmann invited him to lunch at the Algonquin. After a few rounds of drinks, Fleischmann asked Thurber who his favorite candidate was. Thurber asked, 'Candidate for what?' Fleischmann replied that he meant, of course, for Ross's job. 'Whaaat?' Thurber yelled, rising to his feet and swaying slightly. 'What did you say?' He saw a basket of baked potatoes on a nearby table, seized a couple, and threw them at random. As poor Fleischmann, the waiters, and adjacent guests ducked and dodged, Thurber, bellowing denunciations and shouting strange oaths, maintained his potato barrage. When the potatoes were all fired, he turned to hard rolls."

Now, this is a highly implausible story, though it may contain a germ of truth. There *was* talk of replacing Ross in those days, and one story holds that it was Katharine White who was prepared to lead a palace revolution. Nothing came of these purported insurrections, and what makes me suspicious of Sayre's account of the Fleischmann–Thurber encounter is that it sounds to me as if Thurber had made it up, like so many of his other stories. His purpose was not truth-telling but, rather, entertainment and self-aggrandizement: he is always the hero of these vivid episodes and someone else is always the victim or villain. Plainly, the account could only have come from Thurber himself, since Fleischmann wouldn't have wanted it to become known and nobody else in the restaurant could have been aware of what prompted Thurber's indignation. Moreover, I am skeptical of the props employed on that occasion. No restaurant keeps baked potatoes in baskets on tables, where they would immediately grow cold; and at that time the Algonquin served not hard rolls but popovers, a delicacy for which it was celebrated. It is just possible that a drunken Thurber, contemptuous of a scheming Fleischmann, tossed a single warm popover in Fleischmann's direction; the rest is the artist at work.

19

Of the many cases of mistaken identity that I have been party to on the magazine, the one that lasted longest concerned the artists Rea Irvin and Al Frueh. From the beginning, Irvin in fact if not in name was the art editor of the magazine, and when I arrived I assumed that he was still attending the weekly art meetings. Upon seeing a certain figure in the corridors, unmistakably an artist (not least because he was carrying furled drawings under his arm) and of the proper age and jaunty aspect, I assumed that this must be Irvin. In truth, it was Frueh, as I learned several years later, when it occurred to someone to introduce us. Frueh and I became friends; as for Irvin, I was never to meet him at all, though he died only in 1972, at ninety, at his home in St. Croix.

Irvin meant a great deal to Ross in the magazine's earliest days. He helped to prepare the layout for the first issue of the magazine. He drew many of the department headings and was widely credited with having originated the typeface in which those and other headings were set. (It appears to be the case that Irvin was inspired by and modified a typeface designed by the eminent American typographer Carl Purington Rollins.) Irvin also drew the first cover, reproduced every year on the magazine's birthday. A few years ago, an editor wrote to him in St. Croix, "Another year gone by! And soon again the anniversary cover. How are you? Don't forget to write." With his customary playfulness, Irvin returned the note, slightly emended: "to write" had been neatly inked out and "the check" inserted in its place.

Irvin, who was in his forties when the magazine started, was already a highly successful newspaper and magazine artist. He was a familiar figure at the Players Club, and a notable competitor there and elsewhere at pool and poker. Like Ross, he was a Westerner; his mother had reached San Francisco by covered wagon in the eighteen-fifties. Ross was in awe of him, because, for all Irvin's Western background, he seemed so much the consummate

PORTRAIT OF THE FRUEH BY THE FRUEH FOR THE GREENSTEIN.

Eastern insider. Ross was always impressed by insiders, and by people who he mistakenly supposed were insiders; he was sure they possessed secrets unknown to him. A big, amiable man, Irvin had begun his career as an actor, and he dressed in what used to be thought of as a "theatrical" manner; he had an actor's presence. That, too, was something Ross would envy, and with reason. Instead of presence, at weddings and other sizable social occasions Ross radiated a continuous intensity of unease.

Irvin practiced his metier with an old-fashioned equanimity. His style as an artist was decorative and deliberately without depth of perspective; it had the quality of Chinese calligraphy, though with an Occidental boldness of color. He had the patience of a skilled craftsman and could draw in almost any mode. In the thirties, the magazine did a parody of *Punch;* Irvin filled its pages with drawings that one would have sworn were by Belcher, Shepard, Partridge, and du Maurier. When Ross expressed dissatisfaction with the conventional severely straight printer's rule that is used to separate blocks of printed matter, Irvin set about drawing sample wavy lines by the score, and perhaps by the hundred. Ross was especially taken with the one that looks like this: ∿∿

In the days when Irvin was among those who helped to choose drawings at art meetings, Ross once dashed off a note to him in anxious inquiry about a Thurber drawing of a seal. Ross wrote, "Rea — do a seal's whiskers go like this?" Irvin wrote back, "Thurber's seal's whiskers go like this."

My mistaking Frueh for Irvin was all the more ironic because the two men had nothing whatever in common except talent. Irvin was urbane and gregarious; Frueh was a rural loner. The name he chose to be known by was obviously a measure of his intentions about himself. However the surname may originally have been pronounced, Frueh pronounced it "Free," and his given name early reached an irreducible Al. Those two brisk, no-nonsense monosyllables suited him to perfection. One perceives that the name is a near-homonym of "all free," and the hint is worth taking. All free was what Al Frueh wished to become, and he did. Indeed, he was so adroit in escaping the ordinary trammels of life that he gained a considerable reputation as an eccentric. Vigorous into extreme old age — he lived to be eighty-eight and was still making drawings for *The New Yorker* at eighty-two — Frueh would lope barefoot over the rough terrain of his hundred-acre place in Sharon, Connecticut, occasionally scooping up off the forest floor what a visitor described as "débris," which he proffered with a single urgent command, "Chew that!" Few people accepted the invitation, but Frueh would munch with delight whatever berries, nuts, ferns, and leaves the débris happened to consist of. He was genuinely and fearlessly omnivorous, consuming with equal relish squirrels and water lilies. Which is to say that he was a backwoodsman, hugging nature close and striving to keep the false ease of twentieth-century gadgetry at bay. Once Geraghty came to call on Frueh and, failing to find him in or about the house, shouted his name. Frueh gave an answering shout, which Geraghty eventually traced to the bottom of a well, which Frueh was engaged in cleaning out. He liked it down there and was reluctant to come up. For his wife's sake, in their old age he introduced electricity into the Sharon house, for the first time providing mechanically pumped water and a certain amount of central heating, but he was not pleased with these improvements. He was his own man, going his own way, and that way meant contentedly doing without and being left alone. In Frost's phrase, he had chosen the road less travelled by, and he was determined to keep it in that condition. Sometimes the metaphor became a reality. When the town sought to improve the public highway in front of his place, Frueh went out with a pick and shovel and did the job himself, perhaps with a dark intent of disimprovement.

Max Beerbohm, Frueh's peer, lived a life intimately related to the sort of caricatures he drew; he was a London dandy to his gloved fingertips, and in the elegant stitching together of his manifold talents — for he wrote as well as he drew and he spoke as well as he wrote and even his pranks were accomplished works of art — no seam was visible; he was astonishing and yet wholly without surprises. If Frueh's art resembled Beerbohm's in many respects, he was Beerbohm's opposite in being so unlike his handiwork. From the time *The New Yorker* was founded, Frueh drew for it scores of cartoons and hundreds of theatrical caricatures, but it would be hard to imagine anyone who looked less the sophisticated Manhattan theatregoer than he; encountering Frueh at the theatre, one would have wondered what he was doing there — a rube like him should be out pricing the Brooklyn Bridge.

No doubt the discrepancy between the artist and his mask helped Frueh to undertake and carry out so much work over so many years; as all actors know and as the rest of us are too timid to find out, disguise is a formidable source of energy. The Fruehs owned a red-brick house on Perry Street, in the Village, during the period that he was drawing for *The New Yorker*, but the look of Frueh when he came into the office to deliver a drawing was village-like, not Village-like. He wore an old-fashioned broad-brimmed brown fedora and, in winter, unbuckled galoshes, which flopped loosely about his ankles; if the weather was foul, he would carry his drawings — always executed on a particular brand of shiny, coated paper — furled in an old newspaper. He was tall and rangy and (as they used to say up-country) "light-complected," with sandy brown hair and blue eyes, and his face weathered instead of growing old. He was said to be rich, thanks to the fact that he took the advice of a friend and put all of his early savings into A.T. & T. stock. It was the only stock he ever owned and every time new shares were offered he bought some. "The telephone company has kept me poor," he used to tell Geraghty: a countryman's way of confessing to wealth as a countryman's way of saying he is happy is to say that he can't complain.

Since Frueh's death, in 1968, his children have discovered that the stories he told them about his past often fail to jibe; his sense of humor invariably overcame his sense of accuracy and, like a good father, he provided whatever he thought the occasion deserved. Some facts are more plausible than others; it is possible to believe most of what he wrote in answer to a questionnaire in the nineteen-thirties: "Born on Main Street, Lima, Ohio, 1880. Never found out why. Brought up to be a farmer and then a brewer. Percolated through the St. Louis Post-Dispatch school of newspaper art 1904–1908. Loafed in Paris, London, Rome, Munich, Berlin, and Madrid in 1909. Came back and loafed on the New York World 1910 to 1912½. Went to Europe again and married in 1913." After the war, Frueh returned to cartooning for the *World* and left it in 1925 for *The New Yorker.* While abroad, he is reputed to have studied with Matisse and to have Indian-wrestled with Braque; both activities are likely enough for a man who was subsequently to plant seven thousand pine trees and forty varieties of grapes, and who attempted to hybridize a soft-shelled black walnut.

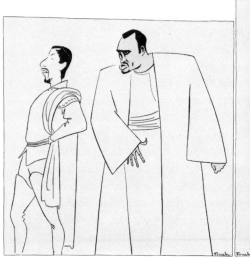

Jose Ferrer and Paul Robeson in Othello.

Raymond Massey, Bramwell Fletcher, and Katharine Cornell in The Doctor's Dilemma.

His relationship with Ross was more tranquil than that of many other artists and writers on the magazine; this was in part because almost nothing that Frueh drew was rejected. Ross was exceptionally hard on others, forcing them to do better than they knew how to do, but Frueh was exceptionally hard on himself. Behind every drawing he submitted lay dozens of rejected sketches. The nearest to a difficulty that editor and artist ever had was when Ross told Frueh, in respect to a drawing he had made of Katharine Cornell, "You've given Cornell a cast in one eye. Gibbs says she hasn't got a cast." Frueh threw the drawing on the floor. "Tell Gibbs to draw her," he said, and strode away. Ross ran the drawing. Some years later, he called Geraghty into his office and said, "I saw Cornell last night. Tell Al that, goddam it, Gibbs was wrong. She *does* have a cast."

Frueh liked that story. It might amuse him to take liberties with his reminiscences but it was a matter of grave concern to him that his drawings be as accurate as they were exquisite. Once, on a dare, he created a caricature that was immediately recognizable, although he had not troubled to give the person depicted a face: the tensely capering body sufficed to reveal that it was George M. Cohan. Frueh had cunning in his eye and skill in his head and no cruelty in him anywhere. His beautiful drawings, neither tender nor harsh, leap off their shiny paper, insouciantly alive. They make us, in whatever darkness, smile.

The most celebrated artist drawing for *The New Yorker* when I joined the staff was Peter Arno. By then, he was rarely in the office; I met him a few times, but the only long conversation I ever had with him was at the party that Katharine and Andy White gave for Shawn shortly after his appointment as editor of the magazine. The party was held at the pleasant little duplex apartment that the Whites then occupied on East Forty-ninth Street, overlooking the gardens of Turtle Bay. Because the Whites were always careful to adhere to the proper etiquette, the invitations read "to meet William Shawn," and many members of the staff, encountering this usage for the first time, were heard to protest, "But I've already *met* Shawn! What the hell's going on here?"

The party turned out to be a very merry, drunken, and melodramatic occasion (there have always been two or three members of the staff that could be counted on in their cups to tear a passion to tatters, hurling accusations and imprecations broadside until the moment was reached when nothing remained for them but to pass out). Among those present was Arno, who had taken the precaution to bring along his own large shakerful of dry martinis. The year was 1952, so Arno must have been forty-eight; to me in my thirties he seemed much older than that, and it may have been the case that my impression was correct and that he was indeed prematurely aged; certainly when he died, in 1968, at the age of sixty-four, he was already an old man. One thought then, sadly, oh, but what an extraordinary young man he must have been! And probably he thought that, too, in the increasing misery and loneliness of his last years.

A rendering by Peter Arno of the racing car that he designed for his personal use in the nineteen-thirties. The car was built in Europe, and a family story has it that the fenders were made of platinum. Once safely past customs in New York, the fenders were detached and replaced by ordinary steel fenders, the platinum then being sold at a great profit.

He was born Peter Arnoux Curtis, of a well-known New York family, and he changed his name in part to protect his family's respectability — his father was a judge and Peter was a classic harum-scarum young man-about-town in that day of the speakeasy, the flapper, and the Stutz Bearcat. He dropped out of Yale in 1923 in order to lead a band in a nightclub called the Rendezvous, presided over by the dancer Gilda Gray. He was tall and lean and handsome, with a big chin and dark crew-cut hair. When *The New Yorker* was launched, Arno began to submit drawings, which the editors speedily accepted. He worked almost entirely in charcoal and wash, and the vigor and simplicity of his line caused him often, and rightfully, to be compared with Daumier.

In the earliest years of the magazine, Arno invented a couple of cartoon characters that caught the public's eye and helped markedly to increase circulation. These were the harridans he called the Whoops Sisters, and their mild misadventures on the streets of New York struck contemporary audiences as being what we now think of as raunchy. By our standards, the Whoops Sisters are not very funny; nevertheless, they were funny to Ross, and they had a particular utility for him as the magazine struggled to acquire a following: the Whoops Sisters manifested conduct revolting to that "old lady in Dubuque" for whom, in the prospectus of the magazine, Ross had promised that the magazine would *not* be edited. They helped him to make good an otherwise unreliable boast.

Arno hard at work in a dinner jacket and opera pumps, and with no fewer than four brushes in hand.

In passing, a word about the possible origin of that curious phrase "the old lady in Dubuque." As I have suggested, the old lady may well have been Ross's way of indirectly mocking his mother, but why Dubuque, which Ross had presumably never visited? Why not Duluth, or, for that matter, Des Moines? The historian Basil Rauch has suggested an explanation. Rauch was growing up in Duluth in the twenties, and living there at the time was a bitter old man known as "Boots" Mulgrew, whose family was prominent in the coal and ice business. "Boots" had gone East and achieved a certain success writing skits for Broadway shows, but liquor had got the better of him and he retreated to Dubuque and the financial protection of his family.

Although Dubuque had a fairly good local newspaper, the more worldly inhabitants preferred reading the Chicago *Tribune,* which among its editorial features ran a column headed "A Line o' Type or Two." The column, which consisted of brief paragraphs of humor, light verse, and the like, was signed "B.L.T.," for Bert Lester Taylor. It was a column widely known throughout the Middle West and was much admired by newspapermen from coast to coast. Franklin Pierce Adams, coming to New York from Chicago, started a column in the New York *World* modelled on Taylor's column; he called it "The Conning Tower" and he imitated Taylor in signing it with his initials only: F.P.A. Many *New Yorker* writers, including Frank Sullivan and E. B. White, were regular contributors to "The Conning Tower."

"Boots" Mulgrew took to sending in squibs to B.L.T., describing some of the provincial absurdities of Dubuque; he signed the pieces "Old Lady in Dubuque." The pieces attained a considerable vogue during the early twenties, and Rauch plausibly assumes that Ross read them, admired them, and, whether consciously or not, got the old lady in Dubuque fixed in his mind as a natural antagonist.

Looking back on Arno's earliest drawings, not only of the Whoops Sisters but of his pert — and unexpectedly busty — flappers and well-brought-up if often thoroughly sozzled young men, one is surprised to notice how many of the drawings have captions consisting of two or three lines. *The New Yorker* pioneered in the general use of the one-line caption but evidently didn't arrive at it without a struggle. Even that celebrated cartoon of 1928, drawn by Carl Rose, in which a mother and her pretty little daughter are at the table and the mother says "It's broccoli, dear," requires a second line from the rebellious child: "I say it's spinach, and I say the hell with it." (A caption written by E. B. White, who had his finger in every pie in those days.) Arno liked to make drawings that needed no captions at all and that were often merely cheerful instead of funny: one remembers racy sketches of wonderful girls naked in bed, with big black dots of nipples and hair black against heaped-up white pillows. Needless to say, these drawings did not appear in the magazine; they would appear in the collections by Arno that were published to high critical praise every few years throughout his lifetime.

Arno aside, surely the most dashing figure on *The New Yorker* in the early days was Lois Long. Ross was often uncertain of what he wanted the magazine to be — or, rather, he was certain only of what he wanted it not to be. This led to many muddles and high hopes dashed, but Ross never doubted that the ideal *New Yorker* writer, to say nothing of the ideal *New Yorker* reader, would be someone as like Lois Long as possible. He felt himself an outsider in New York and something of a hayseed, and in his eyes Miss Long was the embodiment of the glamorous insider. An exceptionally intelligent, good-looking, and high-spirited girl, she had graduated from Vassar in 1922 and had plunged at once, joyously, into a New York that seemed always at play — a city of speakeasies, nightclubs, tea dances, football weekends, and steamers sailing at midnight. She wrote for *Vogue* (her father was both a lexicographer and a minister and he had trained her to respect the hard craft of writing) and she tried her hand at acting as well. For a while, she shared a smart little flat on the East Side with a fellow-actress, Kay Francis; the parties they gave there are still remembered.

In the early years, one of the most important departments in the magazine was "Tables for Two," which reported on fashionable nightclubs, cabarets, and restaurants. The department was written and illustrated by Charles Baskerville, writing under the pseudonym of Top Hat, and when he went off to Paris, late in 1925, to improve his skills as an artist, Ross put Lois Long in his place; Top Hat became Lipstick.

Lois Long and Arno hamming it up during Prohibition at a carnival speakeasy.

"Great Scott! Now what's happened?"

Arno sketched with particular relish the breakdown of mechanical things — trains, planes, ships, and taxicabs. He satirized not only our manners but also the harsh urban context in which we evinced them.

"You have a very penetrating mind, Mr. Harrington — drunk or sober."

Arno made the astonishing discovery that drunkenness could best be depicted by drawing
a man's eyes as crosses — something not to be seen in nature and yet wholly convincing.

Despite Ross's repeated, gloomy expostulations on the subject of office romances, it was perhaps inevitable that Arno and Miss Long should have fallen in love. They married and had a child and — also perhaps inevitably, given their strong temperaments — within four years were divorced; Miss Long subsequently married a proper Pennsylvanian named Harold A. Fox, of whom history records little except that his nickname was Huck and that at bibulous parties he would sooner or later be introduced to strangers as bearing the last name Hox. In 1927, Miss Long was appointed fashion editor of *The New Yorker* and under the heading of "On and Off the Avenue" began to set down the first of what must total several million words of acute and candid fashion criticism.

L. L.'s attitude was a novelty; most writing about fashion then, like most writing about fashion now, amounted to scarcely more than the sedulous puffing of certain favored shops and designers. L. L. cared not a straw for anyone but her readers. Her intention was to instruct and entertain them by the extraordinary device of taking clothes seriously and writing about them honestly. The device succeeded, and she soon acquired an immense following. All her life, she went on telling the truth, with a wit and lack of rancor that made her career an enviable one. She grew stout with age and her eyes began to fail her, and the point was reached when she could no longer accurately distinguish one color from another. She retired in 1970 and four years later she died. Like Arno, she was older than her age; life had proved far different from what that shining Vassar girl had supposed it would be.

Because L. L. had not wanted a funeral service of any kind, her daughter, Patricia Maxwell, gave a little party in her memory at the Algonquin, a few days after her death. Against all odds, the occasion turned out to be a happy one. Shawn, Whitaker, Peppe, Weekes, and other old-timers were there; Whitaker and Carmine Peppe, like L. L., had joined the staff in its founding year. Plenty of drinks were served and anecdotes about Lois were on everyone's lips. People spoke with delight of the latest, and possibly the last, outrageous anecdote of which she was the leading figure. In its long and admiring obituary of her, the *Times* printed a photograph not of the Lois Long with whom the obituary was concerned but of another Lois Long — a dress designer whom L. L., as it happened, had always cordially disliked. What a noisy, comic scene she would have liked to make at the *Times*, denouncing such a gaffe!

The Jazz Age passed, and so did the grim thirties, and with them passed some of the readiest targets of Arno's satire — the imperious dowagers, the choleric, Roosevelt-hating clubmen, rendered extinct by time but in part surely by him. Not that there was ever any dearth of subjects for Arno; his range widened as his social interests narrowed, and if in the years immediately before his death he gave up frequenting bars and nightclubs in favor of a reclusive life in the country, his drawings remained very much of and in the world. He worked hard to give delight, and it must have pleased him to think of thousands of perfect strangers laughing out loud over what had cost him so much serious effort. He never undertook a drawing he didn't have faith in, and it was anguish for him to fail; sometimes he would work for twenty-four hours at a stretch on a single idea, for fear that if he put it aside he would be unable to bear returning to it. Like many artists and writers, he was under the impression that no one had to struggle as painfully to express his talent as he did, and he would swear that he had used up more erasers than all the rest of the artists on the magazine put together.

The very last of the several hundred full-page drawings he made for *The New Yorker* appeared on the week of his death, and in content and composition it was a characteristic piece of work. In the woods of Arcady, a horned and bearded Pan gambols about, playing pipes and making nervous eyes at a lightly clad nymph beneath a tree. Like all Arno girls, she has a gorgeous body and a dismayingly practical nature, and she has but three words for Pan: "Oh, grow up!" The drawing is a matter of some forty or fifty bold strokes of black against white, bound together by a grey wash; it has been built up as solidly as a fortress, though built in fun, and its dominant note is one of youthful zest. Nobody could ever tell that it was the work of an aging man, much less of a dying one. But then, artists are lucky in having it in them to outwit age, as their work outwits death; the longer they live, the younger they dare to become in their art. With every year, Arno's work in black-and-white grew simpler and stronger and more playful, and the colors he employed in his superb covers grew brighter. One could spot them a long way off, blazing with a kindergarten fierceness of sky-blue, apple-red, sea-green.

"Oh, grow up!"

Arno's last drawing for the magazine. Significantly, the scene is a glade and the most complicated mechanism in sight is a set of pipes.

Because he avoided the office, many of his colleagues, though they were directly or indirectly his followers and heirs, had never met him. On hearing of his death, one of them wrote in to the magazine to comment on how universally appealing his drawings had proved to be: "In 1956, I found a copy of an old Arno drawing framed in a bar in Salerno. I came on another last summer in Greece. I expect to be finding Arno drawings for years to come, wherever I go, all over the world. I think he signed his drawings not to identify them, for they could have been nobody else's, but to give more strength to the composition. That bold signature of his was the only unnecessary thing in any Arno drawing."

Ilonka Karasz was making beautiful covers for *The New Yorker* within a few weeks of its founding, and she is making beautiful covers for *The New Yorker* today. For almost forty years I have been grateful to her and have felt her to be a part of all our lives on the magazine, and yet I haven't met her. Worse still, I have never so much as sent her a note of thanks for the pleasure she has given me. Well! This is often the case with the artists and writers we admire. Unwilling to write what we fear may be taken for the mere gush of a fan letter, we keep silent, and we are wrong to do so. For if our colleagues are not actually waiting for our praise, they would certainly be grateful for it if it came. In theory, the execution of a work of art is an act complete in itself, but in practice it is incomplete unless it is responded to, and artists and writers whose handiwork appears in the highly ephemeral form of a magazine publication often experience the uneasy sensation of having performed in a vacuum.

I am on a train and the passenger seated beside me picks up the latest issue of *The New Yorker* and starts thumbing through it. Soon he will reach a short story I have written. I hold my breath. I want very much for him to read it. I want him to glance at the opening sentence ("They were drawing apart, and it was so strange") and be unable to resist reading further. But no — he riffles on past my story, and when other pieces are also ignored, I deduce that he is looking first at the drawings, as I do myself. Still, I am disappointed. I had wanted to observe, however imperfectly, his reaction to my writing. And if later, the train journey over, he

Ilonka Karasz's first cover for the magazine.

turns back at last and reads the story, the chances are that I will never know what he thinks of it. He will not write to tell me how much or little he has liked it. Our readers are as diffident about writing letters as I am; no doubt that is why they are our readers. They have reached a level of sophistication in respect to the arts that causes them to avoid pressing a personal claim upon an au-

Miss Karasz's most recent cover.

thor; they withhold the admiration and even the affection that less sophisticated readers would be apt to give.

Gerard Manley Hopkins wrote that "better late than never" was the dismalest proverb he knew. This paragraph is a fan letter to Ilonka Karasz in the form of an apology. Her perennially youthful art makes me believe, for as long as I am in its presence, that I, too, am young, and I am sorry to be many decades late in telling her so.

Abe Birnbaum, who died in 1966, was one of the most gifted of our cover artists. Nobody was satisfied with the "rough" of this giant robin as it was first seen at the weekly art meeting. At the time, the background consisted merely of landscape. Geraghty suggested the addition of birdwatchers. That simple change changed everything.

So prolific was Birnbaum that at his death a large number of his covers and "spot" drawings remained on the bank. This dazzling white daisy appeared within the year.

Rare as talent is, many millions of Americans believe themselves to be first-rate artists; a very large fraction of this number sends in drawings to *The New Yorker*. Only a few such unsolicited drawings are ever bought, though sometimes an aspiring artist is invited to sell the idea that has prompted his drawing, in order that one of our so-called "regular" artists make something publishable out of it. We have perhaps seventy or eighty regular artists, most of whom depend on other people for ideas. Every week, the magazine buys from fifteen to twenty drawings or ideas for drawings; some of the best ideas come from professional gag-writers, who are able to make substantial livings from their anonymous handiwork. A gag-writer named Richard McAllister contributed most of the ideas used by the artist Helen Hokinson. When Miss Hokinson was killed in a plane crash, editorials in newspapers mourned the country's loss of her satiric intelligence. The truth was that the satiric intelligence remained very much alive and soon found an outlet elsewhere. From time to time, McAllister sells one of his own drawings to the magazine. They appear to be the work of a small, not very gifted child.

Amateur artists and amateur gagmen abound in the professions. Doctors think they know just what *The New Yorker* needs in the way of cartoons; so do lawyers, who invariably notarize their submissions and warn the magazine against plagiarizing them. Psychoanalysts are constantly sending in wretched ideas for drawings about psychoanalysts, and for reasons that nobody fully understands, a large proportion of our would-be artist-contributors are Canadians. In my experience, artists tend to be more cheerful than writers and somewhat more eccentric. One artist who has met with very little success at *The New Yorker* so far regularly brings in rubbings of manhole covers. Certain subjects — desert islands, for example, and drunks in bars — appear to be inexhaustible. Once, Geraghty mentioned to me that the art "bank" contained a deplorably high number of jokes featuring conversations between animals. I proposed that the artwork of an entire issue of the magazine be devoted to talking-animal jokes, thus reducing the bank and just possibly causing our readers to lose their minds. My proposal was accepted, the issue came out, and as far as the magazine could judge, the prank went largely unobserved.

Compared to most *New Yorker* writers and editors, I am gregarious to the point of seeming lunacy. Because I was born with more than ordinary energy and with every passing year appear to have less and less need of sleep, I spend much of my life racing from one pleasant social occasion to the next. A confident believer in Jane Austen's dictum that everything happens at parties, I am present at some five or six public or private gatherings a week and am often hard-pressed to find room in the hours between them to carry out my professional obligations. As a drama critic,

I will sometimes attend a second or third night at the theatre instead of an opening night because the opening conflicts with a promising dance at somebody's house or a birthday celebration in the nearby countryside. In Gatsby's blue gardens "men and girls came and went like moths among the whisperings and the champagne and the stars." I have my Gatsby gardens and other gardens, not all of them under the stars. One consequence of my gregariousness is that I am acquainted with far more people out in the world than anyone else on *The New Yorker* is; I am also in a position to know more people on the magazine itself than anyone except Shawn is likely to know. I am the clownish one chattering his way in high spirits and at high speed among the laconic hermits and dour moles of Sleepy Hollow, and I cannot fail to note that there are times when my colleagues wish I would take my damnable high spirits elsewhere. Those who find it hard to get up in the morning find it intolerable that I should leap out of bed early every morning burning to embrace the day. Once I met Bainbridge on the street outside the office. "Please," he said, holding up his hand. "It's only ten. I haven't had my coffee yet. Not a word about how wonderful a day it is. It would make me ill."

Bernard Malamud was of similar cast of mind at a cocktail party that I remember being held on West Sixty-seventh Street, for a good cause that had enlisted Philip Rahv, Susan Sontag, Larry Rivers, and Dwight Macdonald — *that* sort of solemn good cause. Over drinks, Malamud made the mistake of asking me, "How's everything with you?" I said, "Absolutely marvellous!" Malamud leaned close and shook his head. "Shit," he said.

An advantage of my incorrigible partygoing is that there have been comparatively few Ilonka Karaszes in my life; people I have wanted to know I have mostly come to know. Moreover, at parties I occasionally encounter people of whose existence I have previously been unaware, or who I had assumed were long since dead. Sometimes they are people who have played an important part in the early days of *The New Yorker,* and whom I naturally feel an acute interest in, as having prepared the way for the likes of me. A few months ago, at a cocktail party at the house of Joseph Ryle, I was introduced to Charles Baskerville, who is a well-known painter of portraits of society figures and — the subjects he prefers — of animals and exotic landscapes. Baskerville looks to be in vigorous early middle age, and I asked him if he happened to be any relation of the Baskerville who was writing and drawing for *The New Yorker* back in the spring of 1925. "I *am* that Baskerville," he said, and so he was: despite his youthful appearance, he is old enough to have fought in the First World War and to have been a much-sought-after young man-about-town in those first years of the Jazz Age. He was precisely the sort of dashing New Yorker that Ross was not and never would be and yet, as editor, was supposed to have an intimate knowledge of. Ross asked Baskerville to write a column about nightclubs, illustrating the text with pen sketches. Baskerville was delighted to oblige. "Late at night, I sat down and wrote whatever came into my head," he told me. "Hard to believe how important a part of our lives nightclubs were in those days — Texas Guinan's, Ciro's, the Trocadero, and the rest. We *lived* in them."

As to how much he earned from his weekly column, Baskerville's recollection is not very clear. "It may have been fifty dollars a week, for both text and drawings," he said. "Ross was never one to spoil young folk with high pay."

BILL REARDON BOOSTS EDYTHE BAKER

A FLASK'S EYE VIEW OF A RUM RAID

Charles Baskerville wrote and illustrated a nightclub column for the magazine during the early months of its existence. He signed the column "Top Hat." The drawings were made with pen and brush in India ink on ordinary typewriter paper, immediately after Baskerville's return to his studio from whatever nightclub is identified in the drawing. The dancer at the Club Richman was sketched the evening Harry Richman sang for the first time "The Birth of the Blues."

216

20

Among the artists on the magazine, my oldest friend is Charles Addams. The earliest memories I have of him go back to the Second World War, when, as an enlisted man in the Army, he was not too arduously employed making animations at the Signal Corps Photographic Center on lower Park Avenue. Save for the greying of his hair and a certain thickening of his body, he seems to me remarkably little changed over the years. He has always had a round but not in the least cherubic countenance, with a nose prominent and yet seemingly boneless and therefore capable of being twisted into curious shapes, and it is true that in drawing characters of a diabolical mien he has often fallen back upon making scary faces at himself in a mirror.

"Congratulations! It's a baby."

From boyhood, growing up in harmless Westfield, New Jersey, Charlie has had a genuine bent for Gothic horrors and especially for the outward signs — graves, tombstones, catacombs, coffins, and dangling skeletons — of a necrophilia that he is far from practicing except on paper. Almost from his first appearance in the magazine, a cult sprang up about him and established certain truths as being self-evident, though to anyone who knew Charlie they were but the necessary fictions that worshippers invent to embellish their god and provide the refreshment of gossip for themselves. I used to hear it as an established fact from members of the cult, none of whom had ever met Charlie, that whenever he reached the point of derangement at which he began to sketch again one of the most famous of his drawings — that of a skier who has just skied through the trunk of a tree, the tracks of his skis uninterrupted on either side of the trunk and the skier himself miraculously intact — the office would summon an ambulance and have Charlie hurried off to a sanitarium. It is true that there are some high-strung artists who have drawn for *The New Yorker*, but Charlie is not among them; he is easygoing and pacific, and I am always ready to turn the wildest sort of verbal somersault in order to elicit from him his delightful, squeaky laugh.

Other cultists used to maintain that they had seen in the magazine a drawing by Charlie of one of the more horrid of his man-monsters waiting outside the delivery room of a hospital and saying, to a nurse who holds a newborn baby in her arms, "Don't bother to wrap it — I'll eat it here." Needless to say, no such drawing ever appeared in the magazine; office folklore holds that it was proposed by Gibbs as a parodic extension of an Addams drawing that did appear: one that showed a strange-looking male outside a delivery room and a nurse exclaiming brightly to him, "Congratulations! It's a baby."

In those years of the Second World War, the Gill family lived in a charming old red-brick townhouse on East Seventy-eighth Street. Having grown up in houses, I had found that I disliked life in an apartment, with the occasional impertinences of strangers' heels clicking on the floor above one's head and strangers' voices bawling in the hallway and up and down the service stairs. Moreover, I envied householders their being able to step straight off the street into their own quarters, built upon the hard rock of Manhattan and with a patch of Manhattan soil at the rear, capable of being worried into the semblance of a garden. I had set about looking for a small house on the Upper East Side; in the early forties, hundreds of such houses were on the market. Coming up Third Avenue one afternoon after inspecting a couple of houses that had proved unsatisfactory, I glanced along Seventy-eighth Street toward Lexington Avenue. According to a list of properties I had in my hand, the house at Number 157 was for sale. On the north side of the street stood a row of houses, mostly of three stories, that I reckoned must date back to shortly after the Civil War. At some point around the turn of the century,

"Just the kind of day that makes you feel good to be alive!"

their fourth stories and high stoops had been removed; one gained
access to them from an iron-railed areaway a step or two down
from the public sidewalk. The house nearest Lexington Avenue
had retained its fourth floor, with a steep mansard roof and three
stately dormers emerging from the slates. Sheltering its front door
was a gabled, ecclesiastical-looking little porch of brick and
stone. I willed hard that that house would prove to be Number
157, and it was.

Addams gave me this drawing on my thirty-fifth birthday. The houses in the foreground are not unlike the old mansard-roofed red-brick house that the Gills then lived in on East Seventy-eighth Street, in New York.

The house belonged to the widow of a doctor, who had practiced medicine there for fifty years, in an office fashioned out of a dimly skylighted Victorian conservatory. (The conservatory was a triumph of optimism over geography — it faced north and received only a few hours of sunlight a year.) The living room had high French windows opening onto the street, and a fine white marble fireplace with a black steel grate and brass fittings. It is notorious that animals come with time to resemble their owners, and perhaps plants do so as well; the widow was tall and meager and already inching toward another world, and so were the plants that crowded every window: ferns, Norfolk pines, rubber plants, cactuses, poinsettias saved from Christmas to Christmas, and innumerable lanky geraniums, rising crookedly eight or ten feet into the air without a single blossom. The house had six bedrooms and four bathrooms, a kitchen that smelled deliciously of seventy years of well-spiced cooking, and a dining room that looked out over a garden filled with privet, English ivy, and periwinkle. At the time, we had three children and a nursemaid, so the house would be an excellent size for us, at once cozy and ample.

Then and there, I told the widow I would buy the house. She pinched off a dead leaf or two from the geraniums and said how pleased she was that there would be children playing in the house; for she and the doctor had been childless.

I mentioned earlier that all my life I had lived beyond my means, and the evidence is that it may be wise to do so, or, rather, that it isn't necessarily *un*wise to do so. Nearly thirty-five years after the purchase of Number 157, the ease with which an improvident writer in his twenties was able to carry out the transaction may be amusing if not instructive. The widow's price for the house was nineteen thousand dollars; even in the post-Depression days, to find a ten-room house of exceptional charm in one of the most attractive neighborhoods in New York for under twenty thousand dollars was sufficiently surprising, and I did well to stake my claim to it at once. A bank held a mortgage of fourteen thousand dollars on the property, which I was glad to assume. My father, that indefatigably generous man, gave me thirty-five hundred dollars toward the purchase price and subsequently gave me much more to help pay for furnishing the house with pieces of suitable age and rarity. I borrowed fifteen hundred dollars from the magazine ("advance against future work") to round off the purchase price; my actual cash outlay, for legal fees and the like, came to less than two hundred dollars.

The only person who took a dark view of this transaction was Hawley Truax, then the treasurer of the magazine. Truax on the subject of money has long been an occasion for grim merriment around the office. Having taken care to make himself rich while still a young man, he has since devoted himself to predicting financial disaster for everyone else. Indeed, he has assumed that the country itself was on the verge of collapse for many decades now, and if he lives long enough, it is possible that his opinion may finally be proved of some value. (The office legend is that for over a quarter of a century Truax has had a hundred thousand dollars tucked away in a safety-deposit box at his bank, against the day when the bottom falls out of everything; if the legend is true, then Truax not only has lost thousands of dollars in interest on his money but has also seen its value diminish steadily from year to year.) When I told Truax that I had bought a house for nineteen thousand dollars, he shook his head. "Not a good investment," he said.

A few years later, with the advent of more children, we felt obliged to sell the house and move into a large, semi-ruinous

mock-Tudor mansion in Bronxville, which we still occupy. We sold Number 157 to Harold Henderson — by chance, Truax's friend from earliest boyhood — for about fifty thousand dollars. When the Hendersons, finding themselves in age averse to climbing stairs, decided to move into an apartment, they sold the house to the son of one of their neighbors on Seventy-eighth Street; the price by then was something over a hundred thousand dollars. Today the house is probably worth well over two hundred thou-

sand dollars, but I have no doubt that Truax, if asked his opinion of its worth, would shake his head and say, "Not a good investment."

Be all that as it may, it was in the house at Number 157 that we gave many parties for our *New Yorker* friends and colleagues. I can remember one occasion on which, very late at night, it seemed the most sensible thing in the world for Philip Hamburger, Charlie Addams, and me to mount tricycles belonging to the three Gill children and go racing at top speed round and round the dining-room table. In my mind's eye I see Charlie bent fiercely above the tiny handlebars, a cigar clenched in his teeth, pedalling as if the devil himself were in hot pursuit. Racing came more naturally to Charlie than it did to Philip and me; he has always been a collector of fast cars and in his youth he used to take part in races out on Long Island. He likes both fast cars and very old ones: in the nineteen-forties, he received as a present from the playwright Philip Barry, then living in East Hampton, a 1928 Mercedes-Benz, which Ellen and Philip Barry had driven on the Riviera in the gaudy twenties (the car was sacred for having been occupied by, among others, Sara and Gerald Murphy, Zelda and Scott Fitzgerald, Léger, and Picasso) and which eventually died, much mourned, in Charlie's arms. Today he owns a 1926 Bugatti, a 1933 Aston-Martin, and, for purposes of ordinary transportation, a 1973 Alfa-Romeo.

From time to time, a new and unexpected talent is seen to leap Roman-candle-like straight off the pages of the magazine. Among writers, this has been the case with John O'Hara, Irwin Shaw, John Cheever, Shirley Jackson, J. D. Salinger, and John Updike; of the lot, perhaps the most startling was Salinger. Editors and readers alike were instantly bowled over by his "A Perfect Day for Banana-fish" and "To Esmé — With Love and Squalor" and by his series of later stories about the mysterious Glass family. I had feared that the author's prolonged and obsessive scrutiny of the Glass psyches had led him to still his hand, but Shawn has said that it is not so. Though Salinger's absence from the pages of the magazine is from week to week and from year to year an ob-scurely felt deprivation, the fact is that he goes on writing, and surely someday he will be willing to let us observe the conse-quences.

Among artists, the most startling figure has been that of Saul Steinberg. Born in Rumania, he moved to Italy and at the time of the outbreak of the Second World War was drawing cartoons for a newspaper in Milan. After being held for a period in a detention camp, he managed to make his way to America, or, at any rate, to Ellis Island, well within sight of the promised land. A relative of his came to *The New Yorker* and asked Geraghty if the magazine would undertake to sponsor Steinberg in this country; unless there was some assurance that he wouldn't be-come a public charge, he would have to be deported. Geraghty had never seen any of Steinberg's work and was unable to provide the necessary promise of support. Poor Steinberg retreated to Santo Domingo. From there, he sent some drawings to another local relative, who brought them to Geraghty. At the next Tuesday afternoon art meeting, Geraghty showed the drawings to Ross and spoke approvingly of them, but Ross turned them down. Before returning the originals to Steinberg's relative, Geraghty had them photostated; happening to meet Maloney in the corridor, Geraghty showed him the photostats. Maloney thought they were excellent.

Geraghty said, "Go tell Ross what you think about them. Lay it on thick." Maloney went immediately to Ross and was vehement in his praise of the drawings; with passion, he expressed his incredulity at Ross's having rejected them. Ross called Geraghty on the phone. "Jesus Christ, Geraghty!" he said. "I didn't reject those goddam drawings — I just said I didn't see how we could print them. Not the same thing at all."

Geraghty bought the drawings (which in fact were never printed, though others soon were), and the magazine got in touch with certain friends in the State Department. Soon thereafter Steinberg was admitted to the country by way of Miami. As an alien, he had to register for the draft, and almost at once found himself called up for active duty. Ross telephoned an acquaintance, James V. Forrestal, then Secretary of the Navy, and asked him to take Steinberg under his wing. Forrestal did so to such effect that on a single remarkable day in his life Steinberg was commissioned an ensign in the U.S. Navy and, in the company of a couple of Navy officers, ceremoniously conducted into federal court and made a U.S. citizen. At the time, Steinberg could speak very little English and was of a radically unmilitary posture and deportment; he must have struck his new colleagues as the most unlikely officer in the entire armed forces.

Steinberg is a gifted storyteller, and some of his stories are apt to strike a skeptical listener as being too good to be true. Still, the evidence of his life is that he has nearly always got his way, no matter how preposterous a way it may seem to be. The apparent ease with which he pursued his career as an artist throughout the dark and arduous days of the war isn't necessarily an exaggeration. It is Steinberg's testimony that he was sent out to China with a naval intelligence unit, where one of his tasks was teaching Chinese spies to use Western pens instead of their traditional brushes and little pots of ink in the course of making hasty sketches behind the Japanese lines — so dangerously time-consuming, after all, to be busy mixing one's ink when one is meant to be busy spying! One day he happened to meet General "Wild Bill" Donovan, head of the Office of Strategic Services, which is to say, our head spy; captivated by Steinberg, Donovan invited him to join his personal staff, and so Steinberg set off around the world, touching down in whatever sector of the war theatre was in need of Donovan's attention. Soon the magazine was getting big sheets of Steinberg's drawings out of China, India, North

A present from Steinberg on my thirty-fifth birthday.

Africa, and, ironically, out of the very Italy from which only a few years before he had been at such pains to make good his escape.

Though the subjects of Steinberg's wartime drawings appear to have been approached with a light heart, the drawings were not intended to be funny; they were a form of journalism, serving much the same topical purpose that a "Reporter at Large" piece would serve. They were also, of course, works of art, and it was to Ross's credit that he accepted them as such and, later, respected Steinberg's desire to be not merely an artist who illustrates gags but one whose landscapes are inscapes and whose documentation is devoted largely to the workings of his own mind. As the years have passed, Steinberg's drawings have grown less and less humorous and more and more witty; he has become an epigrammatist whose diction happens to be a sort of lofty doodling. Like most epigrammatists, he sees little to love in human nature and much to satirize, and one feels that he long ago grew weary of a target so difficult to miss; in any event, he is often engaged nowadays in speculations more common among writers than among artists — speculations that take the shape of prankish obiter dicta not about man but about a couple of man's earliest and most intricate inventions: language and numbers. Like Ross and Shawn, he seeks a mastery over the means by which we think, and his message to us is that such a mastery comes hard. Words and numbers are never only what they seem, and though he pokes fun at them, he is in dead earnest; even a single letter or number is perfidious and unpredictable and must be examined with caution.

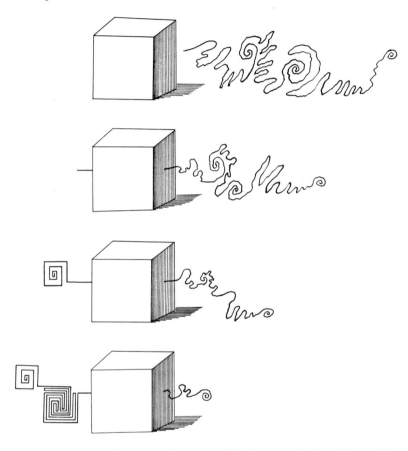

Steinberg is a born pedagogue. He has much that he wishes to tell us about the unreliability of signs, signals, and symbols, and so quickly and easily does he set down his droll warnings that he gives the impression of not needing to take thought; it is as if his hand had the capacity to apprehend as well as execute, without the nuisance of having to be directed by the brain; one thinks of Steinberg's eye as being as much astonished and gratified by the flow of zigzags and curlicues issuing from his pen as any stranger's eye would be. It is a hand inexhaustibly creative, from moment to moment making fresh wonders out of trifles. A match for Picasso in turning found objects into works of art, Steinberg regards the exterior world as existing largely in order to be transformed (a paper plate, scissored and inked, in a few seconds becomes an Indian chief in a feathered headdress) or to be mocked for trying to remain in his presence what it has hitherto been (a bathtub is made to bear on its gleaming white porcelain surface a naked figure outlined in black paint, suave and preposterous in its three dimensions). The nature of Steinberg's interior world one can only make guesses at; it is a vaudeville of tumbling alphabets and numerals, and it is something more. A stranger might fear that the air there was too cold for comfort and perhaps too thin for ordinary folk to breathe, but it is not so.

It is characteristic of Steinberg's bent for pedagogy that in the early years of his success he hired a car and driver and set out to tour the battlefields of the Civil War. He became something of an expert on the subject, not least in order to teach the rest of us what he thought we ought to know. Like so many Europeans, he feels strongly inclined to tell us what America is like; in Steinberg's case, it is worth one's while to listen. He is so persuasive in his speculations that even the most implausible of them, set forth with all the authority of his now formidable command of the language, are apt to go unchallenged. They amount to arias, spoken and not sung, and the very act of testing them might reduce them to nullity.

Once, years ago, I took Steinberg to the Century Association, whose handsome nineteenth-century clubhouse stands but a few doors away from the *New Yorker* building on West Forty-third Street. I was eager to have Steinberg become a member of the Century, and with reason. The club was founded about a hundred and thirty-five years ago, as a gathering place for artists, writers, and "amateurs of arts and letters," and if it has threatened to become the citadel of the Establishment — for among the amateurs are many prominent lawyers, doctors, architects, statesmen, men of God, and even, alas, a few specimens of that filterable virus, the foundation executive — it remains true that artists and writers are favored above all others and that one is elected to the Century on one's merits and not as a consequence of being rich, famous, or well born. ("On one's *merits?*" a member of the Union Club, a citadel of New York WASPs, is said to have exclaimed with incredulity, on learning that this was the basis for election to the Century. ("That's a hell of a way to run a club.")

Steinberg was delighted with the clubhouse, which was designed by Stanford White, in 1889, and has been subjected to a minimum of alteration since, on the principle that the House Committee's responsibility is "to make improvements without making changes." Steinberg was less delighted by the prospect of having to be looked over by members of the Admissions Committee — an ordeal imposed on all candidates for election by the club's venerable bylaws. When Steinberg hinted that the bylaws might well be ignored in his case, I assured him that this was impossible. That he finally consented to be treated like any other candidate was thanks in part to the happy chance of his discovering that the writing tables in the Visitors' Room were furnished not only with old-fashioned steel-nibbed pens and inkwells but also with sticks of red wax, matches, and club seals. Any club so equipped was plainly a club that might prove worthy of Steinberg; at once he sat down and, placing a sheet of club notepaper in front of him, scribbled one of his celebrated nonsense missives — missives that appear at first glance to be important and easily legible documents and that turn out, at a second glance, to be gibberish. Steinberg struck a match, held it to the end of a stick of wax, let a drop or two of warm wax fall onto the paper, and then pressed a club seal into the wax. In something like thirty seconds, he had created a charming little work of calligraphic art, of which I then and there became the honored recipient. It has given me great pleasure ever since.

Despite his remarkable intelligence, not all of Steinberg's intuitions are of a high order. After he had become a member of the Century, he happened one day to notice that a rubber doormat at the front entrance bore the initials C. C. He told Geraghty, "Now I understand Brendan's great devotion to the club. C. C. stands not only for 'Century Club' but for 'Catholic Church' as well." The difficulty with this charming Freudian hypothesis was that Steinberg took me for a devout Catholic, when in fact I was, and am, a totally collapsed one, long known to be the vociferous enemy of the errors and superstitions of Rome. Nothing could be more unlike my feelings in regard to the Century than my feelings in regard to the Church.

Steinberg's misreading of the situation would be unlikely to

THE CENTURY ASSOCIATION
7 WEST FORTY-THIRD STREET
NEW YORK 36, N.Y.

The nonsense missive that Steinberg wrote while visiting the Century Club. The blob at upper left is the club seal in red wax.

embarrass him. A tenacious and adroit debater, he might well silently reverse his field and begin to argue that I love the Century because I love being an apostate, and to prove the point he would

234

call attention to the fact that an accurate abbreviation of "collapsed Catholic" is, of course, C. C.

If one were to ask Steinberg which of the artists on the magazine, himself excepted, was the greatest, I suspect he would answer, "Steig." And if one were to put the same question, with the same exception, to Steig, I suspect he would answer, "Steinberg." They are certainly the two who have gone furthest in the direction of producing works of art that are not jokes; what they draw is almost never based on a gag and almost never needs an explanatory caption. They have escaped the bounds of weekly topical journalism, and in doing so they invite being judged by standards of criticism not usually associated with popular magazines. The fact is that by now they are not so much *New Yorker* artists as artists whose work happens to appear — in both cases, more and more rarely — in *The New Yorker.*

Steig began drawing for the magazine in 1930, when he was in his early twenties. In such extended series of drawings as "Small Fry," "Dreams of Glory," "Holy Wedlock," and "Everyday Histrionics," published over a period of many years, he has demonstrated that his intention has been to give us a view of life

Crybaby

and not simply to make jokes. Steig has a literary gift as well as a gift for graphics, and he has written and illustrated a number of successful children's books; his imagination is obviously allusive and romantic, as Steinberg's is analytical and ironic. Where Steig's

DREAMS OF GLORY

The Case Is as Good as Solved

drawings are, so to speak, warm to the touch, Steinberg's are ice-cold. Steig is the puppet-master of a stage that is peopled with kings, queens, courtiers, and clowns, most of whom one seems to recognize out of some dimly recalled fairy tale of one's youth. Equal in importance to human beings of no matter how high a rank are animals — donkeys, pigs, geese, and the like, all speaking with ease the lingua franca of Cloud Cuckooland. On the occasions when they choose not to speak, we guess that it may be because they are themselves of royal blood and, having long since been put under a spell, await with brute patience a redeeming human kiss.

At the least a kiss, and perhaps more than a kiss. The erotic
has always been implicit in Steig's work, and lately it has become

the theme that preoccupies him and has given a new and unexpected energy to his work. All men growing old dread the loss of their sexual prowess; writers and artists are luckier than their fellows in being able to turn this mounting dread into art. In the genre of the erotic, Picasso, as Steig himself says, "is the father of us all." Like Picasso, Steig celebrates the body both in ripeness and decay; he feels an equal reverence for it whether it be comely or deformed. His Amorous Kingdom is a country that though we have never been there, we feel at once ruefully in exile from: a fresh morning Eden, charged with love — dotty with love — within whose borders everything, whether animate or inanimate, displays a knack for affectionately leaning toward another. Lovers share with the least leaf on the smallest tree a desire to find completion in being touched; differences of age, gender, and species cease to matter in the whirligig of innumerable wooings.

Every year Steig's imagination grows at once bolder and more delicate. My hope is that his drawings in their increased candor will soon pass over into what the conventional opinion of the time would call pornographic. I am a champion of pornography, to the extent that such a subjective topic can be defined; it seems to me obvious that pornography, like all art, is a statement in favor of life and against death. In however clumsy and mutilated a form, it speaks of the intention to reach out and connect by pairing. To the extent that the intention fails, I would place the blame on the timidly unloving nature of our society, for even this late in the twentieth century we fear to express the full amplitude of our appetites; instead, we remain dominated by a grim nineteenth-century Protestant work ethic, which regards sex as necessary but deplorable, and which assumes that life is but a prelude to the rewards and punishments that a just God will be meting out to us after death. (In the words of the well-known Presbyterian hymn, "One more day's work for Jesus, one less of life for me.") Steig's voluptuous men and women and his no less voluptuous flora and fauna assert that life and lovemaking are the only certain goods and that old age and death are horrors, not to be welcomed and embraced but to be yielded to with indignation.

William Steig

At a guess, I would say that the three most prolific artists on *The New Yorker* have been Perry Barlow, Whitney Darrow, Jr., and Alan Dunn. Barlow and Darrow are still alive, and Darrow drawings continue to appear frequently in the magazine. Dunn died last year, of a heart attack, at the age of seventy-three. He sold

Ross disliked "in" jokes and affected to be displeased when it was pointed out to him, after publication, that Darrow had placed my name on the spines of a couple of learned tomes in this drawing of a psychoanalyst's office. As for me, I was delighted. Darrow wished to give me the drawing, but I insisted on buying it; he thereupon presented me with a second drawing — one that had already appeared in the magazine — to which he added my name in ten places, including a dedication.

In the facing drawing, the caption accompanying it reads, "Now, as I've said before, a neurosis often has its basis in conflicts within the family group." (Under Ross's initial on the back of the drawing is the admonition, "Open children's eyes.") In the drawing immediately above, the caption reads, "It isn't that I mind talking to myself, Doctor, but lately I can't think of anything to say."

his first drawing to the magazine in 1926, less than two years after it was founded; since then the astonishing total of nineteen hundred and six drawings by his hand have appeared in its pages — an average of close to a drawing in every issue for forty-eight years. He was by far the most topical of our artists; often it seemed but a matter of minutes, and rarely was it more than a matter of hours, between the time Dunn read of an event in the newspapers and the time he turned in an acute pictorial comment on it. This close scrutiny of his fellow-citizens was a function not of a continuous immersion in the world but of a withdrawal from it; Dunn suffered the burden of several phobias, the most intense of which was a fear of fire. On a few occasions, when he planned to visit a friend in an apartment building new to him, he went so far as to secure copies of the blueprints of the building and ascertain the position of its fire escapes. During the past ten or twelve years, he enjoyed many happy times at the Century Club, which had, for him, the cardinal advantage of possessing a broad flight of stairs leading down to the street. At monthly meetings, he would stroll about sipping a martini and chatting animatedly with friends, at the same time keeping an eye on the front door.

Dunn made this drawing to illustrate an appeal for funds with which to help pay for air-conditioning the clubhouse of the Century Association. It was kind of him to do so, since he intensely disliked air conditioning.

Though Dunn's phobias limited his activities, they increased his alertness to change, and his drawings can be read as a history of the transformations, both physical and psychological, of much of twentieth-century New York. His avocation was architecture, and he lovingly — or, sometimes, sharply — recorded the many alterations in architectural styles that the city underwent in his lifetime. He was funny about them, and he was also bitter; one didn't doubt that behind his courteous demeanor passionate feelings were being held in check.

Dunn was a slender, dapper man with a tiny mustache, which he may have hoped made him look like a dangerous riverboat gambler. In reality, he was the least dangerous man alive, and one of the gentlest. He and Mary Petty, his wife and fellow-artist, were cherished by their friends like prizes that had been won in some incomparable secret lottery; none of these friends wanted to risk making the Dunns known to the world at large, and the Dunns were content within their small circle and with the superb conso-

242

"Uncle Virgil, we're considering having you Astro-Turfed."

Richard McAllister, who has achieved fame among artists and anonymity in the world by providing his colleagues with ideas, occasionally appears in the magazine under his own name.

lation of their work. In the mysterious fashion of nearly all artists above a certain rank, Dunn's talent flowered with age; though his drawings remained as vigorous as ever, they grew lyrical and, in terms of their aesthetic intentions, took greater and greater chances. Right up to his last hours, he never stopped working and learning, and teaching us who we were. To die quickly in one's eighth decade at the very top of one's powers is an enviable end, and not an occasion for mourning.

21

Thinking of Stanley Edgar Hyman, I begin to smile. Whenever we speak of him at *The New Yorker* — and four years after his death, there are not many days when we don't have occasion to speak of him — it is always with a lifting of the heart. He was a merry man, though he aspired from time to time to become a gloomy one, and as a storyteller he was skilled at turning the sorriest of his misadventures into comedy for our sakes. The cluster of his close friends on the magazine — Mitchell, Hamburger, Shawn, Geraghty, me — became not so much participants in the life he actually led as participants in a life that he thought it would amuse us (and nourish us) to imagine his leading. This was a form of kindness as well as art; the most genuine of his protests and wailings would transform themselves into arias of the outrageous, and we would all be laughing with him over what had cost him pain. No doubt there is a Yiddish phrase to cover this situation, and no doubt Hyman in heaven is mocking me for my *goyische* ignorance of it. He loved trafficking in his Jewishness, especially among Christians; the outsider as insider was a favorite disguise of the hard-working confidence man he saw himself as being.

He was the youngest among us and he was also the oldest. He began writing for the magazine — not very well at first, but in a nervous imitation of E. B. White — in the early nineteen-forties, which is to say, during the Second World War. He was drafted and went downtown for a physical examination; according to what Hyman subsequently reported, the doctor told him crisply, "Mr. Hyman, you have the organs of a fifty-year-old man." Stanley was then perhaps twenty-three, but the doctor was right: physically, he was many years older than his chronological age. Early, to our alarm, he grew fat and breathless; all of his teeth went, and then most of his hair; his blood pressure rose; his beard turned from red to brown to gray; and he developed cataracts. Later, when,

Hyman photographed by Philippe Halsman. It is Halsman's custom, at the end of a session, to ask his subjects to allow him to photograph them in the act of leaping into the air. This request has produced remarkable results over the years, none more remarkable than this leap by Hyman, who was one of the most intransigently sedentary men that ever lived.

on doctor's orders, he lost weight, he looked not slender but wasted, and his dowdy businessman's clothes hung in grotesque billows beyond the diminished body. But that, too, was something to be made funny — seated in my office and, a born rabbi, drawing his fingers repeatedly through the forked tip of his beard, he would complain that when he chased girls on the street, the wind catching in his sail-like garments slowed him down and permitted his pretty (and only sometimes imaginary) prey to outdistance him.

As he was at once the youngest and oldest of us, so he was at once more naïve and shrewder than any of us; intellectually, we sat at his feet and learned as he learned. For a time, Lord Raglan, that crotchety but astute anthropologist and authority on myth, became our god; for a time, there could be no other god than Raglan. Freud, Darwin, Marx, Frazer — as the tangled bank of heroes thickened and grew, we took care to grow along with it. We felt lucky to have collided with Hyman and to have observed at first hand the furnishing of that capacious mind, the by no means accidental building of that distinguished career. Nearly all that we learned, we learned over drinks, at Stouffer's, or the Lobster, or in the lobby of the Algonquin, or in a littered bedroom of the Royalton, where the Hymans always stayed. I remember once, in the early days, having breakfast with Hyman and his wife, Shirley Jackson, in the quick-and-dirty that occupied part of the ground floor of the Royalton. Each of them ordered and ate a substantial breakfast of orange juice, buckwheat cakes with maple syrup, buttered toast, and coffee; then they ordered and ate the same breakfast again. They got up hungry.

Hyman's grand passion was, of course, books; he could say, with Wallace Stevens, "Words of the world are the life of the world." Lesser passions, which flared and dwindled, were for chess, poker, baseball on TV, and numismatics. As far as I know, the only machine he ever learned to operate was a typewriter, and he was uneasy with that. When Shirley died and he married Phoebe Pettingell, along with the many gifts of self she brought him, she brought an invaluable skill: she could drive a car, and at Bennington, where he taught for many years, one has to have a car. He knew almost as little about conventional good manners as he did about dress; nevertheless, he gave thoughtful and often quite beautiful presents on ceremonial occasions and he was gleefully aware of how little it pleased me to have him appear at the

Century Club wearing open sandals over multicolored socks. He carried with him whenever he came to the *New Yorker* office what amounted to a magic briefcase. Its magic lay in its being of the same weight at the end of a visit here as it had been at the beginning, though it contents would have changed utterly. He would leave Bennington with the briefcase full of whiskey and he would return to Bennington with the case full of *New Yorker* stationery. There must be hundreds of pounds of *New Yorker* stationery stored somewhere in Bennington. Hyman loved to drink and he loved to write, and it pleases me to recall how that briefcase helped him to make his avocation and vocation one.

Shirley Jackson Hyman wrote under her maiden name. Early in her career, she published a story in *The New Yorker* called "The Lottery," which caused a sensation. It was about a scapegoat chosen by lot to be stoned to death in a community that the author was purposely vague about — perhaps the dreadful events of the story had taken place long ago, in some foreign backwater of civilization, or perhaps (and more likely) they were taking place here in America, in the twentieth century. Hundreds of letters came in from troubled and excited readers, causing a furor not to be equalled until the publication of Salinger's "Franny."

The story made Shirley Jackson famous. She became increasingly preoccupied with witchcraft and claimed, with apparent seriousness, to be able to exercise diabolical powers. Once, when for some reason she was angry with her publisher, Alfred Knopf, she learned that he was journeying up to Vermont to ski. The Hymans had then recently moved to Bennington, so Knopf was unwittingly putting himself within close range of Shirley's evil eye. She made an image of wax and stuck a pin in one leg of the image, and, sure enough, Knopf broke a leg skiing — broke it, indeed, in three places. Shirley would hint darkly that she had enjoyed a good many other triumphs of that nature.

Shirley and Stanley had met as undergraduates at Syracuse University. She was a bluff, good-looking Californian, who wore glasses and weighed too much — a classic fat girl, with the fat girl's air of clowning frivolity to mask no telling what depths of unexamined self-loathing. As for Stanley, he was the classic bright

247

Jewish boy from Brooklyn, also wearing glasses and also a self-mocker. He was a disciple of Kenneth Burke and was burning to become a celebrated critic; until that time came, he would earn a living by journalism and teaching. Though without money, they married and set about having a family; soon there were four children and then almost at once, so it seemed, grandchildren.

The Hymans lived at first in Greenwich Village and later in a forlorn, ill-dusted house in Westport. That house was the scene of many drunken revels, one of them especially notable for its lack of charm. Dylan Thomas was on one of his reading tours in America; somebody brought him to a party at the Hymans', where Thomas took a shine to Shirley. By this stage of his life, Thomas was no longer the promising romantic boy of the Augustus John portrait; he was a tubby little man, with thinning hair and brown teeth with holes in them. Despite his appearance, he enjoyed a considerable sexual success among suggestible college girls, whom he would approach with the honest if unappealing inquiry, "Can I jump you?" At the Hymans', a drunken Thomas put the question to a drunken Shirley, while a drunken Stanley sat contentedly in front of his TV screen, watching a night baseball game. Hearing no negative in response to his question, Thomas made a pass at Shirley, who leapt to her feet and lumbered past Stanley, with Thomas in close pursuit. She mounted the front stairs, ran along the hall, stumbled down the back stairs, and again lumbered past Stanley. Shirley and Thomas made the circuit three or four times before Stanley, irritated at having his view of the ball game repeatedly interrupted by the gross beasts jogging past him, reached out and grabbed Thomas by the belt of his trousers, causing him to fall to the floor, while the winded Shirley mounted the stairs for the last time.

Another drunken occasion (for when I remember the Hymans, it is nearly always under the auspices of alcohol, and I am always every bit as drunk as they): a group of *New Yorker* writers has been invited up to Bennington. We have been asked to conduct a panel discussion on the current state of magazine journalism, and since the panel consists of E. J. Kahn, Jr., John Bainbridge, Philip Hamburger, and me, with Stanley serving as our moderator, there is reason to suppose that something informative may emerge from the discussion. Unfortunately, the hospitality provided by the Bennington girls at a cocktail party held in our honor before the discussion proves far too lavish for our good. We reach the auditorium in a state of total obfuscation. Making matters worse is the fact that we must rely on a public-address system to make ourselves heard and there is only a single microphone to be passed up and down the length of a trestle table. In the course of being fumbled over and shoved back and forth by unsteady hands, the mike quickly falls to pieces. We all babble on more or less inaudibly, often laughing with delight at the good points we are scoring. An intermission has been scheduled, after which the plan is for the audience to return and put questions to the panelists. When the intermission is over and we resume our seats on the platform, there is no audience. It is literally the case that not a single person has returned to ask a question. A few days later, I receive a small check from the bursar of the college, thanking my colleagues and me for our "performance."

Shirley grew so fat that it became painful for her to walk; bones in her feet threatened to break under the heavy burden of her body. The last time Anne and I saw her before she died — death came to her in her sleep, of a heart attack — was at a party we gave to celebrate our twenty-fifth wedding anniversary. The party took place at our country place in Norfolk. On a stretch of lawn between our house and the surrounding woods, we had pitched an enormous white marquee; metal-lined boxes, ordinarily used to hold potted flowers, were filled with ice and scores of bottles of Piper-Heidsieck, and a very satisfactory occasion it turned out to be. Shirley and Stanley had arranged to be driven down from Bennington. Shirley was wearing a shapeless reddish coverall, which served to exaggerate her size and not, as she must have hoped, to diminish it, and with her sharp writer's eye she cannot have failed to note that to many of the other guests she seemed an apparition, impossible to account for in their world of strict bodily discipline. The Hymans stayed late, as they always did, drinking and talking. Stanley sat slumped in a cloud of cigarette smoke on a couch in the living room; at his feet were some boys and girls of college age, a couple of Gills among them. They saw the relish with which Stanley in his cups took the bait of hard questions; joyously he lashed out at them, scolding them and instructing them as he coughed and choked and laughed and scattered ashes and liquor down the front of his rumpled clothes. Shirley in the dining room was determined to be helpful — she would assist Anne and me in drawing up a list of all the presents we had received that day. (One of them was the Hymans' own present, an ingot of pure silver that Stanley had ordered from the Treasury. "A silver anniversary is a *silver* anniversary," Stanley said. He was shocked that one of our Norfolk neighbors had given us a quart-tin of homemade maple syrup.) Shirley scribbled away diligently in the candlelit dusk of the dining room, smiling a child's smile at the accomplishment of the task she had set herself. In the morning, when we looked at the list, not a word of it was legible.

After a brief period of widowerhood, for which he was wholly unsuited, Stanley married Phoebe, who was among the ablest of his students. He accepted a position on the faculty of the State University of New York at Buffalo, found it less agreeable than he had expected, and went back to Bennington and resumed teaching there. On one of his hasty "magic briefcase" visits to New York, I learned that he was in need of more copies of Lord Raglan's *The Hero,* a text that he regularly assigned his students. Raglan's daughter and son-in-law were friends of mine; the son-in-law, who taught at Columbia, happened to mention to me one day shortly after I had seen Stanley that he had hundreds of copies of *The Hero* stored in his office at the university — overstock that he had picked up for a few pennies apiece. I begged for some copies to give Stanley and was told that I could have as many as I liked. I drove my station wagon to Columbia, filled a couple of big cartons with books, and proceeded up to Bennington, to deliver the precious cargo. Stanley and Phoebe had moved into a new house, and Phoebe was pregnant. We had a long, merry visit together. Within a couple of weeks, eating and drinking at a favorite restaurant, Stanley suffered a heart attack and died. The Army doctor of long ago had been proved correct; Stanley was only fifty-one, but he was really seventy. Five months later, Phoebe had their child, a boy whom she named Malcolm.

The book with which Hyman established his reputation was called *The Armed Vision.* Published in 1948, it was a study of the methods of literary criticism, and it contained a detailed attack on Edmund Wilson, accusing him, among other things, of plagiarism. By the time the book came out, Wilson and I were friends;

all I ever heard him say about Hyman was, "That fellow Hyman is bad news." Curiously, I remember him saying this to me in the men's room on the nineteenth floor of the *New Yorker* building, while washing his hands.

Wilson had succeeded Clifton Fadiman as the regular book reviewer for the magazine on January 1, 1944, and he soon made profound changes in the nature of the "Books" department. Fadiman had dealt with the greatest possible number of current books, disposing of them briskly and concisely, often in a single paragraph and often with considerable wit. Wilson was more nearly an essayist than a reviewer; he liked to write at length and he was less interested in reviewing new books as a service to readers than in speaking his mind about writers that mattered to him. Moreover, he was openly scornful of most living writers of fiction. He began his first *New Yorker* review of a book of fiction, "I picked out Kay Boyle's *Avalanche* (Simon and Schuster) in the hope of finding a novel worth reading, and have been somewhat taken aback to get nothing but a piece of pure rubbish."

He was militant, even combative, in print, and was not above showing off; one thinks of those humorless duelling matches about the Russian tongue that he engaged in with Nabokov, in the pages of *The New York Review of Books*. One recollects, however, that the Wilson salvos were hurled not face to face but from what amounted to the snug concrete pillboxes of Wilson's homes in Wellfleet and Talcottville; his favorite battleground was of paper and his favorite weapon was ink, and in person he rarely made a fist at anyone. He had a way of — it was almost a knack for — keeping at a self-protective distance. This was in his nature and was, I would say, a defect in his nature, but like all the rest of us he raised what he could not help about himself into a principle and then congratulated himself upon practicing it. A member of his class at Princeton has described him as a loner there, and in the most serious sense he was a loner all his life. Shyly, awkwardly, he was sometimes willing to be the first to edge sideways into friendship, but more often he would hold back, would huff and puff, would wait and see. Carlos Baker has written of Wilson's telling him that the reason he had been able to maintain any sort of relationship with Hemingway was that he had "intentionally remained somewhat aloof and uninvolved." This decision happened to be a shrewd one in respect to Hemingway — increasingly, toward the end of his life, Hemingway was served by lackeys who were in fact serving only themselves. But "aloof and uninvolved" Wilson remained to many who would have liked to be close to him and whose friendship would have nourished him.

In this connection, I think of a time when Wilson and his wife, Elena, were resident potentates at Wesleyan. Aside from their fellow-potentates Jean Stafford and Father D'Arcy, the cultural pickings in Middletown appear to have struck the Wilsons as pretty thin; they had a good word for the cookies that were served on state occasions there, but for very little else. It was a measure of their plight that they would often repair to Hartford — to Hartford! — to revive their spirits. They would have a few drinks in the bar of the newest hotel and then they would go to the movies. "We never go to the movies *you* recommend," Wilson would say to me, and this was a direct professional blow, for I was then serving as the movie reviewer for *The New Yorker*. "You are *always* wrong about movies." And then he would laugh heartily, much pleased at having left me with nothing to say.

I am a born *shadchan,* and taking pity upon the Wilsons in the wasteland of Middletown, I decided to bring them together with my old friend Wilmarth Lewis, living a few miles away in Farmington. It seemed to me unendurable that Wilson, the greatest man of letters of his time, and "Lefty" Lewis, one of the greatest literary scholars of his time, should never have met. In my small way, I would be making history by bringing them together, these two grey eminences born within a few months of each other, in 1895. I was sure that Wilson would be enchanted with Lewis and Strawberry Hill, his great house in Farmington, filled with eighteenth-century treasures, and I arranged with Lewis to ask the Wilsons, Jean Stafford and me, and a couple of other people to lunch. Lewis has spent most of his life happily immersed in the world of Horace Walpole and other members of the English aristocracy, and he is a man celebrated for the elegance of his dress, the charm of his manner, and the wit of his conversation. I had supposed that one could no more resist Lewis's courtly blandishments than walk on water. Well, I was wrong. Lewis's ease made Wilson edgy; the harder Lewis strove to please, the warier and more prickly Wilson became. Even bourbon, that precious benison, proved of little avail before lunch, except to me. Through the blessed veil of alcohol that lowered over me during what must have been a delicious meal, I can remember little save that when

I got home late that afternoon I went at once to bed, on the pretext that I was coming down with a bad cold.

One of the reasons I have for wishing to live a few more years is to discover what the two principals made of that occasion. We know that Wilson's diaries exist and will someday be available to us, and I assume that Lewis, too, in the good eighteenth-century fashion, has been keeping a diary. It will be instructive to learn what each of them thought of the other. Perhaps Wilson will have written, "Gill is *always* wrong about people."

Wilson himself was *sometimes* wrong about people, me among them. For when he first came to meet some of us staff writers in the long reaches of Sleepy Hollow, I had made a name for myself as a writer of stories about priests, nuns, and sad young men about to be gobbled up by Mother Church. By then, I had long since left the Church — like any renegade Catholic, I was often to be found attacking the Immaculate Conception in the nearest neighborhood bar — but Wilson had pegged me once and for all as a loyal Catholic, and in the most ardently retrograde nineteenth-century fashion, he despised Catholics. It was a confirmed bigotry in him, and he used to mail me, sometimes anonymously, scurrilous doggerel that he had written attacking the Church. I soon saw that there was no way to convince him that his labors on my behalf were in vain — that I was already outside the walls, along with him, and that he should send his lively *pasquinate* to the faithful kneeling inside, among whom they might do some good.

By a pleasing irony, at about the time that Wilson was trying to lure me away from a religion to which I no longer belonged, a new friend, Muriel Spark, was trying in vain to lure me back into it. Out of affection but also, I assume, out of a conviction that all lost souls are worth striving to rescue (for the fiery little Spark is a convert to Catholicism, and converts take their beliefs far more seriously than the rest of us take our disbeliefs), she one day made me a present of a charming gold reliquary, containing a splinter from the skeleton of the distinguished eighteenth-century Jesuit cardinal Saint Robert Bellarmine. I keep the reliquary (along with an affidavit affirming that the splinter is indeed "*ex ossibus S. Roberti Card. Bellarmino*") in a drawer of my desk here at the magazine, not knowing what else to do with it. It is an exquisite piece of jewelry and should be pinned like a brooch on the bodice of a dress, but some remnant of a childhood fear of committing blasphemy keeps me from putting it to such a use. A saint's bone between a pretty girl's breasts! I wish I had the nerve.

Wilson had plenty of other prejudices, including what he called his Hispanophobia, or, rather, his anti-Hispanophilia. Quite late in life, he dared in a book review in *The New Yorker* to make the following extraordinary remarks: "I have been bored by everything about Spain except Spanish painting. I have made a point of learning no Spanish, and I have never been able to get through *Don Quixote* ... I have never visited Spain or any Hispanic country." Well! He was also for a long period an Anglophobe, though the reiterated chorus of praise from over the water that greeted his successive works had an understandably mitigating effect upon him. Since I share his low opinion of detective stories, I will not call his attacks on them manifestations of prejudice but of wisdom. In a celebrated article in *The New Yorker* entitled "Who Cares Who Murdered Roger Ackroyd?" he described a poll he had taken of correspondents who had objected to an earlier article of his, pouring contempt on detective stories and their readers. He had tabulated his readers' preferences and had discovered that Dorothy L. Sayers was by far their favorite. Very well — he would read her supposed masterpiece, *The Nine Tailors.* Anyone who ever knew Wilson will hear his voice — a kind of shrill boom of scorn — in the following passage: "Well, I set out to read *The Nine Tailors* in the hope of tasting some novel excitement, and I declare that it seems to me one of the dullest books I have ever encountered in any field. The first part of it is all about bell-ringing as it is practiced in English churches and contains a lot of information of the kind that you might expect to find in an encyclopedia article on campanology. I skipped a good deal of this, and found myself skipping, also, a large section of the conversations between conventional English village characters: 'Oh, here's Hinkins with the aspidistras,' etc. There was also a dreadful stock English nobleman of the casual and debonair kind, with the embarrassing name of Lord Peter Wimsey, and although he was the focal character in the novel, being Miss Dorothy Sayers's version of the inevitable Sherlock Holmes detective, I had to skip a good deal of him, too. In the meantime, I was losing the story, which had got a firm grip on my attention ..." At the end of his article, Wilson writes: "To detective-story addicts, I say: *Please* do not write me any more letters telling me that I have not read the right books ... With so many fine books to be read, so much to be studied and known, there is no need to bore ourselves with this rubbish."

Wilson felt a scarcely less violent aversion to serious contemporary fiction. One exception was a first novel that, so I remember being told, Wilson was under the impression had been written by a girl in her twenties. He wrote a favorable review, and the author and he subsequently arranged to meet; he was downcast to discover that his promising first novelist was approaching seventy.

Wilson wrote in longhand, at great speed, and it is said that he and Rebecca West have been the two fastest writers on the magazine in our time — a distinction much easier to ascertain than the distinction of which among us is the slowest. Wilson was a fantastically good reporter, and yet how unfit he seemed by temperament for such a role! This short, fat, breathless, diffident man — how did he so quickly gain the confidence of strangers? Given his superlative intelligence, the great books that he quarried out of other books were easy to account for, but where did he find the energy and confidence to turn himself, as he did in the thirties and forties, into an American Defoe? There they stand, shapely volume after shapely volume: over thirty books of fiction, plays, essays, literary criticism, literary and political history, and personal reminiscence. Wilson was a master at devising titles for books, and many of them are so familiar to us by now that the mere recital of them brings back whole reaches of our past: titles like *I Thought of Daisy, Axel's Castle, This Room and This Gin and These Sandwiches, The Triple Thinkers, To the Finland Station, The Boys in the Back Room, The American Jitters, Memoirs of Hecate County, The Shores of Light, Apologies to the Iroquois, Upstate.* Robust titles; robust works. The quality of Wilson's prose — its virile narrative force, coolly advancing over the most difficult terrain — never faltered with age. Because his prose was so much admired by the rest of us, Wilson's opinion of it may be worth giving, as an example of how inaccurate even the ablest literary critic can be in trying to pass judgment on himself. One day in the office, Wilson and Hobey Weekes, who, like Wilson, had attended both Hill and Princeton, were talking about their old English teacher at Hill, who was an Englishman. Wilson felt that he had fallen so far under his spell in respect to forming a prose style that, as he told Weekes — and this in his fifties, at the height of his career! — he was afraid he would never be able to write a really good *American* English.

Before Wilson joined the magazine and therefore some years before I came to know him, he had gone through some hard times financially, and they had left their mark on him. His subsequent cavalier, not to say scandalous, disregard for the payment of income taxes (which he made a feeble attempt to link with his disapproval of the war in Vietnam) no doubt sprang from a feeling, nurtured in the days of his poverty, that the world owed him far more than it would ever be able to pay back. He was always ready to adjust this debt downward by any means that came to hand. In matters of the intellect he had high scruples, and in other matters he had no scruples at all. I remember hearing it said of him in the early nineteen-forties that he had succeeded in obtaining advances from half a dozen publishers for a single unwritten book, and if this was in principle outrageous, still, in the eyes of most of his younger colleagues it was the acceptable and perhaps even laudable conduct of a sort of literary Robin Hood, taking from the rich (that is, from publishers) in order to give to the poor (that is, to writers, though it was true in this case that there was but one writer involved, who happened to be Wilson).

Young people find it hard to credit the radical changes in literary fashions that have taken place over the past few decades. That there was ever a time when nobody read Scott Fitzgerald — how fantastic that seems, and yet it was so. When Fitzgerald died, in 1940, Wilson as his close friend and literary executor put together a volume of Fitzgerald's uncollected work, including his essay on his breakdown, selections from his notebooks, letters to him from Gertrude Stein, Edith Wharton, and John Dos Passos, and poems to him by John Peale Bishop and Wilson. Edmund brought the manuscript to Scribner's, Fitzgerald's regular publishers, whose editors immediately turned it down. They had already let much of Fitzgerald's work go out of print — at one point, *all* of Fitzgerald's work is said to have been out of print — and they saw no reason to believe that the public would be interested in these mere sweepings from a dead author's desk. Wilson carried the manuscript from publisher to publisher, in vain; at last, he brought it to James Laughlin, of New Directions.

Laughlin is easily the most interesting book publisher in the country and, over a period of almost forty years, has proved the most valuable to the world of letters. My high opinion of him is far from being based solely on the fact that he is one of my oldest and dearest friends, for the facts are there and they are incontestable. Laughlin started New Directions in the nineteen-thirties, while he was still an undergraduate at Harvard. He had money — he was a Laughlin of the Jones & Laughlin Steel Company — and he was determined that it be put to a good purpose. He was also a poet (or, as T. S. Eliot would have said, he was a young man who wrote verse) and a friend and protégé of Ezra Pound. "You can publish *me!*" Pound exclaimed, which at the time was less of an inducement for establishing a press than it sounds today. From the beginning, Laughlin made it his concern to bring out unknown young writers — Dylan Thomas, Tennessee Williams, Lorca, Delmore Schwartz — as well as neglected older ones, like Djuna Barnes, Henry Miller, and William Carlos Williams. It was Laughlin who helped launch the revival of interest in Henry James by republishing, in 1943, *The Spoils of Poynton,* and, the following year, *Stories of Artists and Writers,* edited by F. O. Mathiessen. He also revived interest in E. M. Forster by leasing from Knopf for a number of years Forster's *The Longest Journey* and *A Room with a View,* simultaneously commissioning from Lionel Trilling a book-length study of Forster.

Laughlin consented to publish the Fitzgerald volume, and for once Wilson was outwitted: the Fitzgerald estate was to be paid the conventional royalty, but Wilson was paid a fee, amounting to only a few hundred dollars. The outwitting was unintentional and without malice; neither Laughlin nor Wilson expected the book to sell well, a dozen other publishers having declared that it wouldn't sell at all. In those days, moreover, it was the invariable custom to pay the editor of a book, or the author of an introduction to a book, a flat fee. It is a sign of how eager New Directions was to find an audience for the book that the title page was made to serve almost as a table of contents; the book was called *The Crack-Up, with Other Uncollected Pieces, Notebooks, and Unpublished Letters from Gertrude Stein, Edith Wharton,* etc., etc. The assumption was that if there were no longer any readers who cared about Fitzgerald, perhaps there would be some who cared about

Gertrude Stein, Edith Wharton, and the like. The book was published in 1945 and was an immediate and prophetic success. Five years after his death, Fitzgerald was getting ready to be reborn.

James Laughlin

In a sense, Wilson himself enjoyed a form of rebirth a few years later, thanks in part to the interest in his work expressed by a brilliant young editor at Doubleday named Jason Epstein. Epstein had persuaded Doubleday to launch a new line of quality paperbacks, to be called Anchor Books. Among the first ten or twelve titles, he was eager to include *To the Finland Station,* which had long been out of print. Epstein wrote to Wilson at his home in Wellfleet, telling of his admiration for the book and asking if he might reprint it. He offered Wilson an advance on royalties of seven hundred and fifty dollars. Wilson wrote back saying he would be delighted to have the book reprinted and inviting Epstein up to Wellfleet for the weekend. It was the beginning of a close friendship. *To the Finland Station* came out in 1952 and was followed by two other Wilson books in the Anchor series: *A Literary Chronicle* and *Eight Essays.* From that time on, Wilson gained continuously in popularity; he was amused to observe himself becoming a widely sought-after Grand Panjandrum. He had a card printed which served him as an efficient, all-purpose refusal; for years, one of the cards was thumbtacked to the bulletin board on the nineteenth floor at *The New Yorker;*

I perceive that a problem has arisen in the course of my writing about the Hymans and now about Wilson, and it is one that will have to be resolved in order that I not seem to be telling unpleasant tales out of school about intimate friends. The problem is how to deal candidly with the fact that most writers are hard drinkers; it strikes me as necessary and desirable to write openly about a state of affairs I am accustomed to — am, indeed quite happily a party to — but I fear being accused of maligning writers in the very act of praising them.

In this country more than in any other that I know of, the relationship between writers and alcohol is a curiously close one. I have often asked literary scholars for an explanation of the fact that while in the nineteenth century few of our writers except Poe were heavy drinkers, in the twentieth century almost every writer worthy of the name has been one. Among the dead, we have only to think of Faulkner, Hemingway, Fitzgerald, Lardner, Marquand, Sinclair Lewis, O'Hara, Crane, Edwin Arlington Robinson, Wallace Stevens, O'Neill, Barry, Millay, Dorothy Parker, Hammett,

Roethke, Benchley, and Berryman. Among the living, the list is equally long, if not equally distinguished. Surely the provocation to drink that was faced by Melville, James, Twain, and other leading literary figures of the nineteenth century was as great as any provocation we face today, but none of them drank too much and most of us do. It is a mystery, which I am content to leave to scholars; I wish only to be understood as feeling admiration for my colleagues when I speak of their enjoyment of drink and of their willing capitulation to it. The more abstinent of my readers are reminded that "symposium" comes from the Greek word for "drinking party," and that if getting tight was good enough for Socrates, it is surely good enough for the rest of us.

With that caveat, I count myself free to mention what happy times Wilson used to have, drinking in the Algonquin lobby, or at the Princeton Club, or in any number of bars and restaurants around town. He had an enviable gift for seeming to remain sober, or, at any rate, for remaining coherent. He would seat himself on a couch at the Algonquin, surrounded by such young folk as Epstein, the artist Edward Gorey, and Clelia Delafield, who, with Epstein and Gorey, had founded an attractive, financially unsuccessful publishing house for children's books, called The Looking Glass Library. Wilson would order a double martini, or, if he was in his bourbon phase, a double bourbon; that would be followed by another double, and then another. Alcohol banished his shyness and made him eloquent; after a few hours of talk, it was possible that when he attempted to get up, he would fall down. No matter. He was still in command of his beautiful mind, and the abused body must shift for itself as best it could.

An image of Wilson in rickety age, in the old white house in Wellfleet. He shuffles from his desk to take from a bookshelf some heavy volume — he is bent upon correcting what he believes to be some childish error of mine — and as he takes the book from the shelf it falls to the floor. Wilson eyes it with irritation, then begins kicking the book across the floor to his desk, where he can sit down and pick up the book with comparative ease. Yeats's "ignominy of youth" isn't, he assures me, a patch on the ignominy of age.

Edmund Wilson, drawn by George Biddle.

Wilson died in Talcottville, in the big stone house that his mother's family had built in upstate New York and that had become for him in late years a consoling preoccupation. The ghosts there proved friendlier than he had expected. Old Talcotts gathered him in and nourished him as, having weighed the intellectual risks involved, he drew back, in wary unease, from the inimical present. He was seventy-seven when he died, and his mind, though it had changed course, retained to the end its unrivalled powers of discrimination and judgment. He presided with detachment over his bodily decline, noting in his diaries humiliations of age as accurately — and often as zestfully — as he had noted, in the leafy Princeton of long ago, the appetites of youth. It was a sad irony that he found himself increasingly a stranger in the America he had spent a lifetime making the acquaintance of and staking a substantial claim for in the world. Few writers have

261

labored so hard to know a country and its people, and not alone from books. Despite a constitutional diffidence, he became one of the best of journalists, out in all weathers to observe and record at first hand the American jitters of the Depression years, the American experience in Europe during and after the Second World War, the American debacle at home that he saw as the consequence of our intervention in Vietnam. He was tireless in pursuit of facts, tireless in speculation. In middle age, he scrambled hot and breathless among the caves that had held the Dead Sea Scrolls, and his deductions about the possible meanings of the Scrolls caused many a conventional theologian's eyes to pop; in his seventies, he examined with delight the Bomarzo monsters, carved in stone in the thickets of Latium, and when I had the nerve to write to him a few weeks before his death proposing a literary source for the monsters, Wilson wrote back with characteristic energy and terseness, "No! No! What nonsense!"

Wilson's eminence as a literary critic and literary historian overshadowed his distinction as a journalist. For his part, he would perhaps have liked more attention to be paid to his short stories, poems, and plays. In a laudatory piece, the London *Times Literary Supplement* once described him as America's foremost man of letters, and by his standards a man of letters was one who could accomplish any literary task that happened to come his way. His one novel, written in the twenties, continues to read well, and there are from his hand certain fugitive Christmas verses that will go on giving amusement for decades to come. He wrote innumerable book reviews and other articles for *The New Yorker*, and he was always a welcome figure in the office. He would step out of the elevator — a short, overweight man in floppy dark clothes, wearing a floppy hat and carrying a floppy briefcase — and one saw at once that of all the languages he had mastered, dress was the language that concerned him least. He had a big head and handsome, classic features, with fine eyes that would darken frighteningly in the presence of a silly remark. Friends hearing his high and curiously penetrating voice through the thickness of a wall would track him to whatever cubicle he had found an empty desk and chair in and would settle down with him there for a long roller-coaster of a chat. In spite of his shyness, he was a superlative talker; one guesses that Wilson in eruption was not unlike Twain in the range and vigor of his discourse, and, like Twain and other performers, he took pleasure from the pleasure he gave. He had been called Bunny by Scott Fitzgerald and other companions of his early days; to later friends he was a magisterial Edmund. The nickname came from his mother, doting over her pink baby. He was a passionate amateur magician and, for that matter, a magician with words: among contemporary writers, almost no one else has been able to accumulate a manuscript with Wilson's dazzling ease and speed. He had strong opinions, which he voiced without tact, and he cultivated the gifted young in a fashion that made them flourish sooner and to more effect than they could ever otherwise have hoped to do. For a writer, the rarest privilege is not merely to describe his country and time but to help shape them. Wilson was among the fortunate handful of writers who have succeeded in doing this, with books that are like bold deeds and that will live a long time after him, keeping him with us against our need.

22

Oh, but John O'Hara was a difficult man! Indeed, there are those who would describe him as impossible, and they would have their reasons. At a memorial service held for him shortly after his death, in 1970, his publisher, Bennett Cerf, delivered the eulogy. It proved to consist in large part of stories about O'Hara's often wounded feelings and about his many broken-off relationships. Cerf appeared not to notice that he was sketching a thoroughly unpleasant likeness of his close friend. It was said of O'Hara, nobody any longer remembers by whom, that he was a master of the fancied slight. Once it befell that Robert Benchley and his daughter-in-law Marjorie, catching sight of O'Hara at "21," called him over to their table. Marjorie said, "John, we've just been seeing *Pal Joey* again, and, do you know, I like it even better than I did the first time." O'Hara: "What was the matter with it the first time?"

O'Hara is certainly among the greatest short-story writers in English, or in any other language. With Dorothy Parker, Robert M. Coates, Sally Benson, and one or two other writers, he helped to invent what the world came to call the *"New Yorker"* short story, though nobody who has written a short story for *The New Yorker* would ever admit that there was such a thing. O'Hara had begun writing short pieces for us while he was working as a reporter on the *Tribune.* He was encouraged to try more and more ambitious pieces by Katharine White, who by sheer force of character had overcome Ross's fear of publishing anything more literary than "casuals" — those few paragraphs of personal misadventure that were a staple of the humorous magazines of the time. O'Hara's brilliant stories opened the door for all the rest of us to tumble through: Cheever, Shaw, Fuchs, Hazzard, and a score of others. Looking back over O'Hara's early stories, one is struck by how extremely short they are. Their brevity was a function of economics and not of aesthetic intention; in its first ten or twelve years, the magazine had a limited amount of space to devote to text and could run stories of only up to about fifteen hundred words in length. O'Hara appears to have had no difficulty conveying as much within those strict limits as later writers would convey in ten or fifteen thousand words. O'Hara himself became more diffuse as the magazine granted him the space in which to do so; his stories were rarely improved by their greater length.

I met O'Hara for the first time by chance, in the Algonquin lobby. He had been having lunch there with a friend we had in common, John Hersey. O'Hara had been ready to leave; instead, he and I sat down for a moment's chat, and the chat lasted three hours. It was a cold winter's day; one could see through the glass front doors of the hotel snow falling hard in Forty-fourth Street. O'Hara was wearing — wouldn't you know! — a coonskin coat and a plaid Brooks Brothers cap. All the time that we talked he never troubled to take off his heavy coat.

I was startled by O'Hara's ugliness. He was in his middle thirties and had already grown heavy; his head rose out of an exceptionally thick neck and his ears stuck out bizarrely from fleshy cheeks. To make matters worse, he had a bad complexion and a mouthful of decaying teeth, which he was all too slowly having replaced. In spite of his looks and my awe of him, we got on. We were about ten years apart in age, but we found we had much in common besides our friend Hersey: we were both Irish, we were both sons of doctors, we were both from communities that turned their backs on New York and we were both married to New York Protestants. Best of all, I had gone to Yale and made Bones, and O'Hara had wanted desperately to go to Yale and make Bones. He knew all about my particular group in Bones (of which Hersey was also a member), but then, it seemed on that long, snowy afternoon that there wasn't anything he didn't know about in regard to college and prep-school matters, down to the chants of the youngest schoolboy at Lawrenceville. It was, for example, a Bones custom never to speak of the secret society itself but to speak of it in terms of its location in New Haven; one said, "How are things on High Street?" O'Hara knew that, though he didn't tell me he knew it; he revealed it indirectly many years later, when he was anxiously awaiting word of his election to the Century Club. Happening to encounter his neighbor in Princeton, Frederick B. Adams, who is both a Bones man and a Centurion,

O'Hara said, "Tell me, Fred — how are things on Forty-third Street?"

O'Hara envied my being able to write factual pieces for the magazine as well as fiction. He had a number of possible "Reporter at Large" pieces that he wanted to do, but somehow they never worked out. He did succeed in writing one little Department of Amplification, about how it had happened that a race horse named "O'Hara" had been named by him but not after him; the piece must have pleased him, because it established that he was a close friend of the Jock Whitneys and the Charles Paysons, and they were society figures who meant a great deal to him. He also published a single poem in the magazine. It was entitled "Stars in My Eyes" and described, in rhyming couplets, a number of the leading movie actresses of the day; its most notable couplet was:

> Norma Shear'
> Should disappear.

For a time in the forties, Ross let O'Hara have an office at the magazine. It happened to be next to mine, and it was an uncanny experience to observe him at work. He would seat himself at a typewriter, shirt sleeves neatly rolled up and necktie loosened (he was the first person I ever knew to have a button holding down the back of his shirt collar, as well as the usual tab buttons in front. Class, I thought, which was surely what he wanted me to think). He would then proceed to rattle off at top speed a story that would need not a single correction. The fact was that he had worked the story out in his head, over no telling how many hours or days, and what he was setting down with such fiendish ease was simply a fair copy.

Sally Benson followed a similar writing system, with similar miraculous-seeming consequences. She would lie in bed in the dark, putting her stories together sentence by sentence and memorizing them as an actor might memorize the "sides" of a considerable part. The act of finally setting a story down on paper amounted to a delicious reward, which, like a child with a sweet, she would delay indulging herself in for as long as possible. Benson was so prolific that she was obliged to write under two names — her own and a pseudonym, Esther Evarts. As a rule, the Bensons appeared in the front of the book, the Evartses in the back. How envious we all were of her productivity! For though writers know better, sheer abundance always impresses them. In O'Hara's case, we who knew him were impressed not only by the abundance of his work but also by the exceptionally high quality it attained in his youth and early middle years — the years of the short stories collected under the titles of *Files on Parade*, *Pipe Night*, and *Hellbox*.

O'Hara was the best of us and he knew it, and this made him impatient for fame and academic recognition. He received fewer

O'Hara at Quogue, correcting proofs. It was at about this time that O'Hara was pestering the playwright Philip Barry to put him up for the Century Club. Barry demurred, on the grounds that O'Hara, who had many enemies, might be blackballed and that Barry might then feel obliged to resign from the club. O'Hara persisted, Barry proposed him, and, sure enough, O'Hara was turned down. When it developed that Barry had decided not to resign from the club, after all, O'Hara refused to speak to him for a year. After Barry's death, O'Hara persuaded another friend to put him up for the Century, and this time he was elected.

honors than most of his colleagues and he wanted them more. Not a single honorary degree came to him from any university. Having been instrumental in arranging for Yale to grant an honorary degree to Sinclair Lewis, for many years I championed O'Hara's cause at Yale, always in vain. He received the National Book Award in 1955, for *Ten North Frederick,* and grumbled aloud that the award was long overdue. In the same year, he was elected to the National Institute of Arts and Letters; the election was known to be a consequence of persistent campaigning on his part. For all his rancorous air of superiority, he could truckle when he had to. In 1961, finding that he wasn't among those nominated to receive the Gold Medal of the Institute, he resigned. Some years later, the Institute placated him with an Award of Merit medal, which it was able to do because the award goes by tradition only to people who are *not* members of the Institute. Having consented to be reelected to the Institute, he hinted that he stood ready to be invited into the National Academy of Arts and Letters, the smaller and more august body that is drawn from members of the Institute. The invitation never came.

O'Hara's correspondence with officers of the Institute is curious; it consists in large part of requests for rosettes to wear in his lapel. It appears that he was crazy about rosettes. He expected to be given a rosette to wear as a representation of his Award of Merit and was vociferously disappointed to discover that no such rosette existed. When the award was presented to him, he wept, and the tears were bitter as well as grateful. He had had to promote himself with such vigor before his inferiors, and he had had to wait such a long time in the anterooms of the Establishment before its leaders had deigned to acknowledge his presence. He disliked them and admired them and he would take vengeance upon them in his work.

The slight by the academics was genuine, but those many fancied slights he suffered — they were what made it hard to stay friends with him for long. My first estrangement from him was a result of a pleasant, harmless evening on the town; he and his wife, Belle, and Anne and I, having had dinner at "21," had returned to the O'Haras' small apartment on the Upper East Side for a nightcap. In those days, O'Hara was a heavy drinker and he had been pegging away all evening at a succession of Scotches. He had also been lecturing me on how I ought to manage my financial affairs. All my life my failure to take money seriously had induced others to feel alarm in my behalf. If, on earlier occasions, Ross had been fatherly on the subject, O'Hara was now being big-brotherly. Not that he had yet proved any wiser about money than Ross, for he told me that all Belle and he had in the world at that moment was the jewelry he had given her. His big moneymaking period was still in the future, but plainly he intended to be ready for it when it came. And so he was: how good a head he had for business is indicated by the fact that when he died he was said to be a millionaire several times over. Indeed, at the time of his death a newspaper story claimed that his publishers were withholding at his request something like a million dollars in royalties, which for reasons of income tax he presumably felt reluctant to take possession of.

His lecture about money fell upon deaf ears, though of course I enjoyed being worried over. Having finished our nightcaps, Anne and I were ready to say goodbye. O'Hara got unsteadily to his feet, protesting that he had one last treat in store for us. He disappeared into the bedroom, where he remained for some twenty minutes. When he emerged, he was utterly transformed. He had taken off his ordinary clothes and decked himself out in a cowboy outfit of incomparable Reno richness. He was all leather and steel and silk: a bedazzling one-man compilation of boots, spurs, chaps, holsters, and guns with nickelled butts. Above the chaps came a checked shirt and a scarf knotted about the neck, and above the big, boozy face floated a surpassingly broad, high-crowned, creamy sombrero.

O'Hara stood in the living-room doorway, weaving from side to side and evidently taking great satisfaction in his appearance. We realized afterward that he had counted on us to admire him as an embodiment of the Old West, but alas! he seemed merely a comic apparition, coming no closer to reality than his friends the Kriendlers, at "21," came with their indiscriminate litter of Remingtons. Anne and I burst out laughing. O'Hara was incredulous. He saw nothing in his person to laugh about. His cheeks flushed. He was too angry to speak. As the gentle Belle, a born pacifier, fluttered about in apprehension of the storm about to break, we said our farewells and hurried off to our house on nearby Seventy-eighth street.

O'Hara was able to forgive that transgression, but my next proved unforgivable. In 1949, he published a novel called *A Rage to Live,* and I reviewed it in *The New Yorker.* By then I had written a good many book reviews and had grown accustomed to separating the author of a work from the work. For a number of reasons, my unfavorable review of O'Hara's novel had consequences far beyond those that most unfavorable reviews elicit. Best to begin by printing the review in full:

"The present volume is a progress report from a case history study on human sex behavior." So, bumpily but with a certain grandeur, begins the first chapter of the Kinsey-Pomeroy-Martin whodunit, "Sexual Behavior in the Human Male." Translated into less gravelly English, this quotation from last year's romantic best-seller would make a pretty accurate description of what will probably be one of the year's best-sellers, the enormous new novel by John O'Hara, entitled "A Rage to Live" (Random House). The parallels between the Kinsey Report and the O'Hara Report are unmistakable. The authors not only share a major theme but have a similar interest in determining the extent to which the various classes in our society can be distinguished from one another in terms of what they do about sex and then in terms of what they *think* about what they do about sex. Dr. Kinsey is perhaps the leading professional student of this subject and as such has had the advantage of having numerous assistants, as well as the financial backing of the Rockefeller Foundation. Dr. O'Hara, our leading amateur, has had to go it alone, at his own expense. On the other hand, O'Hara has long been one of the most prominent figures in the profession of letters, while Kinsey, an old gall-wasp man, is a taxonomist first and a literary craftsman second.

Granted that Kinsey has the edge in statistics and O'Hara in style, the layman's immediate response to "A Rage to Live," as to the earlier, pioneer work, is likely to be one of uncritical admiration for the amount of scholarly research involved. This feeling is soon displaced, however, by one of depression, and eventually of suffocation, for the reader who begins by being ashamed of having paid so little heed to the true nature of the human condition ends by being convinced, half against his will, that the investigation of sexual practices had better be left, as it always used to be, not to the expert but to the young. It was predicted last year that the Kinsey Report would open our eyes and jolt us into a lively awareness of the complexity of our sexual problems; now it appears that the Report put more people to sleep than it awakened, and numbed our minds instead of jolting them. The recurrent passages of maudlin sexuality in "A Rage to Live," complete even to so worn a stencil as the prostitute with a loving heart and a high I.Q., may have the same effect. If so, it will be all the sadder, because the author has plainly intended to do more than out-Kinsey Kinsey; he has intended, indeed, to write nothing less than a great American novel.

There was reason enough for this ambition. "A Rage to Live" is O'Hara's first novel in eleven years and comes exactly fifteen years after "Appointment in Samarra," which was, and is, an almost perfect book — taut, vivid, tough-minded, and compassionate. In the period between "Appointment in Samarra" and "A Rage to Live," O'Hara published two other novels — the successful "Butterfield 8" and the inconclusive "Hope of Heaven" — and five volumes of short stories, many of which are as good as anything in the language. Within the tight framework of these stories, apparently so small in compass but nearly always so explosive in force, O'Hara was able to take the measure of an astonishing variety of subjects, describing for us, with or without sex but with every appearance of authenticity, the customs of such dissimilar outposts of civilization as Hollywood, Stockbridge, Washington, D.C., and Hobe Sound, as well as half a dozen New Yorks — Wall Street, Jackson Heights, the Village, Fifty-second Street, Beekman Place, Riverside Drive. But it is an unbreakable convention of our time that a man who has written novels goes on writing novels, and perhaps partly for this reason, but surely for other deeper and more compelling reasons, O'Hara sat down and doggedly accumulated "A Rage to Live," which must be about as long as his three previous novels put together and which bears little or no resemblance to any of them.

A sprawling book, discursive and prolix, ranging in time from 1877 to 1947, and full of a multitude of semi-detached characters and subplots, what "A Rage to Live" *does* resemble is one of those "panoramic," three-or-four-generation novels that writers of the third and fourth magnitude turn out in such disheartening abundance. Dr. O'Hara's handy guide to healthy sex practices has been tucked inside the disarming wrapper of the formula family novel, and one result of this odd combination is the loss of the old sure-fire, ice-cold O'Hara dialogue. Here, for example, is Sidney Tate addressing his wife, Grace Caldwell Tate, the heroine of the novel, on the subject of her affair with a cheap, lower-middle-class Irish contractor:

"... you see, in this world you learn a set of rules, or you don't learn them. But assuming you learn them, you stick by them. They may be no damn good, but you're who you are and what you are because they're your rules and you stick by them. And of course when it's easy to stick by them, that's no test. It's when it's hard to obey the rules, that's when they mean something. That's what I believe, and I always thought you did too. I'm the first, God knows, to grant that you, with your beauty, you had opportunities or invitations. But you obeyed the rules, the same rules I obeyed. But then you said the hell with them. What it amounts to is you said the hell with my rules, and the hell with me. So. Grace — the hell with you. I love you, but if I have any luck, that'll pass, in my new life."

Now, if this sounds like something out of an old *Redbook*, one is prepared at first to account for it on the ground that Tate is a Yale man, but no, he is the closest thing to a hero in the novel, and his ethics appear to be those of the author. That passage is, in fact, the intellectual high point of the book, and from there it grinds slowly downhill, through Sidney's death and a few more love affairs for Grace, to a sinister postlude, in which we learn that all the surviving characters have turned more or less physically into swine. In "Appointment in Samarra," there was nothing about Julian English that we did not know and want to know, but Grace Caldwell Tate is a fatally uninteresting woman, and her rage to live rarely amounts to more than pique. It is hard to understand how one of our best writers could have written this book, and it is because of O'Hara's distinction that his failure here seems in the same nature of a catastrophe.

Over a quarter of a century later, the review strikes me as sound — sound in what I singled out to praise in O'Hara and sound in what I condemned. The novel itself has left little mark in literary history, though students of O'Hara will always have to deal with it as a turning point in his career. My review correctly predicted that the novel would become an immense best-seller, but no amount of public approbation could lessen O'Hara's fury over what he considered an act of perfidy on my part. I wasn't simply a reviewer; I was his friend.

All his life, O'Hara was to be the victim of an inexpungeable suspicion that he was encircled by a host of secret enemies; moreover, he felt sure that many of these secret enemies had disguised themselves as intimates. My review indicated to him not so much that I disliked the book — he would have found that hard to credit, since he held the book to be incontestably a masterpiece — as that I had at last exposed myself for what I was: a leading member of the anti-O'Hara conspiracy.

O'Hara roared and howled with indignation, demanding of Ross that I be fired at once. Then he saw to it that his publisher, Bennett Cerf, howled and roared — or, rather, given Cerf's peculiar voice, squeaked and gibbered — to the same effect. Ross took the hurly-burly calmly. He was always at his best when a member of the staff was under attack for having done his work competently and in good faith. Not for the first time and not for the last, Ross sent off a brisk note to Cerf, beginning "Dear Bennett: You are incapable of ratiocination" and ending "You are my natural enemy."

Then something happened that doubled and redoubled O'Hara's wrath, and no wonder. Thurber, that incomparable mischief-maker, informed O'Hara that he had documentary proof of the fact that the review had been written not by me but by Wolcott Gibbs. Now, this was a master stroke on Thurber's part; as Lobrano once told me, Thurber was never so happy as when he could cause two old friends to have a falling-out. (I remember Lobrano's describing a party at Sid Perelman's, in the course of which Thurber had succeeded in making everyone present angry with everyone else, as well as with him. White-faced, trembling with vexation, Perelman finally eased Thurber out of the house. The next morning, Thurber was on the phone to Perelman: "Sid! What a marvellous party! I never had such a good time." And it was true; other people's miseries made Thurber's happiest times.)

With the invention of a single bold lie in respect to my review of *A Rage to Live*, Thurber had done two things: one, he had ensured that O'Hara would see me as a jackal, willing to let my name be used for a nefarious purpose and therefore a person permanently unworthy of forgiveness; and, two, he had ensured that Gibbs and O'Hara would quarrel. Moreover, the most painful of O'Hara's paranoid fantasies would thus have been caused to come true — his oldest and dearest friend stood revealed as his worst enemy. Iago-Thurber took care to point out to O'Hara that my review contained the adjective "discursive," which O'Hara was surely aware was one of Gibbs's favorite words. This was a lucky shot in the dark on Thurber's part; unbeknownst to him, O'Hara had sent Gibbs an advance copy of the novel, and Gibbs, on finishing the book, had written a letter to O'Hara, conveying his disappointment in it and employing that very word "discursive." Desdemona's handkerchief wasn't in the same class with such evidence.

I first learned of Thurber's treacherous misconduct some months later, at the party held at the Ritz to celebrate the twenty-fifth anniversary of the founding of the magazine. From that moment on, I had a hard time not feeling on O'Hara's side. Given Thurber's version of the situation, O'Hara was certainly entitled to despise me. What kept me from seeking a rapprochement with him, as Gibbs eventually did, was the fact that it had got back to me from many quarters that O'Hara was going around town saying that if he ever caught sight of me he would knock my block off — that fate and worse fates, in worse English. Explanations and apologies at such a moment would have seemed self-serving: a mere craven desire to save my skin. I made up my mind that when the inevitable encounter came, since I was a good many years younger than O'Hara and in much better physical condition, I would do my best to knock *his* block off. In my mind's eye, I saw the big, fleshy head rolling unattached along the sidewalk, on the grey face a look of astonishment and dismay.

The supposed sanguinary moment of truth arrived one evening at "21," where the Gills and the Gardner Botsfords had been having dinner. As we walked into the front hall to pick up our gear at the coatroom, I saw O'Hara standing there with a couple of friends. He had been drinking, but then, he was always drinking in those days, and, besides, I had been drinking, too. It appeared to be a fine time to challenge him to put up or shut up. I walked across the room to him and said, "Well, John, here I am. What are you going to do about it?" He stared at me dully, his lips working. At last there began to emerge from his lips a stream of vituperation. The words were conventionally scatological and were spoken with surprisingly little feeling, and when they began to peter out I said in a jeering tone, "Is that the best you can do?" Then I waited for him to take a swing at me. Fear conquered had done its work and adrenalin was racing through me like the headiest ice-cold champagne. O'Hara went on muttering imprecations in the way of the classic sullen barroom bully. I shrugged and turned away.

Out on Fifty-second Street, Botsford said, "That was a close call." In the vainglory of my moral victory, I said, "Not close enough."

Subsequently, O'Hara felt obliged to twist the matter of my adverse book review into something it hadn't been — the occasion for his breaking off relations with the magazine. So often and so eagerly did he and Cerf and other publishing friends repeat the false story that it soon made its way into history. The reason O'Hara pretended that I was to blame for the break was that the real reason was a comparatively sordid one, having to do with money instead of with wounded pride. As the files of the magazine can testify, Ross and O'Hara had long had a difficult relationship, in part because of O'Hara's persistent — and laudable — demands for a better system of payments to contributors. Sometimes he and Ross would be on speaking terms and sometimes not. During the Second World War, for example, O'Hara arranged to be sent abroad as a war correspondent for *Liberty*. He had some properly bespoke uniforms run up for him and was making one of a series of tearful farewell appearances at "21" when he spotted Ross across the room. There was bad blood between them at the time. On the chance that he might be about to die a hero's death in the South Pacific — actually, he spent only a few weeks there and filed a single story — O'Hara sentimentally decided to make it up with Ross. He went over to him, held out his hand, and suggested that they let bygones be bygones. "Go to hell, O'Hara," Ross said and refused to shake hands.

In the early postwar years, O'Hara was agitating for a profound change in the magazine's financial arrangements with its contributors. More accurately, he sought a change in the magazine's arrangements with him alone, but the rest of us would have profited if he had got his way. Something called a "first reading" agreement — what Muriel Spark was later to call a "cross-breeding" agreement — had recently come into existence; by its terms, if an author granted the magazine a first refusal of all his pieces, a twenty-five-percent bonus would be added to his usual payments. O'Hara wanted to amend this agreement in such a way that even if a piece was rejected, the author would receive a sizable fraction of the money he would have received if the piece had been accepted. Ross's nineteenth-century soul was shocked to the core by this suggestion — pay a man for a piece of work that had failed! Reward a man for having bungled! Jesus Christ, what was the world coming to?

In his prime, O'Hara was not only our best short-story writer; he was also our most prolific. By the time he died, he had sold a grand total of two hundred and twenty-five stories to the magazine — far more than any of the rest of us. (To date, Cheever has sold a hundred and nineteen, Updike has sold a hundred and four,

John Cheever

and Salinger has sold thirteen. Coates and Benson each sold around a hundred.) Nevertheless, pieces by O'Hara were often rejected, and it galled him not to be paid for them. He and Ross had a long-drawn-out and characteristically acrimonious dispute on the subject, after which O'Hara stopped writing for the magazine. Soon he was saying that he would never write for it again, unless one condition were to be fulfilled — that he could have Gill's head on a silver platter. *I* had thought of O'Hara's head on a sidewalk, but he thought of mine on silver; he had more expensive tastes than I.

As the years passed, Ross died, Belle O'Hara died (a year later, O'Hara married Katharine Barnes Bryan), Lobrano and Gibbs died. O'Hara became more and more a hermit-writer, luxuriously immured in winter in a house at Princeton and in summer in a house at Quogue. He grew richer and richer and was able to indulge his fondness for exquisite, dandyish clothes and glossy Rollses. Still, his envy of others never grew less. One evening in Princeton, he was invited to a party at the house of my old Yale classmate Merrill Knapp (the same selfish fellow who in Munich, in 1936, had failed to murder Hitler). Merrill had been prevailed upon to play and sing some old Yale songs. O'Hara approached his host at the piano. *"Merde,"* he said.

When O'Hara was proposed for the Century Club, I happened to be a member of the Admissions Committee. I urged his recommendation as a candidate on the grounds that he was a sour son

John Updike

of a bitch and a genius, and that a good club was one in which enemies as well as friends could find themselves at home; no sooner was O'Hara elected to the club than he wrote a stuffy letter to the House Committee, protesting the lack of a club tie. If he could not be seen by the barbarian world to belong to something, what was the use of belonging? He dreamed not only of gold pigs, gold skulls, and rosettes but also of telltale striped ties.

O'Hara on this side of the Atlantic and, on the other side, that equally pushy outsider, Evelyn Waugh, fought hard to prevent the erosion of the social ramparts. Storming them, O'Hara and Waugh had supposed that the ramparts were built of stone; it must have been disconcerting for the two loners to discover that the ramparts were only of sand. Though they had selfish reasons for wishing to keep their discovery a secret, as writers they were quick to plunder it for themes. Waugh succumbed to the temptation of creating retroactively a society worthy of his snobbish ideals *(Brideshead Revisited)*; O'Hara resisted the temptation. The world both high and low fascinated him and revolted him. He assumed that there never had been a time when it wouldn't have fascinated and revolted him. He trusted his eye and ear to the extent that they were free of admiration and pity. Mankind was vile and without surprises for him. He wrote of its vileness with equanimity, page after page. The items of the indictment would last him a lifetime.

One day in the summer of 1960, O'Hara let it be known through his friend McKelway that he had three novellas on hand that would surely prove suitable for *The New Yorker*. Shawn expressed an interest in seeing them. The condition was not that O'Hara was to receive my head on a platter but that the novellas be read at his house at Quogue, out on Long Island — no handing them in as an ordinary author was expected to do. Shawn asked Maxwell to undertake the reading assignment. Maxwell and his wife, Emily, were invited out to Quogue to have dinner and spend the night. In an atmosphere not unlike the opening of an Agatha Christie mystery, O'Hara greeted them on their arrival but failed to join them at dinner. Mrs. O'Hara was charming, as usual, and after dinner Maxwell was given the three novellas to read. It was only then that he fully realized the degree of his entrapment: his head was between the lion's jaws. What if he didn't like the novellas? What if he hated them? He began to feel violent cramps in his stomach. Mrs. O'Hara provided him with a suitable medicament and he settled down to his task. The first novella proved wholly unsuitable. Oh, God. So did the second. Oh, God in spades. Maxwell felt his stomach shrivelling with pain. He took another dose of medicine. The third novella, entitled "Imagine Kissing Pete," turned out to be the best thing by O'Hara that Maxwell had ever read. In the morning he told O'Hara that while he could not speak for Shawn and his fellow fiction editors, he was enchanted with "Imagine Kissing Pete." He brought it back with him to the magazine, where it was universally admired, and it was published in the magazine that September.

Tactfully, no mention was made of the other two novellas.

Shortly afterward, O'Hara mentioned that in the years when he had not been writing for the magazine he had accumulated what amounted to a suitcaseful of short stories. The editors were allowed to look them over, and out of this hoard several stories were purchased. O'Hara went on writing for us, but it was obvious that something had happened to his talent. The stories were longer and looser, to the point of being flaccid; one no longer believed at once in the authority of the dialogue and description. There were a few rejections, but no more roars of protest. O'Hara's heart was in his novels — in those immense earthworks of his late years, which one trudged seeking in vain a clue to their design. Surely the labor of producing them implied a passionate intention of some sort? Sometimes a reviewer says of a novelist that he writes as naturally as he breathes, and one takes this at first as a compliment, but it is not always so. O'Hara came to write as naturally as he breathed and for the same reason: it kept him alive.

For over twenty years, not a word between us. Two or three times, we passed each other in the rooms of the Century, and he seemed not to see me. I, who am so clumsy at cutting people, envied him, who was so skilled at it. The last time I ever encountered him was between the halves of a Yale–Princeton football game, at Princeton. He was coming out of the men's room under the concrete bleachers of the stadium and he looked old and soft and pasty-faced. Again he cut me, without apparent effort, and again I felt the old, reluctant admiration rising in me. What a superlative grudge-bearer he was, and how Irish of him it was to be one — the Irish are a people capable of bearing grudges for generations and even for centuries. O'Hara was a truculent and often mean-spirited man, but he had standards. "You see, in this world you learn a set of rules, *or* you *don't* learn them. But assuming you learn them, you stick by them."

On the gravestone in the Princeton cemetery is carved the epitaph that O'Hara wrote for himself: "Better than anyone else, he told the truth about his time, the first half of the twentieth century. He was a professional. He wrote honestly and well." From the far side of the grave, he remains self-defensive and overbearing. Better than *anyone* else? Not merely better than any other writer of fiction but better than any dramatist, any poet, any biographer, any historian? It is an astonishing claim.

I go back in my mind to that first day at the Algonquin, with the snow falling and the two young sons of doctors — O'Hara in his thirties, I in my twenties — searching out whatever they may have in common in their lives. I am sorry now for that review of *A Rage to Live*, not because of what it said but because it provided Thurber with the opportunity to make our relationship come to nothing. We were not likely to have become close friends, but we need not have become enemies.

23

If Thurber was no longer a regular member of the staff of *The New Yorker* by the time I got there in the late thirties, his presence was still very strongly felt, not only because his drawings and stories were appearing frequently in the magazine but also because he had left behind so many striking souvenirs of himself. Graffiti that he spontaneously dashed off on whatever wall or door happened to be convenient to him at a given moment of inspiration were preserved from year to year by the characteristically slovenly housekeeping of the magazine; which is to say that our walls were not often painted, and the Thurber graffiti lasted much longer upon them than they would have lasted in any conventional latrine.

There were Thurber drawings of men marching up endless flights of stairs, of dogs romping or fighting (it was hard to tell from his dogs' facial expressions whether they were smiling or snarling), and of men and women engaged in contests wholly mysterious to us, thanks to Thurber's having failed to provide any captions for the drawings except in his mind. It was possible for a concerned editor to attempt to rescue such works from a painter by putting a crude border of masking tape around it, or even, as I recall, pencilling next to it the curt message: "Save this." The hazards of asking any painter to save something are twofold; first, painters don't read messages on walls and, two, if they *were* to read such messages, they would regard them as challenges to be defied and outwitted.

The Thurber drawings — in effect, our Sistine Chapel ceiling — survived for several years and remain in existence to this day under many coats of grim yellow and gray paint. Perhaps if I live long enough, devout disciples of the master will have me wheeled through the office, where, cackling with senile self-importance, I will point out upon which walls the sacred works lie hidden. One difficulty about the prospect of their disclosure is that Truax in his prime, in the nineteen-forties and -fifties, was engaged in such a spate of knocking down walls and putting them up again that I suspect much precious Thurbery may have been reduced to rubble in the process.

Every bit as important as Thurber's drawings were the messages that he scribbled or printed in pencil on a hundred random surfaces. With a terrible simplicity, the messages always consisted of the same sorry words: "Too late." Sometimes the message was scrawled with a broad gap between the words, like this: "Too   late." Sometimes it would be printed where the wall took a ninety-degree turn; you could read the "Too" as you approached and the "late" would be waiting for you as you rounded the corner. The message has its ambiguities, now never to be resolved. "Too late," yes, but too late for what? Thurber took care not to say. Surely it's bad enough, he seems to hint, that it should be too late, without our pressing Fate for the dreadful details?

Thurber was one of those very tall men with birdlike bones who are intended by nature always to remain slender, but who, growing slack and paunchy with age, gain a figure that is two-thirds thin man and one-third fat man. At the time that I knew him, his thatch of hair was turning from grey to white; it tumbled from his crown like a disordered nest, and Thurber heightened the disorder by constantly mussing it with his exquisite, long-fingered, nervous hands. His voice was also birdy: very quick and high and capable of infinite modulations of tone. Like Sinclair Lewis — another bird-man gone to paunch — Thurber was a born mimic, and his imitations were sometimes too long and too insistently stage-managed for their own good. As he grew older, one became more and more reluctantly not so much his audience as his prisoner. His increasing blindness may have reinforced his need for auditors; it certainly reinforced his use of the telephone in playing practical jokes. Thurber's passion for practical jokes, like Ross's, sprang in part from his nineteenth-century inheritance — this late in the twentieth century, it is hard for us to believe the cruelty of the pranks our ancestors played on one another, many of them leading to physical mutilation or death — and in part from a comparatively childish sexuality. Ross and Thurber were both atavistic in more ways than one; their natural habitat in time would have been the eighteen-eighties.

Given his remarkably adaptable voice and a telephone (a device that renders blind people equal to the sighted), Thurber could make mischief to his heart's content. Once, when the Thurbers were in residence in London, Katharine and Andy White came to town for a few days. Thurber immediately rang up the hotel where the Whites were staying, asked to be put through to Mr. White, and, having got Andy on the line, identified himself as an English newspaper reporter and photographer. In a clipped Oxford accent, he explained that he would like the favor of an interview with the Whites. Andy demurred; he was sorry, but they were making a private visit to London and had no time for interviews. The reporter grew insistent. When Andy stuck to his guns, the reporter gave way and begged for the favor of a photograph instead. Andy consented to letting Katharine's and his picture be taken, with a simple caption under it and no text. Oh, very well, the reporter said; there was just one other little matter to discuss — the nature of the pose. All politeness, Andy asked what the reporter had in mind. "Why, I think a shot of Mrs. White leapfrogging naked over you," the reporter replied. After enjoying for a minute or two Andy's indignant objections to such a picture, Thurber broke down and confessed his prank. The Whites were not amused.

I had come to know the Thurbers partly by dint of the fact that in summer we often rode the same weekend train up to the northwest corner of Connecticut. The Thurbers had a house in West Cornwall, twenty miles or so from Norfolk, which had once boasted of possessing the highest railroad station in Connecticut. (The line was abandoned in 1935, and today the nearest one can get to Norfolk by train is Canaan, eight or nine miles away.) The weekend train we favored had the drawback of being extremely slow. It seemed to exhaust itself in the effort of reaching Danbury by electric power; from there it proceeded north to Pittsfield by steam, choking and wheezing as it snaked along the east bank of the Housatonic River. On one occasion, rounding a particularly sharp curve, the train fell into the river, but so slowly that no one was injured; passengers scrambled up out of the open windows onto the bank as the train filled with water and sank, sighing a contented, steamy sigh.

I was often accompanied on these weekend trips by my uncle

by marriage, Arthur Knox, a distinguished-looking widower in his late sixties, who practiced law in New York and who, having, like me, married into the Barnard family, had come into possession of their country place in Norfolk. Though Uncle Arthur never set foot on the premises of *The New Yorker*, he became quite a familiar person to the staff; many of his convenient sayings are still in use on the magazine. He was extremely deaf, which he claimed had certain advantages. When he got aboard the train for Canaan, he made a practice of turning off his hearing aid and taking a long nap. While he slept, I visited with the Thurbers. Uncle Arthur had a low opinion of Thurber's looks. "Who's that battered scarecrow you've been talking to?" he would ask, on waking. I would tell Uncle Arthur that he was a well-known humorist named Thurber and that Uncle Arthur would enjoy making his acquaintance. "Never heard of him," said Uncle Arthur. "I knew Twain. Now, *there* was a funny man."

Like many deaf people, Uncle Arthur had a tendency to speak louder than necessary. Once, on the train, he launched out upon a rather racy anecdote, and I borrowed a pencil from him and wrote in the margin of the magazine I had been reading, "Not so loud! There's an elderly virgin behind us." Uncle Arthur retrieved the pencil and wrote, under my warning, "How can you tell?" He had me there.

Uncle Arthur was a great collector of Henry James — many years later, we were to inherit his splendid library — and he had read widely in American literature. Still, there were gaps in his knowledge, and one such gap was Melville, who had been in almost total eclipse when Uncle Arthur was growing up. I urged him to read *Moby Dick*, as being a novel indispensable to the furnishing of any first-rate mind. When I lent him my copy of the book, he asked my permission to annotate it. This was a lifelong practice of his; his posture was that of an alert cross-examiner, and even in his beloved James he would occasionally find an impermissible locution, well worth quarrelling over. His weapon was a little stub of yellow pencil, with which he would indicate his disapproval of the contents of a book, writing in the margins, "Bah!," "Nonsense!," and the like. He never got through *Moby Dick*, but how savagely he fought with Melville throughout the first fifty or a hundred pages! When the book was returned to me, I discovered that at one point early in the novel Uncle

Arthur had written in the margin, "Now, now, enough of that! Enough of that!" Further along, when Melville is describing in detail the process of trying out a harpooned whale, Uncle Arthur had written in the margin (and one could measure his indignation by the force with which the pencil point had been pressed against the page), "Good God, man, get on with your story!"

In the years that I was doing "Talk" rewrite, Shawn would occasionally need to get in touch with me about one or another of the stories I had handed in. The "Talk" department went to press on Thursday, and on Thursdays I generally dined with Uncle Arthur. That was the day that George and Daisy, his butler and cook, took an evening off. Uncle Arthur and I would have drinks in his romantic old apartment on top of a building he had put up on Murray Hill in the twenties, and we would then make our way two or three blocks to a restaurant on Madison Avenue called Sacher's, where Uncle Arthur was a particular favorite. One Thursday evening, Shawn called me at Uncle Arthur's with some inquiry about a "Talk" piece. Uncle Arthur answered the phone. In his usual soft-voiced, mannerly fashion, Shawn asked, "Is Brendan Gill there, by any chance?" To Shawn's astonishment, Uncle Arthur broke out fiercely, in his strong tenor voice, "What the devil do you mean, 'by any chance'? What sort of snivelling cant is that? Good God! Don't you realize that Brendan Gill is either here on purpose, or he is *not* here on purpose? Can't you understand that he would certainly never be here simply by *chance*?" Poor Shawn, cowering at the far end of the line, began to apologize for his good manners and he was still apologizing for them when Uncle Arthur turned the phone over to me.

Another phrase that would set Uncle Arthur off was "by and large." If anyone was unlucky enough to use the phrase in his presence, Uncle Arthur would beg him with a withering solicitude to reveal precisely what it meant. Of course nobody could do so, since it long ago became merely an easy means of making a transition from one sentence to the next. So intimidating on the subject was Uncle Arthur that not once in over thirty years have I ever used "by and large" in *The New Yorker.* By his influence on me and other writers, he did much to help purify *The New Yorker* style, though I cannot remember his reading the magazine with much pleasure. He liked the drawings and the news breaks far better than he did the text.

After my discovery of Thurber's wanton malice in respect to O'Hara, Gibbs, and me, I refused to have anything more to do with him. And so Uncle Arthur never came to meet the battered scarecrow, with whom he had more in common than he may have supposed. They shared a conviction that English, both written and spoken, can convey with perfect accuracy whatever we wish it to convey, and they shared, further, a passion for Henry James, who even in the grand flourishes and alarums of his late years remained every bit as precise in rendering his response to things as he had been in his youth. Thurber and Uncle Arthur — they meet only in my mind, and the conversations that I invent for them I hope do justice to both of them. Sometimes I let James himself join the discussion, and then how the fur flies, because Uncle Arthur, despite his admiration for James, grows impatient with his exquisite hesitancies, and Thurber, scamp that he always was, sometimes cannot resist parodying the Old Pretender to his face.

I've mentioned how difficult I find the art of cutting people. Still, it is easier to cut a blind person than a sighted one, and Thurber was almost totally blind by the time we had our falling out. I would pass him silently in the corridors of the magazine, giving him a wide berth as, accompanied by his wife or Miss Terry, he would make his way boldly enough along one wall, his fingers outspread upon the wall like the most delicate of antennae, and his voice continuously chirruping. Thurber was aware of my feelings about him, and I heard from Shawn how puzzled he was by the fact that, disliking him, I was nevertheless able to write highly favorable reviews of his books. When, late in life, he wrote *The Wonderful O,* I said of him, in a review in *The New Yorker,*

> Mr. Thurber not only invents remarkable stories, he invents remarkable forms to tell them in. Despite appearances, his latest invention — an account of what happens when the inhabitants of a certain far-off island are wickedly prevented from using the letter "o" — is nothing so simple as a fairy tale for children or a parable for adults, though many children and adults will doubtless be pleased to mistake it for one or the other. A short, elegant, and often extremely funny spin through Mr. Thurber's book-lined fancy, it relates an adventure that points a moral, or maybe even two morals (the second being that nobody can remember the first), and is written in a heightened prose that occasionally skips

sidewise into meter and rhyme. If the author of "The Happy Prince" had contrived to write "Treasure Island" under the influence of both Carroll and Joyce, something like the present high-spirited work might have been the result. Like Carroll and Joyce, Mr. Thurber is fascinated by the *mana* that seems to reside in words without regard to their overt meanings. As a medium in the great séance of letters he is incomparable; he has only to utter an incantatory moan, and words levitate, phrases rap out unexpected messages, and whole sentences turn into ectoplasm. A prodigious performance, especially in so small a space.

The relationship between Thurber and White was a curious one, and I observed it with interest and perplexity, because of the unlikelihood of their being close friends. The difference in their temperaments seemed to me every bit as great as the likeness of their intentions as writers. I could understand readily enough why Thurber should be grateful to have White for a friend, but how in the world did White put up with Thurber? Not that this mattered from the point of view of the magazine. The two of them were invaluable. Between them, they had done more than anybody else to set the tone of *The New Yorker*. From the beginning, Ross had been able to provide raw energy and the determination to bring a certain kind of humorous magazine into existence — one that would have a sharper satiric view of contemporary society than the established humorous magazines of the day and that would deal, moreover, with a single city. Ross also had the necessary thick-skinned aggressiveness to bull through issue after issue of the magazine, no matter how subject to unexpected disappointments it might be. He was ulcer-ridden but enduring; recognizing hysteria in others (and half-admiring it in writers and artists), he was on guard against it in himself. Still, what the magazine needed in order to succeed was another quality altogether: one that would express a certain gentle and playful acuteness of sensibility. It was obviously not in Ross to furnish this quality, though he was quick to sense the need for it and to champion it when he came upon it in White's and Thurber's writing. Which is to say that in their common view of the desperate and yet somehow joyous difficulties of ordinary daily New York life, Ross found an attitude around which to construct a magazine.

One can say of that view of life that while it was calculatedly timid, it was also timid in fact. It happened to make good copy, but it was also the only copy that, as honest writers, White and Thurber were capable of producing. They meant every word of the mild apprehensiveness that they described as their natural response to New York. White, born in 1899, was five years younger than Thurber. He had arrived sooner on the magazine and had found an appropriate voice sooner; and he was able to help Thurber find a voice. The two young men had, or affected to have, the usual aspirations of small-town outsiders; White was from Mount Vernon, one of the suburbs of New York, and Thurber was from Columbus, Ohio. If they were far stronger than they pretended, their wariness in the presence of imminent urban disaster was authentic. They were enemies of complexity, wherever it might be found, whether in civic bureaucracy or in the bureaucracy of corporations. Machinery of any size above the pencil sharpener baffled them; and so did domestic crises, no matter how small.

White and Thurber assumed a traditional comic stance toward life, as others about them were doing at the same time; among writers, one thinks of Benchley, Donald Ogden Stewart, Corey Ford, and Frank Sullivan, and one had better not forget, among performers, Keaton, Langdon, Lloyd, and Chaplin. To all of them, the world was a treacherous quicksand, and by bad luck the best they could bring to it was ineptitude and a trusting heart. The fate they shared was to be summed up at the time of the Second World War in what came to be called Murphy's Law, which held that if anything could possibly go wrong, it would.

Ross's perceiving that, though the magazine was his, the persona of the magazine must be White–Thurber is what led to its success. It led also, of course, to the paradox that never ceased to puzzle people meeting Ross for the first time: what connection could be found between this hearty and sometimes boorish roughneck and the sophisticated prose of the magazine he was said to edit? Ross was amused by the paradox; he thought it did him credit, and he was right. He saw his job as encouraging people more talented than he to do their work better than they had hitherto known how to do it, largely by being harder on themselves than they had been accustomed to be. Simple enough, but how rare! The principle that one must be harder on oneself than one knows how to be is, I believe, the only secret means that *The New Yorker* possesses for the achievement of excellence, and it remains a secret after fifty years largely because it is so unappealing.

To what the joint White-Thurber sensibility gave the magazine should be added what Katharine Sergeant Angell, soon to be Mrs. White, was able to give it. As a member of an old Boston family and as a graduate of Bryn Mawr, militantly proud (as the Bryn Mawr graduates of those days especially were) of her fitness to take part in matters of importance in the world, she knew perfectly well who she was; this at a time when Ross, White, and Thurber were not in the least certain of who they were. She had not only a superb confidence in herself and in her eye for quality; she was as stubborn — and, sometimes, as humorless — in pushing for the acceptance of her opinions as some weighty glacier working its way down a narrow Alpine pass. She must often have intimidated Ross and therefore done him good; she certainly gave him what amounted to an intellectual conscience, as Edmund Wilson was said to have done for Fitzgerald. She broadened the boundaries of the permissible in the magazine — not the permis-

Katharine White

sible in terms of language, for we were always to be puritanical in that respect — but in terms of subject matter. Thanks in part to her, we would be not simply a funny magazine; we would be a magazine as serious, and as ambitious, as she was, and we would be much the better for it.

Once she had married Andy White, there were those who, working under her and occasionally disagreeing in vain with her (for she was always a resourceful opponent; when she was not the glacier, she was the narrow Alpine pass), protested that she held White as a sort of hostage, giving her an obvious advantage over every other editor. It was certainly the case that White came as close as anybody on the staff to being indispensable — much more so than Thurber. It was White, indeed, who helped to form Thurber and to ensure that his contributions to the magazine were substantial ones. He did this not least by fetching up out of waste-paper baskets the innumerable crumpled doodles of drawings that Thurber scattered like nervous exclamations throughout the day. White smoothed out the drawings, done in pencil on yellow copy paper, brought them to Ross, and insisted that they were publishable. Later, White inked in a Thurber drawing, covered it with a light wash of color, and so brought into existence the first Thurber cover. He also helped Thurber and most of the other artists with the captions to their drawings. It was crucial that these captions be as succinct and colloquial as possible, and White had a fine ear for the natural rhythms of American speech. His seemingly effortless tinkerings brought thousands of drawings back from the brink of rejection. For nearly fifty years he has been the author of the pithy comments appearing under the so-called "news breaks" that serve as fillers at the ends of columns in the magazine. Nobody could hope to equal White at making them strike just the right note of impish, irreverent truth-telling.

Thurber had much reason to be in White's debt, and White owed nothing that I can think of to Thurber, but Thurber's occasional cruelties to White are not to be accounted for by the notorious fact that gratitude is often expressed in the form of punishment. It was in Thurber's nature to wish to inflict pain, and I suppose it was in White's nature to wish to accept it. Perhaps someday we will learn what Katharine White thought of Thurber. I would surmise that she was often very angry with him.

Katharine and Andy White worked so closely over the years as to become, in most people's minds, one person. It was always the

Whites this and the Whites that about whom one gathered gossip in the corridors. Mrs. White would just have been overheard to say to Miss Terry, "I was up all last night with Andy," and there would be other occasions on which a momentarily restored-to-health White would be up all night with their sick dachshund.

E. B. White looking over a possible news break.

In the late thirties White decided to give up New York, move to his Maine farm, and make his literary voice heard not in the anonymous weekly Notes and Comment that opened the "Talk of the Town" department of *The New Yorker* but in a signed department, "One Man's Meat," in the monthly *Harper's.* Katharine White loyally but not happily went along with his decision. At the time that she resigned her full-time position, she was in charge of fiction on the magazine, but her influence extended far beyond that department; she had helped to invent the magazine as a whole, she and White were owners of a good deal of its stock, and she took care to make her weight felt at every turn.

Gustave Lobrano, who had followed White by a few years at Cornell and had subsequently shared quarters with him and a couple of other bachelors in Greenwich Village, was invited over from *Town and Country* to take Mrs. White's place. A sensitive man, quick to defend his rights, Lobrano would eventually come to tremble with rage at the very mention of Mrs. White's name — she had given up her position but not her interest, and he suffered under the considerable shadow she cast. He suffered still more when, Ross having died, there arose the question of who was to succeed him. The choice would plainly have to be made between the two managing editors — Shawn, managing editor of fact, and Lobrano, managing editor of fiction. Whatever Lobrano's hopes may have been, none of us supposed that there was a chance of the editorship's going to anyone but Shawn. Lobrano took his disappointment bravely, but he was never the man he had been. In a few years he was dead — of cancer, if you think that is how men die; of a broken heart, if you think *that* is how men die. Kind and correct in all things, Shawn would be driven out to Lobrano's house in Chappaqua, to visit with him as he lay dying. What thoughts must have lain behind Lobrano's words when he thanked Shawn for having come to see him?

Lobrano and I had often played tennis and golf together, and I felt that our relationship was based on a conventional bantering rivalry in games and not on the fact that he was an editor and that I was one of his writers. He trusted sports and felt a certain skepticism about writing — he would refer to the poems we published in *The New Yorker* as "doggerel," which they were not — and when he praised writers like Coates and Newhouse, it was always in terms of how well they played ping-pong or badminton. Beneath his debonair manner, I seemed to catch glimpses of an exceptionally troubled man, and now and again his temper would flare up in an unlooked-for quick spitefulness. When he told me how he had secured the immediate dismissal of a lowly smart-aleck of an editorial employee named Seymour Krim (Krim's offense lay partly in his infelicitous custom of working stripped to the waist, which offended his office neighbor Sally Benson, and partly in his still more infelicitious custom of wandering about the office with his fly open), Lobrano crowed with more satisfaction than the event warranted.

Lobrano had won a place for himself in the world, and it meant more to him than he thought it becoming to acknowledge. A new captain in the Algonquin Rose Room, where Lobrano habitually reserved a table for lunch, addressed him as Mr. Shawn, and Lobrano took his custom elsewhere. The reason he gave, whether true or false, was that the Algonquin waiters were kiting his chits. I suspect that he had never recovered from a blow suffered in youth: he and his wife had been running an agency that conducted guided tours of Europe for students; the Depression caused the agency to go broke. The nightmare of economic insecurity that Lobrano experienced in those days, though he concealed it, haunted him; he took a pride surprising in a person of his sophistication in the acquiring of a biggish house and an expensive car, and he spoke with a scarcely concealed contempt of people so rich that they were beyond jeopardy. I wasn't rich, but he rightly supposed that I had never experienced the sense of being in jeopardy. When we gave a housewarming party at our house on Seventy-eighth Street, Lobrano pretended to detect a crack in the façade of the house that might lead to its imminent collapse, and when Anne gave a dance in honor of my thirty-fifth birthday, in the three-story-high gymnasium of our immense old house in Bronxville, Lobrano again uttered, purportedly in fun, grave doubts about the stability of the walls and roof. Friends though we were, he wanted me to suffer a little, because he had suffered a lot.

The Whites had done Lobrano a favor in bringing him to *The New Yorker*, but the favor had ended badly; at any rate, it had ended otherwise than had been hoped, as so many favors do. It was Uncle Arthur who used to say, "No good deed goes unpunished." That is one of the sayings of his that we have inherited on *The New Yorker*. It springs easily and often to one's lips.

The Whites have been married for well over forty years and on the occasions when they have been obliged to be apart, White's conversation is so likely to center on his wife that she becomes all the more present for being absent. They have shared everything, from professional association on the same magazine to preoccupation with a joint ill health that many of their friends have been inclined to regard as imaginary. Years ago, in one of the Christmas lampoons that I mentioned, Edmund Wilson had saluted them for possessing *"mens sana in corpore insano,"* and it was always wonderful to behold the intuitive adjustments by which one of them got well in time for the other to get sick. What a mountain of good work they have accumulated in that seesaw fashion! Certainly they have been the strongest and most productive unhealthy couple that I have ever encountered, but I no longer dare to make fun of their ailments. Now that age is bestowing on them a natural infirmity, they must be sorely tempted to say

to the rest of us, "You see? What did we tell you?" ("Sorely,"
by the way, has been a favorite adverb of White's — a word that
brims with bodily woe and that yet hints of the heroic: back of
White, some dying knight out of Malory lifts his gleaming sword
against the dusk.)

At seventy-five, White is small and wiry, with an unexpectedly
large nose, speckled eyes, and an air of being just about to turn
away, not on an errand of any importance but as a means of
remaining free to cut and run without the nuisance of prolonged
goodbyes. His person is invincibly boyish-seeming, and though
his hair is grey, I learn at the moment of writing this that I do
not consent to the fact; away from him, I remember it as brown,
therefore it is brown to me. White can no more lose his youth-
fulness by the tiresome necessary accident of growing old than
he could ever have been Elwyn by the tiresome unnecessary accident of his having been baptized Elwyn Brooks White. His youth
and his "Andy"-ness are intrinsic and inexpungeable.

Katharine White is a woman so good-looking that nobody has
taken it amiss when her husband has described her in print as
beautiful, but her beauty has a touch of blue-eyed augustness in
it, and her manner is formal. It would never occur to me to go
beyond calling her Katharine, and I have not found it surprising
when her son, Roger Angell, an editor of *The New Yorker*, refers
to her within the office precincts as "Mrs. White."

Angell is one of two children that Mrs. White had by her first
husband, a well-known New York attorney named Ernest Angell.
(The Whites have a son, Joe, who is a naval architect and whose
boatyard is the biggest business enterprise in the Whites' home
town of North Brooklin, Maine.) Before coming to *The New Yorker*,
Roger Angell served a long apprenticeship as an editor at *Holiday*.
Like his colleagues in the fiction department — Maxwell, Robert
Henderson, Rachel MacKenzie — Angell writes fiction; he also
writes on sports, especially baseball. Unlike his colleagues, he is
intensely competitive. Any challenge, mental or physical, exhil-
arates him, and the odder the nature of the challenge the better
he likes it. Given the lack of athletic prowess that distinguishes
most members of the staff of *The New Yorker*, Angell's mastery
of certain unexpected feats — for example, his ability to leap
straight up onto a table from a standing start — fills the rest of
us with awe.

Once, I wrote Angell a note about some unimportant matter,
and as a prank I printed the words in pencil in a very small hand.

Back came a reply from Angell, with words printed on a scale markedly smaller than mine. I sharpened my pencil to a needle-like point and with great effort managed to produce a second note in which the lettering was even tinier than Angell's. Again, a reply. To the naked eye, it appeared to be only a series of fine dots, but on putting it under a powerful magnifying glass I discovered that the dots were words. Angell had won, as with me he always wins.

Several years ago, Angell and the Scots poet Alastair Reid, then a frequent contributor to the magazine, waged a fierce battle of palindromes. Not for them such short-winded trifles as "A man, a plan, a canal: Panama" or "Rats live on no evil star." The well-matched contestants fought on, month after month. Reid eventually achieved a palindrome of truly stunning length and elegance: "T. Eliot, top bard, notes putrid tang emanating, is sad. I'd assign it a name: gnat-dirt upset on drab pot toilet."

Angell refused to be bested. At last he cobbled up a palindrome that was almost twice as long as Reid's, but he looks back on his victory as a comparatively hollow one. His palindrome is not self-explanatory, as Reid's is; it requires the elaborate and not very plausible assumption that the speaker of it is an insane war veteran confined to a government hospital. The palindrome — perhaps the world's longest — goes as follows: "Marge, let dam dogs in. Am on satire: Vow I am Cain. Am on spot, am a Jap sniper. Red, raw murder on G.I.! Ignore drum. (Warder repins pajama tops.) No maniac, Ma! Iwo veritas: no man is God. — Mad Telegram."

At the risk of reducing a man's life to a sort of Merck Manual, I may mention that White's personal physician, Dana Atchley — giving short shrift to a psychosomatic view of his old friend — has often described him to me as having a Rolls Royce mind in a Model T body. With White, this would pass for a compliment, because in the tyranny of his modesty he would always choose to be a Ford instead of a Rolls, but it would be closer to the truth to describe him as a Rolls Royce mind in a Rolls Royce body that unaccountably keeps bumping to a stop and humming to itself, not without infinite pleasure to others along the way. What he achieves must cost him a considerable effort and appears to cost him very little. His speaking voice, like his writing voice, is clear, resonant, and wary. He wanders over the pastures of his Maine farm or, for that matter, along the labyrinthine corridors of *The New Yorker* with the offhand grace of a dancer making up a sequence of steps that the eye follows with delight and that defies any but his own notation. Clues to the bold and delicate nature of those steps are to be discovered in every line he writes, but the man and his work are so closely mingled that try as we will, we cannot tell the dancer from the dance.

My image of White as a dancer would have struck Ross as high-falutin — in a class with comparing these paragraphs to blue butterflies. His own metaphor for White was a good deal earthier than mine. White was the youngest of several children and he is a small man, and *à propos* of his claimed ill health Ross burst out to me one day, "Don't worry about White! White was the runt of the litter! Runts live forever!"

What Ross may have known about animal husbandry I cannot say; I doubt if it was much. If it was sufficiently startling for me to hear him describe the most exquisite of his writers in barnyard terms, what was still more startling was the fact that there was something to it — something in White that coincided with Ross's view of him, for he later wrote a book called *Stuart Little*, about a mouse who was indeed the unexpected runt of a litter of human children. And *Stuart Little* is a masterpiece because, like *Alice in Wonderland*, it is one of the least guarded of autobiographical fantasies.

If to White there was so little sense of rivalry between Thurber and him that he could devote much of his time in the early days to furthering Thurber's career as a writer and artist, on Thurber's side the sense of rivalry that he felt in respect to everyone else appears to have existed in respect to White as well. The best proof of this is what happened on the occasion of Ross's death. It was the most natural thing in the world to ask White to compose the obituary that would be printed in the Notes and Comment section of the next issue of the magazine. White undertook the assignment with his usual fear of failure and produced, as usual, a piece of writing that was exactly suited to its sad purpose. It began:

Ross died in Boston, unexpectedly, on the night of December 6th, and we are writing this in New York (unexpectedly) on the morning of December 7th. This is known, in these offices that Ross was so fond of, as a jam. Ross always knew when we were in a jam, and usually got on the phone to offer advice and comfort and support. When our phone rang just now, and in that split second before the mind focusses, we thought, "Good! Here it comes!" But this old connection is broken beyond fixing. The phone has lost its power to explode at the right moment and in the right way.

Actually, things are not going as badly as they might; the sheet of copy paper in the machine is not as hard to face as we feared. Sometimes a love letter writes itself, and we love Ross so, and bear him such respect, that these quick notes, which purport to record the sorrow that runs through here and dissolves so many people, cannot possibly seem overstated or silly. Ross, even on this terrible day, is a hard man to keep quiet; he obtrudes — his face, his voice, his manner, even his amused interest in the critical proceedings. If he were accorded the questionable privilege of stopping by here for a few minutes, he would gorge himself on the minor technical problems that a magazine faces when it must do something in a hurry and against some sort of odds — in this case, emotional ones of almost overpowering weight. He would be far more interested in the grinding of the machinery than in what was being said about him.

And the obituary ended:

When you took leave of Ross, after a calm or stormy meeting, he always ended with the phrase that has become as much a part of the office as the paint on the walls. He would wave his limp hand, gesturing you away. "All right," he would say. "God bless you." Considering Ross's temperament and habits, this was a rather odd expression. He usually took God's name in vain if he took it at all. But when he sent you away with this benediction, which he uttered briskly and affectionately, and in which he and God seemed all scrambled together, it carried a warmth and sincerity that never failed to carry over. The words are so familiar to his helpers and friends here that they provide the only possible way to conclude this hasty notice and to take our leave. We cannot convey his manner. But with much love in our heart, we say, for everybody, "All right, Ross. God bless you."

Now, nobody could have written a farewell to Ross more touching than that. Yet before it got into the magazine Thurber asked White for a copy of the text, had it read to him, and then

Thurber in 1960, in a dressing room at the Anta Theatre, where something called A Thurber Carnival *was being played.*

pronounced it a rotten piece of work. White was desolated. The fact slowly emerged (as one might have guessed, but as White in his desolation had failed to guess) that Thurber had expected to be the one chosen to prepare the notice. And so he made his best friend the object of his anger. If, as I have said, we are all six years old in our hearts, some of us are more reckless than others in revealing it.

From White's unwritten Guide to Good Writing: "Before I start to write, I always treat myself to a nice dry martini. Just one, to give me the courage to get started. After that, I am on my own."

As the years went by, Thurber became more unpredictable than ever. Afterward, it was surmised that his increased eccentricity was a consequence of the long-undetected brain tumor from which he eventually died. One sign of his changed nature was that he reestablished friendly relations with me. Though I had never indicated the slightest desire for a rapprochement, he started telephoning me at the office and carrying on conversations very like the ones I had stopped listening to some ten years earlier. I was puzzled to know how to deal with this unexpected development. There was little reason to suppose that Thurber would treat me any better than he had before, and, being unaware of the tumor, I had no reason to feel sympathetic to him. By chance, we both gained something from the brief revival of our friendship. Michael Gill, the elder of our sons, was then of college age. He greatly admired Thurber's writing and expressed a wish to meet him. Michael became the occasion for Thurber and me to have drinks in the Algonquin lobby, not once but several times. Thurber was grateful for a new audience. By then he had gone from describing himself as a great American humorist to describing himself as the greatest American humorist who had ever lived. It was not a thesis that many people would have accepted without an argument, but at that period of his life Michael was ready to believe it, or half-believe it. The old, blind, witty, dying cockatoo talked a blue streak at us, on and on, and we sat at his feet in silence, marvelling.

24

During most of the life of the magazine, the nearest bar to *The New Yorker* was a door or two to the west of us, on the ground floor of the National Bar Association Building; unfortunately, it gave way a few years ago to a camera-supply store. The bar was part of a restaurant called the Cortile, which in an earlier incarnation, back in the twenties, had been one of a chain of restaurants founded by Alice Foote McDougall. The decoration of the restaurant, surviving unchanged from decade to decade, was said to have been based on Mrs. McDougall's impression of the Vieux Carré, in New Orleans. It consisted of much heavy black panelling, a beamed ceiling, a red-tiled floor, innumerable wrought-iron candelabra, majolica plates hanging from brass hooks, and a few edifying paintings. Even the nature and dress of the waitresses remained unchanged down the years. The waitresses were capacious, slow-moving black women, who as late as the nineteen-forties and early fifties were still being got up as Southern mammies, with billowing checked aprons and bandannas on their heads.

The Cortile was not celebrated for its cuisine. (To this day, I recollect with revulsion the squares of gelatinous yellow matter on sodden bread that I would be served when I ordered a grilled Cheddar cheese sandwich on rye.) What made the Cortile important to us was its bar, which occupied the northern end of the restaurant, looking out dimly upon Forty-fourth Street. The bar was long and dark and gloomy-spirited; it was furnished with some hard wooden high-chairs and reeked continuously of spilled beer. The bartender kept on the counter behind him a radio with a moon-face as sallow as his own; on it he listened to baseball, football, basketball, and muted soap operas, but never to music. The Cortile was ideally suited to people with a glum view of life, and there have always been many such on the magazine. It was also a handy place to duck into for a quick one, and from morning to night you could count on finding two or three of our serious drinkers there, staring into space.

Characteristic of the drinker-starers was our Mr. Quinn, an accountant in the office, whose task, as far as we were able to make it out, was to measure by the square inch, with a schoolboy's yellow ruler, how much space in the magazine was occupied by different categories of contributors — fact writers, fiction writers, artists, and the like — and then determine whether a just balance was being maintained among them in regard to both space and costs. Ever hoping to run a businesslike enterprise, Ross was sure that this information would prove valuable. Mr. Quinn, a deferent ghost in the corridors, was even more ghostlike at the Cortile, where he appeared to believe that his extended silences served to render him invisible. Given that he was in and out of the Cortile a dozen times between ten and six, it was hard for us to understand how he could carry out his measurings with any degree of accuracy.

In the late afternoons, Geraghty was often to be found at the Cortile, entertaining a cluster of artists. Among other regulars were John McCarten, for a time our movie critic and then for a time our Broadway theatre critic; Freddie Packard, head of the checking department; Kip Orr, who handled correspondence; and Tom Gorman, who, though having an excellent mind, refused to accept any post higher than that of a secretary. He had been a golden-haired boy soprano in the famous Paulist Fathers choir, and nothing in his adult life was able to equal that for glory; slowly he withdrew from the world and soon he was dead, and those of us who had been constantly urging him to seek advancement perceived too late that it was death he had longed for and courted, surely from the start.

Kip Orr, too, sought death, always more directly and recklessly than Tom. He had been a brilliant undergraduate at Dartmouth and had written a successful mystery novel about the college. He sold a few casuals to us and a few pieces for the "Travel" department, in the days when the magazine had such a thing. (The magazine used to maintain many more departments than it does today, perhaps in a youthful attempt to seem more important than it was; such headings as "Polo" and "The Sky Line" have long lain dormant in the make-up department.) Alcoholic and homosexual, Kip took terrible chances with his life, and it became a wonder that he wasn't murdered; more than once, he was rolled, beaten up, and left for dead in some dirty doorway in the Village, and yet he survived to die sadly in the small college town where, for a little while, he had known good fortune.

When I first encountered him, he was perhaps in his early forties; his reddish pompadour was going grey and his large light-green eyes had lids shocking in their rolled-back redness. He had an air about him of ruined insouciance, and this was heightened by the fact that he wore good-looking, old-fashioned tweeds and English brogans with the exceptionally thick light-colored crepe soles that were in vogue in the twenties. Thanks to those soles, Kip was able to steal up behind one in the corridors and suddenly whisper some abrupt, catty remark, or offer the latest gossip about some fresh office disaster, and one was more startled by the fact of his presence at one's ear than by anything he said. He liked having things go wrong in the office; he wanted to see tables turned and to observe the discomfiture of people of importance, and in those days of Rossian experiment and upheaval his wishes were often fulfilled.

When the Shawns, then still childless, lived in a small apartment on Murray Hill, they gave pleasant evening parties, at which Shawn would sit playing, hour after hour, popular music and twenties jazz; his painted upright piano was rigged to give a true honky-tonk sound. Orr would stand at one end of the piano, drink in hand, listening raptly. As the evening wore on, his eyes would grow more and more watery, and it was odd and touching to see him, as happy in those moments as he would ever be, apparently dissolved in tears. He had a historic personal connection with popular music, having written the lyrics for a song that became a hit and earned him a regular income from ASCAP. The song was called "I May Be Wrong But I Think You're Wonderful," and, given Orr's sexual orientation, the singer's negative approach to the girl to whom the words are presumably addressed is understandable, if also insulting.

Like many alcoholics, Orr strongly disliked eating. Sometimes he would accompany a group of us having lunch at a Stouffer's restaurant near the office. (The unforgettable mock veal choplets that Mother Stouffer served us during the dark days of the Second World War! And the plump Irish waitresses, fresh from the old country, one of whom sang a ballad of which I remember the consoling finale: "If dogs have a heaven, there's this much I know, Old Shep has a wonderful home.") For lunch Orr would drink a series of sweet Manhattans, signalling so discreetly to the waitress for a second, third, and fourth that in my earliest acquaintance with him I supposed him always to be sipping daintily at his first.

Alcoholics suffer from various consequences of their malnutrition; perhaps the most horrifying consequence is something called cortical atrophy. The cerebral cortex of the brain, giving us among other things our ability to reason, requires to be furnished with the richest possible blood, which the ill-nourished alcoholic is unable to provide; atrophy may then set in, with the result that the alcoholic becomes progressively less intelligent and more childlike. As the years passed, Orr began to bring toys of all sorts into the office, which he would occasionally take the trouble to demonstrate to me, kneeling on the floor and winding them up with evident pleasure. I was under the impression that he had bought the toys for some young niece or nephew, but not at all — his mind was going and he had bought them for himself.

One day I had undertaken to entertain a French journalist, who, making his first visit to New York, was eager to see the sort of bar frequented by his American counterparts. I led him to Bleeck's, on West Forty-first Street, next door to the New York *Herald Tribune*. Bleeck's was a favorite hangout not only of *Herald Tribune* employees but also of reporters on other newspapers, magazine writers, press agents, and theatre people. The Frenchman and I were standing at the bar, which was, as usual, extremely crowded. Suddenly, along the surface of the bar cluttered with beer glasses came a little toy automobile — one of the first of those toys that by an ingenious mechanism was able, on reaching an obstruction of any kind, to retreat, change direction, and move forward again. The little car made its way along the bar, bumping into glasses, backing up, on occasion hovering at the edge of the bar and then correcting itself, and so continuously advancing, advancing. The Frenchman was beside himself with delight. So this was what an American newspaperman's bar was like! I let him suppose that it was, but I knew better. For at the far end of the bar I had caught sight of a tweedy arm, a trembling hand: poor Orr at play.

For many years, the favorite bar of *New Yorker* writers and editors was Costello's, on Third Avenue. Originally, the bar and restaurant occupied a hundred-year-old two-story brick building on the southeastern corner of Forty-fourth Street and Third Avenue, with the traditional "family entrance" at the rear of the premises, fifteen or twenty paces in from the avenue. Later, the building being sold, the bar was shifted to a similar building next door. In appearance, the first Costello's had little more to recommend it than the second; both buildings were thrown down last year to make way for still another skyscraper.

Costello's was a long, narrow shoebox of a space, with the bar itself running along the south wall and a number of cheap wooden booths facing it on the opposite wall. In the space that remained between the last booth and the serving pantry were a few tables, covered with white, much-mended tablecloths. The chairs around the tables were of the usual bentwood Thonet design, with seats of wood instead of cane. When the two brothers, Tim and Joe Costello, opened their bar, the hand-me-down furnishings of it may have cost them a couple of hundred dollars, and they took care to make few improvements. The men's room, unnervingly close to both the serving pantry and the bar, was a tiny, shantylike room, compared to which the lavatory at P. J. Clarke's, farther up the avenue, with its solid porcelain urinals and stained-glass decoration, was a basilica.

Above the booths, on cheap Celotex panels that had evidently been placed there to conceal cracks in the plaster walls, were some drawings by Thurber; as they faded with time, they were touched up or redrawn by increasingly unskillful hands. The bar-back was mirrored, and from the heavy woodwork that framed the mirror were suspended a few immemorial souvenirs, including a couple of blackthorn canes. Many tall stories were repeated and enlarged upon at Costello's, and one of them was to the effect that a contentious Hemingway, encountering an equally contentious O'Hara at the bar, as a demonstration of superior machismo broke a blackthorn cane in two by bringing it down hard on the top of his own head. Somewhere in that story lies a kernel of truth, but of the story itself I have my doubts. Still, in those days Hemingway *did* seem twice life-sized and was capable of feats prodigious as well as foolish.

At about that time, I wrote a piece about him for "Talk of the Town" and because he struck me as so awesomely strong and full of life I headed the piece "Indestructible." In the light of his miserable last years, it was just the wrong word for me to have chosen, and yet Hemingway believed it of himself at the time; and not alone of himself but of his whole family. In our talk, he

Lillian Ross and Ernest Hemingway at the Hemingway place in Ketchum, Idaho. Miss Ross was then preparing a Profile of Hemingway's friend Sidney Franklin, the American matador. A few years later, she would be writing the celebrated Profile of Hemingway himself. Also in the picture, from left to right, are Hemingway's three sons — Patrick, Gregory, and John — his wife, Mary, and an old hunting and fishing companion. Miss Ross and Hemingway were good friends and they kept up an intimate correspondence until his illness and death. He liked to feel close to the writers on The New Yorker *whose work he admired.*

outlined his theory that no Hemingway had ever died a natural death. "That's one reason I've written so little about my family," he said. "I can't say everything I want to say about it as long as certain people are still alive." This was, at his request, a deliberately oblique reference to his mother, whom he hated. He told me of how she had sent him the gun with which his father had shot himself, and Hemingway spoke of his certainty that he would never follow in his father's footsteps. Brash young reporter that I was, I asked him his opinion of a then fairly common critical theory that his preoccupation with virility in the form of hunting, fishing, boxing, and other sports was a sign that his true bent was to be a homosexual. Hemingway was newly married to his fourth wife, Mary. "What a question!" he said, his black eyes shining with amusement. "Let's just say I think life would have been a whole lot simpler for me if I had been."

Tim and Joe Costello were old-country Irish, of the same tough peasant stock as Paddy Kavanagh. Joe was small and wiry and quick to utter a sarcastic word. Considering how comparatively well the world had treated him, one felt puzzled at first by his bitterness; later in life, when he had to have a leg amputated, the bitterness came to seem a natural thing in him as he sat crouched on the counter of the bar-back, watching his customers like prey. Tim was a big man, or, rather, a big-seeming one, with a plump face and small, canny, light-colored eyes. He wore a white apron-coverall, drawn tight about the waist with strings, and he worked hard. He sat at table with a dignity more like that of a small-town judge than the proprietor of a bar.

Tim liked telling stories and he liked hearing them told. His brogue was very broad; he pronounced the word "car" in such a way that it sounded as if it had three syllables — "key — ee — yaar." When, to his astonishment and pleasure, he found himself something of a literary lion, it cost him no effort to remain unchanged. He was a close friend of Thurber and John McNulty and Joseph Mitchell and a dozen or so other *New Yorker* writers, and after it became the vogue for well-known literary figures and their hangers-on to frequent Costello's, he was grateful for their patronage, but he wouldn't truckle to them. He was a devoted family man and he paid me many compliments upon my family for the only thing he knew about it — that it was big. Being Irish, he believed that big families possessed some special grace, but he wouldn't have dared to attempt a big family himself. The thought of the cost intimidated him. "It must be fierce, paying for it all," he would say. "Fierce! Fierce!"

Tim was a Catholic and in his eyes an errant one. He neglected going to Mass and no doubt he neglected his daily prayers as well, and he made a joke of the fact that there were two fears at war in him, preventing him from flying over to Ireland for a holiday. First of all, he was afraid that the plane would crash and that he would die in a state of mortal sin, not having been to confession since he couldn't remember when. Why not go to confession, then, and die as pure as a child? Ah, that was just it! That was his second fear. The only thing he was even more afraid of than flying was having to face a priest in a confessional.

In the thirties and forties, there were scores of bars more or less similar to Costello's up and down Third Avenue. In the early part of that period, the elevated railroad still darkened the avenue with its Piranesi crosshatch of heavy black steel uprights and sooty crossties. Trolleys ran under the El, rocking along in a sort of permanent twilight even on the brightest days. The avenue was a dirty and yet snug cave, and in winter, when the drifts piled up like soiled laundry about the El uprights and the wind blew stinging ashes into your eyes along with the snow, the lights in the bars, three or four to the block, let you know that others of your kind were still alive and had found some measure of solace there, and so could you. If it wasn't the best life in the world, something was present in those bars — at the bleakest, a shared loneliness — that kept it from being the worst.

As soon as the El was pulled down and the trolley tracks pulled up, the avenue was seen to be unexpectedly handsome, all the broader and more boulevard-like because of the low height of the old buildings on either side. Thus it befell that after the Second World War the avenue was ready to be plundered by real-estate speculators, who turned it into the sterile sequence of tiresome glass-walled, high-rise office buildings that crowd it now. Faster and faster as the land under them rose in value, the old bars were sold and reduced to rubble. Some of them were to be reborn thirty or forty blocks to the north, in the German section of Manhattan called Yorkville, but most of them simply vanished. Those that remained, like P. J. Clarke's, shrewdly married themselves to the calamity of the skyscrapers all round them and became not the homely comfort of the serious, often notably morose drinker, but of the social show-off and account executive. The Irish bar in New York, like the pub in Dublin, though it was reputed to be the citadel of brilliant conversational improvisations, was mostly silent; the air in it was as heavy with mortality as that of any wake save Finnegan's. Given our plight here below, so the bent figures at the bar seemed to imply, there might be much to deplore in it but very little to say. That sort of drinker has long since left Third Avenue; if he is anywhere, he is in the nearby exhausted suburbs, putting off by not taking thought the dark necessity of going home.

At one point in the postwar period, Tim and Joe were given the opportunity to buy their small corner building on Forty-fourth Street for just under fifty thousand dollars. Nothing could have been more certain at the time than that the price of property on Third Avenue would continue to multiply at a Western boom-town rate; the price was a bargain. But Tim and Joe were miserly. Not only did they dread having to spend money, they took pleasure in withholding it. They dared not risk the gamble, lovely as it was. Soon, somebody else had bought the corner and the Costellos moved to rented quarters next door. And soon again the corner building was sold, this time for over a quarter of a million dollars. The Costellos took the news hard. They had missed the chance of their lives and they knew it. Being intelligent men, they also knew that they had missed it out of a countryman's primitive fear of taking chances. I think that they never fully recovered from this manifestation of their failed avarice. It diminished all their previous good fortune — two stout immigrant lads that had succeeded against high odds in the New World — and caused them to lose hope for the future; worse still, to lose interest in it. And so they began to die.

John McNulty on Third Avenue.

The man who made Costello's famous was John McNulty. What a marvellous writer he was! As far as I know, he is almost totally forgotten nowadays, except by his friends. Still, his stories will survive somehow and find their proper audience, and perhaps they will seem all the more remarkable to a later generation for the reason that both the time and the place that they celebrated have disappeared without a trace — brick and stone as thoroughly ground to dust as man. McNulty had been a newspaper rewrite man, working in the city room on stories that were telephoned in by reporters on the scene. He was well known not only for his speed (all rewrite men have to possess that skill) but also for his acute ear. One heard that he had once been well known for his drinking, but by the time he and I became good friends he had long been careful not to drink at all.

McNulty was a small, passionate man, with bright blue eyes, a bold nose, a mustache, and the small man's gift for wearing natty clothes. He was an irresistible raconteur, in part because of the evident pleasure he gained from practicing the art. His stories as they began to appear in *The New Yorker* took the public by surprise. They were so offhand, so modest-seeming: paragraphs that gave the impression of having been struck off at random, like tiny sparks off flint. They were nearly always about a certain bar and its customers, and the bar was plainly enough Costello's, but the customers were not so readily identified; they were versions — especially the extraordinary old men, as crabbed and demanding and death-haunted as Lear — of people that McNulty had been observing with sympathy since childhood. No doubt many of them had been dead for fifty years before McNulty, a late starter at fiction, got around to writing about them.

McNulty made a romance of Costello's, and few of us were able to observe it with accuracy after reading him. Even the waiters struck me as more interesting at Costello's than at other bars, thanks to McNulty. The waiter who must have enjoyed the longest tenure there was Emil, who had a curiously mutilated finger and the air of a boulevardier, and who when he quit the bar at night was dressed like an old-time matinée idol, in a handsome grey homburg and rich-looking dark overcoat. The steaks and chops and hamburgers at Costello's were very good, and it was hard to do harm to a baked potato, but peas, string beans, and other green vegetables were allowed to simmer by the hour and would come to the table blanched and waterlogged. I would protest in vain to Emil, who argued that since I liked my hamburger charred, I was beyond passing sound judgment on cooked food of any kind. No ice cream was served at Costello's, though other forms of dessert were available, and coffee, usually execrable, was served in thick white crockery cups. It was not a distinguished place to eat, and it didn't matter; people went there for other and more serious reasons.

Freddie Packard, for long the head of our checking department and from time to time a contributor of drawings and casuals, frequented Costello's from its earliest days. Freddie was a rotund man with smooth dark hair and a diffident manner, who yet would stand his ground when he had some characteristic misadventure to relate. He would speak slowly, with measured intakes of breath, clearings of throat, and pattings of his small mustache, until all had been uttered to his satisfaction. He was a born injustice-collector; things went wrong for him that would never go wrong for anyone else, and he bound these wrongs to him with a practiced skill. When Thomas E. Dewey, whom Freddie regarded as a dwarfish nonentity, was elected Governor of New York, Freddie reported that he had begun to be mistaken for him in the street, though the resemblance between the two was certainly slight. And once Maxwell, encountering Freddie in a corridor, thought to pass the time of day with a conventional "How are you?" To Maxwell's surprise Freddie took the question seriously and prepared a reply. With grave deliberation, scratching the backs of his hands, he said, "I have two colds." It happened that, without waiting for Freddie to accomplish a cure, a second cold had unconscionably ridden in piggyback upon the first. Who but Freddie would be called on to put up with such a burden?

On an occasion when there were still trolley cars in Times Square, Freddie, laden with a number of bundles, books, magazines, and an outsize umbrella, signalled in vain for several crowded trolley cars to pick him up. At last he spotted one that had stopped a block or so away. In spite of his heavy gear, Freddie ran up and boarded it, breathing hard. Though vaguely surprised to note that the trolley car was empty, he was too grateful for a seat to speculate on the reason why. Soon he started to reflect indignantly on the poor service that the trolley-car company was rendering. A letter to the president of the company was by no means out of the question. And again it turned out that a maleficent fate was pursuing Freddie, for the trolley car was afire. That was the reason Freddie had been able to board it and find a seat on it. Smoke billowed toward him, and out of the smoke emerged a panic-stricken conductor, insisting that Freddie leave the car at once. Freddie refused. He not only refused — he issued a counter-demand: fire or no, he wished to be taken to his destination at once. It was some time before the conductor, assisted by several firemen and a police captain, could talk Freddie into leaving the blazing car.

I stopped in at the checking department one morning to verify some obscure fact or other (*not* that Saint Ambrose was the first person in history to be able to read without moving his lips) and found Freddie in a state of extreme distress. Somebody had sent him a poison-pen letter, calling him, in so many words, a fat, shiftless no-good. Understandably, Freddie was anxious to track down the miscreant. He was prepared to believe that it was someone who knew him and bore a grudge against him, but there was a difficulty: the letter was addressed "Dear Fred." He scratched the backs of his hands. "No friend of mine would ever call me Fred," he said. I pointed out that no friend of his would ever write such a letter. Freddie looked at me suspiciously. He was afraid that the injustice of his situation would be taken away from him. The alternative possibilities were that the letter had been written by a friend who didn't like him or by a total stranger who didn't like him. Plainly, the latter alternative represented the greater and therefore more desirable injustice. Freddie shook his head in wonder: who but he would receive a poison-pen letter from somebody who didn't even know him?

Freddie was not beyond creating an occasional injustice by his own efforts. One day Geraghty was talking something over with him as they made their way to Freddie's cluttered desk. The mail had just been delivered and on top of the pile was a letter from a bank in Philadelphia. Freddie snatched it up in a rage — he and the bank had been engaged in some dispute about a monthly statement that by Freddie's reckoning unjustly favored the bank in the amount of a dollar or two. He ripped the envelope to pieces. As he dropped the torn fragments back onto the desk, he and Geraghty both noticed that among them were pieces of what looked like a check. Freddie fitted the pieces together as best he could. Oh, yes, it was indeed a check — a partial settlement of his mother's estate, in the amount of eighteen thousand dollars.

One of the great marine disasters of our time was the sinking of the *Andrea Doria* off Nantucket Island, after a collision with the S.S. *Stockholm.* It was a sensational story, and Shawn was eager for the magazine to share in the reporting of it. For a while, it looked as if he might even have a scoop, because Freddie was among the passengers aboard the *Stockholm*. Shawn sent him off a wireless, urging him to send back soonest as many details of the disaster as possible. I was asked to stand by for a quick job of rewrite; the whole "Talk" department might well be given over to the collision if the story reached us in time. At last the waited-for message arrived; it said, "No story this end." We were all baffled, though less baffled than if the person involved had been anyone but Freddie. We suspected that he would somehow have contrived to become a victim of the accident — in his eyes, perhaps the leading one.

On Freddie's return to New York, we learned that our surmise was correct. Freddie was still indignant over the entire episode. It turned out that on the night of the collision he had retired to his cabin early, feeling somewhat indisposed; the cuisine of the *Stockholm* had not lived up to expectations. During the night, he had been awakened by the sound of people running up and down the passageway outside his cabin and by occasional inexcusably loud shouts and cries. He kept ringing for the steward in order to protest against this unmannerly behavior, but the steward never troubled to answer his ring. At last Freddie succeeded in getting the man's attention. By then it was morning, and the steward arrived at Freddie's cabin looking haggard and ill-shaved. He was wearing a life preserver, and after a prolonged tongue-lashing by Freddie, he explained that he had been up all night rescuing passengers from the *Andrea Doria*.

So it was that Freddie heard of the collision, and so it was that we failed to get our scoop.

Often there seemed (but this may have been the spell cast by McNulty) a dangerous pressure in the air at Costello's, leading to hysteria. How many quarrels between lovers took place at that dreary bar, under Joe's not in the least astonished eye! And sometimes they were quarrels of the worst sort, which are those that are carried out in silence, leaving nothing to retract, nothing to forgive. I think of one of the most gifted of our writers, a pretty girl always immaculately groomed, and of how she would sit beside her lover, smoking cigarette after cigarette and drinking drink after drink, never speaking a word, until in the early morning the moment had come for her to punish him by passing out, and her exquisite head would pitch forward upon the bar, as if guillotined.

For many, Costello's was an extension of home and therefore a place to pursue, with the advantage of an audience, a domestic crisis that would otherwise not have been worth the effort of inventing. We had an intelligent, slovenly young writer on the magazine, who died in Asia almost at the beginning of his career. He had a wife as intelligent and as slovenly as he, and one night they were both at the bar at Costello's and both were crying. What were they crying about? Why, about their three small children, over in their drafty house in Brooklyn, in the care of an elderly, incompetent, half-blind, half-deaf crone. The young couple could not fail to be moved by their children's plight, but neither one of them had the slightest intention of leaving the warmth and coziness of Costello's, where, tears and all, they were having a particularly good time.

Another story about tears — McKelway's story. He is sitting at the bar at Costello's, drinking and feeling sorry for himself. Having just bought a package of cigarettes, he turns it round and round in his hands, fumbling for a purchase on the taut cellophane wrapping. Somehow his fingers fail him; the one thing he needs more than anything else in the world at that moment — a smoke — eludes him. He stares down helplessly at the package and feels tears springing into his eyes.

In the opinion of many (which is a by no means modest way of saying "in my opinion"), the finest writer on *The New Yorker* is Joseph Mitchell. Born in the tobacco country of North Carolina, where his numerous family lives and where he continues to own a farm, Mitchell was a reporter on the *World-Telegram* before coming to *The New Yorker*. As a newspaperman, he was expected to turn out a considerable amount of copy every day; on *The New Yorker*, his writing has been accomplished at a pace increasingly slow. Whether Mitchell or any of the rest of us would write more (or, at least, would write more rapidly) if the magazine were more sternly businesslike in its demands upon us remains, after all these years, an open question. The fact is that although productivity is rewarded by a scale of payments that increases with the number of pieces sold during the course of a year, lack of productivity is neither rebuked nor deplored. On the contrary, it may be sneakingly admired, as proof that the magazine considers writing an occupation often difficult and sometimes, for the best writers, impossible.

A snapshot by Lillian Ross of Joseph Mitchell and A. J. Liebling outside the New Yorker *building on West Forty-fourth Street. It was a cold day, and the white blur at Liebling's mouth is his breath.*

Mitchell, who is in his sixties, used to take months over a piece and now takes years. One consequence of that long period of composition is the interest it arouses among his editors and fellow-writers; everyone speculates about the nature of the piece upon which Mitchell is at work and about when it may be handed in. Nobody would dream of putting such questions to Mitchell directly; that would be an unthinkable violation of our custom of pretending that each of us is engaged upon a project of great size and extreme delicacy, the slightest reference to which might cause it to shred away into dust. More than any other writer on the magazine, Mitchell cherishes the secret nature of his labors up to the last possible moment. Even when one of his pieces has been put in galleys and is being circulated among editors and checkers, he begs friends to wait until it has actually been published in the magazine before reading it; of the ten or fifteen thousand words that the piece may contain, Mitchell, after a final agony of indecision, may wish to alter two or three adjectives and he wishes only the immaculate finished version to be seen and judged.

This appears to be a Daily News *shot of a New York City detective bringing in a notorious con man. Instead, it is a snapshot by Therese Mitchell of her husband, Joseph, and their friend S. J. Perelman, out for a pleasant stroll in the Village.*

Henry James spoke of Flaubert's "gouging out" his works in his country house overlooking the Seine, and I have always a sense of Mitchell's gouging out *his* works in his little cell overlooking Sleepy Hollow. It is a notably austere cell even by *The New Yorker's* high standards of austerity, not only because Mitchell is a tidy man but also because he is a worrier. He keeps his office as bare as he can and he keeps under lock and key as much of his written materials as he can, apparently out of fear that some literary cat burglar may come in and pilfer a paragraph or two. Now, a Mitchell sentence, to say nothing of a Mitchell paragraph, is as unmistakable as a sentence by Twain or Hemingway, so it would be of no value whatever to anyone else, but if Mitchell worried less about such matters and were less miserable in the long-drawn-out process of accumulating his inimitable prose, the results might be to that degree less joyous and carefree-seeming. For what we read in a Mitchell piece has the air of having sprung by the happiest chance, with no effort, from a playful superfluity of energy and talent on the part of the writer; not a groan in it anywhere.

Mitchell was an especially close friend of Tim Costello, but one could rightly say of Costello's that it belonged, as a literary property, to McNulty, and Mitchell was content to give fame to another and much older bar — McSorley's — and to a hotel, the Hartford House, down near Peck Slip, in the decayed waterfront section of the oldest part of New York. According to Mitchell, the most distinguished resident of the hotel was a peppery retired house-wrecking contractor named Hugh J. Flood, about whom Mitchell wrote a Profile in the magazine. Readers were enchanted with Mr. Flood and many of them made strenuous efforts to get in touch with him at the hotel. For his part, Mitchell made strenuous efforts as well: he had to see to it that Mr. Flood was said to be visiting his daughter in South Norwalk when anybody sought an audience with the old gentleman. For the truth of the matter was that although Mitchell had written about him as if he were a real person, Mr. Flood was an invention — a composite of several old men that Mitchell had known and, more importantly, of Mitchell's own reveries on age and death. Literary historians may pigeonhole

Mr. Mitchell:

        I have read the piece on Mr. Flood and ⚡ am a great admirer of it. I may be prejudiced because my father ~~we~~ was Scotch Irish and would have been like this old fellow if he'd lived long enough. My Uncle John, ~~~~~ the famous founder of the Pillar of Fire was more like Mr. "all in that he got in his rut and stayed there despite everything, by God. He lived with his daughter, though, which this fellow didn't. I syggested a couple of little additions from on points I was honestly interested in, but you know what to do about those if you don't agree.~~~~

                  Ross

Mitchell as a factual writer, but he has been no more concerned with run-of-the-mill facts than Twain was. He happens to be one of those writers who are more at ease when they are writing fiction in disguise; there exists a long and honorable tradition among writers in several languages to mingle and make the best of the two worlds of fact and fiction, and Mitchell and some of the rest of us were disdainful of Truman Capote for hailing the "non-fiction" novel as an entirely new art form. Capote said of himself at the time, "A boy must hustle his book," and no doubt his new art form was but a manifestation of this industrious hustling, for Capote promotes himself as other people promote lipstick or baby powder, with an endearing and profitable assiduity.

In his teens, Capote served for a time as an office boy on *The New Yorker*. He was a tiny, round-faced, slender creature, as exotic as an osprey. He and Daise Terry, who was in charge of the office help and who also took charge of running the weekly art meetings, doted on each other. There was a gap of fifty years or so between them in respect to age, but they were a close couple, alike in size, in their relish for gossip, and in their cynical view of other members of the staff. Capote dressed with an eccentricity that wasn't to become a commonplace among the young for another twenty-five years; I recall him sweeping through the corridors of the magazine in a black opera cape, his long golden hair falling to his shoulders: an apparition that put one in mind of Oscar Wilde in Nevada, in his velvets and lilies.

The story goes that after Capote's departure from the magazine it was discovered that he had been serving as a sort of self-appointed art editor. One of his tasks was to open the envelopes that contained drawings sent in by artists from all round the country; when Capote didn't like a drawing, he dropped it over the far edge of the big table at which he worked. Years passed, and someone thought to move the table. Behind it were found hundreds of drawings that Capote had peremptorily rejected, instead of sending them along to Geraghty and Ross. True or false? Nobody knows, for Capote anecdotes are hard to check. If he didn't invent the non-fiction novel, he early became the master of the self-serving anecdote, many of them composed out of the thinnest possible air, but told with a zestful self-love that renders them irresistible.

When Capote's first novel, *Other Voices, Other Rooms*, was published, Gibbs went striding up and down the corridor outside his office, jingling the coins in his pockets and exclaiming, in an astonished voice, "But the kid can write! The kid can write!" And indeed he could and indeed he has and does, quite often for us. The Capote pictured on the dust jacket, lounging soulfully

Truman Capote

like an adolescent male Madame Récamier on an antique sofa, has transformed himself into a stout burgher of the arts, pontificating on TV. He and Shawn worked together for several years on *In Cold Blood*, which in spite of Capote's high opinion of it, uttered in too many places before too many audiences, remains a model of how to combine diligent reporting with an appropriate literary form. This is an art that Shawn has helped many writers to master; among them, one thinks of Rachel Carson and her *Silent Spring* and S. N. Behrman and his delightful *Duveen*. Few writers are as clever at organizing their information as they are at amassing it; Shawn's exceptional lucidity of mind finds a structure for the most intractably diverse materials, and it is obvious that the New Testament would make far more satisfactory reading if it had been the handiwork of Matthew, Mark, Luke, and Shawn.

Tim Costello on Mitchell: "Joe has been workin' hard at bein' an old man since he was in short pants. It's as good an ambition as any, since barrin' a bus in your path or an angry husband or, in Joe's case, the side of a buildin' tumblin' in on you, you can't help but succeed. He's a great one, Joe is, for pawin' over other people's fallin'-down properties. If he ever disappears, start lookin' for him under fifty foot of brick, with a rusty fire escape on his chest and a pleased smile on his face. 'Jesus, Mary, and Joseph,' my grandmother said, 'we're all born, but we're not all buried!' "

Mitchell's closest friend was A. J. Liebling, whom I picture in my mind not only at the Cortile, Bleeck's, and Costello's but also at one or another of the Italian restaurants that used to flourish in the West Forties, within easy reach of *The New Yorker* — the Villa Nova, the Red Devil, Del Pezzo, and the like. Nobody in our time has written more accurately and more lovingly about food than Liebling, and nobody, I suppose, has eaten more of it than he. The A. J. in his name stood for Abbot Joseph, though it appears that even in school nobody ever called him anything except Joe. A pity, because as he grew older and his weight increased, he came to deserve the "Abbot" not as a name but as a title. When I first knew him, he looked exactly like some eighteenth-century Franciscan monk, with a big belly, a bald pate, and small, lively eyes behind old-fashioned, thick-lensed, metal-rimmed glasses — a worldly monk, none too strict in the observance of his vows and, as a confessor, an easy mark for sinners. One wanted to see him dressed not in conventional twentieth-century street clothes, which didn't suit him, but in a cowled robe of brown wool, girdled by a wooden rosary, and with stout sandals on his feet. When he laughed, which was likely to be unabashedly at some remark of his own making, his whole body would shake with pleasure. He was sensual and vain and talented and extremely hard-working, and he was just beginning to enjoy the fame he had counted on and long waited for when, in 1963, he died.

Mitchell and Liebling had much in common; what they didn't have in common was rate of composition. If Mitchell was one of the slowest writers in the world, Liebling was one of the fastest. He wrote an extraordinary number of pieces for the magazine, especially after he had come into his own as an overseas correspondent during the Second World War, in England, North Africa, and France. His most ambitious work was a series on the three Parises he had known: that of his childhood visits with his family, then the wartime Paris, and then the Paris of after the war.

The series conveyed so strong a sense of the mingling of time, memory, and emotion that one could compare Liebling to Proust without seeming to risk staking too bold a claim in his behalf.

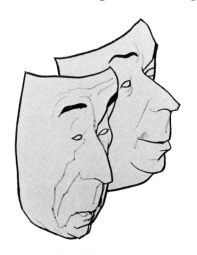

A portrait by William Auerbach-Levy of Lee and J. J. Shubert, drawn to illustrate Liebling's Profile of the Shuberts. No New Yorker artist has ever surpassed Auerbach-Levy at getting a likeness and then getting more than a likeness.

Not that Liebling would have believed there was any such risk involved. It happened that he preferred to compare himself to Stendhal. He admired his own writing without the least taint of modesty and, again unlike Mitchell, was always eager to call attention to it, even in an unfinished state. More than once, I would encounter him seated at his typewriter, staring at a sentence on the sheet of paper in front of him and chuckling — bouncing, joggling — with satisfaction. Sometimes, impatient to share the fruits of his wit with others, he would pull a still incomplete paragraph from the typewriter and shuffle down the hall to Mitchell's or Hamburger's office to give them an impromptu reading. In my experience, most writers, and in particular most *New Yorker* writers, have little confidence in their gifts; Liebling's confidence was unbounded. Again and again the high quality of his work would wring compliments from me that I was reluctant to give, knowing that they would fail to measure up to that ideal compliment which Liebling was ever ready to entertain. The second of his Paris series of pieces struck me as so brilliant that against my better judgment I rushed to his office the moment I had finished reading it to say that I thought it the finest thing he had ever done. Liebling stared at me through those little round glasses of his. "Wait till you read the next one," he said.

Liebling had a singular, highly successful method of interviewing people. He would sit facing the person from whom he intended to elicit information; and then sit there and sit there, silently. Soon the person being interviewed would begin to break down. Most reporters plunge into an interview asking too many questions, among which the interviewee is free to pick and choose, concentrating upon the questions that are easiest to deal with and skirting without seeming to do so those that might prove embarrassing to him. Liebling's method left the interviewee unnerved and at a loss as to what he was expected to defend himself against; by the time Liebling had put the first question to him, he was ready to babble almost any indiscretion.

One day I was a silent observer at a historic encounter in Liebling's office between him and Edmund Wilson. Each of them liked to talk and each wished to talk *at* the other man but not with him. Liebling launched out on an extended aria, to which Wilson affected to listen; in reality, he was simply watching Liebling's chest and waiting for the moment when Liebling would have to stop talking in order to draw breath. The moment came at last, and Wilson leapt with a torrent of words into the momentary gap. Liebling then sat staring glumly at Wilson until Wilson, too, had reached the necessary point of inhalation. It was a battle of titans, which neither of them was able to win, though from out in the corridor it might have been supposed that Wilson had done so: Liebling spoke in a low, sometimes inaudible voice and Wilson's voice could penetrate a foot-thick brick wall. What made the battle all the more remarkable was that neither opponent relinquished the tiniest part of his hold on his own topic of conversation. Wilson, who was then at the height of his interest in the Dead Sea Scrolls, roared on contentedly about their significance, while Liebling mumbled about a favorite figure of his, the learned sportsman Colonel Stingo.

The traditional Fifth Avenue parades in honor of various national holidays — Columbus Day, Pulaski Day, St. Patrick's Day, and the like — use West Forty-fourth Street as an assembly point for the scores of high-school bands that march and play on these occasions. It seems to me that no matter whose Day it may be, the same plump young drum majorettes, their thighs goose-pimpled with cold, are forever leading the same brightly costumed ragamuffin musicians out onto the avenue. They block our side street, making it difficult to cross, and we tend to grow impatient with them and their shouting, tootling mindlessness. Once, Liebling, Mitchell, and I were waiting in vain on the curb as the band of Our Lady of Sorrows blocked every foot of space in front of us. "One of the great things about the Jews," I said to Liebling, "is that they're the only large group in New York that doesn't insist on a parade. Why should that be?" Liebling thought and thought. "Their feet hurt," he said at last.

Liebling liked making bets and, naturally enough, hated losing them. When the office-building boom in New York was still in its infancy, he was convinced that it was almost at an end. I bet him an expensive lunch — no set price — that in the following year he would see at least a score of new high-rise office buildings begun in New York. He accepted the bet with alacrity. Of course he lost, but the bitterness of defeat was somewhat mitigated by the fact that he was paying me off in food, not cash, and that he

Liebling and his wife, the novelist and critic Jean Stafford, at their country place on Long Island.

was seated beside me, eating two or three times as much as I was and therefore, by his standards, proving himself a better man than I.

It is said to be a weakness in my character not to be much interested in food, and Liebling was a true trencherman, whose appetite astonished and appalled me. I saw that he was, in the old saying, digging his grave with his teeth, but there was nothing to be done about it; the pleasure he took in gormandizing was obviously identical to the pleasure other people took in listening to a Chopin nocturne. One day at lunch at the Villa Nova, during a period when, on doctor's orders, Liebling was making a valiant effort to eat lightly, he ordered a succulent dish of veal, peppers, and eggplant, which, in the Villa Nova tradition, arrived at the table aswim and asizzle in a large pewter platter. Liebling quickly polished off the entire platter, then, breaking chunks of bread from a long loaf on the table, soaked up the remaining gravy, all but literally licking the platter clean. It was a meal the very thought of which was enough to keep me from feeling hungry for a week. Liebling beckoned to the waiter. I thought he would be asking for the check, but not at all. "I'll have one more of the same," he said.

Mitchell and Liebling often repaired to the Red Devil, where they consumed a variety of repellent, hairy crustacea, as well as octopus, squid, and other creatures best left, to my mind, in the shallows and deeps from which they had been fetched. Around Christmastime one year, the proprietor of the Red Devil placed on their table at the end of a substantial meal a bottle of brandy and two glasses and invited them to drink their fill. No sooner had they filled their glasses than it was discovered that a grease-fire had broken out in the kitchen. Smoke poured out into the dining room and the fierce crackle of flames could be heard. The situation posed a dilemma for Mitchell and Liebling. It was the first time they had ever been so generously treated by the proprietor and they certainly intended to take full advantage of the gesture. At the same time, they wished to save their lives. Either they could remain where they were, go on drinking, and perhaps die; or they could abandon the brandy for safety's sake; or they could take the brandy with them, which, given that the proprietor's precious property was being destroyed all round him, had the look of unbecoming greed. Luckily, there was a contrary factor: if they were to leave the brandy behind, it would add to the already terrifying combustibility of the premises. Firemen were smashing the glass in the kitchen skylights; it would be of the greatest possible help to them, and to the distracted proprietor as well, if they carried the bottle of brandy and their two glasses out into the street and toasted the spirit of Christmas there. Heavily laden and with clear consciences, they made good their escape.

A late, sad-funny glimpse of Liebling: he and Hamburger are walking down Sixth Avenue toward the office. Liebling is dressed, as usual, in a tightly buttoned overcoat that is too small for him and a strange little high-crowned bowler hat, which he wears tipped down over his forehead. He makes a radically eccentric figure, and pedestrians take more than a casual look at him as, shoes splaying sharply east and west, he shuffles along in his slow, rocking-horse fashion. He has recently appeared on some local TV programs and has scored a certain success with them; he feels that the day of his real fame is about to dawn at last. "Notice them looking at me?" he asks Hamburger. "That's because they've seen me on TV."

25

To our readers, there appears to be a hierarchy of importance in respect to the various categories of contributors to the magazine. It is a hierarchy that strikes most of us who work here as interesting in large part because it is so arbitrary. On learning that I am a member of the staff of *The New Yorker*, people tend to ask me first of all about certain artists — Addams, Darrow, Steinberg, Steig, Price, Saxon, Stevenson, Lorenz, and, especially in recent years, Weber, Booth, Hamilton, and Koren, the last of whom draws furry creatures of indeterminate species that evidently incline his admirers to assume that Koren himself must be quite a furry creature. Which to tell the truth he is, with a drooping, dark mustache that I fear must make heavy demands on his energy.

"Happy?"

After the artists come, in the world's eyes, the writers of short stories — Updike, Woiwode, Barthelme, and the like — and then several writers of factual pieces, among them John McPhee, Calvin Trillin, and Calvin Tomkins. (Ever since the days of sour old Calvin Coolidge, it may have become an unbreakable rule of nomenclature that if you are named Calvin you are not called Calvin. In any event, Trillin is called "Bud" and Tomkins is called

"Congratulations, Schaeffer! You are now the captain."

"Tad.") With the exception of James Merrill, Anne Sexton, and James Dickey, I am rarely asked what any of the scores of poets we publish are "really" like. By now, Dickey is as much a public figure as he is a poet, and curiosity about him is to be expected; a big, hearty, noisy, hard-drinking man, he calls attention to himself as naturally as most poets shrink from doing so. I met him in a way that I found charming and that I think deserves to be recalled. Dickey happened into the office one day, intending to

A drawing by Frank Modell for an office Christmas party that I gave once in Sleepy Hollow. We are not much for parties at the New Yorker; people worry about them. When the Whites gave a party for Shawn at their house in Turtle Bay, Truax sent an engineer over to see whether the floors were sturdy enough to support the gathering. They were, but it took a New Yorker worrier to anticipate that they might not be.

visit with our poetry editor, Howard Moss. Moss being out, Dickey asked the receptionist to ring a couple of other people whom he knew in the office; they, too, were out. He then racked his brains for a name — any name — familiar to him, and hit on mine. He asked the receptionist to discover whether I was in; I was, and so we met. I admire a man who, even though he suspects that he may be scraping the bottom of the barrel, scrapes the bottom of the barrel.

Robert Graves has published many poems in *The New Yorker*. I once made the mistake of trying to write a Profile of him for the magazine. It was a mistake, not alone because it violated the Rossian injunction against writers writing about writers (especially base was it in Ross's eyes for *New Yorker* writers to write about other *New Yorker* writers), but also because, both in verse and prose, Graves had told so much of his life story himself, in his innumerable books. Moreover, I discovered that the remnant that remained untold I would not be at liberty to tell. In spite of all this, it was an error well worth making; I spent a pleasant week or so with Graves in Majorca, subjecting him to what he pretended was a painful psychoanalysis and writing up many pages of notes on him. Returning home, I put my notes in order and then sat staring at my typewriter for months in vain; not so much as an opening sentence emerged from all that conscientious labor.

Graves was the undisputed monarch of the little Majorcan village of Deya, where he has lived since the twenties, and it was amusing to become for a time a member of his substantial court. He showed off for me splendidly, in what was then but the beginning of his vigorous old age, diving off high rocks into the sea, working hard in his garden, and, over food and wine, uttering dazzling obiter dicta on a thousand favorite topics, from Judas to the divine mushroom. The grey, frizzy tangle of hair that rose above his brow was prophetic; so were his broken nose, his cold grey-blue eyes, and even the absence of teeth (for his false teeth irritated him). He was a spellbinder out of another time, and he knew it.

Graves put me up in his guest house, which a local bishop some centuries earlier had built as a sort of lean-to against one side of the village church and which Graves had succeeded in restoring with his own hands. Lying abed on a Sunday morning, the renegade Catholic in me enjoyed listening to the distant murmur of Mass on the far side of the bedroom wall. Water at the *posada* had to be drawn from a deep well in the courtyard. For a shower, one hoisted bucketful after bucketful of water into a tin container fastened high on a wall; one then pulled a string and the icy water gushed down tumultuously until the container was empty. In those days, a burro named Isabella dwelt in a nearby byre, a corner of which served as the makeshift jakes of the *posada*. One was instructed to take care lest Isabella escape when one entered the byre, but it was a tradition in Deya that the wily beast nearly always managed to outwit human beings; whenever she was to be seen strolling through the streets of the village, it indicated that Señor Graves had still another hapless guest at stool.

Graves, a devoted gardener, has long been in the habit of naming compost heaps after friends. During my visit he honored me by naming his latest compost heap after me. A friend that Graves and I have in common — the banker-scholar, R. Gordon Wasson — had recently been honored in a similar fashion. I was understandably proud when, some months after my visit to Deya, I received a letter from Graves, in which he mentioned that "the Gordon Wasson is something of a disappointment, but the Brendan Gill is rotting nicely."

The founders of an expensive restaurant in New York called the Forum of the Twelve Caesars drew much of their information about Roman times from the Graves translation of Suetonius's *Lives of the* [Twelve] *Caesars.* In acknowledgment of their literary debt, the restaurant owners wrote to Graves in far-off Majorca, thanking him for the assistance he had provided by means of his book and adding that if he should ever happen to visit New York, he and a number of his friends must accept the present of a luncheon at the Forum. Little did the owners know about the suggestibility of poets! They may have supposed that Graves was a safe person to issue such a blanket invitation to at a distance of some four thousand miles, but not at all — within a few days, Graves was in New York and was eagerly on the telephone to me. Dropping everything else, I must help him locate some suitable companions for a luncheon party at the Forum on that very day.

I had been planning to have lunch at the Century Club with C. P. Snow, who was then at the height of his fame as a novelist and whom I had never met. Would Graves like me to bring him along? By all means! When Snow arrived at the Century at the agreed-on hour, I asked him if he would care to join Graves and his group at the Forum; Sir Charles said he would be delighted. Graves and he were strangers and, save for such a chance meeting, would perhaps always have remained strangers. The Forum party was an outstanding success, with Graves and Snow dominating the table and taking a great interest in each other's company. As for the owners of the restaurant, Graves was ruthless; the meal he ordered was an enormous one, and when it came to the wines that accompanied it, he wasn't above asking for a few bottles of "a wine that was named for my people." This proved to be Château Haut Brion, which is indeed a graves, if not a Graves.

Another poet who was often published in *The New Yorker* and who became a good friend of the Gills was Marianne Moore. Up to her late seventies, she was something of a literary gadabout, turning up at parties with an ever-surprising girlish eagerness. When we first knew her, she was living in Brooklyn, in the apartment she had shared with her mother; in late old age, she moved to an apartment on West Ninth Street, in Greenwich Village. Once, at the end of a cocktail party somewhere far uptown, Anne and I offered to drive Miss Moore home. We were on our way to Brooklyn when it occurred to me that she might like to stop off somewhere in midtown for dinner. Why, gracious! Nothing would suit her better! By what amounted to a miracle, I was able to find a parking space not far from Gino's, a well-known Italian restaurant on Lexington Avenue in the Sixties. Hurrying into the restaurant ahead of Miss Moore and Anne, I discovered that it was, as usual, desperately crowded, with a large number of people waiting at the bar. I drew Gino aside and explained that I had in my company one of the leading poets in America; would he do her the honor of finding a place for her? Gino bowed; *d'accordo*, he understood perfectly.

When Miss Moore came in, dressed in black and with the invariable black velvet tricorne nesting atop her white hair, Gino was in no doubt of her distinction. Her blue eyes beamed up at him; murmuring solicitudes, Gino ushered us to a table that had just been cleared. Though reservations are not permitted at Gino's, the crowd at the bar must have understood that an event of some moment was under way; all the more so when, at the end of our dinner, Gino brought out from the cloakroom a large, old-fashioned guest book, which he begged Miss Moore to sign. Pen pressed to her lips, she thought hard and long; at last, very slowly and taking care to make her penmanship as clear as possible, she wrote on a blank page of the book, "That was the nicest veal à la marsala I ever ate. Marianne Moore."

Later, Miss Moore wrote a poem about Gino's; that is, she wrote a poem that included mention of the spirited zebras that decorate the walls of the restaurant. I was able to buy a copy of the book in which the poem appears, have Miss Moore autograph it, and present it to Gino; a happy ending to the episode. Knowing how mad about animals Miss Moore was, I wasn't surprised at her having found room for Gino's zebras in her verse. I congratulated myself on having served as a sort of broker in this aesthetic transaction, but some years afterward I performed a more remarkable feat — I commanded Miss Moore to bring a poem into being on a topic of my choosing, and she did so.

Shortly before the opening of the New York World's Fair of 1964, a public relations firm representing the fair sent me a press release about the historic background of the land upon which the fair was to be built. With the release came a glossy eight-by-ten-inch photograph of a race track at an amusement park that had occupied the site a hundred years earlier. The grass track was surrounded by a white wooden fence, and leaning against the fence in the photograph (and no doubt standing very still in order not to spoil the time exposure, which would have been a long one) was a little boy in white sailor blouse and trousers, with black stockings and high-buttoned shoes. It was a curiously haunting photograph and on an impulse I mailed it off to Miss Moore, adjuring her to write a poem about what was taking place in the mind of the little boy. I heard never a word from Miss Moore, but a few months later I was riffling through the latest issue of *The New Yorker* and I saw a poem entitled "Old Amusement Park" and signed "Marianne Moore." And, sure enough, it was "my" poem, about the little boy and his thoughts; that day, I felt veritably godlike.

Once, I was riding in from Brooklyn on the subway with Miss Moore. At a stop, ten or fifteen black children, all carrying band instruments, rushed headlong into the car and seated themselves in helter-skelter high spirits around us. They were evidently members of a high-school band, on their way to a parade in midtown Manhattan. Two very tall, skinny boys were carrying between them a bright-red bass drum, trimmed with brass. They squeezed themselves into an empty place next to Miss Moore. Miss Moore stared with admiration at the drum, then said to the boy holding the drumsticks, "Sonny, when the time comes, give it a big bang just for me."

Miss Moore had a handsome brother, a Navy man, with whom she liked to go on long walks. Brother and sister were very close, and Miss Moore told me that her sister-in-law was often put out to observe that closeness. "I declare, I don't understand such a feeling," Miss Moore said primly, understanding it perfectly.

I failed in my attempt to write a Profile of Graves, and I failed also in an attempt to write one of William Carlos Williams. He was among the poets I admired most in my youth, and I wanted to set down my impression of him in the magazine while he was still active. Though only in his late fifties, he had suffered an ominous heart attack and had been warned that there might be more. He was a physician, practicing pediatrics in Rutherford, New Jersey, and it was my thought that by writing about him in terms of his medical practice, I could avoid the difficulty of his being, from the magazine's point of view, "literary."

My friend James Laughlin was Williams's publisher and friend, and he arranged for me to meet Williams at his combined home-and-office in Rutherford. Whatever Rutherford may be today, twenty-odd years ago it was a decaying middle-class community, and Williams devoted himself largely to caring for the families of blue-collar workers. Even by the standards of that time, he was an old-fashioned doctor, selflessly making house calls at all hours of the night and day. So exceptionally kind-hearted was he, and therefore such a soft "touch," that it was wonderful that he could bring himself to earn a living at all. He was also an exceptionally passionate man, and as I followed him on his rounds it soon turned out that his interest was aroused not only by the sick children who were under his care. Despite his age and damaged heart, he was lacerated by sexual excitement; every young mother we encountered seemed to strike him as a Venus.

Williams and I would pull up in his car in front of some not very savory-looking bungalow, and Williams would slap my knee and say, "Wait till you get a look at this one!" We would ring the bell, and the door would be opened by some slatternly woman in her late twenties or early thirties, wearing a soiled rayon dressing gown and with her dyed hair done up in a dozen or so pink plastic curlers. She would have an infant in her arms, purple-faced from screaming and with diapers unpleasantly tapestried, and the odds were that however sick the infant was, the mother was suffering from something equally unpleasant — at the very least, so I seem to remember, a severe case of post-nasal drip. Williams wouldn't be daunted. He would examine the baby, write out a prescription, and then spend five or ten minutes in happy banter with the dull, distracted, and wholly undesirable mother. Back in the car, he would be breathing hard and radiant. "What a girl!"

One day his wife, Floss, to whom Williams was devoted, asked him with understandable impatience, "Bill, tell me the truth. Do you want to make love with every single woman you meet?" Williams took the question seriously, and after a minute or two of grave thought he replied, "Yes. I do."

Because there was no way to tell the truth about Williams and his joyful, indiscriminate amorousness, I abandoned the Profile. Certain failures make me happier when I look back on them than certain successes.

Next in degree of interest to our readers, after artists, writers of fiction, and writers of fact, come people who write departments: Pauline Kael and Penelope Gilliatt, say, of "The Current Cinema," and Audax Minor, of "The Race Track." George T. Ryall employs that archaic pseudonym because when he began writing for us there was a correspondent on an English racing paper who signed his dispatches "Audax." In calling himself "Audax Minor," Ryall, a transplanted Englishman, followed a principle employed in English public schools, where, if there are two Joneses enrolled, the elder Jones is known as Jones Major and the younger as Jones Minor. Ryall is a spry little man in his middle eighties, with fine brown hair, sharp eyes, and a droll way of speaking; tips on horses emerge sideways and downward out of a corner of his puckered mouth, as if that were the very fashion in which he had received the tips from the horses themselves, warily circling the paddock and sizing up their adversaries. Many people are eager to read Ryall's column who have never been to a race track in their lives; to them, his world is a romantic fiction, and they are grateful when they learn that, with his green tweeds, his binoculars slung smartly athwart his chest, and his jaunty stride, Ryall resembles a character out of some sunny Edwardian novel. Bertie Wooster might well have stumbled against him in the press of the crowd on a corking afternoon at Goodwood. Bertie would have burst out, "Sorry, old chap!," and Ryall would have told him what he thought of him, in a courteous, sidelong snarl.

What can I do but salute with admiration the two brilliant women, Pauline Kael and Penelope Gilliatt, who, seven or eight years ago, took my place reviewing movies for the magazine? They divide the department between them, in terms of six months apiece, but Kael has been notoriously impatient with the arrangement, and for a simple reason: she is insatiable and wishes nothing less than to see every movie ever made and to give her opinion of it in print. Her memory matches her ambition, and it is uncanny to hear her in conversation casting a net of movie titles, studios, actors, directors, producers, and screenwriters so wide that it covers far more countries than she can possibly be acquainted with at first hand, and far more years than she has lived. As a social being, she is always witty and sometimes a holy terror; among other things, she has the distinction of being the only person I know who has made her fellow-reviewer John Simon blanch with terror, and that by means of a mere throw-away ethnic slur on the place of his birth. With relish, she turns Simon's viperish *ad hominem* tactics against him, and he finds them wounding. An irrepressible rictus of anticipated triumph crosses Simon's features as he prepares to deliver some cruel blow, but Kael is always ahead of him: he stands disemboweled and incredulous as her foul-mouthed schoolgirl voice speeds on.

Kael's only fault as a writer is an occasional garrulousness. Instead of gathering up her materials in her mind and putting them into some sort of concise order there, she begins to write and then lures herself, by one impromptu divagation after another, into a loosely strung-out judgment of a movie; the series of *aperçus* to which we are treated may prove dazzling, but we find it hard to forgive her for having led us on such a prolonged ramble when, from almost the first paragraph, her goal was in sight and not beyond our ability to attain. I blame the prolixity of her style

Pauline Kael   Penelope Gilliatt

on the fact that in youth she used to give talks about movies over
the radio; the ear forgives much more than the eye and welcomes
repetition as a necessary *aide-mémoire;* on the page it implies that
the reader cannot follow a straightforward line of reasoning. With
Kael, as long ago my Uncle Arthur found himself with Melville,
I am sometimes tempted to cry aloud, "Good God, woman! Get
on with your story!"

Gilliatt writes fiction for the magazine, as well as movie reviews, and her stories are so good that she must often hear, to
her despair, that many of her readers wish that she would devote
herself exclusively to them. Her movie reviews tend to contain
highly personal views of what America is like and what England
is like; from time to time, she will even tell us at length what
Henry James thought America was like, or what Fitzgerald thought
it was like, and these obiter dicta, though not without a certain
scholarly appeal, have little to do with reviewing movies like *Daisy
Miller* and *The Great Gatsby.* One reads her for the pleasingness
of her mind; at the very moment that, radically disagreeing with
some opinion that Gilliatt has expressed, I wish to begin a quarrel
with her, her lucidity and wit disarm me. Who would wish to turn
so blithe a companion into an opponent?

When, in 1967, I switched from writing movie reviews to writing play reviews, most of my younger friends were sure that I had taken a humiliating step downward, movies being the only art form that could be said to amount to anything this late in the twentieth century. My elder friends assumed, on the contrary, that I had taken a step up, theatre having always counted for them as the real thing and movies as some sort of engaging but fundamentally trivial counterfeit. As for me, I felt only that I had taken a step sideways, into an area already as familiar to me as movies and one that had a value, in terms of its aesthetic worth, neither greater nor less than any other area. There they were and are, theatre and movies, staking their own superlative claims and having much less in common with each other than most people suppose.

Young as she was, the receptionist on the twentieth floor was under the impression when I changed jobs that any change must represent an improvement in my lot, and she concluded therefore that my new appointment would lead to an increase in my pay (as it did not). Soon after she heard the news, she said with a grave sweetness, "Oh, Mr. Gill, I think it's *so* nice about your new job! Now you'll be able to afford to buy better clothes." There was little that one could say in answer to this peculiar compliment except "Thank you."

Perhaps as a consequence of the receptionist's opinion of my low standard of dress, I make a point of putting on a black tie for opening nights. I am alone among reviewers in always doing so; my only recruit in the cause of honoring the theatre by dressing up for it has been Leonard Harris, of C.B.S., and even he is not to be counted on, his turtleneck sweaters and tweed jackets occasionally letting down the side.

Thirty-five years ago, all the reviewers except Richard Watts, Jr., habitually wore dinner jackets to openings. The Second World War apparently sufficed to put an end to this tradition and so turned Watts from a maverick into a ringleader. My colleagues in the Critics Circle now affect a slovenliness of dress and deportment that would be hard to surpass in a Bowery saloon; our meetings, which mercifully take place but twice a year, are remarkable for a rumpledness of mental activity that exactly matches our manners. We cannot even contrive to vote for the best play of the year without falling into acrimonious debate over the total of votes cast for different plays; again and again, we must repeat our votes, sometimes orally, sometimes with a show of hands, sometimes on ballots. Watts, who is in his late seventies, observes these contrarious goings-on with the skepticism of one who has been persuaded against his better judgment to visit the snake pit of an ill-kept zoo; the longer and more confused our discussions, the farther down on his nose he allows his glasses to slip and the thicker the cloud of cigarette smoke behind which he takes refuge.

My fellow-reviewers practice many foolish customs, one of which is, at intermission, not to discuss the show they are in the midst of watching. It would be the most shocking of gaucheries if anyone were to blurt out the least hint of what he is thinking at such a moment; the pretext is that one has no opinion, and banter and small talk take the place of what I would consider useful discussion. Watts and Walter Kerr follow this absurd practice with the devotion of a couple of old Galway priests, as they follow the equally absurd practice of never applauding the performers. They stand on the curb outside the theatre for as long as possible on opening nights, determined to be among the last to enter. Not too much need be read into this in respect to their confidence, or lack of confidence, in the evening ahead; they wait there less because of distrust than because they dislike being run down by first-nighters, many of whom are aggressive middle-aged businessmen with Coppertone tans and money in the show.

I often hear praise of my colleague in the "Theatre" department, Edith Oliver, who covers Off Broadway. As the reviewer for Broadway, I must have some sort of following, but what it is I cannot tell. From time to time, some imperious ten-year-old will write in to complain of my obtuseness and beg me to pull myself together, and I always write back that I will do my best, but I get comparatively little mail except from people who, in an exchange of correspondence, eventually reveal themselves to

Edith Oliver

be relatives or close friends of the author, director, or performers in some play or musical that I have reviewed adversely. Now and then an actor — James Stewart, for one — will risk violating the age-old tabu against actors thanking a reviewer for a favorable review; now and then an Edward Albee will write in to agree or disagree with my interpretation of one of his plays, and I am grateful to find myself in a colloquy with him, fruitful for me and perhaps fruitful for him. The closest I come to gaining the impression that as a writer on the magazine I may be an object of curiosity to readers is when I learn by chance that somebody has been speculating upon my appearance. I happen to be tall and thin, but on being introduced to me at a cocktail party an elderly lady once said, with indignation, "You Brendan Gill? What nonsense! I can tell by his writing that Brendan Gill is short and fat."

As a variation on the hypothesis that a writer's style may resemble his person as well as his nature, what of the possibility that a writer's style accurately reflects his preoccupations as well? If one writes quickly, and especially if one writes under pressure, are the figures of speech that spring to mind likely to embody certain suppressed wishes and needs? Ross long ago said that I talked like a goddam fool because I found his typos pregnant with meaning, but figures of speech make a far richer field of study. A charming piece of literary detective work on this topic was once performed by a *New Yorker* writer, Susan Black (now Susan Sheehan). Her subject, or victim, was Walter Kerr.

Reading Kerr's drama criticism from day to day in the *Herald Tribune,* Miss Black came to realize that most of his metaphors and similes were drawn from the world of food. He wrote that he hoped someone would create a "sirloin steak of a play" for Bette Davis. He described *The Hostage* as a "pot-au-feu" and "a broth," and he said of its author, Brendan Behan, that he was "an original piece of salt." Margaret Rutherford was said to resemble "a shark about to feast on a bather," while the music in *Irma la Douce* was "jelly-roll" and the play as a whole had "no staying power, no hearty filling inside the showy meringue."

Having kept track of Kerr's metaphors and similes for several weeks, Miss Black was able to make a convincing case for the probability that Kerr was on a diet and that the diet was giving him a good deal of difficulty. Only once in the period in which she kept him under observation did Kerr abandon his gastronomic analogies, and that was over the Thanksgiving weekend, when, presumably, he let himself go a little.

26

Among the best-known writers of departments are Mollie Panter-Downes, with her "Letter from London," and Janet Flanner, with her "Letter from Paris." Mollie Panter-Downes has been writing for the magazine since 1939; during the Second World War, her dispatches from bombed, burning, and, for all we knew at the time, dying England were unforgettable; to us and to our readers, she was as much an embodiment of the gallant English spirit as Churchill himself. And having doubted the possibility that there could be any connection between a person's writing and his appearance, to say nothing of his name, I have to confess that in this case the appearance, the prose style, and even the name are indisputably one. Mollie is a classic English beauty — fair, blue-eyed, erect — and just such a person as should bear the hyphenated patronymic Panter-Downes. Moreover, during most of her career on the magazine she has lived in the verdant, rose-embowered English countryside, in a house every bit as well named as she: Rapplegh's, in Haslemere, Surrey.

Janet Flanner has been writing her "Letter from Paris" since 1925. How she came to do so and how she came to acquire her famous pseudonym, "Genêt," she has told in a witty introduction to Jane Grant's autobiography, *Ross, The New Yorker and Me.* (Ross would have objected strongly to his ex-wife's omission from the title of a comma after the name of the magazine; no doubt he would also have objected to the title itself, which strains to embrace too much and puts one in mind of that mythical all-time best-seller, "Lincoln's Doctor's Dog.") Flanner wrote in her introduction, in part:

> . . . I occasionally wrote to Jane to tell her what was going on in the boulevard theatres and the Opéra, to both of which she was addicted. In the summer of 1925, she wrote me, saying, "You remember that magazine Ross always talked about starting? Well,

Mollie Panter-Downes at Rappleghs.

he has it in print at last. Why don't you write a fortnightly Paris letter for us?" I wrote back asking what Ross's magazine was called and if it was any good, to which Jane replied it was called "The New Yorker" and was not any good, as yet, but that Ross was laboring over it, on some days believed in it optimistically and particularly in some of his new ideas. I sent two sample "Letters from Paris," which were also not good, especially after Ross condensed them into one, which, when I finally saw it, published early in September, somewhat surprised me by being signed Genêt, apparently my "nom de plume." Months later, out of curiosity, I wrote and asked him which of the three well-known, if rather objectionable, Genêts he had had in mind in choosing it. Had he named me for Citizen Genêt, the first minister from the First French Republic sent to the United States after the French

Janet Flanner in 1933, pretending to be Eustace Tilley. The portrait was taken by her friend Horst.

Revolution, whose recall was demanded by President George Washington as a brash French diplomat historically noted for his tactless lack of democratic diplomacy? Or had he named me for the yellow broom flower, that leguminous weed that overruns French heaths and is viewed by peasants as a pest? The third I cited was the feline Genêt, or civet, a small French relative of the polecat. Ross very sensibly ignored my letter. Office gossip in New York reported that it seemed unlikely he had ever heard of any of the three Genêts. He had apparently fallen on the name at random, and to his eyes and ears it seemed like a Frenchification of Janet, so it was merely a pleasant compliment, after all.

Contrary to what Flanner writes, her first "Letter" was very good indeed. Since then, she has written many hundreds of them, in a style at once graceful and austere, with an occasional word — "fastuous," for example, borrowed unconsciously by her from the French — that sends us all in haste to Webster's, to discover that it is admirable English. Flanner is now in her eighties, but her perspicacity is undiminished and her speech remains as elegant and aphoristic as ever. Speaking recently of a friend of hers who has been a lifelong womanizer, she said, "I cannot tell you how many women he has ruined and delighted." The friend, to whom, as Flanner was well aware, the remark was sure to be repeated, accepted the judgment she had pronounced on him as if it were the highest of compliments — and of the fact that he would do so, Flanner had also been well aware.

I speak of her aphoristic style, but she has another side: as a storyteller, she is superbly, fearlessly anfractuous. She sets forth upon what seems a broad, straight highway of an anecdote, strays as if for only a moment from the highway onto to some inviting country lane, leaves the lane for a mere grassy track, vaults a gate or two, crosses a field, fords a brook, and threatens at every moment to leave us, her bewitched auditors, not only far behind but also totally baffled as to the link between the direction in which she set out and the direction in which she appears to be heading. Then presto-magico! a last gate, a sudden, easy turn through what had appeared to be an impenetrable underbrush, the highway is regained, and we have arrived triumphantly at our promised destination. Not for a moment has she lost her way, or let us be tempted to follow any way but hers; and all the while she has held us bound to her not alone by her beautiful low voice but by her beautiful dark eyes, immense with the adventure of high, fanciful talk.

Flanner's only rival as a teller of complicated tales is her old friend Hawley Truax, the retired chairman of the board of directors of *The New Yorker*. They are contemporaries in age and close comrades in their championship of precision in thought and speech. In the old days, when Flanner spent nearly all of her time abroad, Alethea and Hawley Truax could be counted on to give a grand party for her whenever she returned to the States; at these parties the only person likely to tell a story richer in incident and more devious in syntax than one of Flanner's would be Truax. Botsford and I remember a Flanner party, in the days when the Truaxes were living in a cozy little duplex on Murray Hill, at which Truax, intending to be a good host but irresistibly tempted to begin a story at the very moment in which he had also been about to open a magnum of champagne, stood in the center of the room spellbinding his guests and now and again gesturing with the bottle of champagne, though with every indication of no longer remembering what it was that he held in his hands. None of us had yet had a drink and the story promised to be a long one, with many an adroit detour for the purpose of visiting attractive sub-episodes and footnotes along the way. Botsford was unable to stand the strain of this unnatural abstinence in the midst of plenty; gently but firmly he detached the bottle from Truax's arms, popped the cork, and started pouring drinks, while Truax, entirely unaware of Botsford, a radiant smile on his face, proceeded to lead us step by step into the heart of his intricate maze and then joyfully out again.

A Truax family anecdote, to illustrate how fiercely compelling Truax could be in his prime. One day he was waiting at the railroad station in Stockbridge for a friend who was expected to spend the weekend with the Truaxes at their country place in Tyringham. Truax has such extremely poor vision that I have never seen him without at least one pair of gold-rimmed spectacles dinting the bridge of his beaky nose and another pair about to take its place. As the train pulled into the station, Truax eagerly observed the passengers stepping down onto the platform. No sign of his friend. Impatient as always and determined to act decisively at all costs, Truax marched up and down the platform, peering up into the windows. At last, the man he had been looking for! He beckoned energetically to him, mouthing through the window-glass the words "Hurry! Hurry!" After some hesitancy, the man stood up, took his luggage from the overhead rack, made his way along the aisle, and stepped down onto the platform just as the train started out of the station. It was then that, changing his spectacles, Truax got his first clear look at the man. Not his friend at all, but a suggestible stranger, who had been unable to withstand Truax's importunacy. Damnation! Gravely embarrassed and at the same time furious with the stranger for his deplorable lack of character, Truax grimly volunteered to drive him at top speed to the next station, which with luck they would reach in time for the weakling to resume his journey.

I have already mentioned Truax's exceptional fiscal prudence, which to my mind has nearly always amounted to folly. He has practiced other forms of prudence as well, especially when it comes to taking every precaution against possible future accidents or misadventures. Once Truax and Ross were driving up to Tyringham for the weekend. They stopped off in Norfolk (where the Gills were subsequently to have their summer place), in order for Truax to transact some minor piece of legal business; they were then obliged to put up overnight in the only available quarters — a decayed hostelry known as the Norfolk Inn. This was a great rambling wooden wreck of a place, sagging like a grey-skinned, tipsy elephant, which uncannily survived into the nineteen-sixties. The only bedroom left in the inn was a musty cell on the top floor. The building was all too obviously a firetrap, and Truax looked around at once for a means of escape in case a fire should break out during the night. To his relief, under the single window in the room was a wooden box and in the box was a rope ladder. Tired as Truax was and determined as Ross was to turn out the light and go to sleep, nothing would do but that Truax make sure that the rope ladder was in good working order. The window had been sealed tight for years with court plaster and old newspapers — Norfolk is the coldest town in Connecticut, as well as the highest — but Truax finally worried it open and began paying out the ladder. It fell readily enough; so readily, indeed, that the last of it suddenly slipped through Truax's fingers and vanished into the dark, leaving him to discover that someone had unaccountably failed to fasten the end of the rope to the bottom of the box. As Ross snored on, Truax spent a sleepless night in a rocker by the window, awaiting the holocaust.

Early in my friendship with Truax, I encountered his remarkable system of mnemonics. It turned out to depend not on his efforts but on those of Alethea Truax, a wife so patient that whenever her name is uttered it is invariably followed by a sigh of wonder. I went one morning to Truax's office, to ask his advice on some matter concerning the magazine's first-reading agreement. (The agreement stipulated, among other things, that writers signing it would be provided with a desk and a typewriter, "such as they are." A Rossian touch, which has long since been dropped from the agreement.) Truax decided that the point I had raised would require cogitation. He picked up a phone and put through a call to his wife. "Alethea, dear, will you please take a piece of paper and write down on it the name of Brendan Gill, and then take the piece of paper into the bathroom and place it in the top of my shaving mug?"

Cogitation would take place the following morning, while Truax shaved.

Self-imposed squalor: my office at the end of Sleepy Hollow. The clock on the wall hung in my grandmother's kitchen in Southington, Connecticut, a hundred years ago. Often the papers mount so high on either side of my typewriter that I am reduced to writing poems in iambic trimeter. Now and then an old Ross outline for a "Talk" story surfaces on the sofa and then sinks again from sight.

A bust high on my office wall. It was given to me by Jo Mielziner, as a souvenir of a catastrophic play — The Day the Money Stopped — of which I was, with Maxwell Anderson, the co-author and of which Mielziner was the designer. The play was based on my novel of the same name and lasted three days on Broadway. Mielziner had used the bust as a prop in a score of plays, beginning with The Barretts of Wimpole Street.

Truax has always been a solicitous host, if a maddening one. A familiar scene: coming home late from the office, he finds half a dozen people, members of the family and close friends, seated comfortably about the living room, enjoying a quiet chat. What a pleasant picture, and how glad he is that everyone appears to be so content! But stay a moment — surely Mary D. would prefer being seated in the chair next to Alan's, while Betty would be far better off if she were to move over next to Tom? Nor must Will be left out of it — Will must go sit where Alethea has been sitting, so would Alethea please sit in the chair formerly occupied by Betty? And thus, within five minutes this domestic von Clausewitz has everyone in the room on his feet, frantically engaged in maneuvers half military and half musical chairs — maneuvers that are all the harder to face because there has never been any telling how far Truax is prepared to go in his determination to make everyone attain the greatest possible happiness.

Truax was in charge of the highly successful party held at the Ritz Hotel in 1950, in honor of the twenty-fifth anniversary of the founding of the magazine. The Ritz, then already marked for demolition, was a delightful place in which to give big parties, and Truax had outdone himself in the care he had taken with the preparations. Nothing had been left to chance; characteristically, there were rooms reserved uptstairs in the hotel not only for guests who had come from distant places but for guests who, however nearby they happened to live, might find themselves unable to undertake the difficult, zigzag journey home. When the Truaxes arrived at the party, Alethea stopped in the lobby and glanced about in mock astonishment. She had listened long and long to the number of potential disasters that Truax had anticipated and by shrewd precautions was confident of having outwitted. Now she said, "But, Hawley, no boats?"

Truax blinked. "Boats, my dear?"

"What if there were to be some sudden, terrible flood later in the evening? Surely you must have thought of having a few boats in readiness here in the lobby?"

In the late nineteen-fifties, the Truaxes spent a good deal of time in Paris, where they saw much of Flanner and other members of the American circle there. Truax was as prudent abroad as he was at home; he would never frequent what he called "those tourist traps," by which he meant any of the really first-rate restaurants in Paris. He knew of plenty of little side-street restaurants that Michelin ought to have heard of and hadn't; *tant pis* for Michelin and the American innocents abroad who trusted it!

One summer, the Truaxes and their son and daughter-in-law went on a tour by car through the French countryside. Back in

Hawley Truax

this country, Truax complained that agreeable as the trip had been, he disliked being obliged to go without meat for so long a time. Alethea Truax and the children protested that this was nonsense — they recollected instance after instance in which all of them, and especially Hawley, had enjoyed a certain veal dish at such-and-such a restaurant, and still another veal dish at a restaurant farther along the road . . . Truax held up his hand. His voice was magisterial. "Veal is not meat," he said.

The last big building boom on the *New Yorker* premises took place in the fifties, and Truax was to that peculiar series of operations precisely what Baron Haussmann was to nineteenth-century Paris. Walls came down and went up, men's rooms became ladies' rooms and ladies' rooms men's rooms, and stairways were pierced from floor to floor (for years, we had been content to go back and forth between the nineteenth and twentieth floors by way of an outdoor fire escape, not easy to negotiate in wet weather). Truax is an ebullient and resourceful amateur architect. Though trained as a lawyer, he laid the foundation of his fortune as a developer of real estate on Long Island, and it was he who, in the twenties, drew up the plans for turning two derelict old houses on West Forty-seventh Street into a "commune" for Ross, Jane Grant, Alexander Woollcott, and himself. He is a born problem-solver — some would call him a born inventor of problems where none had previously been seen to exist — and the more difficult the problem, the more pleased he is to fiddle with it. There have always been plenty of problems in respect to the efficient use of space at *The New Yorker,* especially since every writer expects to possess his own cubicle and, once installed, will rarely consent to move out, however much the space may be needed for other purposes.

Truax must have had great fun during this last fling as a Haussmann. He is willing to admit that two or three of the more out-of-the-way offices can scarcely be located except by measuring the total square footage of a given floor and then subtracting the square footage of the offices one already knows. The story goes that there is at least one office on the premises that can be entered only by climbing the face of the building and entering it through a window; certainly it is true that the corridors have many doors that lead nowhere; they remain locked, awaiting the day when a new arrangement of offices will be worked out behind them. Truax's most ambitious accomplishment was the driving through of what I call his Avenue de l'Opéra — a broad corridor that instead of having to take an abrupt right-angle turn, as in the old Rossian days, simply veers off at an angle of approximately forty-five degrees. This stroke of engineering genius has unquestionably improved visibility, causing fewer unwary pedestrians to collide with each other, but it has also led to some mighty unusual shapes in the way of offices, viz:

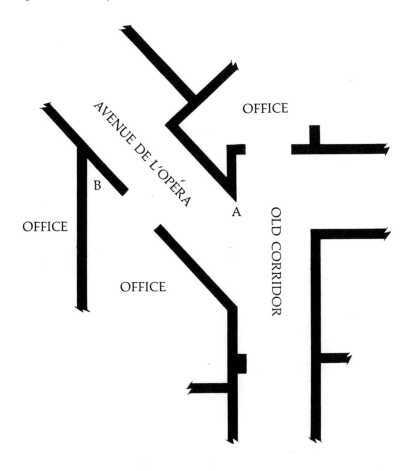

Milton Greenstein, who was Truax's protégé and learned at his knee the art of anticipating imaginary disasters, has often worried lest some overzealous office boy, rounding the bend into the Avenue de l'Opéra, split his skull open against the sharp-edged angle marked "A" in the diagram. Not dangerous but inexcusable in terms of effective design is the acute angle marked "B" in the diagram. I pointed it out to Truax one day, asking, with the exaggerated indignation of a rival amateur of architecture, how he could possibly justify such a waste of space. "Not a waste at all," said Truax benignly. "It's a perfect place to put a wet umbrella."

Truax is exceedingly cautious with money; he can also be generous.

An example of his caution: For a time, Truax made it a habit to eat inexpensive lunches at his desk. On his way to the office, he would stop off at an Automat on Sixth Avenue and pick up a sandwich wrapped in wax paper. One day a wino stopped him

At first glance, one would imagine that the complex series of plane surfaces that make up one wall of The New Yorker *library was the handiwork of a confirmed Bauhaus enthusiast. Not at all — it is the underside of a Truax stairway.*

on Forty-fourth Street and begged for a handout, purportedly to stay his hunger. It was plain to Truax that he wanted money not for food but for drink and he took satisfaction in outwitting him. "I won't give you any money," he said, "but I *will* give you lunch," and digging down into his overcoat pocket he fetched up the wax-paper-wrapped sandwich.

An example of his generosity: Knowing that Truax had become interested in the Pierpont Morgan Library, I urged upon him the fact that the library, despite its proud name and its innumerable treasures, in terms of endowment and funds for new purchases was comparatively poor. One day at the office I received a phone call; it was Truax, calling from the library — calling, in fact, from a coin-box telephone in a closet at the library. "Help!" he said. "I'm trying to give away some money and they won't let me." What had happened was that, crippled as he was with arthritis, he had hobbled on foot to the library and had attempted to hand somebody a check for five thousand dollars as the first of a projected series of annual contributions. The director, Frederick Adams, was out of town, and so was his secretary; nobody else was willing to accept the check. Truax, dressed as usual like a Balkan spy, seemed an unlikely person to be offering the library so handsome a gift. I promised to correct the difficulty by making a phone call to one of the curators, which I did. Later, I thanked Truax for his munificence. Not at all, not at all; he assured me that he was being as prudent as ever. "When I was younger," he said, "I might have thought twice about starting to give such sums. Nowadays, when I consider the multiplier . . ."

One of the most gifted and original of our writers, Niccolo Tucci, spoke of the imminence of death in something like the same bantering terms when some months ago he described to me a period of depression through which he had recently passed. "For a while, I considered taking my life," he said. "Then I put it to myself that at my age and with my prospects, committing suicide would be very much like turning in a Rumanian passport."

Truax is indomitable. He is also a Calvinist, with, on some probably not often examined level of his mind, a conviction that suffering is natural to man, that it may be deserved, that in any event it must be given a value, just as pleasure is, and, finally, that with sufficient discipline it can be profited from. For years, in extreme pain, he dragged himself about the city by public

transport when he could easily have afforded a chauffeur and
limousine. Now he is largely confined to his wheelchair, but his
spirits remain high. When, thanks to pain, his nights have been
sleepless, he has refused to let that pain go to waste — he has
forced it to serve a worthy end, which turns out to be nothing
less than the composition of poetry. At the beginning of this
chapter, I noted that our readers appear to show much less curiosity about the poets who are published in the magazine than they
do about the artists and short-story writers. One of these poets
is Truax and he is entitled to more attention than he has received
so far. Not many poets have begun their careers in their seventies;
not many have taken their inspiration so purely from suffering
transformed. The following poem by Truax is a classic example
of how a work of art can be shaped out of the sorriest materials
that happen to be at hand. Was there ever a more joyful apostro-
phe to a wheelchair than

NOW AND THEN

Now that the sawdust of threescore and ten
is running out through legs that will not bear
the body that outlives them, how and where
to park becomes the question. Not on Central's carpet, wall to wall — so boundless when
it flew beneath the feet of boyhood's hare
and hounds — or in the Luxembourg, a fair
hour's walk to the Bois for me at twenty, "Paris twenties" still in store.
                                    Where, then?
Settle for peddling in a pinwheel chair,
forever seated, in my hand a stick,
before I take no turns about and sip
the last time from too long a stirrup cup?
No! Fistfuls of balloons shall bear me up!

27

Shawn has always ruefully accepted the fact that it would be necessary to keep the median age of members of the staff of the magazine as low as possible, in order that *The New Yorker*, though it cannot help but grow old, would yet remain young. The matter of the aging of members of the staff is comparatively easy to control; in recent years, a retirement plan that calls for obligatory retirement at sixty-five has been put into operation. Only Shawn, as editor, and the people who write for departments ("The Theatre," "The Race Track," and the like) are exempt. As for artists and writers, they are likely to retire themselves, often unintentionally; either they draw and write less as their energy diminishes or they encounter a steadily increasing degree of rejection of their work. It is in the nature of things to be superseded, in part because fashions in drawing and writing change with the years, like fashions in everything else, and in part because even if a fashion hasn't changed or even — what is rarer — if one manages to accommodate to a new fashion, one may lose the knack of successfully embodying it. The old King of the Wood is on guard both night and day, but sooner or later some young usurper will bring him to his knees; the most one can hope for is to behave well instead of badly at the moment of inevitable defeat. One should practice a smile and a cheerful wave of the hand in anticipation of that day, but who among us has ever done so?

Thurber made a drawing once of a wife staring down with unseemly relish at her writer-husband, where he sits crouched in despair before his typewriter. She is asking him something like, "What's the matter, hon? Lost the old know-how?" Poor wretch, indeed he has; poor wretches, we all face, sooner or later, the same harsh fate. Still, there are a few contributors to *The New Yorker* who have enjoyed careers lasting well into extreme old age, and one plucks up courage by taking note of them. In the past, there have been Al Frueh and Samuel Hopkins Adams, active in their

Gardner Botsford

Hobart E. Weekes

Howard Moss

Roger Angell

eighties, and at present, among the fiction writers who contribute regularly to the magazine, we have Sylvia Townsend Warner, who is surely close to eighty and who writes with the zest and candor of a twenty-year-old. (A recent story began, "She planted a high Spanish comb in her pubic hair and resumed her horn-rimmed spectacles." Who could resist reading the next sentence of such a story?) Flanner and Ryall are hard at work in their eighties; among our poets, surely the oldest is John Hall Wheelock, at eighty-eight a match for Miss Warner in ardor and in the keenness of his observation of natural things.

Among factual writers, by far the most productive has been Geoffrey T. Hellman, who began writing for *The New Yorker* in 1929, when he was twenty-two and a year out of Yale, and who has since written dozens of Profiles, hundreds and perhaps even thousands of "Talk" pieces, and innumerable casuals, including a very funny one that began, "Many of my friends wonder why I give so little money to charity." Hellman was hired by Ingersoll as a "Talk" reporter at thirty dollars a week. (One of his first "Talk" pieces was about butterflies. He is *still* writing about butterflies.) Ingersoll told him, "At the end of six weeks, you'll either be fired or receive a substantial raise." Six weeks having passed, Hellman went to Ingersoll to learn his fate. Ingersoll said that he was doing fine and afterward, at a meeting with Ross, suggested that Hellman's salary be raised to fifty dollars a week. Ross hit the ceiling. Jesus Christ! Highway robbery! After a prolonged discussion, Ingersoll returned to Hellman with the news that his salary would be raised from thirty dollars a week to thirty-seven dollars and fifty cents a week.

That first fiscal disappointment may have marked the beginning of Hellman's lifelong feud with *The New Yorker* over suitable payment for his work. It has been like a miserable, tumultuous, and yet undissolvable love affair, with this difference — that money takes the place of sex. The feud continues to this day, though in a milder form. Not that Hellman cares less about money; it is only that he needs it less and, in his sixties, would rather be writing than fighting.

Hellman's first skirmishes were carried out against Fleischmann as well as Ross. In those early days, Hellman was unaware of the fact that Ross hated Fleischmann, so, after heated but vain debate with Ross over how much he should be paid, Hellman accepted in good faith Ross's suggestion that he talk to Fleisch-

Benjamin Sonnenberg, drawn by Saul Steinberg to illustrate a Profile by Geoffrey T. Hellman.

mann about it. "After all," Ross said, "he's the one with the money." An innocent-sounding remark; later, Hellman realized that Ross had gained a double satisfaction from it. He had simultaneously got rid of that goddam Hellman nuisance and he had inflicted him on his enemy.

Fleischmann received Hellman with his accustomed charm; he liked meeting writers and rejecting their naïve demands. "My dear boy, how is your mother?" he began.

"Very well, thank you, sir." Hellman was wondering how to direct the conversation toward money.

"A beautiful girl," Fleischmann said. "Haven't seen her in thirty years." It turned out that Fleischmann's father, Louis Fleischmann, and Hellman's mother's father, Louis Josephthal, had owned adjoining country places in the Catskills. "Your grandfather was a fine old gentleman," Fleischmann said, and then opened the very door that Hellman had been groping for. "He was said to have been an extremely wealthy man," Fleischmann went on. "I hope he left all of you plenty of jack."

Hellman protested that his grandfather had been far less wealthy than many people appeared to assume; in any event, none of the "jack" had yet filtered down to him. (Forty-five years later, the "jack" still hasn't filtered down to him; Hellman's mother, in her nineties, retains tenacious control of it.) Hellman's disclaimers went unheard. It was plain that Fleischmann had put him down for a rich boy, not alone because of his connections on his mother's side but because, on his father's side, he had Seligman connections; the Seligmans were well known to be in the category of the rich-rich. Fleischmann brought the interview to a close with a shower of complimentary remembrances to Hellman's mother, father, sister, and to his innumerable Seligman cousins; the question of a raise never came up.

Hellman has quit *The New Yorker* twice. The first time, seeking more money, he went to work on *Fortune,* from which he was soon fired for being unable to write a piece about the Federal Reserve Bank (a topic that one would have expected to enchant Hellman). The second time, he went to work on the newly founded *Life,* not altogether in pursuit of better pay. He had been understandably affronted by a remark that Fleischmann made to him one day at lunch, surely after his second martini. With unexpected rudeness, Fleischmann said, "There are times, Hellman, when we think very well of you here on the magazine, and there are other times when we think of you as a horse's ass." Thurber subsequently reported to Hellman that it was as a consequence of this remark, and of Hellman's indignant reaction to it, that Ross pronounced anathema upon Fleischmann; he was never to be allowed to speak to a *New Yorker* writer again. The ban was upheld for a long time and abandoned with reluctance.

For over twenty years, Ross and Hellman conducted a running battle of memoranda about money, with occasional surprising cease-fires on Ross's part in order to praise something that Hellman had written, or to mention some social occasion that Ross hoped Hellman and his first wife, Daphne, would be able to share with him. What is extraordinary about the exchange is Hellman's continuous bad temper and Ross's continuous good temper. Plainly, Ross considered Hellman a valuable member of the staff, worth placating even when he was at his most outrageous. Besides, Hellman was a writer, and by definition writers were crazy. As an editor, Ross had learned to put up with them, but surely there was more to his patience than that; he must have admired their craziness as a part of their talent, and perhaps even to some extent as a proof of it. Moreover, once upon a time he had hoped to be a writer himself — a Jack London, say, or a Richard Harding Davis. When Hellman, hoping to better his economic circumstances, for a while consented to become a *New Yorker* editor, Ross was incredulous. Despite his early taunts to Thurber and others that writers were a dime a dozen, he had learned better, or had always known better. "You mean you don't *want* to be a writer?" he asked Hellman, his monkey-face agape. "You mean you wouldn't mind *not* being one?"

When Hellman came back to *The New Yorker* from *Life*, he brought with him a large supply of *Time* memorandum pads. He gave some of them to Ross, in order, he said, that any memoranda exchanged between them would not prove an expense to the magazine. "Very handsome of you, Hellman," Ross said, accepting the gift. He was pleased to have proved an expense to Henry Luce, however indirectly.

Excerpts from a characteristic exchange, Ross to Hellman: "I have your note about payment on Talk originals, and will investigate this subject, to find out how much you are getting — to begin with. I know the base prince [Ross would not have welcomed a Freudian analysis of this slip of the typewriter] but not what the frills figure out to. I will advise you later."

Five days later, Ross sent Hellman a long memo, explaining the base pay for "Talk" stories, the so-called "breakage" (payment for stories that didn't work out), and the Cola, or cost-of-living adjustment, and giving the total amount of payment per "Talk" story that Hellman was receiving. "It seems like a fair price to me," Ross wrote, "but I am willing to listen to any argument for higher pay, and will take it up with Mr. Truax, who is counselling me in such matters now, and with Mr. Shawn, whose say is important . . . I don't object to being prompted in these things, this being a business undertaking that should be run on businesslike lines."

Hellman replied crossly, "Yes, I knew what I was getting for Talk. I wrote you that note because I wanted to know whether I had reached a permanent financial plateau in this office, or whether I could look forward to any sort of raise in future. Your answer, to the latter question, would appear to be No.

TIME
INCORPORATED

OFFICE MEMORANDUM
FORM 34

TIME · LIFE · FORTUNE · MARCH OF TIME · ARCHITECTURAL FORUM

To___Mr. Hellman_____   New York Office

From___Mr.Ross_____   Date___(June 10)_____

I have your noteaoout payment on Talk originals, and will ᵻᵼᵼᵼᵼ investigate this subject, to find out how much you are now getting--to begin with. I know the base prince but not what the frills figure out to. I will

advise you later.

H.W.Ross.

One of the hundreds of memos on the subject of money that went back and forth between Hellman and Ross.

"I have no intention of offering any argument for higher pay, or making a 'case,' as you suggest. I have not forgotten that last February I asked Mr. Shawn to bring up for consideration your docking me $255.28 (counting Cola) on the Crowninshield That Was New York, which ran two thousand words short, after having refused me extra pay on the Corbusier Profiles, which ran 5000 words long, and that I have still received no reply. (And I am mindful that Thurber's Onward and Upward on soap operas, which I will mercifully refrain from characterizing, ran for two weeks in the Profile position, and received top Profile rates.)

"My case is my work, which you and Mr. Shawn have had ample opportunity to evaluate. It doesn't make sense for you to drag in Mr. Truax, who hasn't."

Ross to Hellman:

"I do not regard myself as having answered definitely the question of whether or not you have reached a permanent financial plateau in this office. I wouldn't undertake to make any kind of an answer to that question, or any prediction as to the financial future of this undertaking. By and large [Uncle Arthur had never met Ross], the money put out is governed by the money taken in. The money coming in has increased greatly in the last seven or eight years and, accordingly, editorial prices have been increased. They are several times what they were. If income warrants higher editorial expenditures in the future there will be higher editorial expenditures. That has been and is the policy of the business.

"I have to consult Mr. Truax because he knows how much money there is around and may be able to make a guess as to how much there will be, although only God knows much about the future, really. It isn't a question of raising one man's rates in a case like this, but of considering the whole price setup.

"As to the Crowninshield piece, I do not regard that you were 'docked.' That was definitely a sort of long-Talk piece rather than a piece of the Reporter type, and in a different class than a Reporter. I suggest that in future if you do not get a reply from Mr. Shawn on such matters you query me, as you usually do. Mr. Shawn is, God knows, swamped a great deal of the time."

One notes Ross's determination to pretend that he is presiding over a business like any other and not over a madhouse. Further to this point, he wrote Hellman a memorandum on another occasion stating his dark view of the economics of being a magazine writer: "You say that you have been here eighteen years and are not treated better than a good writer a couple of years out of college would be, so far as pay for individual articles is concerned, and ask me to correct you if you are wrong. You are not wrong, I guess. My firm viewpoint is that we ought to pay what a piece is worth, regardless of age, race, color, creed, financial status or any other consideration. I don't know how, in an enterprise of this sort, one in my position can take into consideration anything beyond the actual value of the things he buys — and I write this as one who buys hundreds of thousands of dollars' worth of stuff of a wide assortment annually — drawings, spots, anecdotes, fiction pieces, art ideas, and so on. I be damned if I want to inject into that the long-and-faithful element or any other element than sheer value. How in the hell could I do that? I wish you'd tell me ... You say you get no vacation pay, which I argue. My viewpoint is that you are paid enough for your work to finance your own vacation. Writers are small-businessmen in the last analysis, manufacturing and selling their wares, and are subject to the lonely responsibilities and hazards of small-businessmen. I don't see how it can be otherwise. I've been in the business of buying things from writers and artists for thirty years and have never worked out a workable scheme to pay writers' and artists' salaries, to remove them from the state of being a free-lance, or a small-businessman. Or a professional man. You can put it that way. Doctors, architects, lawyers, writers are all in the same boat. No other magazine has ever worked out a scheme for paying writers except by the piece. This magazine made an effort to beat this game a couple of years ago, an effort that will be a final one so far as I am concerned, I trust. Shawn worked out a scheme that guaranteed writers a certain income for exclusive services, and I approved it. It collapsed immediately. It was cried down by the writers because of the exclusive service provision ... Writers want their independence, to a greater or less extent, or the right to it. I don't blame them for this. I am now glad the scheme failed, for it cleared the air, and convinced me once and for all that nothing can be done to better the cruel fundamentals of the magazine-writer relationship ... You don't have, you say, 'much security.' That is true, but who does? You have as much security as I have. There is no such thing as security, and that's that."

Looking back, Hellman thinks that Ross may have put up with Hellman's innumerable harangues about money in part because he enjoyed dealing with figures. "Ross always liked to get people's incomes and personal fortunes into 'Talk' pieces and Profiles," Hellman says. "Once I wrote a Profile of Nelson Rockefeller, and I didn't feel inclined to bring up any personal financial questions with him. Ross was ashamed of me. He sent me back to Rockefeller, saying I was to ask him exactly how much money he had. So I did, and Rockefeller said, 'I don't think people are interested in that sort of thing nowadays, do you, Geoffrey?' "

Ross took as much pleasure in working out sums as he did in working out grammatical constructions. One senses this pleasure in the following excerpt from a memo to Shawn, the occasion for which was a complaint by Hellman about the amount of "Talk" breakage he was getting: "I have no means of knowing how many stories Mr. Hellman went out on that didn't materialize, but I'll speculate a little: If he made twenty false starts, he was paid an average of $31.625 for them. If he made ten false starts, he was paid an average of $63.25 for them. If he lost 100 hours, he was paid at the rate of $6.325 an hour — just to sit there and meditate. If he lost 50 hours, he was paid at a rate of $12.65 an hour."

At the end of the memo, which was a fairly lengthy one, Ross added a hasty postscript: "I now realize I have figured the above wrong. Hellman got considerably more than $820 in breakage. The Cola should be added to that. As Cola has averaged around 25%, all the figures in the foregoing breakdown should be increased in that percentage. The $820 should read $1,025, the $12.65 per hour figure should read $15.81."

Ross sent a copy of the memo to Hellman, who fired off an immediate rejoinder. It read in part, "Editors sit and meditate; writers of Talk originals don't. They take subways and taxis (at their own expense), interview people, beg for anecdotes, trudge through long hotel corridors, traipse around ocean liners, drink with possible subjects (at their own expense), and in general have a hell of a time physically, which can only end in a coronary thrombosis."

Since offering that dire medical prognostication in respect to himself and his fellow "Talk" reporters, Hellman has spent over a quarter of a century eating and drinking with subjects and trudging through long hotel corridors, and his health remains unimpaired. The fact is that aside from what Ross called his "money-mania," Hellman is not given to complaining; on the contrary, he is a notably genial man, who likes going to parties (he has been known to turn up at three or four cocktail parties in a single afternoon) and who enjoys himself thoroughly both at work and at play. One can tell that he is in the office, because unlike most *New Yorker* writers he keeps his door wide-open and the delicious aroma of his pipe tobacco — Wally Frank's "Istanbul" mixture — works its way out into Sleepy Hollow as the day goes on; Hellman himself, crouched at his typewriter with a *Who's Who* and a *Social Register* near at hand, tends to vanish gradually into an autumnal blue haze. Tall, good-looking, and well-tailored, he is an admirable raconteur; his favorite stories concern people of distinguished lineage and somewhat dotty conduct. Gibbs said once, speaking of a colleague on the magazine, "— would rather fuck a prominent girl than a pretty one," and with Hellman it is certainly the case that his preference is for names that resound when they are dropped. Here is Hellman reminiscing about the late Edward R. Hewitt: "He was a grandson of Peter Cooper and the country's leading dry-fly trout fisherman. He also designed the original motor used in Mack trucks. He was America's outstanding example of the inability of man, however much inclined, to turn himself into a brook trout. At his fishing camp on the Neversink, in the Catskills, he descended into glass-bottomed tanks in order to inspect things from the trout's point of view.

"Mr. Hewitt and I got on friendly terms, and he provided me with the material for three long pieces — a Profile of himself; an institutional Profile of Cooper Union, which was founded by his grandfather; and a 'Reporter at Large' on his grandfather's house, a block north of Gramercy Park on Lexington Avenue, which has long since been torn down. This was a square, four-story, red-brick structure with thirty-five rooms. It had a marble stairway with stuffed peacocks on the balustrades, copper-lined bathtubs, clocks with busts of Napoleon on them, and a ballroom with eleven identical mirrors, each five feet wide and running from floor to ceiling.

"Its final occupant was Mr. Hewitt's brother Erskine, a rather idiosyncratic bachelor, who camped out in a little suite on the top floor and rarely used the rest of the house. Except for breakfast, he took most of his meals at the Union Club. Erskine had been born at Ringwood Manor, the family place in New Jersey, and his brother told me that he never had a first name until he was three. I don't know what they called him until then. He was christened at three, at the suggestion of the local minister. According to his brother, the baptismal ceremony got under way before the minister had been briefed as to the infant's name. As he paused for a clue, the eyes of the child's father — Mr. Abram Hewitt, at one time Mayor of New York — fell on the tombstone of Robert Erskine, a Scottish engineer who had managed the Ringwood mining property in the eighteenth century and had been buried on the place. 'Erskine was named after the tombstone,' Mr. Hewitt told me. 'He grew up rather gloomy.' "

Hellman on longevity:

"I don't suppose I can take credit for it, but my subjects often live to a respectable age. Mr. Hewitt was ninety when he died, and another of my subjects, Gilbert Grosvenor, was ninety-one. General Henry C. Hodges, U.S.A., was just under ninety-seven when I buttonholed him. He lived to be a hundred and six. He was brought to my attention by his nephew, Reginald T. Townsend, a man I have long admired because his middle name is Townsend. Some years ago, I wrote a 'Talk' piece about Charles C. Burlingham, an admiralty lawyer, who was then ninety-one. The editors of *The New Yorker* daringly kept this around the office, in proof, on what we call the bank, for three years and then ran it off. Five years later, when Mr. Burlingham was approaching his hundredth birthday, they asked me to write him up again. I called him up, and he begged off. He said he didn't care for publicity and that he was delighted that my previous article on him had not been published. 'But it was,' I said. 'I sent you a proof and we ran it several years ago.' 'No, you didn't,' he said. 'I tore it up and threw it in the scrap basket.'

"Mr. Burlingham was one of the subjects of an intermittent series that we ran on spry oldsters — men of eighty or over who were still active. We gave up the octogenarians, as such, after a while, because there were too many of them. While the series was still running, a man wrote in that he was eighty-one, the editor of a yachting magazine, a Yale man, and spry. He suggested himself as a candidate. I went around to see him, and, as the material seemed a little thin, I looked him up in his college class yearbook. I had hoped to find that he was voted the Most Color-blind man in his class, or some such nugget as that, but what I *did* find out was that he was only seventy-eight. I confronted him with this, and he confessed that he had tacked on a few years in order to appear eligible. We wrote him up, anyway, as a resourceful septuagenarian."

Hellman again, on some of the risks and rewards of *New Yorker* reporting: "I've been threatened with violence only once in my professional career. That was by a brother of the late Charles M. Schwab, the steel magnate. After Mr. Schwab's death, his brother

Geoffrey T. Hellman

showed me through the Schwab house — a great château on Riverside Drive, occupying an entire block, with eighty-five rooms. Many of these were furnished with tapestried rocking chairs and statues of naked ladies. I described them in the piece, of which I sent a copy, before publication, to Mr. Schwab's brother. He called me up and said that if I didn't take out the statuary he would personally come over to the office and beat me up. He was a large, powerful man, so I took the matter up with Shawn, who suggested changing the word 'naked' to 'nude.' This made everybody happy.

"I've been threatened with lawsuits more than once. I did a Profile of the architect Le Corbusier, who didn't like to be called 'Mr.' and didn't like to be called Swiss, either, though he was Swiss by birth. When I mentioned his birthplace in the Profile, he threatened to sue me, on the peculiar grounds that the Swiss were a nation of hotel-keepers.

"Sherman Fairchild, the airplane manufacturer, after reading the proofs of a Profile I had written on him, took me to task for a passage in which I had characterized his butler as a man who insulted his employer's weekend women guests, many of whom were models, and who aired his political views while passing the dishes. Mr. Fairchild's lawyer called me up and said, 'What you say about the butler may well be true, but if you print it Sherman will fire him, and the butler will sue *you* for loss of livelihood.' I relayed this disconcerting prophecy to the *New Yorker*'s lawyers, who advised me to delete the passage.

"When I wrote a Profile of Henry Morgenthau, Jr., then the Secretary of the Treasury, he read the proofs and objected to a sentence that stated that he had no interest in finance. I changed the sentence to read, 'Finance is not Morgenthau's favorite subject,' and he wrote me a grateful letter after the piece came out. Frank Crowninshield was so favorably disposed toward me because of a Profile I had done of him that he handed along to me a gold pencil that had been a gift to him from the banker James Speyer. Crowninshield informed me that he had taken the pencil to Cartier's for an appraisal and that it was worth ninety dollars.

"At least one man tried to give me a present *before* being written up. At the end of an interview I had with him, when we were shaking hands goodbye, or when I thought we were shaking hands goodbye, I found that he was pressing a bill in my palm. I declined it in an ill-advised reflex action, which hurt his feelings and made me feel unhappy as well, as I have often wondered how much it was."

28

I began to write for *The New Yorker* when I was twenty-one and now I am almost sixty. Looking back, I shake my head, not without wonder, at that arrogant, confident beginner. He was not long for this world — easy as life was to prove for him, there were cuffings enough, both personal and professional, to turn him after a few years into another man and, again after a few years, into still another man, and another. Today I feel emerging on the threshold of old age the latest of the many persons I have been, and even this person may prove, with luck and discipline, only the latest me and not the last.

Yeats says somewhere that after forty we must all wither into the truth. Withering is easy; it is the truth that is difficult.

I have reached the age now that my father was when he was showering all those benedictions of love and benefactions of money and household goods upon me and my sisters and brothers. Even this late I only begin to take in how easy he was on us and how he spoiled us. In his old age, I drifted away from him, in part because I became impatient with his having forgotten the suffering it had cost him to bring up five motherless children. Enfeebled, a blanket over his knees, he would sit in a big wing chair in his bedroom and say, "You were all such good children — such good children!" And it was not so. Silently, staring into the face made bland by diminished intellect, I would insist *No, don't think that, we were often dreadful, we quarrelled murderously with each other and with the servants and neighbors, we dropped out of school, we ran away, year after year we took every advantage of your kindness. If you forget that dark side of our young lives, then you will have lost your own life as well. Blessed old father, you will have lived it all in vain.*

When he lay dying in the hospital, I was able to make him a present of an early copy of my first novel, *The Trouble of One*

House. The nurse placed it upright on the bureau across from the foot of his bed, where his eyes rested on it with pride. He was far too sick to read a word of it, and that was lucky; there were things in it that would have injured him and made him sad. They were statements that would have struck him as judgments directed against him, though in fact they were directed against me. He lay there smiling and nodding and murmuring to visitors how grand it was that his Brendan had done precisely what he had always wanted to do: had become a writer, as the whole world could see. And I would lean over the foot of the bed and — again silently — would say to him, "Ah, die! Please die! Then I can get back the father I knew, the father I loved."

How hard I was on him, an old man needing only my piety!

And how hard I was on Ross as well! Even now, in this book, I see that the emotion with which I have written of him has been largely that of the impertinent young man who sent him a wooden skunk for Christmas — who wanted more of Ross than Ross was able to give, or, for that matter, had any reason to give. In those days, I forgave him nothing. Because he was rude to my wife, I saw him as unmannerly to all women, and I was wrong. Adele Lovett was a close friend of his for over twenty-five years; the first word that springs to her lips in describing his conduct toward her is "gentle." Mrs. Lovett was much younger than he; older women found him courtly, and so did children.

Ross was gentle, even docile, with women whose competence in certain fields was obviously greater than his. Dorothy Silberberg, the wife of Ross's close friend Dan Silberberg, decorated several apartments for Ross and helped to design his country house in Stamford. Perhaps in recollection of the steep, rushing mountain streams of his Aspen boyhood, Ross was all for having the house built on the banks of a brook that flowed through the property. Mrs. Silberberg persuaded him that a house by his Connecticut brook might often be underwater. The house was built uphill from the brook; even so, to Ross's alarm, the basement was often awash. Ross was far from being handy when it came to solving household problems. If something went wrong with the plumbing or the electricity, he simply moved out of the house and stayed away until the necessary repairs had been made.

When it came to furnishing his country place, Ross issued but one command to Mrs. Silberberg. It concerned his study. "Keep sort of a big corridor all round my desk, so I can pace," he said.

"I do a lot of pacing." Once, between marriages, Ross was occupying an apartment too stark even for his rough-and-ready tastes. He reached into his pocket, drew out two or three hundred dollars in loose bills, handed them to a woman friend, and said, "Go out and buy a lot of those goddam things — those gewgaws — that make a place look lived in." The only articles of furniture that Ross took seriously were ashtrays. There had to be a good many of them in any room that Ross occupied; otherwise, ashes and cigarette butts fell on the nearest flat surface, whether it was of crystal, china, rare wood, or cloth.

Ross's women friends occasionally made an effort to spruce up his wardrobe. Ordinarily, he wore the kind of dark suit and laced high shoes that a small-town undertaker might have worn in, say, 1920. When it became the vogue to wear sports jackets to work, Ross made a single abortive effort to strike a note of debonairness. I remember his recounting the episode to me with a pleased grin on his face — nineteenth-century storyteller that he was (like Twain, like Nasby), for him much of the humor of the episode lay in the fact that he was its humiliated victim. That morning he had dropped in at Brooks Brothers and had asked to be fitted to a sports jacket. He was a conspicuously round-shoul-dered man, with a caved-in chest and arms that hung almost to his knees, and the salesman he spoke to — elderly, dignified — evidently felt certain professional misgivings from the start. Jacket after jacket was taken off the rack, slipped onto Ross's peculiar body, and then slipped off again. Nothing fitted. Finally, the sales-man could stand the strain of failure no longer. "Sir," he said, "I have to tell you that it is impossible to fit you in this store. I must ask you to take your custom elsewhere." Upon which with a stern forefinger he pointed Ross the way to the elevators. "Jeesus!" Ross said. "You'd 'a thought I was some kind of oorang-ootan."

That day, in that mood, an endearing man.

On another occasion, learning that a kind of fern that grew abundantly on his place in Stamford was considered a delicacy in high gourmet circles, Ross dashed off a "Talk" outline, in the course of which I recall his writing, "If, by God, there's any value to these so-called fiddlehead ferns, than I'm going to be the fid-dlehead fern king of America, because I got millions of them." Pretty soon our readers were being treated, surely to their aston-ishment, to a long disquisition on fiddlehead ferns. Ross assumed

Philip Hamburger   *S. J. Perelman*

as a matter of course that anything that interested him was bound
to interest a couple of hundred thousand other people, and he
didn't want more readers than that. When the circulation of the
magazine went over three hundred thousand, Ross said nervously,
"Too many people. We must be doing something wrong." (The
current circulation of the magazine is around half a million. In
proportion to the total population of the country, the circulation
may not be quite as great as it was twenty-five years ago; in which
case, by Ross's standards, we must be doing something right.)

Ross attracted as if out of thin air innumerable scraps of information, which he would jot down on the back of an envelope,
a blank check, or the like, and subsequently turn into "Talk" or
Profile outlines. How dark is it legally permissible for a bar to
be? Not so dark that you can't read a newspaper by the available
light — isn't that interesting? What's broken glass called? Cullet.
And what's cullet used for? Why, for making new glass — a great
"Talk" idea. In Vienna, you can dial a number and get the musical
note "A." In that case, let's dial Vienna long-distance and listen
to "A" for "Talk."

In all the years that I was doing "Talk" rewrite, only once did
Ross express impatience with my performance. Early on a Thursday evening, he phoned my office to ask how much longer such-
and-such a piece of "Talk" was going to take me. I promised that

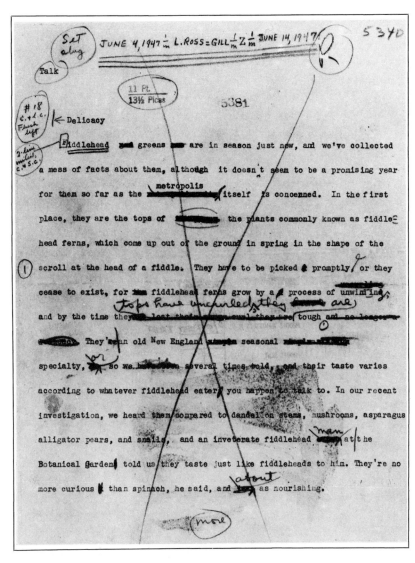

Some Ross corrections on the "Talk" story by Lillian Ross and me about fiddlehead ferns. The story was Ross's idea and he plunged joyously into disimproving it.

it would be ready in a few minutes, and it was. Later, Ross phoned a second time, in order to apologize. Whatever amount of time I took on a piece was the correct amount of time to take; the thing was that he had promised to go to a movie with his daughter Patty, then in her teens, and he was afraid of keeping her waiting. "My fault, mixing my social life with my work. Won't happen again."

Ross had generous impulses, but they were not always easy to carry out — life would blunderingly intervene to remind him of his own selfish necessities. Carmine Peppe has been head of the editorial make-up department of *The New Yorker* since 1932. He came to work for the magazine in 1925 and for several years served an apprenticeship in make-up under Whitaker. It was obvious to everyone that he was an exceptionally intelligent and gifted young man. One day in the late twenties, Ross called Peppe into his office and, out of the blue, suggested that he would be glad to send him to college. Peppe was overwhelmed. "Mr. Ross, I can't thank you enough," he said. "All my life, the one thing I've wanted most is to become a doctor."

"Jesus Christ, I didn't say I'd turn you into a *doctor!*" Ross roared, in consternation. "I meant for you to go to college, then come back here and keep on working for me. Now, get your ass the hell out of here!"

Ross was always fascinated by the workings of the make-up department. He admired the ingenuity with which Peppe and his

The house at 601 West Bleeker Street, Aspen, Colorado, in which Ross was born, on November 6, 1892. His parents had borrowed six hundred dollars the previous summer with which to buy the house and two adjoining lots. By the time the family moved away, in 1901, the silver boom had collapsed, and Aspen, built upon the richest silver lode on earth, was already becoming a ghost town. The Rosses sold the house and lots for three hundred dollars. As a child, Ross was an able scholar. When he was eight and in the third grade in Aspen, all his grades were in the high nineties except deportment, in which he received an eighty-five. The Ross birthplace is still standing, and Aspen has begun to take pride in showing it off to visitors.

Carmine Peppe

four or five veteran assistants were able to solve certain problems of space that were sure to arise whenever a piece came in late and proved to be of much greater length than had been expected. Unlike the practice at many magazines, at *The New Yorker* we write as copiously as we please (too copiously for some of our readers), and the magazine miraculously accommodates its limited space to us. Perhaps half a dozen times in forty years has anyone asked me to cut so much as a single sentence on the grounds that it couldn't be fitted into the magazine. Drawings are switched or omitted, news breaks are added or taken away; one's sacred prose is spared.

Ross's manner of admiring Peppe's handiwork was to begin by denouncing him. He would summon him to his office, slap a palm down hard on the latest galleys for "A" issue, and say in fury, "Peppe, what in Christ's name have you done this time?"

Peppe would explain step by step what he had done, and why, and in a few minutes Ross would be smiling and exhilarated; his anger, he would tell Peppe, was all the fault of some dam-fool nonsense that had been going on in the advertising department and had just been brought to his attention. And at once Peppe forgave him, as nearly everyone forgave Ross.

"In the Beginning," saith the Law
(As true today as then),
"God looked upon the Earth and saw
That it was good"—for men.

Aware of Ross's disapproval of sex in the magazine, Peppe felt obliged one day to call Ross's attention to the fact that a soon-to-be-published drawing by Clarence Day contained that forbidden thing, a woman's nipple. He showed the drawing to Ross, who at once saw an opportunity to make Peppe suffer. "Take that goddam tit up to Mrs. White and ask her what to do about it," Ross said. Peppe was a shy young man, and he protested that he couldn't face doing such a thing. "Now, for Christ's sake, Peppe!" Ross said. "That's an order!" The miserable Peppe carried the drawing up to Mrs. White and stammeringly pointed out the problem. Mrs. White saw no reason for stammering or perturbation: let the engraver excise the offending protuberance. And so he did, as the drawing shows.

One of Ross's favorite sayings was "You can't win." I once wrote a Profile that was so little flattering to the subject's image of himself that, reading the piece in galleys, he threatened to sue the magazine for libel. I reported the threat to Ross, who urged me to hold fast. The Profile was published, and many of the subject's friends advised him that I had drawn an excellent likeness of him. He thereupon telephoned the magazine to ask if he might purchase several hundred copies of the issue that contained his Profile; he was eager to undertake a mass mailing. When I reported the latest development to Ross, he had his usual rueful statement ready: "You can't win."

In a somewhat similar vein, this footnote to Bainbridge's excoriating three-part Profile of Toots Shor, a restaurateur who often boasted in print of his drunkenness and bad manners. One of Shor's favorite ways of greeting an old friend was to punch him in the belly, then give him a big hug. When Shor and his buddies were not punching and hugging each other, they devoted a large part of their time to crying over lost companions. The only women they respected were mothers, preferably dead ones. Bainbridge's close examination of the sadistic, sexually regressive conduct of Shor and company might have been expected to give offense; instead, Shor invited Bainbridge to his restaurant shortly after the pieces appeared and presented him with a gold watch from Tiffany's. On the back was inscribed, in a replica of Shor's handwriting, "Thanks a lot, pal."

Despairingly, Ross to Bainbridge: "You can't win."

There were times when it was hard to tell whether Ross was acting on a generous impulse or being defensive. Archibald MacLeish wrote a long poem entitled "The Hamlet of A. MacLeish," and Edmund Wilson wrote a cruel, witty parody of it for *The New Yorker,* which he called "The Omelet of A. MacLeish." Immediately after the parody appeared, MacLeish happened to be having lunch in the Oak Room of the Algonquin. Ross was also in the room, and on leaving it he found that he had to walk past MacLeish's table. Making a curious protective gesture with one arm, he stopped, leaned over MacLeish, and said in a loud voice, "That must have hurt! That must have *hurt!*" To this day, MacLeish is puzzled as to whether Ross, fearing that MacLeish might swing at him, spoke the words out of fear or out of sympathy. Ross used to announce grimly that no reporter or editor could have friends, but that didn't mean that he welcomed having enemies. He was every bit as timid as his mother used to say he was.

Despite our differences of age and temperament, I would certainly have understood Ross far better in his lifetime if I had taken the trouble to learn more about his birthplace. Visiting Aspen for the first time a year or so ago, I found it wholly unlike the Aspen of my imagination. At the time that Ross was born there, in 1892, I had supposed that Aspen resembled any one of a hundred or so silver- and gold-mining boom towns in the Far West, running helter-skelter up and down a few raw gulches in the face of a mountain, with wooden sidewalks and crude, unpainted false-front saloons and general stores. The fact is that Aspen, founded upon the richest deposit of silver ever discovered in this country and enjoying unprecedented prosperity until the federal government abandoned silver as a backing for currency, was a town of considerable elegance, laid out in a setting of exceptional natural beauty, upon hundreds of acres of gently rolling mountain meadows, open to the sky and girdled round by mountains higher than any mountains in the Alps except Mont Blanc. There were many mansions in the town, some of them of brick and stone, as well as the usual "opera" house and a substantial fireproof hotel.

The cultural aspirations of Aspen in the nineties were very high. Having been a schoolteacher, Ross's mother was among the women in the community who sponsored poetry readings and similar occasions of an edifying nature, and it was always a cause of shame to her that her only child should have been a total failure in school, dropping out forever in his early teens. When the silver boom ended, the Ross family, like most of the other residents of Aspen, had to move elsewhere. For a time they lived in nearby Silverton, and then they moved on to Salt Lake City, where Ross's father ran a small construction business.

Ross was proud of having been born in Aspen and he liked to return there on fishing trips, stopping off on his way to and from Hollywood. He became friends with Walter and Elizabeth Paepcke, who, happening upon Aspen in the early thirties, had found it a virtual ghost town, with a population of only a few hundred people. (At its peak, it had had a population of something like twelve thousand.) A wealthy businessman from Chicago, full of energy and bold ideas, Paepcke almost single-handedly turned Aspen into the celebrated ski resort and cultural center that it is today, successfully mingling well-tanned, skinny young men and women in jeans with physicists, musicians, artists, and writers.

Paepcke died in 1964. Mrs. Paepcke, who lives in a charming old house in the heart of town, told me on my visit to Aspen of Ross's delight in being Aspen's most famous native. He often reminisced with her about his early days there and in Silverton. At one time, he worked as a delivery boy for the local grocery in Silverton, and he soon learned that the madams and girls in the red-light district in Silverton were cheerful, attractive women who gave big tips, while the women in this mother's circle tended to be morose and sour-faced, rarely bestowed a kind word on him, and gave him small tips or none at all. He would sometimes lie on the floor outside his mother's parlor while she was entertaining women friends at tea; he would listen in bewilderment as those pious souls gossiped in harsh terms about the finest people he had ever met.

One of my lifelong preoccupations has been the subject of early memory. There was a time when I went around the office, asking everyone to tell me his earliest memory; some of my colleagues astonished me by being unable to remember anything before the age of five or six, while others remembered, or claimed to remember, events that took place in the cradle. Eventually, I put the question to Ross. It obviously interested him and he spent a long time silently turning the matter over in his mind. "Here it is," he said. "I'm just past two. I'm sitting in the front parlor of our house in Aspen, which is territory forbidden to me. In front of me is a small white coffin. In the coffin is the body of my baby brother. I'm all alone and I don't know why."

It must have been at about the time I was asking Ross for his earliest childhood recollections that I put a similar question to Shawn. One episode that he recounted, though it is by no means his earliest memory, is so vivid a witness to his lifelong attitude toward nature that it is surely worth setting down. Over sixty years ago, he and his mother and father are paying a visit to the Dells, outside Chicago — a park-like area notable for curious rock formations dating back to the last Ice Age. Among these formations is something known as Lovers' Leap. It consists of a steep cliff, a gap of many feet beyond the face of the cliff, and then a single flat-topped pinnacle, chimney-shaped and rising to the same height as the cliff. Reckless young men make a practice of leaping off the edge of the cliff onto the pinnacle and then leaping back. The hazard lies in having to jump sufficiently far to land on the pinnacle, without jumping so far — and at such a speed — that one cannot bring oneself to a halt before pitching headlong over the outer edge of the pinnacle.

Shawn's father is a vigorous, athletic man, who likes to take chances. At that moment, nothing will do but that he attempt the perilous feat. Shawn's mother bursts into tears. Shawn, too, is soon in tears. He is perhaps five or six at the time; he clings to his mother's skirts and wails in company with her as the brave father leaps through space, successfully halts on the pinnacle, and with equal success leaps back across the gulf to safety.

A happy end to the adventure, but not a happy end for little Shawn. From that episode and perhaps a dozen others, many of them centering inexplicably on the pleasant Dells, Shawn comes to regard rocks, trees, and other natural phenomena as inimical. They are a menace to him and to those he loves and he must take care to avoid them.

In the nineteen forties, I gave Shawn a brisk tour of the big old house that we had just bought in Bronxville. It was four stories high, in a style that the architect evidently believed to be Elizabethan, and, among other unexpected exterior decorations, it had affixed to its highest gable a carved-oak owl. The house contained twenty-five rooms and had three-quarters of an acre of red-slate roof, all in bad repair. It stood on a granite hillside high above the village, and its thick stone walls and chimneys had been cut out of the living rock. The basement of the house had served as a convenient quarry, out of which the materials for the upper portions of the house had been obtained. Here and there in the basement the stonemasons had left random outcroppings of ancient, jagged cliff. In one shadowy room, where coal had once been stored in bins, a shelf of rock thrust itself up out of the floor at a sharp angle. As I was leading Shawn past the shelf, he started; the shelf threatened him as powerfully as if it had been a thug in a dark alley. Oddly enough, Shawn's distress communicated itself to me, and from having taken pleasure in the outcropping as evidence of the fact that the hillside and the house were one, I soon came to dislike it. Within a few months, I had called in workmen with electric jackhammers and had had the shelf of rock removed and the newly leveled floor covered with a fresh surface of concrete.

When Ross went up to Boston, to the hospital where he was to be operated on for cancer, he phoned a number of his associates in the office, not so much to give them information that they might someday have need of as to feel himself in continued touch with them. Talking with Geraghty about the art department, Ross said how bad he felt about the extra burden his repeated absences had placed on Geraghty's shoulders. The two men had worked closely since the day that Geraghty joined the magazine, in 1939. As Ross spoke, Geraghty was recalling one of the first art meetings that he had attended; it was an especially memorable day for him, because the sharpness of his observation in respect to a certain drawing had startled and impressed Ross. They were sitting around the table — Ross, Miss Terry, Lobrano, and Geraghty — and staring glumly at a picture that didn't work. It had been drawn by Robert Day and it showed some white hunters in Africa, crouched on a platform built high up among some trees at the edge of a water hole. Gathered around the water hole were innumerable animals of assorted species — elephants, tigers, antelopes, serpents, ducks, and the like. The caption to the joke seemed as if it might be past fixing, and Ross asked Geraghty if he had any suggestions. Geraghty said, "Why not have one of the hunters say, 'Well, I don't know. I sort of had my heart set on a lion'?" Ross leaned forward and jabbed at the drawing with the large knitting needle that always served him as a pointer. Click, click, click, animal after animal. "Well, I'll be a son of a bitch!" he burst out, and then, "Pardon me, Miss Terry, but Geraghty's right — there *isn't* any lion in the picture!"

Now Ross was on the telephone saying that he had been advised that after the operation he would have to remain away from the office for at least six months. The burden on Geraghty and the others would be even greater than it had been; moreover, Ross wasn't looking forward to six months of enforced idleness. To cheer him up, Geraghty said, "Well, you always claimed that if only you had the time you'd be a great idea man for drawings. Here's your chance."

James M. Geraghty

"Go to hell, Geraghty," Ross said, with something like his old vigor. That was the last time they spoke before Ross died, and Geraghty thinks that the characteristic roughneck "Go to hell" was Ross's blessing and perhaps his farewell.

Hard to imagine Ross old; if he were alive today, he would be approaching eighty-three, and how could the violent and opinionated man we knew and marvelled at have learned to accept gracefully the many ignominies of age? There would surely have been a shocking gap for us to take the measure of between Ross in eruption at fifty and Ross trying in impotent bad temper to erupt at eighty. I predict that no such gap will manifest itself to us as Shawn grows old. The fact is that he marches into the enemy country at such an equable pace that he seems always to be precisely the same age. Though he is seven years older than I, by some mischievous acrobatics of time and chance I appear to have vaulted over him and now outrank him in the unenviable precedence of seniority. Soon Shawn will have been editor of the magazine longer than Ross was. We are celebrating our fiftieth birthday this year, and I will not be surprised if, when the sixtieth birthday anniversary rolls around, Shawn is still in charge of the premises — is still saying in his soft voice, his blue eyes bright with amusement, "Go out and mill!"

If Shawn were to give up some of his duties as editor, it might have the welcome effect of freeing him to write more. For it is as a writer that he could still achieve, if he so wishes, a second and equally distinguished career. On the magazine, we cherish the published but anonymous evidences of his talent and skill. Here, for example, is Shawn writing with affection of his friend and mentor, Sam Behrman, who died in 1973:

Some days ago, S. N. Behrman died, at the age of eighty. The space he occupied was more than that of one man, and with his death this crowded city seemed suddenly vacant. Decade after decade, his brilliant writing kept streaming down from wherever he lived uptown — plays, articles, fiction, memoirs — and, for those who were lucky enough to be his friends, his talk flowed along in parallel bounty and with equal brilliance. A telephone call from Sam Behrman was an event; he could be as inventive and witty on the telephone as he could be on paper. A lunch or a tea or a companionable evening with him was an even bigger event; he had an endless supply of stories to tell, and they tended to be funnier than anyone else's stories. He called himself, half seriously, a mild manic-depressive, but that was imprecise. True, he suffered throughout his life from depressions, but "manic" is not the word for what he achieved in the course of lifting himself out of the depths, which was a true blitheness, a self-forgetfulness, a spirit of fun that, while it may have made things merely tolerable for him, had an exhilarating effect on everybody around him. The world presented itself to him as comedy, so his literary style was comic. Almost every piece of formal writing he did, like every letter or note he wrote to a friend, bore the Behrman mark: the unexpected inversion or inflection of thought, the surprising placement of a word, the idiosyncratic phrase, the droll shift in tempo, the pure funniness. He wrote twenty-one plays, which were in a vein that was rare in the American theatre at the time and is no longer found there at all: high comedy. Among them were "The Second Man," "Serena Blandish," "Biography," "Rain from Heaven," "End of Summer," and "No Time for Comedy." They are among the finest plays in our theatre, and no doubt they will be rediscovered in due course and will again be seen on our stages. On occasion, he went to Hollywood to write dialogue for films; among those he worked on were several for Greta Garbo, including "Queen Christina" and "Anna Karenina." He always stayed in Hollywood as briefly as possible, and always returned with a new fund of marvellous stories to tell his friends. For many people, still, Behrman's Hollywood *is* Hollywood.

In 1929, Behrman wrote his first article for *The New Yorker* — a Profile of George Gershwin. In the next twenty-five years, he wrote mostly plays. Then he turned more and more to what he jokingly called "prose" — as distinguished from whatever it was he was writing when he wrote plays. For reasons he could not explain, he did not care much for the actual writing of plays; he knew how difficult it was to write a play, but when he had written one, and even when it had been acclaimed (as it usually was), he was not quite sure that he had done anything. The writing of prose seemed to him somehow more substantial, and it gave him profound satisfaction. He made a trip to London during the Second World War and wrote a report for *The New Yorker* called "The Suspended Drawing Room." He went on from that to write a Profile of the Hungarian playwright Ferenc Molnár, his famous Profiles of the English art dealer Joseph Duveen and of Max Beerbohm, a series of stories about his childhood and youth in Worcester, Massachusetts, and much else. His work habits were such that he had to do his writing at home or in country inns, but he enjoyed the fanciful notion that he was one of the magazine's "staff writers" — that he had an office on the premises and came to work each morning, took off his jacket, and sat down at a typewriter like a workaday journalist. If ever *The New Yorker* had an honorary staff writer, it was Sam Behrman. At the same time, he was *The New Yorker's* ideal reader. He read every word of every issue, including the Race Track department, even though he had no interest whatever in race tracks, and he wrote in or called in regularly to report on what he particularly liked.

Behrman's admiration for other people's writing was extraordinary. Not only did he have no envy of any other writer (surely he had no reason to have) but he expended so much enthusiasm on the work of others that he had little left over for his own. He egregiously underestimated his own writing, but, fortunately, other people were not misled. His literary heroes were many; in addition to Beerbohm, there were, among others, Siegfried Sassoon, Wolcott Gibbs, St. Clair McKelway, and — perhaps most important of all to him — Montaigne. All but Montaigne were close friends as well. (He would not have excepted Montaigne.) And among his other heroes and heroines — and close friends — were Gershwin, Rudolf Kommer, Ernst Lubitsch, Alfred Lunt, Lynn Fontanne, Ina Claire, Oscar Karlweis, Harold Freedman, Isaiah Berlin, and Harold Ross. Friendship was his second great talent. It is not easy, within a span of eighty years, to do as much good writing as Behrman did and at the same time be a devoted husband and father and maintain a large number of intimate friendships, but he managed. He loved his friends, and they loved him.

In his early seventies, Behrman became distressed by the American intervention in the war in Vietnam. At the age of seventy-seven, when his health had failed and he thought he didn't have long to live, he wrote, "I have been terribly upset by the Vietnam war. The country has taken on a frightening aspect. It seems to have become a plutocracy, cruel, capable of atrocities, which has darkened its image all over the world. I say to myself: Why should I care? In a short time, I will know nothing about anything. But I care. I care deeply." And that was true. He did. Underlying all his humor, when he was thirty, when he was sixty, when he was eighty, were his passionate curiosity about human behavior and his concern for other human beings. He called Beerbohm a well-wisher. He, too, was a well-wisher. In the last few years of his life, he was subjected to one physical affliction after another. The time came when he could no longer walk, and was confined to his apartment. One day, as he sat in his bedroom in an armchair, he said to a visitor, with amusement, "I never knew what a wonderful thing it was just to be able to get up and walk down to the corner for an ice-cream soda." A year or so later, he began to lose his eyesight. An ardent reader, he was painfully forced to give up most of his reading, and what little he did he had to do with a complicated magnifying device attached to his chair. To entertain another visitor, he spun out some delightful nonsense about stratagems for learning to read with a piece of machinery. Finally, no magnification was strong enough; the words he adored and tried to read receded toward invisibility, and members of his family took over for him. Immobilized, nearly sightless, he sat in his room and sent out messages to his friends — to the world, really. It was clear that he still cared deeply about what was going wrong, he still thought most things were funny, and he wished us well.

It is by no means surprising that autobiography should flourish in the form of the obituary. When writing of a dead friend, I am always aware that the mood in which I write is one of sympathy for the precariousness of my own life and fear lest such gifts as I may possess and such joy as I may be capable of be taken from me before I have gained, at no matter what late age, a suitable mastery over them. Perhaps the closest that Shawn has come to making what I consider an autobiographical statement is to be found in an obituary he wrote to his fellow-editor, Bob Gerdy; it is at least his statement of what the ideal editor should be:

Robert S. Gerdy was born on January 21, 1919, in New York City, and on the sunny morning of December 23, 1965, walking along lower Fifth Avenue, in this city he loved, he fell to the ground and died. He was only a few steps from his own home and his parents' home, and within strolling distance of his office at *The New Yorker,* where for the last thirteen years of his life he was an associate editor. His work was nearby, and so were friends. He was in the midst of everything he cared about most. He died quietly, just as he had lived. His specific work at *The New Yorker* was to help prepare some of the longer articles for publication — for want of a more satisfactory word, to "edit" them. It is one of the comic burdens of that particular kind of editor not to be able to explain to anyone else exactly what he does. As he works with a writer over a manuscript or a proof, placing his technical and aesthetic judgment at the writer's service, giving counsel when counsel is asked for, lending an objective eye, acting on occasion as a conscience, helping the writer in any way possible to say what he wants to say, only the editor and the writer can know what passes between them. The work of a good editor, like the work of a good teacher, does not reveal itself directly; it is reflected in the accomplishments of others. Bob Gerdy was a consummately good editor. He had the qualities that were needed. He was generous, he was sensitive, he was tactful, he was modest, he was patient, he was imaginative, he was unfailingly tuned in. A physically fragile man, with a strong intelligence, he clearly had no wish to impose his will on anyone, and was content to help each writer attain in each piece of writing whatever it was that the writer himself aspired to. He never suffered from the editor's occupational delusion that he is writing the writer's work. It was enough for him to know that he was doing his own job. In a period in which celebrity is so widely pursued, he chose to practice an anonymous art; in a period dense with publicity, he had no desire to become public; in a period of rampant self-assertion, he was self-effacing; in a violent period, he was extremely gentle; in a noisy period, he spoke softly. He found his own form of joy in helping other people bring their writings to a state of something like perfection. His other joy was to bask in the warmth of his family and his friends. It is a tribute to his extraordinary talent as an editor that many of those friends were the writers he had worked with. All of us, the writers and the artists and the editors who were his colleagues, will profoundly miss him.

Springtime, and the Shawns are giving a party at their apartment on upper Fifth Avenue. It is in honor of a couple of young friends of theirs, who are soon to marry. The parents of the bridegroom are neighbors of the Shawns when the Shawns move to Bronxville for the summer. (To Shawn, Bronxville is as remote a rural retreat as Goose Bay, Labrador, and often as chilly. If the temperature falls below eighty, one can be sure that the windows and doors of the Shawns' house will be shut tight and the furnace will be throbbing.) The Shawns' two sons, Wallace and Allen — one an actor and playwright, the other a musician — are at the party, along with their girl friends; also present among the guests are Edith Oliver, Kennedy Fraser, and Richard Harris.

I arrive late, having just flown back from Buffalo, where, as a substitute for Shawn, I have accepted an award from the New York State Council on the Arts. (If Bronxville is Goose Bay to Shawn, Buffalo is in another galaxy. Shawn is grateful for the award but incapable of receiving it in person.) I stand in the doorway, as yet unnoticed. Shawn is at the piano, which is a glossy black Steinway. He is playing popular songs out of the twenties and thirties: Kern, Gershwin, Porter. The young man whom I remember playing a fixed honky-tonk piano in the little apartment on Park Avenue sits apparently unchanged, immured in music. It appears that he is at ease inside his captivity. I am put in mind of the fact that I once told Shawn that my impression of the unconscious was of some immense, well-armored bank vault, which I was struggling to enter and ransack, and Shawn said, "That's strange. I think of it as a place that I struggle to get out of, always in vain."

Tonight, when the last guest has gone, Shawn will return to work on the galleys for the forthcoming issue. By now, he has read every word of well over two thousand issues of the magazine. As far as anyone can tell, he never tires of the great flood of paper rushing in upon him. None of the rest of us can imagine surviving the demands of such a career; Shawn flourishes. It is a sufficient mystery, all the more pleasing to us because we have no other. The stories we tell about him are a form of incantation; they serve to conjure him up and make him vivid to us even when he is already in our presence.

Some stories about Shawn: a taxi-driver is taking him home at what strikes Shawn as a recklessly high speed. He taps on the plastic divider. "I'll tip you just twice as much," he says, "if you'll drive me just half as fast." And this one, about the galleys of a short story that Shawn has been looking over. In one of the opening paragraphs, the author has made reference to cow-paddies, and Shawn has somehow deduced that the word means "excrement." He has written in the margin of the galley, "Oh, dear." Further down on the galley, the author again refers to cow-paddies; this time, in extreme discomfort, Shawn writes, "Surely once is enough?"

Luncheon at the beautiful, vanished Ritz. Present are Marshall Best, an editor at Viking Press; Henry Green, author of the newly published novel *Loving;* and Shawn and me. A few weeks earlier, *The New Yorker* had published my favorable review of the novel, and on coming to this country the usually reticent author had expressed a wish to thank *The New Yorker* and me. We are talking with Green about what prompts the creation of a novel, especially one as exquisite and unworldly as *Loving.* With his usual hushed delicacy of speech and manner, Shawn inquires of Green whether he could possibly tell us what had led him to undertake the writing of *Loving.* Green affirms that he can. "I once asked an old butler in Ireland what had been the happiest times of his life," he says. "The butler replied, 'Lying in bed on Sunday morning, eating tea and toast with cunty fingers.' " This was not the explanation that Shawn has been looking forward to. Discs of bright red begin to burn in his cheeks.

Shawn is learning to drive a car, and he is not finding it easy. The difficulties appear to be in large part conceptual and aesthetic. "It seems to me," he says, "that if one is disengaging the gears, one ought to have to let the clutch *out,* instead of pushing it *in.* To me, 'in' represents engagement and 'out' represents disengagement." "Aw, come on now, Mr. Shawn-baby," the instructor says. "Let's get the show on the road, awright?"

The award from the State Council on the Arts has arrived at the office. It is a small burnished-steel sculpture by Beverly Pepper. The shape is that of a triangular wedge, slanted back from a base that is also a triangle. It is surprisingly heavy for its size and each of its many angles comes to a razor-sharp point. Shawn has arranged for it to be placed on a table in the nineteenth-floor corridor, some distance from the doors to his office. It will rest there for two or three years, until somebody in a fit of house-

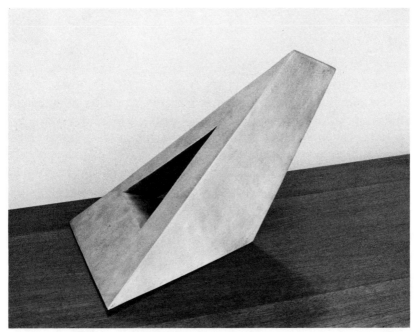

The prize that Shawn and The New Yorker *received in 1974 from the New York State Council on the Arts. The sculpture is by Beverly Pepper.*

cleaning orders it removed to a shelf in the storeroom, where it will join Ross's typewriter and other dusty artifacts. It will certainly not become a cherished Shawn memento. For upon examining it, Shawn has seen that however handsome an object it may be as sculpture, it is also dangerous. Looking at it, he shakes his head. "It is not only a prize," he says. "It is also a weapon."

A note on the bulletin board, posted at the height of a fierce February blizzard: "Everyone should feel free to leave as early as conveniently possible today." Shawn's masterly, unmistakable prose, which Ross would have envied for its lack of interior punctuation and for the phrase "conveniently possible." Who but Shawn would have put those two words together and made them bear such a weight of meaning? It is plain that the convenience Shawn refers to is not merely one's own but also that of one's fellow-workers; blizzard or no, the magazine must be got out on schedule, and the kindness of management is not to be taken unfair advantage of, especially at the expense of a colleague.

Shawn on Ross:

"Harold Ross presented himself to the world as a raucous, clumsy, primitive, somewhat comic figure. He said extremely funny things spontaneously and intentionally, and in his conversation and in his physical bearing he was funny unintentionally, or almost unintentionally, as well. He lent himself to anecdote. Because of this, and because his personal qualities were large in scale and included a formidable charm and magnetism, the serious and inspired work that he did as an editor tended at times to be lost sight of. Occasionally, when contemporaries of Ross talked about the old days on *The New Yorker,* one got the impression that he did very little to create it or run it — that in spite of his inadequacies, and somehow over his protest, a number of other people did what was necessary to put out the magazine each week. The implication was that Ross spent much of his time getting in the way of the talented people who worked for him. None of this, of course, is true. Ross founded *The New Yorker,* but he did far more. He gave it its character, he shaped it, he guided it through its formative period, he determined its basic policies and principles, and he edited it in its every detail for twenty-seven years. Some of the magazine's innovations — the characteristic literate, observant, very particularized, light-handed, timely writing that was to revolutionize the American magazine article; the Profile, the 'Talk of the Town' story, the 'letter' from abroad, all three in form and intention unlike anything that had gone before; the cartoon with the one-line caption — were there from the beginning. So was the then novel orientation toward New York City.

"Of all the people Ross might have gathered around him, he selected those who had the talent, the temperament, and the outlook that were right for *The New Yorker.* They gravitated to *The New Yorker* for a reason, and they remained for a reason. Whatever gaps there were in Ross's own taste and understanding and appreciation he tried to compensate for through other editors. Once he had found his way, by trial and error, to a number of editors who supplied him with what he knew was missing in him, he came to trust them utterly. He would sometimes say of a piece of writing, 'This is over my head,' by which he meant that it was slightly beyond the normal boundaries of his taste; but he trusted the judgment of the other editors, and, besides, it *wasn't* over his head. With a few exceptions, Ross was not adept at working directly with writers and artists. From a distance, he greatly admired them, and he was sympathetic to their professional and personal problems; in their presence, he was ill-at-ease, and could be awkward, tactless, or confusing. But he swiftly discovered, or developed, a remarkable group of editors which included Katharine White, Wolcott Gibbs, William Maxwell, Gus Lobrano, and James Geraghty. By nature strikingly unsystematic, Ross dreamed of systems that would take care of virtually everything: a system that would serve as the magazine's memory; a system that would anticipate as many 'operational contingencies' as possible; a system that would keep track of the flow of proofs and memoranda; a system that would coordinate what the various members of the staff were doing; a system that could jump into the breach and turn out an issue by itself if necessary. He found an editor to design systems and watch over them. Ross wanted the magazine to be accurate. What he had in mind, however, was not approximate, or human, accuracy; it was absolute accuracy. Therefore, he established the first magazine checking department, the purpose of which was to back up the writers by checking every checkable fact that went into print, and he placed at its head an erudite editor equipped to take accuracy as far as it could go. Ross knew, roughly, what he wanted the magazine to look like, but he had no idea of how to go about making it look that way. His knowledge of typography and layout was sketchy. Nevertheless, within months he found the one make-up editor in the world, the legendary Carmine Peppe, who could provide him with the chaste and lovely pages that would properly set off whatever we published — and to this day the pages are Peppe's pages. Ross had no aptitude for keeping an organization running smoothly and in a relatively happy state, but he found people who could help him do that, too. He presided over it all — justly, nervously, and, for the most part, benevolently.

"Every issue of *The New Yorker* represented hundreds of editorial choices, hundreds of decisions; Ross chose, and Ross decided. Somebody had to say what went into the magazine and what stayed out; Ross was the one who said it. He read proofs of everything that went into the magazine, and respectfully 'queried' anything he thought was questionable; his queries, in the course of time, influenced writers and other editors, set technical and literary standards, established a canon of taste, and laid the basis for a tradition of good writing which still flourishes. It was not someone else who led the magazine to avoid whatever was shoddy, shabby, cynical, petty, sensational, gossipy, exploitative, opportunistic, coarse, pedestrian, or banal; it was Ross.

"Ross was an enormously intelligent man who worked almost entirely by instinct and intuition. He was not naturally analytical in his approach to a piece of writing or to a drawing. If he had a favorable response to something, or an unfavorable one, he felt no need to know why. If he laughed at a cartoon, that was enough for him; that meant it was funny, and he didn't think that his reaction or the humor itself should be, or could be, analyzed. He was unintellectual, at times even anti-intellectual. He once told me, half seriously, that he didn't want to know what any writer *thought*. And in a way he didn't. He was not at home with ideas, theory, speculation — abstract thought of any kind. He liked what he regarded as pure information. His working assumption, at least, was that there was such a thing as objective reporting. He wanted to know about events; he did not want to know what a writer's subjective response to the events was. It was hard for him to face the rumored possibility that a writer could approach a journalistic story with preconceptions, with a bias, with a point of view; and he appeared to hope that if these impurities were present, the writer would transcend them. At a minimum, he expected that the writer's point of view would not be expressed explicitly but would be implicit in the facts. Because Ross was suspicious of 'thinking,' the magazine that he founded and edited did not publish either essays or what are called articles of opinion. It was, fundamentally, a magazine of reporting, humor, fiction, and criticism. His feeling for reporting, humor, and criticism was sure and confident; his feeling for fiction was less so, and his feeling for poetry still less, and in these spheres he therefore relied rather more on the judgment of others. He shied away from the words 'art' and 'literature.' For many years, the word 'literary,' applied to some piece of writing — including fiction — was a house pejorative. But Ross enjoyed and was stirred by, valued and encouraged much that was in fact literary.

"Ross was an editor who doted on immaculate writing and on stylish writing, which is to say writing that had style. He had a natural taste for simple, direct, colloquial writing, but he never failed to take delight in good writing of any sort, even writing that was elaborate or exquisite. He was equally open-minded in the field of comic art. He may have had his preferences in styles, but he was receptive to as many styles as there were talented and original comic artists. He never talked aesthetics — again, he would have shunned the word — but he was highly sensitive to graphic art. And, though he would have been embarrassed to admit it, he recognized beauty when it appeared. It was certainly not the least of Ross's talents that he was able to see talent in writers and artists before it was plainly visible to everyone. Also, he understood that talent developed more slowly in some than in others, and he was willing to wait. He gradually learned that the primary function of the magazine's editors, including him, was to create a structure and an atmosphere — a little world apart from the world — within which the writers and artists could fulfill themselves. The entire editorial staff was there, Ross realized, to serve the writers and artists, and then to bring their work to the reader in an appropriate setting.

"Every publication must consider itself to be interested in the high quality of the work it publishes, but in Ross, I think, this interest ran especially deep. Not only was he determined to publish the best writers and artists he could find; once he had found them, he did everything possible to stimulate and encourage them to do the best work they were capable of. By being hospitable to the best, and expecting the best, he often received the best. Something else contributed to the high quality of the work published in *The New Yorker.* Unlike some editors, Ross was not diverted by external considerations. He did not care about 'names' or reputations; he published material he thought had merit, no matter who had done it. If a writer had a name, or acquired one, that did not rule him out, but it did not rule him in, either; he was treated like anyone else. If his work was seen to have merit and to be right for *The New Yorker,* it was accepted; if not, it was rejected. Unknown writers and artists were as welcome as known writers and artists; it was the quality of the work that mattered. Also, Ross did not have commercial considerations on his mind. He did not worry about whether what we published attracted advertisers or drove them off. Nor did he concern himself with building a large circulation. He concentrated on the quality of the magazine, and let the circulation find its own level. He did not think of how many people might like what we published. And he was indifferent to fashion. We published what pleased us, and we ignored the question of whether or not it was fashionable.

"I have never been sure just what Ross really thought about facts. All I know is that he loved them. They were an end in themselves; they were self-justifying. I doubt whether he gave any thought to why it was good to gather facts and present them in journalistic form; he simply took it for granted that that was worth doing. As a young editor working for Ross, I never questioned the usefulness of facts. It was only in later years that I realized that facts in themselves might be meaningless or worthless, or might need defending. Ross was not tormented by questions of this kind. Scores of articles were written for *The New Yorker* because he himself was curious about something; he wanted to find out about a particular situation or person or event. He wanted the magazine to report on something not because he thought the public — or some hypothetical reader — wanted to know about it, or ought to know about it, but because *he* wanted to know. The impulse was not professional, it was personal. He used to say, 'We don't cover the news; we parallel the news.' But he had marvellous news judgment, and he knew what news to parallel. He had a vast, though not indiscriminate, curiosity, and it was that curiosity which set the magazine on the course it is still following. His appetite for facts was not unlimited, but it was large, and perhaps this explains why the magazine's reporting became as thorough as it did — for among the new standards he set were standards of thoroughness. Facts steadied him and comforted him. Facts also amused him. They didn't need to be funny facts — just facts. A series of factual statements set down with complete gravity could make him laugh because they took him by surprise or amazed him in some inconsequential way. Above all, facts — or some facts — were interesting to him. What was interesting to Ross, I always thought, really was interesting. What was dull to Ross really was dull. As far as I was concerned, Ross was the final authority on facts. Ross was also the final authority on humor. His element was humor. He generated it, he sought it out, he elicited it, he needed it, and he lived by it. If he thought something was funny, it was funny.

"Ross was devoted to clarity and stood in awe of grammar. Poets, he recognized — with some displeasure — had to be ambiguous and obscure at times, but he saw no excuse for ambiguity or obscurity in prose. He wanted every sentence of prose in the magazine to be intelligible, and he struggled hard to achieve that aim. The words 'fuzzy,' 'cloudy,' and simply 'unclear' turned up often in his queries. He also wanted impeccable grammar. This seeming fanaticism about clarity and grammar, I think, was a form of courtesy to the reader. He didn't want the reader to be stumbling around in the murk, or to have to take time to decipher what someone was trying to say, or to be distracted from what was being said by the faulty mechanics of how it was said. 'We don't print riddles,' he often remarked. And we don't. (Being a non-formulator, he would not have thought of it this way, but his high standards of accuracy were a token of his more important high standards of truthfulness. In the same way, his high standards of grammar were a token of his more important high standards of journalistic and literary content, and of style.) In a refinement of his effort to attain total clarity, Ross tried to do away with indirection in writing — particularly in factual writing. He did not want facts to come in one moment later than they should. He wanted the reader to know everything he should know at each step of the way, and not be taken unawares by information he should have had at an earlier point. He did not want a writer to say that a character took off his hat unless it had been established that the character was wearing a hat. I interpret this avoidance of indirection, too, as a form of courtesy. Moreover, he did not want a writer to raise questions of any sort in the reader's mind (synonymous with his own mind) without answering them — if possible, immediately: he did not want the reader to be, as he said, 'tantalized.' (He said, 'A writer should never arouse curiosity without satisfying it' — and he was a man whose curiosity was easily aroused.) Finally, Ross asked for sense. He wanted everything in the magazine to make sense, to be rigorously logical. To assist him in his pursuit of clarity, grammar, and sense, he assembled a group of gifted editors who specialized in those matters.

"Ross's ability to detect falseness of any sort and in any form was one of his important attributes as an editor. He was naturally drawn to what was genuine, authentic, real, true. His eye and his ear — and another sense or two that he peculiarly possessed — were affronted by a word, a phrase, a sentence, a thought, a bit of information, a line of dialogue, a short story, a piece of reporting, that was not the real thing, that was in one way or another specious, spurious, meretricious, dishonest. Although the branch of writing he knew best was journalism, his senses worked just as reliably with fiction. Even when a piece of writing was too rarefied for his taste, or outside the normal range of his interests or knowledge, or — in extreme cases — basically incomprehensible to him, he could tell whether it was the real thing or counterfeit. He could spot any kind of pretension or affectation instantly. Conversely, he looked for truth in a piece of fiction, a reporting piece, a cartoon, and he knew just what it was when he saw it. Without, I'm sure, realizing it, he was a connoisseur of authenticity.

"Of Ross's own qualities, perhaps the most important was his honesty. The idea of distorting information, of tampering with facts, of saying something that you knew was incorrect or that you didn't mean, repelled him. From time to time, he referred to 'journalistic integrity,' by which he meant many things, some of which he could identify and some of which he could not. In any event, journalistic integrity was a religious matter for him. When, once, he said that *The New Yorker* was not a magazine but a cause — and Ross was a man who fled from 'causes' — he was speaking, in a sense, of integrity. Ross was no moral philosopher, and his social conscience was shaky, and he knew nothing whatever about politics, but he had a profound ethical sense when it came to journalism. The truthfulness and accuracy were part of it. The aversion to falseness was part. But there was something more. He held to some resolve — scarcely ever hinted at in words — never to publish anything, never to have something written, for a hidden reason: to promote somebody or something, to pander to somebody, to build somebody up or tear somebody down, to indulge a personal friendship or animosity, or to propagandize. There were no ulterior motives, no hidden purposes, however worthy; no concealed explanations. Everything that was published in *The New Yorker* was precisely what it purported to be, was published for its own sake. In addition, Ross was fair-minded, and he saw to it that the magazine was fair-minded. That meant being fair to every person we wrote about, and also being fair to the facts, whatever they were. These aims were seldom articulated. Ross was a secret idealist. He would have been unable to formulate his journalistic principles, but the principles were there, in his bones.

"As a managing editor working for Ross, I always felt that he had some vision — never defined, never described, never mentioned — of what he thought a magazine should be, what he wanted *The New Yorker* to be, and I was trying to give it to him. I imagine that it was much the same for several other editors. If those of us now who are loosely bound together in this common enterprise manage every once in a long while to bring out an entire issue that might be called a work of art, it is because Ross, who thought he scorned works of art, prepared the way. In the early days, a small company of writers, artists, and editors — E. B.

White, James Thurber, Peter Arno, and Katharine White among them — did more to make the magazine what it is than can be measured. Over the years, many other people contributed heroically to the mixture. But at the source, abounding in promise, was Ross."

Shawn on Ross — yes, but one perceives that it is Shawn on Shawn as well. And this is not surprising, since the older man had so large a part in the shaping of his successor. If we are lucky, we find ourselves with many fathers and perhaps, with still more luck, a few sons. Anyhow, that is how things are, here at *The New Yorker.* Looking back and looking forward, I wouldn't want them any different.

Index

Abbey Theatre, 59
Adams, Franklin Pierce, 38, 39, 202
Adams, Frederick B., 265–66, 351
Adams, Samuel Hopkins, 353–55
Addams, Charles, 111, 220–22, 227, 228, 325
Adler, Polly, 132
Albee, Edward, 338
Algonquin Hotel, 30–31, 171, 192, 206, 246, 260, 265, 280, 299, 375
Alice in Wonderland (Carroll), 296
All Aboard with E. M. Frimbo (Whitaker and Hiss), 137
American Jitters, The (Wilson), 255
American Society of Composers, Authors, and Publishers, 302
Anderson, Malcolm, 177
Andrea Doria (ship), 311–12
Angell, Ernest, 294
Angell, Katharine Sergeant, *see* White, Katharine
Angell, Roger, 294–95
Anthony, Joseph, 39
Apologies to the Iroquois (Wilson), 255
Armed Vision, The (Hyman), 250
Arno, Peter, 74, 140, 159, 169, 199–204, 206, 207–9, 395
Arrowsmith (Lewis), 63
Astounding Crime on the Torrington Road, The (Gillette), 94
Atchley, Dana, 295
Atkinson, Brooks, 134
Atlanta University, 174
Auerbach family, 73
Austen, Jane, 213
Avalanche (Boyle), 251
Award of Merit medal (National Institute of Arts and Letters), 268
Axel's Castle (Wilson), 255

Babbitt (Lewis), 63

Bachrach, Fabian, 108
Bainbridge, John, 115, 214, 248–49, 375
Baker, Carlos, 251
Bangkok (Siam) *Daily Mail*, 146
Bankhead, Eugenia, 177–78
Bankhead, Tallulah, 122–23, 177
Barlow, Perry, 240
Barnard, Anne, *see* Gill, Mrs. Anne
Barnard family, 75–76, 158, 159, 284
Barnes, Djuna, 257
Barry, Ellen, 227
Barry, Philip, 34, 63, 227, 259
Barthelme, Donald, 326
Baskerville, Charles, 203, 214–15
Beardsley, Aubrey, 80
Beebe, Lucius, 121, 122
Beer, Thomas, 63, 157
Beerbohm, Max, 119, 197, 382, 383
Behan, Brendan, 338
Behrman, S. N., 154, 168, 318, 381–83
Belcher, George, 196
Bellarmine, Saint Robert, 253
Benchley, Marjorie, 264
Benchley, Robert, 128–29, 132, 153, 159, 260, 264, 288
Benét, Stephen Vincent, 63
Bennington College, 246, 247, 248, 250
Benson, Sally, 159, 264, 266, 276, 292
Berlin, Isaiah, 382
Bernstein, Jeremy, 112
Bernstein, Walter, 168
Berryman, John, 260
Best, Marshall, 386
Bishop, John Peale, 256
Black, Susan, 338
Bleeck's (bar), 122, 303, 319
Bliven, Bruce, Jr., 152
Booth, George, 325